TARTESSIAN

CELTIC STUDIES PUBLICATIONS
series editor: John T. Koch

CELTIC STUDIES PUBLICATIONS I
The Celtic Heroic Age: Literary Sources for Ancient Celtic Europe and Early Ireland and Wales, ed. John T. Koch with John Carey (Fourth edition, revised and expanded, 2003) Pp. x + 440
ISBN 1–891271–09–1

CELTIC STUDIES PUBLICATIONS II
A Celtic Florilegium: Studies in Memory of Brendan O Hehir, ed. Kathryn Klar, Eve Sweetser, and †Claire Thomas (1996) Pp. xxxvi + 227
ISBN *hc* 0–9642446–3–2 *pb* 0–9642446–6–7

CELTIC STUDIES PUBLICATIONS III
A Single Ray of the Sun: Religious Speculation in Early Ireland, John Carey (Second edition 2011)
ISBN 978–1–891271–18–2

CELTIC STUDIES PUBLICATIONS IV
Ildánach Ildírech. A Festschrift for Proinsias Mac Cana, ed. John Carey, John T. Koch, and Pierre-Yves Lambert (1999) Pp. xvii + 312
ISBN 1–891271–01–6

CELTIC STUDIES PUBLICATIONS VII
Yr Hen Iaith: Studies in Early Welsh, ed. Paul Russell (2003) Pp. viii + 224
ISBN 1–891271–10–5

CELTIC STUDIES PUBLICATIONS VIII
Landscape Perception in Early Celtic Literature, Francesco Benozzo (2004) Pp. xvi + 272
ISBN 1–891271–11–3

CELTIC STUDIES PUBLICATIONS IX
Cín Chille Cúile—Texts, Saints and Places: Essays in Honour of Pádraig Ó Riain, ed. John Carey, Máire Herbert, and Kevin Murray (2004) Pp. xxiv + 405
ISBN 1–891271–13–X

CELTIC STUDIES PUBLICATIONS X
Archæologia Britannica: Texts and Translations, Edward Lhwyd, ed. Dewi W. Evans and Brynley F. Roberts (2009) Pp. xii + 262
ISBN 978–1–891271–14–4

CELTIC STUDIES PUBLICATIONS XI
Ireland and the Grail, John Carey (2007) Pp. xxii + 421
ISBN 978–1–891271–15–1

CELTIC STUDIES PUBLICATIONS XII
An Atlas for Celtic Studies: Archaeology and Names in Ancient Europe and Early Medieval Ireland, Britain, and Brittany, John T. Koch with Raimund Karl, Antone Minard, and Simon Ó Faoláin (2007) Pp. viii + 216
ISBN 978–1–84217–309–1

CELTIC STUDIES PUBLICATIONS XIII
Tartessian: Celtic in the South-west at the Dawn of History, John T. Koch (Second edition, revised & expanded 2013) Pp. xii + 332
ISBN 978–1–891271–19–9

CELTIC STUDIES PUBLICATIONS XIV
Moment of Earth: Poems & Essays in Honour of Jeremy Hooker, ed. Christopher Meredith (2007) Pp. xvi + 313
ISBN 978–1–891271–16–8

CELTIC STUDIES PUBLICATIONS XV
Celtic from the West: Alternative Perspectives from Archaeology, Genetics, Language and Literature, ed. Barry Cunliffe and John T. Koch (Softcover edition 2012) Pp. xii + 383
ISBN 978–1–84217–475-3

CELTIC STUDIES PUBLICATIONS XVI
Celtic from the West 2: Rethinking the Bronze Age and the Arrival of Indo-European in Atlantic Europe, ed. John T. Koch and Barry Cunliffe (2013) Pp. viii + 237
ISBN 978–1–84217–529–3

CELTIC STUDIES PUBLICATIONS XIII

TARTESSIAN

Celtic in the South-west at the Dawn of History

Second edition, revised & expanded

John T. Koch

ABERYSTWYTH

2013

First published 2009
Second edition 2013

Copyright © John T. Koch

All rights reserved. No part of this publication
may be reproduced in any form or by any means,
without permission from the Publisher.

John T. Koch has asserted his rights under the Copyright, Designs and Patents Act, 1988, to be
identified as the author of this work.

Typeset in the Cynrhan and Sudoeste type families by CSP-Cymru Cyf

Cover design by CSP-Cymru Cyf

A Catalogue record for this book is available from the British Library.

ISBN 978–1–891271–19–9

Celtic Studies Publications

for customers in North America:

Celtic Studies Publications
c/o The David Brown Book Co.
P. O. Box 511, 28 Main Street
Oakville, CT 06779
USA

editorial correspondence:

CSP-Cymru Cyf
Centre for Advanced Welsh and Celtic Studies
National Library of Wales
Aberystwyth, Ceredigion SY23 3HH
Wales

i JA

ac

er cof am Jürgen Untermann
(24-x-1928 – 7-ii-2013)

THE AUTHOR. John T. Koch is research professor at the University of Wales Centre for Advanced Welsh and Celtic Studies in Aberystwyth. His publications include *The Celtic Heroic Age* with John Carey (4th edition 2003); *An Atlas for Celtic Studies* with Karl, Minard, and Ó Faoláin (2007); *The Gododdin of Aneirin* (1997); *Celtic Culture: A Historical Encyclopedia* (2006); and *Tartessian 2* (2011). With Barry Cunliffe, he co-edited *Celtic from the West* (2010; 2012).

ILLUSTRATIONS. Back cover photograph: warrior stela with Tartessian inscription from Abóboda, Almodôvar, south Portugal, now in the Museu da Escrita do Sudoeste, photo: Jane Aaron. Except as otherwise noted, the drawings in this book are by Martin Crampin (supported by a British Academy grant), the photographs by Jane Aaron, and the maps by the author. The essential assistance of the following museums is gratefully acknowledged: Museu da Escrita do Sudoeste (Almodôvar), Museu Nacional de Arqueologia (Lisbon), Museu Regional (Beja), Museu Municipal (Faro), Museu Municipal (Lagos), Museu Municipal (Loulé), Museu Municipal (Olhão), Museu Municipal (Silves), Museo Arqueológico (Sevilla), Museo de Cádiz, Museo Provincial de Huelva, Museo Arqueológico Provincial de Badajoz.

PREFACE TO THE FIRST EDITION

BEYOND *the Aegean, some of the earliest written records of Europe come from the south-west, what is now southern Portugal and south-west Spain. Herodotus, the 'Father of History', locates the Keltoí or 'Celts' in this region, as neighbours of the Kunētes of the Algarve. He calls the latter the 'westernmost people of Europe'. However, modern scholars have been disinclined—until recently—to consider the possibility that the South-western inscriptions and other early linguistic evidence from the kingdom of Tartessos were Celtic. The aim of this book is to show how much of this material closely resembles the attested Celtic languages: Celtiberian spoken in east-central Spain, Gaulish on the other side of the Pyrenees, as well as the longer surviving languages of Ireland, Britain, and Brittany. In many cases, the approximately 85 Tartessian inscriptions of the period c. 750–c. 450 BC reveal more than isolated Celtic names and words and can be interpreted as continuous statements written in an Ancient Celtic language. It is worth emphasizing that most of Tartessian's Celtic comparanda are not drawn from poorly attested and rare words or vocabulary otherwise attested only in non-Celtic Indo-European languages; rather they are straightforward items of core vocabulary in one, or most often more than one, Celtic language. To recognize the Tartessian language as Celtic has profound historical implications. By a century or more, it is the earliest attested Celtic language. Its early date and its extreme situation on Europe's south-western edge call for reconsideration of the standard account of the origins of the Celts and the Celtic languages in central Europe.*

This book is the result of research and ideas which unfolded rapidly between February 2007 and July 2008, none of which would have been possible without a wide variety of stimulating feedback and generous support from numerous friends and colleagues. The following list is no doubt incomplete and does not imply endorsement of the proposals presented here: Jane Aaron, Wil Aaron, Gareth Bevan, John Carey, Marc Clement, José Correa, Rui Cortes, Barry Cunliffe, Katherine Forsyth, William Gillies, Amílcar Guerra, Richard Harrison, Glenys Howells, Ricardina Inácio, Nicolas Jacobs, Geraint Jenkins, Raimund Karl, Marion Löffler, J. P. Mallory, Francisco Marco Simón, Luis Filipe de Matos Raposo, Prys Morgan, Kevin Murray, Brendan O'Connor, Rui Santana, Peter Schrijver, Jürgen Untermann, Dagmar Wodtko, Alex Woolf. This study is published now in the hope that it may continue to stimulate new ideas—and possibly new discoveries—and lead to a fuller understanding of the Tartessian language, Tartessos, and broader issues in historical linguistics and European protohistory.

Sevilha, 11 July 2008

[vii]

PREFACE TO THE SECOND EDITION

I N 2010 *the first edition of* Tartessian: Celtic from the South-west at the Dawn of History *(2009) went out of print. That book was written between February 2007 and July 2008. The longest of the South-western or 'Tartessian' inscriptions, the stela from Mesas do Castelinho (Almodôvar) was discovered in September 2008. I did not see the MdC stone or know of its existence until the occasion of the X Colóquio Internacional sobre Línguas e Culturas Paleo-hispánicas held at the Museu Nacional de Arqueologia in Lisbon in February 2009, where the stone was slyly revealed to us without fanfare at the first coffee break. I was able to add some references to this find in my contribution to* Celtic from the West: Alternative Perspectives from Archaeology, Genetics, Language and Literature *(2010), alongside Guerra's report of the discovery. However, the impact of the Mesas do Castelinho text could only be taken into account fully in* Tartessian 2: The Inscription of Mesas do Castelinho, ro and the verbal complex, Preliminaries to Historical Phonology *(2011). Recent excavations at Medellín, Abul, Abóboda, Alcorrín, and other sites have also brought major advances with the archaeological background and dating of the Tartessian corpus. I am therefore now taking the opportunity of the impending reprinting of* Tartessian *to bring this work up to date in line with* Tartessian 2, *so as now to include the MdC and other subsequently discovered inscriptions, to update the references, interpretations of the inscriptions, lexicographical and grammatical notes, and to add further new materials and cross-references. It should as a result be easier to use the two books together.*

Readers following the subject closely will see that my thinking has evolved substantially on many points. Thus, some new ideas are offered, some previously proposed ideas can now be strengthened and elaborated upon, others must be revised or downgraded to less likely alternative possibilities, and others simply withdrawn as unlikely or too uncertain. The intention is for this new edition to reflect the present state of work on the South-western corpus and my current thinking so as to ease the difficulties facing researchers in this rapidly developing and important field, as well as clarifying matters for all interested general readers. Having made detailed arguments for the Celtic classification of the language of the corpus in Celtic from the West *and* Tartessian 2, *as well as the first edition of this book, efforts are made here in the expanded notes to move on to focus more broadly on questions of interpretation. What kind of Celtic language was Tartessian? And what kind of cultural concepts are expressed in the inscriptions? Readers should not assume that every idea presented here is an inescapable consequence of, or even closely bound up with, the initial conclusion that the principal language of the inscriptions belongs to the Celtic family of the Indo-European macro-family. To be a contribution to progress, this book should not be taken as final or authoritative, but lead readers to the breadth of publications on the subject and, most importantly, back to re-examine the primary material itself.*

All of those thanked in the Preface to the First Edition have continued to be supportive and I thank them again, noting especially Amílcar Guerra for providing news, readings, and images of new discoveries. Jaime Alvar, Manuel Álvarez, Martín Almagro, Ana Arruda, Xaverio Ballester, Pedro Barros, Walter Bodmer, David Brown, Juan Campos, Mary-Ann Constantine, Vergilio Correia, Joseph Eska, Carlos Fabião, Andrew Fitzpatrick, Andrew Garrett, Chris Gosden, Gwen Gruffudd, Geraint Gruffydd, Eric Hamp, Barbara Hillers, Dafydd Johnston, Carlos Jordán, Kristian Kristiansen, Daniel Le Brise, Jean Le Dû, Clare Litt, William Mahon, Ranko Matasović, Wolfgang Meid, Joseph Nagy, Stuart Needham, Stephen Oppenheimer, Blanca Prósper, Colin Renfrew, Marisa Ruiz-Gálvez, John Shaw, Gregory Toner, Francisco Villar, Fernando Wulff, and Nicholas Zair have helped with aspects of the work in various ways during the intervening years. No one on this list or the previous should be presumed to endorse any of the ideas expressed here.

Aberystwyth, Dydd Gwener y Groglith 2012

CONTENTS

¶ NOTE. For editorial clarity, italicized transliterations given between vertical lines | | will be used to represent Tartessian forms so as to be more readily compared with other attested Ancient Celtic languages, such as Gaulish, and reconstructions of Primitive Irish and British. These transliterations are closer to phonemic structure, but it is not their chief purpose to be strictly phonemic, and there remain unresolved aspects of the Tartessian phoneme inventory.

Starred italicized forms, unless identified as another reconstructed language, stand for Proto-Celtic.

Introduction

BACKGROUND

THE idea that 'Tartessian'—the name now often given to the written language used in the south-west of the Iberian Peninsula in the mid 1st millennium BC—is partly or wholly Celtic is not new. Several variants of the idea had been expressed before the first edition of this book appeared in February 2009. Interpreting several strings of signs in the inscriptions as Celtic names, Correa (1989 and especially 1992) concluded that Tartessian was a Celtic language. Thus, we could simply add Tartessian as another ancient Celtic language to the established list: Lepontic, Celtiberian, Gaulish, Galatian, Primitive Irish, and British. Prior to this book's first edition, however, no one to my knowledge had unreservedly embraced this conclusion in print, and Correa himself has since revised his views coming to regard the language as unclassified though containing borrowed Celtic names. Untermann in Ellis Evans's festschrift (1995) and in his imposing *Monumenta Linguarum Hispanicarum 4* (1997) recognized the likelihood of several Indo-European and specifically Celtic elements in the Tartessian inscriptions, though viewing the language as a whole as still undeciphered. Thus, fifteen years ago, when the Tartessian corpus became widely available in an authoritative edition and amid preliminary indications of Celticity, the question might have received more attention from international Celtic studies and historical linguistics than it did. In a lucid and densely informative survey, Villar (2004) suggested that the Tartessian inscriptions contain items of 'ein frühes Gallisch' within a non-Celtic and probably non-Indo-European matrix language. Villar made the important point—anticipating some of the findings here—that the Celtic in the Tartessian inscriptions, like the Celtic theonyms found in Latin inscriptions of Galicia dating to the Roman period, shows some linguistic features more akin to what is found in Gaulish than in Celtiberian. Ballester (2004) provided a detailed list, not limited to onomastics, of forms resembling Celtic from the South-western [SW] inscriptions. In a general introduction to Indo-European, Fortson allowed that the SW corpus contains 'some Celtic material in its personal names' (2004,

278). Jordán (2005, 8; 2007, 751) provided a chart classifying the pre-Roman languages of the Hispanic Peninsula in which the 'South-west Language or Tartessian'
is listed as 'Indo-European macrofamily? Celtic family?' Although cautious, Jordán's
position was a noteworthy step away from the question-raising 'Celtic admixture'
position—what is this matrix language? which words in the inscriptions do we assign
to it?—towards a more straightforward classification and implicit directive for future
work. Lorrio and Ruiz Zapatero (2005, 18) briefly mentioned the possibility that the
SW inscriptions were written in a 'western Indo-European' and specifically Celtic
language, but also expressed 'some doubt' about that. Thus, before I began to study
the subject in 2006, degrees of Celticity had been proposed for Tartessian by several
authors, but none had worked through the entire SW corpus, either in support of
the strong position (simply a Celtic language throughout) or a comprehensive case
for a Celtic admixture.

On the other hand, the claim that 'Tartessian' was a non-Indo-European language
has likewise been made repeatedly. (In the briefer formulations, not citing specific
evidence, it is sometimes unclear whether 'Tartessian' or 'tartésico' means the language
of the pre-Roman place-names of western Andalucía or that of the SW inscriptions,
or both.) Schulten many years ago saw connections with the also poorly understood
Etruscan language. Schulten's ideas have had an extraordinarily long-lived impact.
Mallory (1989) classified Tartessian as non-Indo-European. Regarding the Correa/
Untermann transcriptions of the SW texts as 'unpronounceable', Sverdrup and
Guardans (2002) presented radically altered transliterations and then proposed:
'The Tartessian language is morphologically and structurally different enough from
Indoeuropean to exclude any genetic relationships'. Rodríguez Ramos (2002) force-
fully concluded that the 'Sudlusitanian–Tartessian inscriptions' are 'definitely neither
Celtic nor Anatolian, and probably also not Indo-European'. Isaac (2004) called
Tartessian 'equally non-Indo-European' as/to 'Basque'. Salinas de Frías (2006, 26)
recognized the Tartessian king's name *Argantonios* as Indo-European but thought
that the SW inscriptions look non-Indo-European, acknowledging this disparity
as a problem. In another general introduction to Indo-European, Clackson (2007,
4) used Tartessian as an example of an ancient non-Indo-European language. The
description of the Hesperia collaborative project on the pre-Roman languages of
ancient Hispania (based at the Department of Greek Philology and Indo-European
Linguistics of the Universidad Complutense de Madrid) views the language of
'south-western (or "Tartessian") inscriptions' as 'unidentified', thus making no claim
either as to what Tartessian is nor what it is not.

Several relevant publications became available since the first edition of this book
went to press in 2008. De Hoz (2010) contains a substantial treatment of the
SW corpus, characteristically erudite and nuanced, but largely sceptical on issues of
the Celticity of the language and even its decipherability. That author evidently did

not have access to publications newer than 2007 and so was unaware of the Mesas do Castelinho discovery of September 2008. In the third volume of the series on the Medellín necropolis (2008b, 1050–2), Almagro-Gorbea, Lorrio, Mederos, and Torres present a list of identifiable Hispano-Celtic personal names in the SW corpus, as well as emphasizing the Celticity of *Argantonios*, in making a case for the Atlantic Celtic background of the population of Early Iron Age Medellín/Konisturgis. Broderick (2010, 304–6) has published a discussion of the SW corpus based largely on the first edition of this book (as acknowledged), but itself uncommitted on the classification issue. In a substantial collaborative publication by Villar, Prósper, Jordán, and Fernández Álvarez, they conclude (2011, 100): 'Más reciemente J. T. Koch ha proporcionado argumentos lingüísticos de mayor enjundia en favor de la tesis de la filiación celta, de manera que en la actualidad conviene retirar, al menos provisionalmente la lengua de las inscripciones del suroeste como miembro del listado no indoeuropeo.' Current materials on the internet from linguist Terrence Kaufman treat Tartessian as Celtic. At any rate, had it been the de facto consensus a few years ago that the language of the SW corpus was probably non-Indo-European, movement away from that position is more evident today.

PURPOSE, METHODS, AND A FEW TENTATIVE CONCLUSIONS

An important factor in the rising awareness of the SW inscriptions was the opening in October 2007 of the dedicated Museu da Escrita do Sudoeste in Almodôvar (MESA), south Portugal. MESA has played a key role in bringing together inscribed stones from collections across Portugal and acting as a focal point for excavations and other new research on the corpus through the Projecto Estela. The language or languages of Tartessos were also an essential component within the multidisciplinary international congress 'Tarteso: el emporio del metal' held in Huelva in December 2011. That well-attended event has lent impetus to a campaign to launch a dedicated Museo Tartésico in Huelva's historic centre. It is, therefore, against a current background of recent discoveries and intensified interest—both locally and internationally—that this new edition is intended to provide further stimulus to progress on the subject.

The approach of the first edition was to see how much of the corpus of Tartessian inscriptions (then about 84, now a few more than the 95 recognized in Correia 2009) might suggest comparanda in the earlier Celtic languages: the Ancient Celtic languages listed above, as well as Old Irish, Old Breton, Old and Middle Welsh. I also included with the inscriptions a few further proper names from the region of Tartessos dating back to the mid 1st millennium BC. What I generally did not do in my initial work for the first edition, in 2007–8, nor during the subsequent resifting of 2011–12, was to seek out Indo-European words not attested in any (other) Celtic language and then run these through the requisite sound changes to see how these Indo-European preforms might have appeared in an Ancient Celtic language, assuming that the root had once existed in Celtic, but had then either simply died out in all sub-branches except Tartessian, or somehow otherwise failed to be attested in all other Celtic languages. This procedure was not motivated by an ethos of methodological purism—though etymological interpretations based solely on evidence from other branches of Indo-European are sometimes less conclusive—but rather the view that a more worthwhile contribution might result from keeping to the usual area of my previous work in the earlier Celtic languages.

The one glaring exception to this limitation of methodology was demanded by the most often repeated of the 'formula words' of the Tartessian inscriptions: naŕkᵉe ⊙)|ᴎAᴧ (J.27.1), naŕkᵉe ⊙)|ᴎAᴧ (S. Martinho), naŕ[kᵉ]e ⊙)|]ᴎAᴧ (J.1.1), naŕkᵉ[e] [⊙])|ᴎAᴧ (J.26.1, J.57.1, MdC), na]ŕkᵉe ⊙)|ᴎ[(J.16.2), naŕkᵉetⁱi ᴧ⊕⊙)|ᴎAᴧ (J.56.1), naŕkᵉe(n) (ᴧ)⊙)|ᴎAᴧ (J.7.8), naŕkᵉeni (J.1.2, J.1.3), naŕkᵉenii ᴧᴧᴧ⊙)|ᴎAᴧ (J.2.1, J.21.1), n[aŕkᵉ]enii (J.6.1), naŕkᵉentⁱi ᴧ⊕ᴧ⊙)|ᴎAᴧ (J.12.1, J.16.1, J.17.2, J.18.1), naŕkᵉen↑ⁱi ᴧ↑ᴧ⊙)|ᴎAᴧ (J.19.2), [n]aŕkᵉentⁱi (J.1.5), na]ŕkᵉentⁱi[(J.4.3), n(a)ŕkᵉenii ᴧᴧᴧ⊙)|ᴎᴧ (J.11.1), n]aŕkᵉenii ᴧ]Aᴎ⟨⊙ᴧᴧᴧ (J.11.3), na]ŕkᵉeni ᴧA]ᴎ⟨⊙ᴧᴧ (Corte Pinheiro) naŕ]kᵉenii (J.19.1), naŕrkᵉe:n: | ᴧ | ⊙)|9ᴎAᴧ (J.23.1), n[a]ŕkᵉen ᴧ⊙)|ᴎAᴧ (Cabeza del Buey IV), na[ŕ]kᵉen (Monte Gordo), naŕkᵉenai ᴧAᴧ⊙)|ᴎAᴧ (J.7.1, J.55.1),]naŕkᵉeuu[ ]ᴧᴧ⊙)|ᴎAᴧ[(Corte do Freixo 2). On the face of it, the forms appear, as Untermann has remarked (1995), to be inflected as an Indo-European verb, but no Celtic root immediately comes to mind. Nonetheless, so prevalent and pivotal is this naŕkᵉentⁱi, &c., that something has to be attempted. The funerary formula at its most minimal, and transparent, occurs in the clear and complete inscription of Almoroquí (J.56.1) akᵒo(l)ioś naŕkᵉetⁱi, the basic message of which can hardly be far from 'Akolios now lies/rests [here]'. Furthermore, as discussed in the notes on Linguistic Forms below, the stem or stems lak-, which Untermann also recognized as being inflected like Indo-European verbs in the SW corpus, is arguably interchangeable with naŕkᵉe- in the diction of the inscriptions. In a funerary context, lak- | lăg- | is plausibly assigned to Indo-European root *legʰ- 'lie down', which is well attested with suitable meanings in Celtic languages. Therefore, in counter distinction to the approach usually followed and described above, the etymological proposal is that naŕkᵉentⁱi, &c., is the cognate of Greek ναρκάω 'grow stiff, numb, dead' (< Indo-European *[s]nerk- 'bind', cf. Old High German in-snerahan 'bind' [Rix 2001, 574])—both in the literal sense, suiting funerary inscriptions, but also more abstractly 'to bind, fix, make inalterable, carve in stone', hence 'so be it, amen'—an Indo-European formation which has otherwise died out or failed to be attested in Celtic. It should be noted, on the other hand, that Beekes (2010) has assigned the Greek form to the non-Indo-European pre-Greek substratum. However, the semantic link with the Germanic ('bind' > 'become stiff') is plausible enough. (Arguably, despite their seeming 'Indo-European-ness', the apparent non-Celticity of naŕkᵉentⁱi, &c., has been a significant factor in inspiring reluctance on the part of some scholars to accept the language as a whole as Celtic, indirectly propping up a persistent—but linguistically baseless—idea that the Tartessian language, like the script, was an import from the east, akin to Anatolian or Phrygian.)

The readings here generally follow Untermann (1997) as the authoritative starting point, based on both his transcriptions and the accompanying photographs and line drawings. There is usually close agreement between the readings of Untermann and those in the various publications of J. A. Correa, and for most points the Untermann/Correa transliterations agree also with those of Rodríguez Ramos. V. H. Correia (1996) usefully provides transcriptions in standardized SW signs, but not Romanized transliterations. There remain some basic uncertainties in making out the signs on the stones, as well as interpreting those signs (see 'Script and Transliteration' below). In addition to using published sources, in March and July 2008 and February 2009 and August 2010 I was able to examine (and was often permitted to photograph) the many Tartessian inscribed stones kept at the following museums: the new Museu da Escrita do Sudoeste (Almodôvar) = MESA, Museu Regional (Beja), Museu Municipal (Faro), Museu Municipal (Lagos), Museu Nacional de Arqueologia (Lisbon), Museu Municipal (Loulé), Museu Municipal (Olhão), Museu Municipal (Silves), the inscription of Villamanrique de la Condesa at Museo Arqueológico (Sevilla), and Museo Arqueológico Provincial de Badajoz. I wish to express my sincere gratitude to these institutions, their directors, and staff.

The procedure sketched above—essentially fishing for any further Celtic forms within a corpus of inscriptions in which a few promising examples had already been recognized—had the unexpected result of identifying a sufficient number of 'Celtic-looking' forms (very often with comparanda in the core vocabulary of more than one Celtic language) as to call into question the hybrid positions taken by Untermann and Villar. (In personal correspondence of 2009, Francisco Villar informs me that he now accepts that 'la lengua de las inscripciones del suroeste es de la familia celta'.) The Celtic-looking elements in Tartessian identified by earlier writers had remained small as an absolute number and as a relative proportion of the corpus. With a writing system that did not show word divisions or distinguish voiced from voiceless stops (along with the remaining uncertain details of the script), such a small number of resemblances might be coincidental. That is not to say that all elements in all the inscriptions have now simply fallen neatly into place as Celtic. But rather, there is no coherent residue of recurrent and systematic linguistic features that lack fairly obvious Indo-European (and most often Celtic) analogues. The inscriptions most devoid of Celtic-looking features are those that

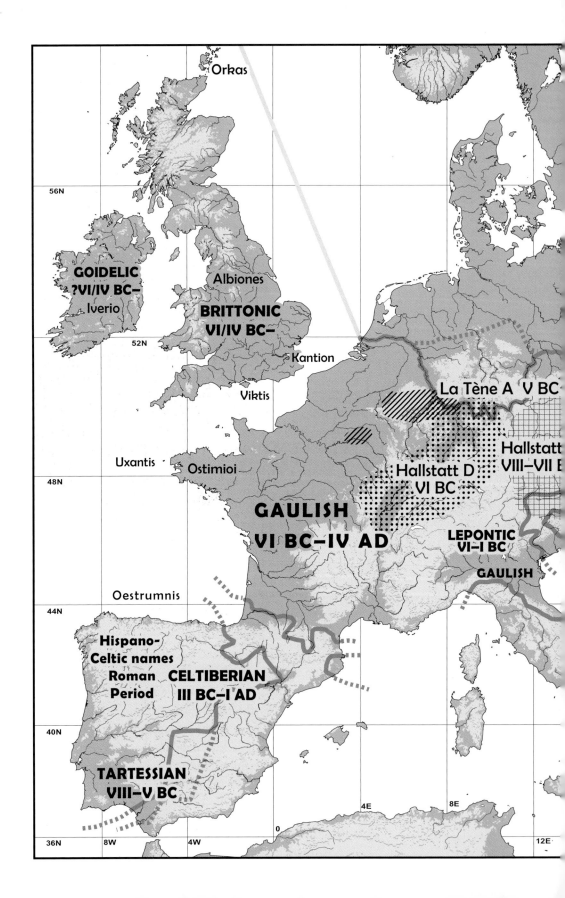

Orkas

56N

GOIDELIC
?VI/IV BC–
Iverio

Albiones

BRITTONIC
VI/IV BC–

52N

Kantion

Viktis

Uxantis

Ostimioi

48N

La Tène A V BC

Hallstatt
VIII–VII E

Hallstatt D
VI BC

GAULISH

VI BC–IV AD

LEPONTIC
VI–I BC

GAULISH

Oestrumnis

44N

Hispano-
Celtic names
Roman   CELTIBERIAN
Period   III BC–I AD

40N

TARTESSIAN
VIII–V BC

4E   8E

0

36N   8W   4W   12E

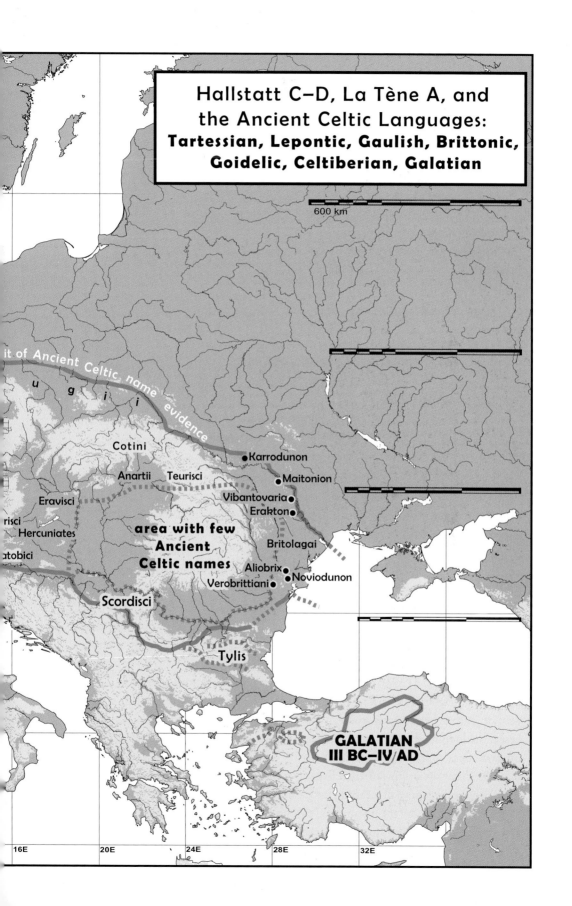

Hallstatt C–D, La Tène A, and the Ancient Celtic Languages: Tartessian, Lepontic, Gaulish, Brittonic, Goidelic, Celtiberian, Galatian

600 km

it of Ancient Celtic name evidence

u g i i

Cotini

Karrodunon

Anartii Teurisci

Maitonion

Eravisci

Vibantovaria

Erakton

risci

Hercuniates

area with few Ancient Celtic names

Britolagai

atobici

Aliobrix

Noviodunon

Verobrittiani

Scordisci

Tylis

GALATIAN III BC–IV AD

16E 20E 24E 28E 32E

are generally of poorest quality—briefest, badly fragmented, poorly carved, badly worn, known only through old drawings, or using anomalous letter forms of uncertain phonetic value. In many of the inscriptions, especially the longer ones that are complete and unbroken, the Celtic-looking elements—names, common nouns, pronouns, preverbs, verbs, and inflexional terminations—accumulate to the point that the inscrutable forms that had implied the hypothetical non-Celtic matrix language are nearly, or wholly, absent. Consequently, it was possible to offer in the first edition several original translations for words, for groups of words, and for some complete inscriptional texts.

Owing to subsequent discoveries and the further work made possible by them, the method used for this second edition could achieve greater critical control. Two types of patterns have become more visible in the enlarged corpus, which can be used as guides to decide between more likely interpretations, that conform to the recurrent patterns, and less likely ones, that do not. First, syntactic structures are now evident, including the basic elements and order of the Tartessian epigraphic formula—surely a funerary formula—as well as more and less obvious variations on it (see Appendix C below). Secondly, to formulate and test the hypothesis of the Celticity of the material, I had at first expected Tartessian to be an archaic, but fairly generic Ancient Celtic language glimpsed through the distorting screen of an ill-fitting writing system imperfectly adapted from a non-Indo-European language. However, as explained in *Tartessian 2*, it is now clear that the representation of the language with the SW signs bears a closer and more systematic relationship to the Proto-Celtic sound system than I had at first realized. This recognition permits a detailed account of the innovations separating Tartessian from its reconstructed ancestor. It must still be emphasized that at the present stage of the work, all translations remain provisional and open to revision. They are offered mostly to aid non-linguists, for whom the implications of the proposed grammatical identifications and etymologies would otherwise be opaque.

As to broader implications—historical, linguistic, and archaeological—these are potentially significant, once they have been explored at length, but no more than a few broad strokes are attempted presently. It matters only secondarily whether the Tartessian inscriptions have Celtic elements within a non-Celtic (probably non-Indo-European) matrix language or whether the inscriptions are simply Celtic throughout. Either way, we have speakers of a Celtic language in the extreme southwest of Europe by the Early Iron Age or even the Bronze–Iron Transition. In either event, the long-held spell of the Hallstatt and La Tène archaeological cultures on modern ideas concerning the origins of the Celts must begin to loosen. In terms of ideas about the origins of the Hispano-Celts, the Tartessian evidence shifts the focus from the coming of central European Late Bronze Age Urnfield influences to the eastern Meseta (the historical Celtiberia) as the key event, usually imagined as crossing overland the formidable central Pyrenees with subsequent westward penetration to Galicia and Portugal. Attention now turns from Herodotus's oft-quoted, but fuzzy, formulation concerning the Keltoí inhabiting the upper Danube and to his too often ignored, but much clearer and better informed, statement that the Keltoí were the immediate neighbours of the Kunētes, that is, the inhabitants of what is now the Algarve and the vicinity of Tartessos, in the extreme south-west of Europe.[1] In short, we now have another set of data coming from another discipline for reconsidering some version of Cunliffe's (2001; 2009; 2010) theory of the expansionist ancient Celtic speech as a lingua franca developing due to prolonged maritime contacts, which culminated during the Atlantic Bronze Age.

That the territory of Tartessos had formed an integral part of the Atlantic Bronze Age can be seen abundantly in the archaeological evidence, such as the spectacular Huelva deposition of the 10th century BC (Ruiz-Gálvez 1995; Harrison 2004). There is at least an inkling of textual confirmation in *Ora Maritima* of Rufus Festus Avienus. Despite its remaining uncertainties and apparent confusions, this late 705-line poem (as extant) has unique value in its claims of detailed use of lost early Greek and Carthaginian sources, sometimes recording *their* view of *their* past. Avienus's statement concerning the Straits of Gibraltar, *hic Gadir urbs est dicta Tartessus prius* 'here is Cádiz formerly called Tartessos' (line 85; Freeman 2010, 307) is intelligible as it stands as describing the state of affairs at the Bronze-Iron Transition before Phoenician Gadir was founded. We need not assume confusion of two neighbouring Early Iron Age centres (Cádiz and Huelva), rather Tartessos and Gadir belong to earlier and later ages for Avienus. *Ora Maritima* continues that the Tartessians had been wont to trade as far as the 'Oestrumnides' (*Tartessiisque in terminos Oestrumnidum negotiandi mos erat*), islands rich with tin and lead mines and situated two days sailing from the island thickly inhabited by the *gens Hiernorum* 'Irish people', which itself was near *insula Albionum*, i.e. Britain (lines 94–7, 110–16; Freeman 2010, 308). This passage sits alongside, and is perhaps part of, information derived from the Carthaginian navigator Himilco, who flourished in the later 6th or earlier 5th century BC. The case for continuity in the south-western Iberian Peninsula across the Bronze-Iron Transition, canvassed under 'Dating' below, is less easily harmonized with the alternative possibility of Celtic speech arriving in western Iberia with an influx of Urnfielders from central Europe. Thus, in general terms, the impact of accepting Tartessian as Celtic can be summarized as follows. As to *date*—a century or two before the oldest Lepontic—it requires a significant but containable revision of the standard introduction to Celtic studies; on the other hand, Tartessian's *place*—far from the La Tène, Hallstatt, and Urnfield core areas—jars some conditioned expectations.

---

1   It is not impossible that the long inscriptions of Bemsafrim [J.1.1 'Fonte Velha 6'] and Mesas do Castelinho are referring to their honorands, as 'Celt' and/or 'Gaul', if we read Tartessian **kᵃaltᵉe** as a case form corresponding to Greek nominative plural Γαλάται *Galátai* and/or Latin *Celtae*.

DATING AND ARCHAEOLOGICAL BACKGROUND

There is today a general consensus that the South-western or Tartessian corpus is the earliest of the Palaeohispanic *corpora*, predating Iberian, Celtiberian, and Lusitanian, and that the SW script is, primarily, an adaptation of the Phoenician 'alephat' (consonantal alphabet), that is, the first alphabet, which had been invented to write West Semitic (Correa 2005). The subsequent development was apparently that the Iberian scripts (the South-eastern 'Meridional' and then the North-eastern 'Levantine') were then adapted from the SW signary, both before the end of the 5th century BC, and afterwards the Celtiberian scripts were developed from the NE Iberian script. It is increasingly evident that the SW and SE scripts are closely similar from the standpoint of both the form of the signs and their phonetic values (cf. Ferrer i Jané 2010), so we might now think of them as a single 'Southern' Palaeohispanic writing system with two regional or language-specific sub-systems (following Correa 2011). The Iberian (SE and NE) and Celtiberian scripts are semi-syllabaries (some of the signs represent two phonemes: consonant+vowel), rather than true alphabets. Lusitanian and later Celtiberian were written in Roman letters.

As to when the first step in this chain of events could have happened, several old thorny issues about the arrival of the Phoenicians beyond the Straits of Gibraltar must be revived. According to the chronology of the Roman historian Velleius Paterculus (1.2.3; 1.8.4; he lived *c.* 19 BC–post AD 30), Tyre's colony at Cádiz (Latin *Gades*, Attic Γάδειρα, Phoenician *Gadir*), near Tartessos and a short voyage north-west of the straits, was founded 80 years after the fall of Troy. The date was, therefore, either 1110/1109 or 1104/3 BC depending on the reckoning used for the Trojan war. Though less exact, Strabo (1.3.2), Pliny (*Naturalis Historia* 19.216), and Pomponius Mela (3.6.46) were broadly in agreement with Velleius, writing that Gades was founded not long after the fall of Troy. If the ocean-going 'ships of Tarshish' mentioned in the Old Testament (e.g. Kings 1: 10.22, Ezekiel: 27.12; see the collected biblical passages in Freeman 2010, 331–3) as bringing silver, gold, and other luxuries mean 'ships of Tartessos', as has long been believed (Blázquez 1993; though disputed by Aubet 2001), then major commercial links between the Phoenicians and Tartessians would date back to the period of the joint venture of King Solomon (961–922 BC) and Hiram I of Tyre (971–939 BC).

In the archaeological record, we see that luxury manufactured Phoenician items —goldwork, armour, and bronze buckets—entered the Atlantic trading networks by the 10th century BC, the date of the Huelva hoard, a marine deposit of the Late Bronze Age and earliest Iron Age, which contained 400 items (Ruiz-Gálvez 1995; Kristiansen 1998, 126), more probably a ritual deposition than a shipwreck (Cunliffe 2001, 279). For the 'Pre-Colonial Period' in Iberia, Ruiz-Gálvez has identified weights and writing implements amongst the Huelva finds and persuasively links these with beginnings of literacy in the west (2000; 2008). One might regard this eastern material as representing a Phoenician 'pre-colonization' and a 'first orientalization' of Late Bronze Age Tartessos and Atlantic Hispania beyond. In the light of the analysis by Burgess and O'Connor (2008), intense Phoenician influence had catalysed a 'precocious' Iberian First Iron Age—and brought an end to the Atlantic Bronze Age in Iberia—as early as *c.* 950, contemporary with the carp's-tongue industries of the Late Bronze Age in Atlantic Gaul and Ewart Park Phase of LBA Britain. Ruiz-Gálvez (2000; 2008; 2009) has suggested that it was contact with Semitic, specifically Canaanite, alphabetic literacy at this stage that first inspired the phenomenon of Tartessian literacy. Full-blown Phoenician colonies become archaeologically visible along the Mediterranean in the southern Iberian Peninsula before 800 BC, with datable Phoenician material from Cádiz/Gadir on the Atlantic beginning by *c.* 770.

Regarding the SW script, Rodríguez Ramos (2000) has made the point that some characters most closely resemble specific Phoenician letter forms found in inscriptions closely dated to *c.* 825 BC. The recently-excavated, orientalizing site at Castillejos de Alcorrín has produced graffiti on two ceramic sherds. The longer graffito from that site was inscribed before firing. Alcorrín was strategically situated between Málaga and Gibraltar, within view of the straits 25 km to the south-west. It was a massively-fortified hilltop town, with a circuit of 2,380 metres of defensive walls on stone foundations, including nine bastions evenly spaced along the most vulnerable side. Marzoli et al. (2010) find the closest analogues for the letter forms of the Alcorrín graffiti in Phoenician inscriptions from the Levant, Cyprus, and Nora (Sardinia) over a range of dates from the 12th–8th centuries BC with clearest parallels in examples of the period 1000–850. Thirteen C14 dates establish that the occupation at Alcorrín began during the last quarter of the 9th century BC and that it continued through the 8th, with Phoenician amphora sherds of the 7th being the latest finds. It was soon after abandoned. The sparse occupation materials within the stronghold were mostly native ceramic types of the Bronze-Iron Transition, thus favouring the site's interpretation as a centre of indigenous (Tartessian?) power under Phoenician influence, rather than a Phoenician colony. In any event, it now appears that alphabetic writing was known at a key indigenous strong point, verging on the Atlantic, by about 800–750 BC.

Nevertheless, a long time lag could have passed between the adoption of the West Semitic alephats by indigenous people(s) in the south-west and the oldest of the surviving SW inscriptions. On the later limit, Phoenician influence in Hispania slackened during and after Nebuchadnezzar of Babylon's siege of Tyre *c.* 586–*c.* 573 BC. The evident decline at the end of the 'Late Orientalizing Phase' of the Tartessian material culture from *c.* 550 BC (Chamorro 1987, 204) might be a consequence of these disruptions in the east. Against this background, we can understand why

Arganthonios, the ruler of Tartessos, was so eager, about 550 BC, for the Phokaian Greeks to found a colony 'anywhere they liked' in his territory (Herodotus 1.163–5; see below pp. 148–50, 266–7, 273). The loss of most of the Phokaian fleet *c.* 539 BC off Alalia in eastern Corsica against a combined Etruscan/Carthaginian force, as well as the Persian conquest of Phokaia itself *c.* 540, precluded any such possibility, further constricting the Tartessian élite's economic lifeline to the eastern Mediterranean. However, the Tartessian inscriptions need not have stopped at that time, unless we suppose that competition with Phoenician and/or Greek literacy had been the sole *raison d'être* for the tradition. The Tartessian signs are not similar to attested forms of the Carthaginian or 'Punic' version of the Phoenician alphabet; therefore, the influence of Carthage in southern Hispania *c.* 539–208 BC cannot explain the genesis of Tartessian literacy. (A true Carthaginian military empire in the southern peninsula comes only at the end of this period, with Hamilcar in 237 BC.)

Untermann (1995) has proposed 700–500 BC as the date range for the inscriptions, likewise Villar (2004, 268), while Rodríguez Ramos (2002) dates them to certainly post-800 BC and probably belonging to the 6th and 5th centuries, adducing some archaeological finds, and Correia (2005) generally 7th–5th century BC. If we agree with Untermann that the Tartessian script was partly of alphabetic Greek inspiration—as opposed to being wholly derived from the Phoenician—the starting point is unlikely to precede *c.* 700 BC. A recently discovered Tartessian graffito on a Phoenician sherd found at Doña Blanca near Cádiz has now been dated with confidence to the first half of the 7th century (Correa & Zamora 2008; Correa 2009, 277).

According to Almagro-Gorbea (1988, 72), the highly 'orientalizing' proto-urban Tartessian archaeological culture reached its apogee in the second half of the 7th century BC. The Tartessian material culture was characterized in part by rich complex burials, and several of the inscriptions have been found in necropolises of the Early Iron Age, though the datable contexts have been in most cases only with a given necropolis as a whole. Nonetheless, the datable contexts we do have, today most especially those from Medellín (see below), decisively exclude the possibility that the entire SW corpus could post-date *c.* 450 BC (contrary to Broderick 2010, 287). A graffito on grey ceramic from Abul (Alcácer do Sal, Setúbal, ancient Salacia) has recently been shown to be Tartessian by Correa (2011) and belongs to an archaeological context closely datable to 650–550 BC. With this find Salacia now counts as the north-westernmost distribution point for the SW corpus. The necropolis of Fonte Velha (Bemsafrim) is the find site of inscriptions J.1–5 below and has been dated 8th–6th century BC (De Hoz 1989, 540). De Mello Beirão (1993) found 8th- and 7th-century associations in finds from the south Portuguese necropolis of Pardieiro where Tartessian inscribed stones were also discovered (J.15.1–3). In the case of the Herdade do Mealha Nova stelae (J.18.1–2), the excavation of the two associated necropolises recovered an Egyptian scarab with the hieroglyph of

Pharaoh Petubaste of the 23rd Dynasty (817–763 BC; Chamorro 1987, 229). Scarabs were common as imported antiquities, but had gone out of fashion by c. 400 BC (Harrison 1988, 135). For the necropolises in the district of Seville (the find sites of inscriptions J.52.1 and J.53.1), Catalán (1993) lists datable associations, the earliest of which is another scarab of Petubaste, followed by 7th-century pottery, and the latest are native annular fibulae of the 5th or 4th century BC. The famous 'Guerreiro' stela of Gomes Aires ('Abóboda 1', J.12.1) is dated by Harrison (2004, 310) to the 7th century BC. That stone, which had originally stood upright, was unearthed in 1972 in an Iron Age necropolis, where it had been reused face-down as a covering slab over a burial cavity, which contained a large ceramic urn filled with cremated bones. Abóboda was re-excavated in 2010–2011. A large iron spearhead in excellent condition typologically datable c. 450–c. 350 BC was found near the urn at that time, establishing the horizon of the stela's reuse within the newer funerary rite.

The well-excavated and admirably published Early Iron Age necropolis of Medellín, Badajoz, Spain (Almagro-Gorbea et al. 2007; 2008; 2008b; Almagro-Gorbea 2010; Almagro-Gorbea & Torres 2009), provides a solid anchoring for Tartessian studies in more than one respect, including chronology. In the first place, the evidence from Medellín makes it clear that applying the name 'Tartessian' to the language and the South-western script in which it was written are not misnomers. Iron Age Medellín is 'Tartessian' in the archaeological sense of exemplifying the orientalizing material culture of the south-western Peninsula in the Earlier Iron Age and in the historical sense of being associated with—if not simply belonging to— the flourishing polity of Ταρτησσος during the 7th and 6th centuries BC. Medellín is also 'Tartessian' in the epigraphic and linguistic senses, as the find site of three graffitos in SW script scratched on ceramics (Medellín T2, 86H/13–1 c. 625–600 BC; T3, 86/TP–1 c. 550–500 BC) and one contextualized funerary stela (J.57.1 = Medellín T1, 86H/EN12–1 c. 650–625 BC), all closely datable. The stela not only uses SW script, but is clearly in the same language as the stelae of the less-urbanized Algarve 200+ kilometres to the west. It reads:]ЖИᗉᐱ ᓭ‡ꓓ**ᓭ‡Ⴟ‡ꓓ[ ]lok°on kᵉeloia naŕkᵉe[. . . The text thus shares items of vocabulary (lok°on and naŕkᵉe) with, for example, the well-known 'Fonte Velha 6' (J.1.1) inscription. In other words, although the linguistic and archaeological senses of 'Tartessian' may be less than exactly co-terminous, they coincide at this key site on the upper Guadiana. Formally, lok°on suits an o-stem accusative singular or nominative/accusative neuter, for the meaning cf. Cisalpine Gaulish LOKAN 'interment, funerary urn', corresponding to VRNVM in the parallel Latin text at Todi (1st century BC). Thus, as an item of Common Celtic funerary vocabulary, occurring in the SW corpus alongside Hispano-Celtic names and forms inflected as Indo-European verbs, lok°on is a significant point in favour of the Celticity of the language. A tentative translation for the Medellín stela can be offered: '. . . the burial/funerary urn . . . the daughter of Kelaos rests . . .'.

A further linguistic link is Medellín's pre-Roman name *Konisturgis*, which, though the second element is apparently non-Celtic, probably means 'town of the Konioi', as also most probably the clearly Celtic *Conimbrigā* (modern Coimbra, Portugal). The group name Κονιοι *Conii* is generally recognized as a variant of Κυνητες *Kunētes*, the name of the ancient inhabitants of the Algarve. In other words, the ancient people of the region with the densest distribution of SW inscriptions (the 'linguistic Tartessians') and the cosmopolitan orientalizing 'archaeological Tartessians' of Medellín identified themselves with the same group name. Both *Konioi* and *Kunētes* are probably based on Celtic *kū, *kun-, *kon- 'hound, warrior', likewise the Κονισκοι of the north-central Peninsula (see Joseph 1990 on the forms of this root). In the light of the recurring links between this group name and the inscriptions, any infelicitous ambiguities inherent in the use of the term *Tartessian* (Spanish *tartésico*, German *Tartessisch*, Welsh *Tarteseg*, &c.) for the language of the SW corpus might be avoided if we were to call it instead *Cynetian, cinético, Kynetisch, Cynwydeg*.

Amongst the important conclusions drawn by Almagro-Gorbea and his colleagues concerning the implications of the finds from the Medellín necropolis is the key point that it does not represent the beginning of the written tradition in the 7th-century material, at which stage one would expect uniformity strictly maintained under a royal monopoly or some similar restricted order of specialists. Rather, we are at the mid-point, with writing employed in more than one social domain and the development of local epigraphic schools. On the double graffito of Medellín T2, one string of signs on this bowl reads right-to-left (as does funerary stela J.57.1 = T1) and the other left-to-right. T3, a graffito on a second vessel reads left-to-right and is assigned to the later 6th century BC. From these data, Almagro-Gorbea plausibly proposes that we are seeing a changeover in scribal practice (right-to-left to left-to-right) *ante c.* 550 BC, due to contact with Greek alphabetic literacy, and that the same change might have occurred at about the same time at other centres. Rising Greek influence from the late 7th century BC is amply borne out by the exotic finds in the Medellín necropolis itself. In the historical context for such developments, we may recall the constriction of Gadir's mother city Tyre under prolonged Babylonian pressure from 586 BC and the favouritism shown the Phokaian Greeks by the Tartessian ruler Arganthonios about 550 BC. The important inscription of Alcalá del Río (J.53.1), near Seville, atypically reads left-to-right/clockwise and also shows six lapses in the 'principle of redundancy' (on which see below), both of which are probably later features. Note also the left-to-right Moura graffito]*ꟼⵜⵊΑɅΑ[ ]*rob^a na[, for which a later date has been proposed. Therefore, we have potentially a powerful criterion for dividing the SW corpus chronologically on the basis of the primary orientation of the writing.

Harrison dates the inscriptions added to the Late Bronze Age warrior stela of Capote (J.54.1) to 700–600 BC (2004, 51, 79). Note now also the more recently

Detail of a reconstruction of the La Joya funerary chariot, Museo Provincial de Huelva

discovered warrior stela with Tartessian inscription from Cabeza del Buey IV below (p. 124). As argued by Kristiansen (1998, 157–60), the funerary stones with Tartessian inscriptions probably form a continuum with the Late Bronze Age 'warrior stelae' of the south-western peninsula (on these pre-literate stelae in general, see further Pingel 1993; Celestino 1990; 2001; Harrison 2004; Celestino & López-Ruiz 2006; Díaz-Guardamino 2008; 2010). Another link between the warrior stelae and the SW corpus can be drawn in the context of the present study. Wheeled vehicles are a common motif in the LBA warrior stelae, and forms that can be taken as a Tartessian verbal noun **oretᵒo** (J.4.1.), probably in the genitive case, 'of help, of deliverance, of salvation', literally 'of running under', and its perfect 3rd person singular form **kᵒtᵘuaratᵉe** 'has delivered to', literally 'has run under towards' (J.53.1), express the action of horses and/or wheeled vehicles. Note that the Old Irish cognate *fod·rethat* 'that run under him' is used specifically of a king's chariot wheels in the 7th-century wisdom text *Audacht Morainn*; similarly in the Early Welsh *Gododdin* the words *ae gwaredei* 'used to run under him' describe the horses of a hero. These various forms are all from Proto-Celtic **u(p)o-ret-*. Harrison (2004, 147) collects a total of 24 examples of two-wheeled chariots from the warrior stelae. One subsequent discovery is the Cabeza del Buey IV stela with a chariot and an added Tartessian inscription. The rich Tartessian burial from tomb 17 at La Joya, Huelva (700–600 BC), included a luxurious two-wheeled chariot of walnut wood with lion-headed hub caps.

Chamorro (1987, 230) and Harrison (2004, 312) identified swords on the pre-

Swords of the 11th/10th century BC from the Huelva deposition, Museo Provincial de Huelva

literate stelae as specifically of the Atlantic 'carp's-tongue' type (which we can now identify more specifically as the distinct and earlier 'Huelva' type), at least 84 examples of which were included in the Huelva deposition of *c.* 950 BC. In the discussion of Burgess and O'Connor, the identifiable weapon types of these stelae belong to their Hío Phase of *c.* 1150–*c.* 950 BC.

In reviewing the pre-literate stelae, Almagro-Gorbea (2005) draws attention to a number of images of musical instruments, including lyres, which he argues show oral poetry flourishing at this stage, possibly a key prerequisite for the inception of funerary epigraphy. Harrison (2004, 146) notes six lyres on the stelae: Luna (Zaragoza) with 15 carefully carved strings (Harrison dates this stela as one of the earliest, at the 13th or 12th century BC), Herrera de Duque/Quinterías (Badajoz), and Capilla I, III, and IV (Badajoz). The stela from Capote, Higuera la Real (Badajoz), which shows both a lyre and a chariot, was reused for two short Tartessian inscriptions (J.54.1 below). The fact that the lyres are generally shown together with shields and other items of the warrior's panoply might imply that bards belonged to the class of the arms-bearing warrior élite. The instrument would therefore have been one of the status symbols of the deceased (cf. the suggestion of Harrison 1988, 32). Alternatively, the idea may be that a lyric elegy has been translated into pictures on the stone, in which case it was the bard, and not the lyre on its own, that was the status symbol.

Although briefly and rather mysteriously reported (Murillo et al. 2005, 17–19; Criado 1996), the two stelae of Cerro Muriano II (near Córdoba to the north), a copper-rich area, are potentially significant. The site was discovered during construction work in a wooded area in the mid 1970s, then reconcealed to prevent looting. It comprises a low circular feature about 20 metres in diameter, which yielded large quantities of charcoal and abundant bones of cattle, sheep/goats, and horses, some showing signs of butchering and burning, indicating feasting or sacrificial activities. The stelae were found in the same context, marking either side of the circle. One (measuring 1 m × 40 cm showed iconography typical of the warrior stelae: spear, sword, v-notched shield, a conventionally stylized two-horse chariot, and a large central 'stick' figure with horned headgear and splayed fingers and toes (cf. below pp. 124, 284). On the sole basis of images on this first stela a date in the range 11th–9th century BC is indicated. The surviving field sketch of the second stela is illegible, but it is clearly a Tartessian inscribed stone with an anti-clockwise series of signs following an incised rectangle. If these finds could be re-excavated and the reports confirmed, they would point to the literate and preliterate traditions overlapping, and sharing a ritual context, preceding the Orientalizing Period proper, as well as adding a point near the south-eastern limits of the distribution of the SW inscribed stones.

According to Harrison (2004), the Late Bronze Age warrior stelae went out of favour rapidly in the period 800–750 BC. That period also saw a change of funerary rite, from an absence of burials—a general negative characteristic of Atlantic Late Bronze Age cultures—to burials with grave goods and tumuli. (The warrior stela of Solona de Cabañas, Logrosán, Cáceres, is thus exceptional in being placed above a warrior's burial.) This transition coincides with the opening of the Phoenician-catalysed 'Early Orientalizing Phase' of the Tartessian material culture c. 750–c. 650 (Chamorro 1987, 204; but beginning somewhat earlier in the scheme of Burgess and O'Connor 2008). The revival of the burial rite at this stage, after a hiatus of several centuries, is probably itself of eastern Mediterranean inspiration, as the Early Iron Age burials of the western Peninsular regions show less influence from the central-European Urnfield tradition.

There can be no obvious or predetermined answer to the question of whether the adoption of alphabetic writing and its application to an indigenous language necessarily came sooner or later—requiring a more or less intense, more or less prolonged Phoenician contact—than the other aspects of the revolutionary orientalization of the Tartessian material culture. It is likely enough that a relatively abrupt transition to written funerary stones came as yet another facet of the sweeping 'orientalizing package' taking hold in the 8th century. But this is not yet certain.

Writing has not been found evenly distributed throughout the orientalizing area. Tartessian inscriptions are known from only a few of the orientalizing burial grounds of south-west Spain. As Rodríguez Ramos (2002) notes, the most intensive evidence of writing does not come from the Tartessian regions richest in imported luxuries. Future discoveries may alter this picture. The distribution of Ancient Celtic place-names in the Peninsula suggests a possible explanation. They appear densely in southern Portugal and nearby parts of south-west Spain, while they progressively thin out and are intermixed with clearly non-Celtic place-names as one moves eastward across Andalucía (Sims-Williams 2006; Koch 2007). That probably means that, by the beginning of the Roman period at least, the region around and west of the Guadiana was more heavily Celtic speaking than the basin of the Guadalquivir. As what now appears to be a literate tradition based in Celtic speech, the distribution of SW inscriptions simply follows other indicators of Celticity in the southern Peninsula.

As I proposed in *Tartessian 2* (§§124–32), the authors of the SW corpus might best be understood as having received their literacy second-hand as part of a two-stage process. The Peninsula's Mediterranean coast came first into primary and strengthening contact from a succession of literate peoples from the east, including possibly the Minoans initially, then Mycenaeans, Cypriots, and Phoenicians, the last eventually becoming full-blown colonists. In this zone, knowledge of literacy came together with direct contact with exotic languages bringing opportunities for cultural advancement. For example, at Alcorrín (Marzoli et al. 2010), we find Phoenician literacy at an extraordinary centre of indigenous power by the 8th or even late 9th century BC. That site overlooks Gibraltar from a western Mediterranean coastal zone devoid of Celtic place-names, but verging upon, and no doubt in contact with, areas where pre-Roman Celtic names are well attested, in south Portugal and along the Guadiana. Thus, in Atlantic-facing regions, groups such as the Kunētes/Konioi would have encountered literacy both from the most far-ranging of the mariners from the eastern Mediterranean, but also as a prestigious cultural attribute adopted by their most powerful indigenous neighbours. Almagro-Gorbea et al. (2008, 1033–59) envision a process of expansionism or colonization from the core zone of Tartessos, along the lower Baetis/Guadalquivir, to the Kunētes/Konioi of south Portugal and up along the Anas/Guadiana. Within such a scenario, the secondary indigenous group faced the challenge of retaining their distinctive identity while at the same time seizing new economic opportunities and embracing cultural innovation. They could achieve this by developing literacy in their own (Western Indo-European) language. The process would have been broadly comparable to the beginnings of literacy in Ireland a millennium afterwards. The Britons were Roman citizens and so demonstrated their cultural attainments through the medium of Latin. The Irish, experiencing prolonged Roman influence on the Empire's fringe, maintained a distinct non-Roman identity while adopting Christianity and other aspects of *romanitas* (mostly from the Romanized Britons), by enthusiastically cultivating literacy in their own language. This included inventing their own ogam script on a disguised Latin basis and an imaginary national history and history of Gaelic stretching back to Old Testament times. Nearer the period of Tartessian literacy, the Greek adaptation of the Phoenician alephat is also comparable, as an innovation not intended merely to emulate Phoenicians, but to express (even to assert) their distinct Hellenic tradition and identity through a new medium.

It is relevant in this connection that the pre-Roman names of Tartessian towns (in the archaeological and historical senses) often contain the non-Celtic and possibly non-Indo-European elements *ip(p)o* and *-(m)urgi-*. The latter type has the more constricted and probably earlier distribution, going back to the Late Bronze Age as proposed by Almagro-Gorbea (2010). For a variety of reasons, some fairly obvious, it is inherently likely that more than one language had been in use within the south-western quarter of the Iberian Peninsula during later prehistory and the cusp of pre-Roman protohistory. First of all, Europe and Africa, the Atlantic and Mediterranean, come together here. Secondly, we find pre-Roman place- and group names in the region of both Indo-European (often clearly Celtic) type, mostly to the north and west, and of non-Indo-European type, mostly to the south and east, with a wide zone of intermixing between the two. For example, the names in Celtic *-brigā* and *Eburo-* extend well into the zones of *ip(p)o* and *-(m)urgi-*. Hecataeus's statement (*c.* 500 BC) that there was a πόλις of Ταρτησσος called Ἐλιβυργη *Elibyrgē* at least raises the possibility that the 'Tartessian' place-name element *-(m)urgi-* might have assumed that form as an Iberianization of Celtic *brig-* 'hillfort, town' < Indo-European *$b^h\mathring{r}g^h$-*. Thirdly, the archaeological record shows that the south-western Peninsula had been in contact with speakers of a variety of exotic languages from the eastern Mediterranean, including the Mycenaean Greeks from about 1500 BC followed by the Cypriots and Phoenicians (Ruiz-Gálvez 2008; 2009; Mederos 2008; 2009). And fourthly, the genesis of Palaeohispanic literacy itself requires intense intellectual contact between speakers of different languages. In short, we should not be at all surprised to find evidence for more than one language within the historically and archaeologically defined limits of Tartessos. In fact, the proximity and overlapping of Indo-European and non-Indo-European idioms in this region may help to elucidate some of the peculiar typological features that distinguish the Celtic languages from the other branches of Indo-European (see further below, pp. 266–7).

The only certain examples of the Tartessian script used in the Peninsular Later Iron Age (thus after the collapse of Tartessos and coeval with the Palaeohispanic scripts derived from the South-western) involve other media and other functions: for example, a graffito on a bowl dated to the later 4th or 3rd century BC from Garvão (Ourique, Beja, south Portugal) has been interpreted by Correa (2002) as a Tartessian personal name **aiot'ii**, and now the graffito on ceramic]**rob**ᵃ**a(n)**[(alternatively](**n**)**abor**[) from Castelo de Moura, possibly of the earlier 4th century BC.

SCRIPT AND TRANSLITERATION

For discoveries predating 1997, the readings and Romanized transliterations of Untermann in *Monumenta Linguarum Hispanicarum* 4 have been adopted as the authoritative starting point. His numbering system is followed in the present catalogue of inscriptions (pp. 29–134) and cross-references. Untermann's transliteration system of the SW script is largely consistent with that developed in the work of Correa. Both build on Schmoll's breakthrough in the decoding, which recognized the 'principle of redundancy', that is, the agreement between the stop consonants and the following vowel signs. It is important to point out in this connection that the decoding of the phonetic values of the SW script has been carried out independently and by different researchers from the present work, which is concerned more with the classification issue and the hypothesis of the Celticity of the inscriptions' language. Therefore, the two stages of decipherment have not been determined by the same principles. Unlike the assignment of phonetic values to the signs, the proposed word divisions here are often my own, though some of these follow the earlier segmentations published by Untermann in MLH 4. It is now possible to confirm most of the word divisions given in the 2009 edition of this book and to revise a few others in the light of the Mesas do Castelinho inscription (unearthed in September 2008). As explained in detail in *Tartessian 2*, this newly discovered text contains many of the same sequences of signs previously recognized as word stems, inflexional endings, and prefixes, recombined so as to confirm their earlier indentification as isolatable syntactic units.

The version of the Untermann/Correa transliteration system used here is as follows:

a e i o u
b^a b^e b^i b^o b^u
$k^a g^a$ $k^e g^e$ $k^i g^i$?? $k^o g^o$ $k^u g^u$
$t^a d^a$ $t^e d^e$ $t^i d^i$? $t^o d^o$ $t^u d^u$
l m m n r ? ŕ
s ś ?φ :

The Espanca stone (J.25.1), with two complete 27-sign sequences of the Tartessian abekatu, or a closely related archaic Palaeohispanic signary [Câmara Municipal, Castro Verde; MESA]; 25 signs are transcribed above with the names of corresponding Phoenician and Greek letters noted.

A a	9 be	Λ ka	Δ tu	Ɣi	)(ke	ꓩl	}ba	ꓨn
ALEPH	BETH	GIMEL	DALETH	YODH	KAPH	LAMEDH	(MEM)	NUN
ALPH	BETA	GAMMA	DELTA	IOTA	KAPPA	LAMBDA	(MU)	NU

Ɣm	)(?r	M ś	X ta	Ɑu	ꝯr	≡ ?φ	Ⓘ ti
MEM		SHIN	TAW	WAW	RESH	HE	TETH
MU		SIGMA	TAU	UPSILON	RHO	EPSILON	THETA

目 ku	ꛛ bo	Ψ ?	↑ bi	≠o	Z ?	Ǝꓓ ?	⋈ ko
HETH	PE						
ETA	PI						

Although probably representing the same sound, �/Ꮇ and Ꮤ are distinguished in the Romanized transliterations here as **m** and sans-seriph m respectively.

The system of Rodríguez Ramos differs from Correa/Untermann over a few key details. Where his published transcriptions diverge from the texts adopted here, these variants are given at the end of entries on the individual inscriptions below. I have accepted Rodríguez Ramos' and Correa's interpretation of Ᵽ as k^i/ g^i, but retain the Correa/Untermann transliteration of Ⴙ as b^u (which can also stand for **m^u**, notionally also p^u), rather than as Rodríguez Ramos' k^u/g^u. (It should be remembered, in considering these alternative proposals for Tartessian Ⴙ, that the allophonic alternation of [k^w] and [p] was a characteristic tendency of the Ancient Celtic sound systems.) ↑ clearly represents a stop consonant before the vowel Ⴖ **i**; its appearance in the verbal endings in recurrent formulaic language suggests a transcription t^i (as an alternative for the grapheme Ꝋ t^i), at least in some occurrences. (A similar sign occurs for *ti* in the North-eastern Iberian script and also, though perhaps coincidentally, the Cypriot syllabary.) However, the transcription followed in this edition as a first option is b^i, as proposed by Correa and Rodríguez Ramos. Along with the Greek spelling Ἀργανθωνιος (for etymological *Argantonios*), the orthographic variation -nt^{i}i, -nii seen in the Tartessian inscriptions may reflect a general instability in clusters of nasal + stop consonants (as in Insular Celtic) and in the combination -*nt*- in particular. There is also uncertainty over the value of some other (mostly infrequently occurring) signs. The current state of our knowledge of the Tartessian script is thus relatively less advanced than that of the North-eastern Iberian and Celtiberian scripts. Against this background, the Tartessian script is sometimes still termed 'undeciphered'. It is more accurate to say 'not wholly deciphered/decoded' (cf. Villar 2004). There are broad areas of agreement among the experts concerning the values of most of the frequently occurring Tartessian signs. And the accepted values for the 'Meridional' or South-eastern Palaeohispanic signary are closely similar (Ferrer i Jané 2010). There is thus consensus concerning most of the readings that first suggested Celticity and which provided compelling motivation for widening comparisons with the early Celtic languages. At this stage, the ongoing work with the script and work with the language can inform and stimulate one another.

Two copies of an inscribed Tartessian, or closely related, signary occur on the inscription from Espanca, Castro Verde, within the zone in south Portugal where most of the extant Tartessian inscriptions have been found (Correa 1993; De Hoz 1996; Untermann 1997, 327–9, J.25.1). The opening sequence of signs is related to that of the Phoenician alephat: aleph, beth, gimel, daleth (see p. 21).

In Espanca, as in most of the Tartessian inscriptions, we are to read from right to left, though left-to-right and boustrophedon (alternating lines, right-to-left and left-to-right) also occur in the SW corpus. The more common shape of the signs is most often reversed (as a mirror image) in lines to be read from left to right, leaving little doubt over the intended direction. In the edited transcriptions below, arrows are inserted at the beginning of lines to clarify the direction of the reading. The romanized transliterations are all written left-to-right here. Undivided *scriptio continua* is usual in Tartessian. Line breaks do not systematically correspond to word divisions, and vertical lines | infrequently carved between letters and transliterated as colons [:] in the romanizations do not consistently mark word divisions.

Untermann has suggested some influence from the Greek alphabet on the invention of the Tartessian alphabet. Note the implications of the 6th-century BC graffito NIEΘΩI from Huelva, possibly a Celtic theonym ('to [the wargod] Nētos'), which would thus be evidence that Greek script could sometimes be used to write Tartessian or a related indigenous language in the Later Orientalizing Period (Almagro-Gorbea 2005, 55, discussed in the word-list below). However, it is clear that the primary source of the Tartessian script was most directly a West Semitic alephat (De Hoz 1996), specifically of the later 9th century BC. Rodríguez Ramos (2000) has argued for a direct Phoenician-to-Tartessian monogenesis drawing special attention to the point that the Tartessian and Greek alphabets have added vowels to the vowel-less Phoenician alephat according to different principles: for example, the symbol for the Phoenician laryngeal 'ayin' O is the source of Greek 'omicron' /o/, but Tartessian |e|. De Hoz envisions a rather complex descent of the extant SW script from the Phoenician, which allows for a lost Proto-Palaeohispanic intermediary system and the possibility of a secondary contributing source from the eastern Mediterranean. On the other hand, the more straightforward formulation of Rodríguez Ramos has appealing clarity: the Phoenician script is the 'madre' of the Tartessian script (escritura sudlusitana), and South-east Iberian script (Meridional) is its 'hija', or alternatively its 'sobrina'. The scheme of descent has obvious implications for absolute dating. Graffiti in the Phoenician script (the mother of the Tartessian script according to Rodríguez Ramos) found at the native sites of El Carambolo, Castillo de Doña Blanca (Cádiz), and Alcorrín date back to the 8th century BC (or possibly 9th for the last). The oldest known inscriptions recognized as being written in the SE script (the daughter or niece) have an archaeological context of the 4th century BC. However, the graffiti from Medellín (T2 86H/13–1 c. 625–600 BC and T3 86/TP–1 c. 550–500 BC; see Almagro-Gorbea 2008, 751–71) employ a system of Palaeohispanic writing lacking redundancy, i.e. they are truly semi-syllabic, and thus anticipate the SE writing system. These examples of what resembles, in this particular feature, an early form of Meridional occur alongside—in fact amongst the finds at the same necropolis—as the findspot of a fragmentary stela (J.57.1 = T1 86H/En 12–1 c. 650–625 BC) inscribed with the conventional 'redundant' form of the SW script and re-buried c. 525–500 BC.

There is a methodological observation in connection with the parentage of the scripts. The North-east Iberian script, used along the Mediterranean coast and adjacent regions (including part of south-west Gaul) during the last centuries BC, appears to be a direct or collateral descendant of the Tartessian or SW script. Progress on the Tartessian script has thus been informed by advances with the far more copiously attested NE script and its corpus, and similar approaches have naturally been applied to both corpora. Although the SE script and its corpus are less extensive and less well understood than its north-eastern relative, there is now wide agreement that most of the frequently occurring signs in it have the same or similar phonetic values to those of the SW system, though the principle of redundancy is not a feature of the SE system. Thus, there is universal agreement on SE A *a* Ꜷ *i* ꓇ *l* Ꜹ *n* ꟼ *r̄* ⧧ *s* ꟽ *ś* + *t* △ *tu* ⋀ *ka*)| *ke* ⋈ *ko.* In recent publications, there has also been general agreement regarding SE ⧧ *o* ⏀ *ti* Ꜹ *u* ◇ *e* and significant support for ꟼ *ki* ⋏ *r* Ꜹ *u* ꓷ *te* ▢ *bo* (Ferrer i Jané 2010).

Unlike the scripts derived from Tartessian (or its Proto-Palaeohispanic source), Tartessian itself is a true alphabet, in the sense that each character represents a single phoneme. There are, however, two extraordinary features of the Tartessian script which might be thought to raise the possibility that the alphabet was originally devised for a language which differed phonetically from Tartessian—such as Iberian, which is likely for geographic reasons to have come into contact with Phoenician at an early date—and also call into question the general intellectual merit of the invention of the SW script. First, whereas the language itself surely distinguished voiceless from voiced stops as phonemes—/t/ vs. /d/, /k/ vs. /g/—these opposed series were not distinguished in writing. The phoneme /p/ quite possibly did not exist in Tartessian. There are two signs that can be read as /m/— ꟽ and ꟺ —but these are rare in the inscriptions, and it seems that /m/ is often represented by the series ꓛ bᵃ, ꝯ bᵉ, ↑ bⁱ, ▢ bᵒ, ⋈ bᵘ, or bᵃ, bᵉ, bⁱ, bᵒ, bᵘ preceded by Ꜹ n.

Secondly, by far the most striking feature of the Tartessian writing system is that different symbols are employed for the stop consonants depending on the following vowel, even though the vowel itself is written, unlike the derivative system in the Iberian and Celtiberian semisyllabaries, in which the redundant vowel is omitted. Thus ✕ is the Tartessian letter for [t] or [d] before **a** A, △ for [t] or [d] before **o** +, △ for [t] or [d] before **u** Ꜹ, ⏀ for [t] or [d] before **i** ꟽ, &c. This redundant system—considered alongside the absence of any graphic distinction between voiced and voicelesss stop consonants—may seem simply bizarre or intellectually deficient. On the other hand, as those involved with the decipherment will appreciate, the redundancy does help in reading the texts in that one sign often confirms its neighbour. It is hard to imagine that anyone could have devised such a system unless there was already a perception—or even a fully phonologized principle—that the quality of consonants agreed with those of the following vowels. In fact, precisely this feature is one of the pervasive earmarks of the medieval and modern Goidelic languages. It is often assumed that the contrasting consonant qualities would not have already existed (at a grammaticalized or phonemic level) at the earliest stage of Primitive Irish written in the ogam script. But as the ogam alphabet's structure is closely modelled on that of Latin, the script had no means to represent such a feature of the sound system whether or not it had already been phonemicized. (On the evidence for phonemic consonant quality in Tartessian, see further *Tartessian 2*, 140–4). In any event, there is no reason that a phonetic tendency in a proto-language could not have been phonologized at widely different dates in two of its daughter languages.

Geography and the history of writing remind us that literacy first came to the Iberian Peninsula as a result of contacts with mariners from the eastern Mediterranean, who spoke a variety of languages, including Semitic and Greek. Literate peoples also first made their landfall in the Peninsula along its non-Indo-European-speaking Mediterranean coast before passing on to the Atlantic west. Therefore, we should not expect the SW corpus to exhibit a linguistic immunity to external influences, either in its writing system or the language itself, the corpus being the outcome of prolonged and intense intellectual contacts between different languages, as one of many innovations stirred by 'orientalizing' cultural aspirations (see further *Tartessian 2*, 163–72). The fact that the Tartessian writing system is as different from the Phoenician as it is implies an intentional creative reformation and that indigenous linguistic ideas already existed, including a native analysis of the sound system.

The single most consistent disparity between the Tartessian evidence and the reconstructed Proto-Celtic sound system comes with the reflexes of $*/w/$ (or $*/u̯/$). Tartessian often writes nothing in this sound's etymological position, raising the possibility that it had simply been lost as in most dialects of ancient Greek and the Old Irish outcome of the more weakly articulated allophone. However, in other examples Tartessian **o ✚** or **u Ч** continue Proto-Celtic $*/w/$. In some instances where $*/w-/$ has vanished, the immediately following vowel has doubled: for example **eertᵃaune** OЧЧA✕9OO [J.55.1] , where the first e- stands in the position of Celtiberian *u* /w/ in Celtiberian *uertaunei*. The evidence pertaining to this problem is examined in detail in *Tartessian 2*, 137–40, where the following explanation is offered. **u Ч**, derived from $*/w-/$ and probably pronounced [w], was most stable preceding **a A**. Preeceeding other vowels, the glide's quality first centralized to [ǫ] then became fully assimilated to the articulation of the following vowel. For example, **ooŕoir** (J.19.2) can be analysed as | Qorǫir | and traced back to *Worwiros.* **lebᵒoiire** (MdC) and **linbᵒoire** (J.11.2) (both from *Lemo-wiroi*) represent subsequent successive stages, in which the glide is at first assimilated to the quality of the following vowel | Lemo-i̯irē | and then either fully vocalized | Lɪmo-irē | or merely omitted from representation for graphic economy.

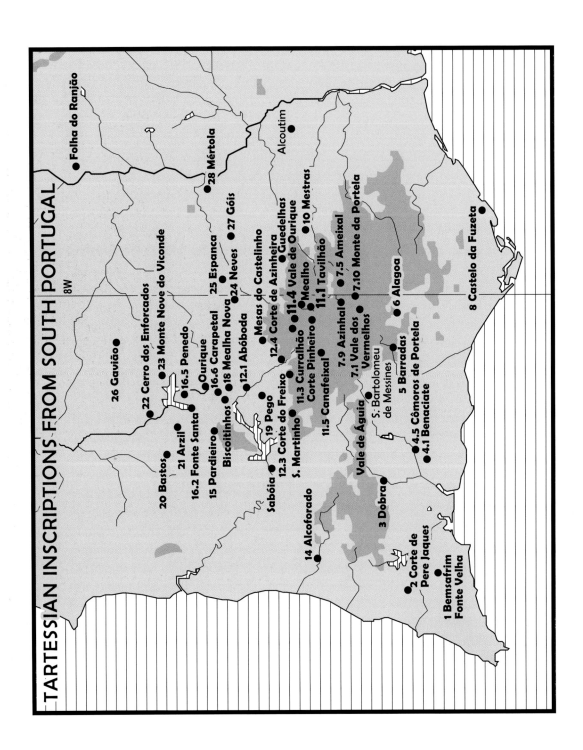

TARTESSIAN INSCRIPTIONS FROM SOUTH PORTUGAL

8W

Folha do Ranjão

28 Mértola

25 Espanca
27 Góis
24 Neves

26 Gavião
22 Cerro dos Enforcados
23 Monte Nove do Viconde
16.5 Penedo
Ourique
16.6 Carapetal
18 Mealha Nova
12.1 Abóboda

Mesas do Castelinho
12.4 Corte de Azinheira
Guedelhas
11.4 Vale de Ourique
Mealho
10 Mestras
11.1 Tavilhão
7.5 Ameixal
7.10 Monte da Portela

Alcoutim

20 Bastos
21 Arzil
16.2 Fonte Santa
15 Pardieiro
Biscoitinhos

19 Pego
12.3 Corte do Freixo
S. Martinho
11.3 Curralhão
Corte Pinheiro
11.5 Canafeixal
7.9 Azinhal
7.1 Vale dos Vermelhos
S. Bartolomeu de Messines
5 Barradas
6 Alagoa
8 Castelo da Fuzeta

Sabóia

14 Alcoforado

Vale de Águia
4.5 Cômoros de Portela
4.1 Benaciate

3 Dobra

2 Corte de Pere Jaques

1 Bemsafrim Fonte Velha

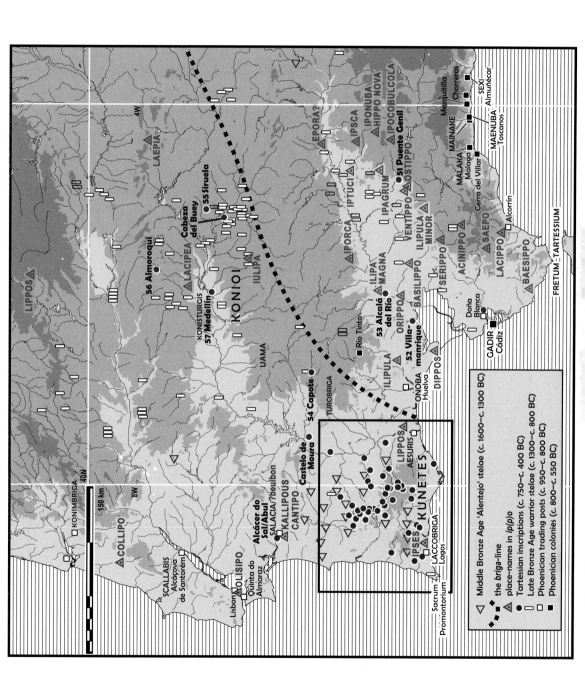

KONIMBRIGA

COLLIPO

SCALLABIS
Alcáçova
de Santarém

Lisbon
OLISIPO
Quinta do
Almaraz

Alcácer do
Sal/Abul
SALACIA/?beuibon

KALLIPOUS
CANTIPO

Castelo de
Moura

TUROBRIGA

54 Capote

56 Almoroquí

LACIPEA Cabeza
del Buey

55 Siruela

LAEPIA

4W

KONISTURGIS
57 Medellín

KON·IOI

UAMA

IULIPA

IPORCA

ILIPA
MAGNA

53 Alcalá
del Río

ORIPPO

52 Villa-
manrique

Río Tinto

ILIPULA

ONOBA
Huelva

DIPPOS

BASILIPPO

SERIPPO

EPORA?

IPTUCI

IPSCA

IPAGRUM

IPONUBA
HIPPO NOVA

IPOCOBULCOLA

VENTIPPO
OSTIPPO

51 Puente Genil

ILIPULA
MINOR

ACINIPPO

SAEPO

LACIPPO

BAESIPPO

MALAKA
Malaga

Cerro del Villar

Alcorrín

MAINAKE

Mezquitilla
Chorreras

MAENUBA:
Toscanos

SEXI
Almuñécar

FRETUM·TARTESSIUM

GADIR
Cádiz

Doña
Blanca

40N

3W

150 km

LIPPOS

LIPPOS
AESURIS

KUNETES

IPSES

LACCOBRIGA
Lagos

Sacrum
Promontorium

Legend:
⬇ Middle Bronze Age 'Alentejo' stelae (c. 1600–c. 1300 BC)
◆ the briga-line
△ place-names in ip(p)o
● Tartessian inscriptions (c. 750–c. 400 BC)
◗ Late Bronze Age warrior stelae (c. 1300–c. 800 BC)
▭ Phoenician trading posts (c. 950–c. 800 BC)
◻ Phoenician colonies (c. 800–c. 550 BC)

Tartessian Inscriptions

¶NOTE 1. Where variant readings are given below, for convenience of comparison, the superficial differences in the varying transcription conventions of individual scholars are not replicated here. At the time of writing, the Museu da Escrita do Sudoeste, Almodôvar (MESA), displays many inscribed stones belonging to the permanent collections of other museums in Portugal; as a rule, both institutions will be noted here.

¶NOTE 2. Suggested syntactic functions are labelled as follows: N = noun; V = verb; E = enclitic; dat. = dative; nom. = nominative; acc. = accusative; gen. = genitive; loc. = locative; sg. = singular; pl. = plural; fem. = feminine; pvb = preverb; prep. = preposition; pf = perfective particle; neg. = negative particle; rel. = relative pronoun; demon. = demonstrative; attrib. = attributive of relationship; adv. = adverb; cjt. = conjunction. Probable co-ordinative (*dvandva*) compounds are indicated with the symbol ≡.

¶NOTE 3. 'THE FORMULA'. The recognition of a recurrent formulaic pattern—consisting of a 'naming phrase'+**uar(n)b^{a}an+t^{e}e(e)·ro-b^{a}are+(b^a)nařk^eent^{i}i**—aids in the interpretation of many of the inscriptions. Although that is the most usual order, there are numerous ellipses, variations, rewordings, and elaborations. See further Appendix C; *Tartessian 2*, 101–2.

J.1.1

'Fonte Velha 6' Bemsafrim, Lagos, south Portugal [Museu Municipal
Figueira de Foz; Museu da Escrita do Sudoeste, Almodôvar] (Correia no. 15)
136 X 73 X 15cm

Tartessian text

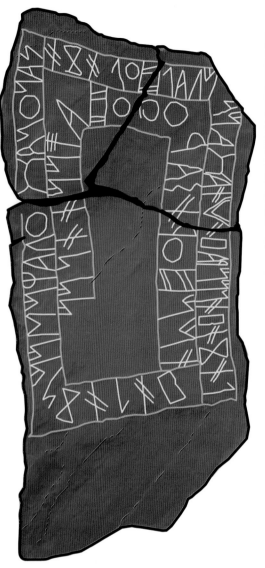

J.1.1. 'Fonte Velha 6' (photo: Jane Aaron)

Transliteration

1   lokᵒobᵒ≡niirabᵒo tᵒo aŕaia

2   i kᵃaltᵉe lokᵒo

3   n ane naŕkᵉe kᵃakⁱiśiin

4   kᵒolobᵒ

5   o ii tᵉeˑro-bᵃar

6   e (bᵉ)e tᵉa

7   siioonii

Syntactic analysis

lokᵒobᵒo≡niirabᵒo tᵒo   aŕaia͟|i kᵃaltᵉe lokᵒo|n ane naŕkᵉe
dat.pl.   dat.pl.   prep. dat.sg. loc.sg.? acc.sg.   V 3sg.?

kᵃak͟iśĺln|kᵛolobᵛ|o ii tᵉe·ro-bᵃar|e (bᵉ)e   tᵉa|siioonii
dat.pl. ?   pvb pf V.3sg.   ?   N? *or* V 3pl.

suggested phrasing and some possible glosses

For the divine Lugoues [and] for the chief men	*| Lugubo≡nirabo |*
to araiā (= ?'the ploughed land'),	*| to araiāi |*
in the grove (i.e. necropolis).	*| kaldē |* or
or for a 'Celt, Gaul'	*| Kaltē |* or *| Galtē |*
a burial deposition/urn,	*| logon |*
rests unmoving within	*| an(d)e nar'ke(t) |*
—and invoking all the Eχskingoloi 'heroic ones'—	*| k⁽ᵘ⁾āk͟iśinkolobo |*
it has carried [the offering/deceased] away,	*| ii de·ro-bāre |*
so they might give [benefit]	*| me dāsi̯onji (< *dāsi̯onti) |*
or the child of Taskio(o̯)onos	*| Tas(k)i̯o(o̯)oni̯i |*

'For the divine Lugoues and for the chief men—and for all the "heroic ones"—a burial rests unmoving within the sacred grove that has carried away [the offering/deceased] towards the ploughland, so they might give [benefit].'

Commentary

The parallels to other Palaeohispanic texts provide the most secure core of the interpretation. In other words, we start from the assumptions that the resemblance of **lokᵒobᵒo≡niirabᵒo** to Callaecian ʟᴠᴄᴠʙᴏ ᴀʀǫᴠɪᴇɴᴏʙᴏ (&c.) is probably not mere coincidence, and that neither is the resemblance of **lokᵒobᵒo≡niirabᵒo tᵒo araia͟i** to Celtiberian ᴛᴏ ʟᴠɢᴠᴇɪ ᴀʀᴀɪᴀɴᴏᴍ (Peñalba de Villastar, K.3.3). Therefore, this starting point provides double evidence for a relationship between the language of the South-western inscriptions and two indigenous Indo-European (specifically Celtic) languages in use in the Iberian Peninsula at the beginning of the Roman Period. It also follows from the Celtiberian comparandum that it is somewhat less likely that **araia͟i** is the name of the deceased (i.e. '[a grave] for Araiā') and more likely that the form is an item of Hispano-Celtic vocabulary specifically connected with the cult of the divinity Lugus (plural *Lugoues*) and widespread associated cult practices. The gloss 'ploughland' for ᴀʀᴀɪᴀɴᴏᴍ goes back to Schwerteck (1979; see further Wodtko 2000; Jordán 2006) and might suit Tartessian **araia͟i** as well. Incidentally, the Middle Welsh variant spelling *Maeth ap Mathonwy* for Math of the Mabinogi, where he is a central character in the heroic biography of Lleu (< *Lugus*), suggests his former identity with the mythological ploughman *Amaethon* < **Ambaχtonos*, the unaccented initial *A-* being prone to loss in Old Welsh (see further Koch 1990, 2–4). **tᵒo araiai** beside TO LVGVEI shows that *to*, whatever its etymology and precise meaning, functions as a preposition assigning dative case (De Bernardo Stempel 2008).

This external basis of the interpretation can then be extended along two lines internal to the SW corpus. First, the initial co-ordinated datives/ablatives plural (**lokᵒobᵒo≡niirabᵒo**, cf. LVCVBO ARQVIENOBO) are echoed further on by a third (**kᵃakⁱiśinkᵒolobᵒo**). There are also the 'verbal' formula words, which recur frequently in the corpus (**naŕkᵉe . . . tᵉe·ro-bᵃare**). In the light of the examination of the verbal complex in *Tartessian 2*, it is notable that **naŕkᵉe** and **tᵉe·ro-bᵃare** are not in their more usual order and that **naŕkᵉe** does not show one of its most frequent forms with present-tense (Indo-European primary) marking, namely **naŕkᵉentⁱi** or what is probably a secondary phonological development of that, **naŕkᵉeni(i)**. The epigraphy is not crowded on the stone, and there would have been plenty of room for one of the longer forms. Furthermore, what is the most common final word in the extant complete inscriptions is **naŕkᵉentⁱi** or **naŕkᵉeni(i)**, where here we find the hapax **tᵉasiioonii**. These details suggest the possibility that **tᵉasiioonii**, rather than being a name (though it resembles British *Tasciouanos* < **Taskio-gᵘonos*, specifically a case form of the adjectival patronymic **Taskio-gᵘonios, -iā*), might more probably be a verb with distinctive primary marking, distinguishing the most recent action or state in the narrative succession of tenses. In particular, we should consider as one fairly obvious possibility reading this form as a 3rd plural future/desiderative | *dāsiionji* | < Pre-Celtic **dōsiiónti* 'they will give' ~ Vedic *dāsyánti* 'they will give', Gaulish 3rd singular *bissiet* ?'will be', relative 3rd plural *toncsiiont-io* (cf. Lambert 1994, 63); for the meaning and function, note also Lusitanian DOENTI 'they give' (once more with a primary ending) in an inscription commemorating offerings to the gods. If this is the correct analysis, **bᵉe tᵉasiioonii** is comparable in form, syntax, and function to the recurrent concluding phrase **bᵃa naŕkᵉeni** (J.1.2), **bᵃa naŕkᵉentⁱi** (J.16.1, J.16.3, J.18.1), where the preverbal segment can be taken as an affirmative conjunction, meaning approximately 'so' (~ Old Irish *ma* 'if'; see *Tartessian 2*, 104–6). That would leave us with no personal names in J.1.1; however, the prominence given to the divine name **lokᵒobᵒo** by its initial position already raises the possibility that this is not a conventional funerary inscription preoccupied with the identity of the deceased. In the Phoenician and Punic worlds, it was common to erect inscribed stelae commemorating sacrifices and naming the gods honoured. Such a practice may be reflected here and similarly in J.5.1, where there are again no likely personal names, and prominent triple co-ordinated datives/ablatives plural take up most of the text. A further notable absence in this connection is the formula word **uar(n)bᵃan** | *uar_aman* | < **u(p)er_amām** 'highest place, state, being' or anything obviously taking that word's place as an accusative of destination and/or expression of the sublime afterlife of the deceased.

J.1.2

'Fonte Velha 3' Bemsafrim, Lagos, south Portugal [Museu Nacional de Arqueologia, Lisbon] (Correia no. 11) 117 × 51 × 15cm

J.1.2 'Fonte Velha 3' Bemsafrim

kᵒo-bᵉelibᵒo na-kⁱi·bᵘu oira uarbᵃan
tⁱirtᵒos ne-bᵃa naŕkᵉeni

[Rodríguez Ramos: **kobelibona*kikuoirauarban tirtosnebanaŕrkeni**]

Syntactic analysis

> **kᵒo- bᵉelibᵒo na-kⁱi·bᵘu　oira-uarbᵃan　tⁱirtᵒos　ne　-bᵃa**
> prep. dat.pl.　　neg.　V.3sg. N　acc.sg.fem. nom.sg.　neg. adv/cjt.

> **naŕkᵉeni**
> V.3pl.

Commentary

The name **tⁱirtᵒos** was probably in origin the Celtic ordinal number 'third' (Gaulish *tritos*, Latin *Tertius*, which was used as a man's name) or was similar enough in form to have been felt to mean that. Therefore, the poetry of the epitaph, as interpreted, would play on the name, to say that 'Third' had attained the highest, i.e. the first. The syntax juxtaposes the contrasting **uarbᵃan** and **tⁱirtᵒos**. Dative plural **bᵉelibᵒo** could be either a group name or a common noun, 'strong ones' being one possible meaning (see further 160–1 below). Along the lines suggested before (Koch 2010, 211–12; *Tartessian 2*, 105), the negation of the recurring **bᵃa naŕkᵉentⁱi** would have to be understood as reversed in meaning by the preceding negative **na-kⁱi·bᵘu**, so approximately:

'By no means does Tirtos now rest [here]
| *Tirtos ne-ma narken ́n ́i* |

in the company of the *Beles* (?"strong ones")
| *koᵐ Belibo* |

as one who has not been to the heroic summit.'
| *na-kⁱi bū(V) o̧ira-u̯ar₄man* |　　　　< **ne-kʷī+bou̯(e)*

J.1.3

'Fonte Velha 1' Bemsafrim, Lagos, south Portugal [Museu Nacional de
Arqueologia, Lisbon] (Correia no. 9) 67 × 53 × 9cm

→] ⋉AHⱢⱣMƎO⋛APOⱯⱯ⋊IOⱯⱯ

→ ΑΛ**ⱯⱣⱯ‡ⱯΑ[

Syntactic analysis

1)]ŕak^{u}urś t^{e}e·b^{a}are naŕk^{e}eni
        pvb V   V.3pl.

2) ak^a<u>a</u>**ir-ion   a[
        V?   rel.acc.?

'(the named deceased) [this grave/death] has carried away. "They" now rest [here]
//. . . . ?who have been buried under stones. . .'

Compare line 2 ak^a<u>a</u>**iriona with J.7.2 k^{a}aŕner-ion ?'who has been buried under
a cairn', so we may consider reading here likewise a k^a<u>a</u>[ŕn]ir-ion a[.

J.1.4

'Fonte Velha 2' Bemsafrim, Lagos, south Portugal [Museu Nacional de
Arqueologia, Lisbon] (Correia no. 10) 43 × 68 × 12cm

←] * ᚺ∧∧໑○Ͱ⧻○)ꟼ५५ᛑ५Ⴗ○‡[

←]∆⇂∆∆○⇂‡○∆Ⴙ○∆[

Syntactic analysis

]sek^uui uurk^ee   ot^eerk^aa ŕ*[*or* ot^eerk^aaŕ*[

dat.sg.   V.3sg.?   N nom.sg.?

]aeⱧaeoḷeaala[

'. . . has made the grave(s) for a man of the kindred of . . .' *or* 'for (-)Segos . . .' *or*
'. . . for Degos, -(s)-ek̯uos, Tegos'

Commentary

The engraving is well executed. The shape and size of the broken stone and
arrangement of the signs on it indicate that half or more of the text is missing.
Therefore the full syntax of the statement is not recoverable. **uurk^ee** resembles a
verb (preterite < Indo-European perfect; see notes). But alternatively, it could be a
name: compare Celtiberian *urkala* and the Hispano-Celtic names *Urcala*, *Urcalonis*,
Urcalocus, and *Urcico*, as well as the second element of Tartessian **tⁱilek^uurk^uu**
(MdC). Note that *urke* also occurs in Iberian as a personal name element (Wodtko
2000, 461–2). The pre-Roman place-name element *-urgi-* is found in the south-
central Peninsula applied to towns. In favour of the segmentation **ot^eerk^aaŕ*[**,
there are no other likely examples of ᚼŕ at the beginning of a word. Though
near a break and partly obscured, the reading ᚼŕ is not in doubt.

J.1.5

'Fonte Velha 5' Bemsafrim, Lagos, south Portugal
[Museu Nacional de Arqueologia, Lisbon]
(Correia no. 13) 115 × 43 × 12cm

←]9A3AO9ᴹᕼᗡᕼᴹ

← ᴹⵁ𐤌Oᐣᕼᗅᒪ[

→ Ａ*ᗰᕼ⧻⧻ᐸO⧻ᕟᕟ

Syntactic analysis

1) **mutᵘuirea bᵃar[e n]aŕkᵉentⁱi**
   N   V   V 3pl.

                           (*or* **śutᵘuirea**)

            [Rodríguez Ramos: **śutᵘuirea . . .**]

'The daughter of Muturos: [this grave/death] has taken; they now remain [here].'

It is possible alternatively to segment an initial masculine dative singular **mutᵘui** (*or* **śutᵘui**), with **r'-ea·bᵃar[**e as a preverb+infix+verb (< *(p)ro* + feminine nominative singular relative *iā + *bōre*); cf. the element prefixed to the verb in J.6.1 tᵉ]**ea·bᵃare**:

1) **mutᵘui r'-ea·   bᵃar[e n]aŕkᵉentⁱi**   (*or* **śutᵘui**)
   N dat.sg. pf rel.fem.sg. V   V 3pl.

'for Mutos [this grave] that has borne [him]. . .'; they now remain fixed in place.'

2) **a(a/m)musokᵉeonii**
   N? *or* V 3pl.?

Commentary

Sequence (1) of signs begins in the lower right and continues, upwards right-to-left on the right-hand side of stone, then down on the lefthand side. The basic reading is complete and, apart from the two possible phonetic values of the sign resembling

M, not in doubt. Sequence (2) running left-to-right across the bottom of the stone is virtually illegible on the left-hand side, nor is it clear whether it should be read as a continuation of (1) or as a separate text. Within (1) one can recognize the last two words of the recurrent formula **uar(n)bᵃan tᵉe-ro-bᵃare naŕkᵉentⁱi** in there usual order and orthography. Simplex **bᵃar[e** with no preverbs is unusual, indicating that the diction is compressed and possibly elliptical. That leaves **mutᵘuirea** *or* **śutᵘuirea** as the naming clause, also in its normal position at the beginning of the text, starting at the lower right of the stone. Since the formula does not occur in its full form and we do not have a double name with agreement markers (e.g. **lokᵒobᵒo niirabᵒo, iru alkᵘu**), it is uncertain where the naming sequence ends and the verbal formula begins. **mutᵘuirea** could be the nominative of *i̯ā*-stem, used as a feminine patronym, 'daughter of Muturos'. This segmentation is favoured by Celtiberian *muturiskum*, four times in the long Botorrita text (K.1.3) and there once again 'mispelled' as *muturskum*. That Celtiberian name is undoubtedly a genitive plural of a family name, implying as its base a Hispano-Celtic man's name *Muturos*. From the Roman Period a MVTIA M[V]TVRRAE is attested at Talavera de la Reina, Toledo (Wodtko 2000, 268). If we take the single term **mutᵘuirea** as standing for a fuller naming phrase ('X≡daughter of Muturos'), a nominative/accusative dual co-ordinative compound, that would allow **mutᵘuirea** to be the object of **bᵃar[e** and subject n]aŕkᵉentⁱi, but a fossilized formula is also possible.

A possible but less likely alternative interpretation would understand the sequence **rea** as a variant of the **ro** of the usual verbal formula, possibly with a feminine singular infix, cf. Vedic nominative feminine singular relative *yā*, in which case the lowering to **ea** is a regular Tartessian sound change (see *Tartessian 2*, 126–7). That would leave **mutᵘui** as a regular masculine singular dative ('[a grave] for Mutos'). The **mutᵘuirea** reading would have the advantage of being comparable to an attested western Palaeohispanic name MVTVRRA. **mutᵘui**, on the other hand, would eliminate the single example of the precociously Gaelic-looking *i*-epenthesis in **mutᵘuirea**.

The readings of the second–fourth signs of sequence (2) **a(a/m)musokᵉeonii** are uncertain. (**)**sokᵉeonii** could be construed as a 3rd plural verb of the Indo-European type characterized by a -*éi̯e/o*- suffix and the vowel -*o*- in the verbal root. The problem with that interpretation is that **naŕkᵉentⁱi** occurs on the same stone as **a(a/m)musokᵉeonii**, so that the Indo-European primary verbal ending, 3rd plural active *-nti*, would show the *t* preserved in one form and lost by innovation in the other. As **naŕkᵉentⁱi** is formulaic, an archaic representation is possible; that objection is therefore not insurmountable. A second anomaly would be that taking **a(a/m)musokᵉeonii** as a verb with a primary ending would make J.1.5 the only example of primary endings occurring twice on one Tartessian inscription. Nevertheless, (1) and (2) may be separate statements, even carved at different times.

J.1.6

Fonte Velha, Bemsafrim, Lagos, south Portugal [Museu Nacional de Arqueologia, Lisbon] 8.4 x 6.0 x 1.3cm

→ X A ʒ A *   1) tᵃabᵃa*

→ Ͱ P   2) ur

J.2.1

Corte de Pére Jaques, Aljezur, south Portugal [Museu Municipal, Lagos] (Correia no. 24) 97 x 42 x 5cm

→] ☐ / ‡A٩AͰ⋊⋊O / ⋎⋌⋎

Syntactic analysis

]bᵒoara narᵏᵉenii
V 1 sg.   V 3 pl.

'. . .I [the grave] have borne. . . They rest unmoving.'

J.3.1

Dobra, Monchique, south Portugal [Museu Municipal, Lagos] (Correia no. 25)

124 X 82 X 10cm

←]‡ᛉᛈ᛫ᛗᛉᛉ	aibᵘuris[
← ᛉ↑ᛉᛉᚨᛉᛉᛈᛈᴀ[	]a kⁱinbᵃai↑ⁱi
← ᴀᛒᴀ↑‡ᚦ	ro-laᛒa
←]ᛉᛉᛉᚨᛉᚨᛉ	uarbᵃan ubᵘ[u
ᛉ[	]i

Syntactic analysis

aibᵘuris[|]a̠ kⁱinbᵃai↑ⁱi | ro·lak̠ᵘa | uarbᵃan ubᵘ[u |]i
N.nom.sg.   N   pf V.1sg.   acc.sg.fem

'Aiburis . . . I [this stone/grave] have buried (< caused to lie down) with/by the Cimbii (Cempsi) . . . to the highest destination . . . (?they remain).'

or

'I Aiburis . . . have lain down with the Cimbii (Cempsi) . . . to the highest destination . . . (?they remain).'

Commentary

The reading is given here following the text right-to-left anti-clockwise from the lower right-hand corner, as occurs in J.1.1 and several other inscriptions. The inscription has been carefully laid out. It was clearly carved with evenly spaced signs, all of similar size. It is unusual in that, as the text continues and changes direction, it turns a full right angle immediately, rather than curving gradually with one or more oblique signs with intermediate orientation. Also, each 'panel' seems to represent a discrete word or phrase, or comes close to that, though this may be fortuitous. It is therefore probably intentional that the name **aibᵘuris** is physically parallel to, and centred above, **uarbᵃan** 'highest destination'. The stranded ⑂ **i** of the last line shows that we have lost at least one line of text, possibly more. A plausible restoration in this position would be the usual last segment of the recurrent formula, **naŕkᵉentⁱi** ⑂Φ⑂Ο)⑂ΛΑ⑂ or **naŕkᵉenii** ⑂⑂⑂Ο)⑂ΛΑ⑂ (see Appendix C). It is possible that a more sizeable chunk of text has been lost vertically above what survives.

    kⁱinbᵃai↑ⁱi is possibly related to the name *Cempsi* used for a group residing west of the Anas (river Guadiana) near Tartessos and the Cynetes (see Κυνητες below) according to the *Ora Maritima* of Avienus (lines 179, 192–8, 251–5, 297–8). **kⁱinbᵃai↑ⁱi** and/or *Cempsi* may be related to *Cimbii*, a name applied by Livy (28.37) to a location near the coast not far from Gades where the fleet of the Carthaginian Mago was able to land safely in 206 BC. In addition or alternatively, we can compare **kⁱinbᵃai↑ⁱi** to Old Irish *cimbid* 'captive, condemned man', probably based on Old Irish *cimb* 'tribute' (cf. *Lexique* 1960– , C99–100). Both these Irish words may be related to both **kⁱinbᵃai↑ⁱi** and *Cimbii*. Hawkes argued (1977) that Avienus's Cempsi lived in the western Algarve. If so, their territory included Dobra where this inscription was found, strengthening the possible identification. For the connection with Old Irish *cimbid* and *cimb*, it is likely enough that the Cimbii/Cempsi, as inhabitants of this marginal district, were a tributary people of Tartessos and/

ro-la𝔅a

or of the Kunētes/Konioi and that their name articulated their subordinate status.

It is likely that **aibᵘuris** reflects **Aibo-rixs*, that is, a name of the type common in Gaulish and British (though possibly not Celtiberian) that incorporated the Proto-Celtic word for 'king'. (On Tartessian **u** < Proto-Celtic **o* regularly after a labial consonant and before **-rĭ-*, see *Tartessian 2*, 132.) If such *rix*-names were still literally meaningful in the Early Iron Age, does **kⁱinbᵃai↑ⁱi** refer specifically to the subjects of **aibᵘuris**? If we transliterate **kⁱinbᵃai↑ⁱi** as **kⁱinbᵃaibⁱi**—the least problematic Romanization—the case form would be instrumental plural (cf. Gaulish *eiabi* 'with them', GOBEDBI 'with/by means of the smiths'). Therefore, translate 'with the Cimbii/tributaries' or 'by means of the Cimbii/tributaries'; they are buried with him or commissioned this (fine) funerary monument for him.

The unique **ro-la𝔅a** can be analysed as taking the place of the frequent **ro·bᵃare**, **tᵉe-ro·bᵃare**, &c., though it is not inconceivable that a form of that verb had orginally been present on the now missing portion of the stone. The phonetic value of the sign 𝔅 is uncertain, but the prefixed **ro** indicates a verb, bringing our attention to **lakᵉentⁱi** (J.53.1), which is inflected as an Indo-European verb. On funerary inscriptions, an obvious likelihood for both is Indo-European **legʰ-* 'lie down', Old Irish *laigid* 'lies down', *fo·luigi* 'conceals', Early Welsh *go-lo* 'inters'. Formally, the verb in **-a** conforms to a 1st person singular perfect, as opposed to 3rd person singular **-e**. The sense here could therefore be either intransitive 'I, Aiburis, have lain down' or causative 'I (this talking stone) have laid down/concealed/interred'. The latter possibility would make **aibᵘuris** a hanging nominative, a topic loosely connected syntactically to the rest of the statement.

J.4.1
'Benaciate 2', S. Bartolomeu de Messines (Concelho de Silves), south Portugal
[now lost] (Correia no. 51) 120 × 60 × 12cm

Syntactic analysis

?ibᵒoi	ion	asune≡		uarbᵃan	(*or* ib̲ᵒo̲n̲ ion)
loc/dat.sg.?	?rel.acc.sg.	fem.dual *or* loc./dat.sg. acc.sg.			

≡ ekᵘuŕine	obᵃar	bᵃara*******tᵃa	oretᵒo/
fem.dual	?	V.1.sg.	VN gen.sg.
or loc./dat.sg.			

A partial and tentative translation can be suggested, taking **asune≡ ≡ekᵘuŕine** as a discontinuous *dvandva* or co-ordinative compound:

'In the town(??) . . . I [this stone monument] have carried to the highest one, to Asunā (??the divine she-ass/mare) and Ekᵘu-ŕī(g)nī (the horse queen) . . . . of deliverance (< coursing under).'

Commentary

The script continues anti-clockwise along a continuous rectangle with round corners, beginning and ending with an incised box at the lower right-hand corner containing a hapax sign resembling a dollar symbol. The signs are arranged carefully between two incised lines. There is a large section broken away and missing in the lower left of the stone between **bᵃara**[** and]**tᵃa oretᵒo**, which presumably contained 6–9 signs. It is conceivable that **bᵃara** 'I have received, have carried' refers not to remains received by the grave, but to the image of the horsewoman (Ekurīnī herself?) carved on stone J.4.2 from the same site (see next item). An overall interpretation remains difficult. There is a lack of Hispano-Celtic parallels for the opening segment **?ib̲ᵒo̲i̲**. Could **ib̲ᵒoi** be the Indo-European locative form of a borrowing of the non-Indo-European place-name element *ip(p)o* ?'town, hill-fort, prominent place' (see *Tartessian 2* §133)? More probably **?ibᵒoi** is to be read with an uncertain word-initial phoneme preceding **i-**. There is also the question of the function of the text. The probable divine name **ekᵘuŕine** = 'Epona regina', the compound verb **oretᵒo** 'coursing under', and the image of the stately horsewoman on the related inscribed stone from the same site, 'Benaciate 1' (J.4.2), suggest a common theme and raise the possibility that J.4.1 is not (primarily) a funerary statement, but a dedication to a goddess.

J.4.2

'Benaciate 1', S. Bartolomeu de Messines (Concelho de Silves), south Portugal
[Museu Municipal, Silves; Museu da Escrita do Sudoeste, Almodôvar]
(Correia no. 50) 42.5 × 41 × 12cm

photo: Jane Aaron

←]* ꓤ WO[   ]e**ṣi***[

Commentary

Though the remains of the fragmentary inscription are too short to be interpreted,
it is accompanied on the stela with a figure of a relief of a broad-hipped female
figure brandishing a long wand, sceptre, weapon, or possibly thick reins and riding a horse side-saddle. She appears to wear a helmet with noseguard, which is
comparable to the Corinthian helmet of the earlier 7th century BC found in the
river Guadelete, up-river from Cádiz (Olmos 1989, figure 1). What appears to be
a circlular feature carved near her chin may represent a neckring shown from a
turned perspective. This female rider is reminiscent of some images of the goddess
Epona in Gaul and may be related to the form **ekᵘuŕine** 'to the horse-queen',
which occurs on inscription J.4.1. above from the same site carved on the same

sculpture from the horse cult centre at Marchena, south-west Spain, 5th–4th century BC,
Museo Arqueológico, Sevilla (photos: Jane Aaron)

type and thickness of stone. Inscription J.4.1 ends with the verbal noun **oret°o**
'running under, deliver', signifying the action of a vehicle or steed. Several of the
images from the 'horse sanctuary' at Marchena, Sevilla, Spain (6th–4th century BC,
now held in the Museo Arqueológico de Sevilla) are reminiscent of the Benaciate
1 figure, especially the gracefully curving back and neck of the galloping horse
carved on an altar-shaped stela (above left). Another significant comparison is
that some of the Marchena horse carvings, grouped in pairs, clearly continue the
tradition of the stick-figure chariot teams that appear on 25+ of the Late Bronze
Age warrior stelae. These points suggest that the figure called **ekᵘuŕine** on J.4.1
had a deep and widespread basis in myth and cult of the south-western Peninsula.

J.4.3

'Cômoros de Portela 2', S. Bartolomeu de Messines, south Portugal [Museu Municipal, Silves] (Correia no. 24) 64 X 53 X 15cm

←] A ᴼᵞ≠ᴹAOᕼꟼ* [   ]*r tᵉeaion(kᵃ)a[

←] ᴹⲪᵞOↃᴋ* [...na]ŕkᵉentⁱi[

'... the goddess(es) (Deiu̯onā(-)) ... They now remain.'

Examination of the stone favours the reading **tᵉeaiona**[over Untermann's **tᵉeaionkᵃa**[. It appears that the text panel originally continued as an arc over the top; so at least eight signs have been lost. The find site is very near to Benaciate (J.4.1 and J.4.2); therefore, **tᵉeaiona**['goddess' may reflect a form of the same goddess cult as seen in the dedication to **ekᵘuŕi̱ne** (J.4.1) and the equestrian figure (J.4.2). On the phonology of **tᵉeaiona**[| D ʹê(ǫ)onā | < *Deiu̯onā, see the note on **tᵉeaiona**[below and *Tartessian 2*, 135, 143. Dative singular or nominative/accusative dual **tᵉeaion(kᵃ)a**[i | D ʹê(ǫ)onāi |, accusative **tᵉeaion(kᵃ)a**[n | D ʹê(ǫ)onan, or dative plural **tᵉeaion(kᵃ)a**[bo | D ʹê(ǫ)onabo | are also possible readings.

J.4.4

'A e B de Cômores da Portela', S. Bartolomeu de Messines, south Portugal
[Museu Municipal, Silves] (Correia no. 14) 27 × 25 × 12.5cm; 24 × 18 × 12.5cm

←] ᕿᕿᖻ≠Oᒣ*[   ]*r̲e̲o̲n̲uu[

←] *⟩*ᑫᖻ[   ]u̲[a]rbᵃa[an . . .

←] ᖻᕐᕐO[⟫ᴎᙁᖻ   . . . naᒋkᵉ]enii[

' . . . | . . . to the highest destination . . . | (. . .) They remain . . . '

J.5.1

Barradas, Benafim (Concelho de Loulé), south Portugal [Museu Municipal,
Loulé; Museu da Escrita do Sudoeste, Almodôvar] (On the text, see also
Correa 2002.) 114 × 73 × 13cm

← ✕≠ᖻ | ᖻ≠ᗯA≠   sab°oi : ist̲ᵃa̲

→ ᴎᗯ≠ᒍᴎᖻ≠Oᗯ≠   ib°o rino̲eb°o

← O|ᙁAᖻOᙁAᖻA   anakᵉenak̲ᵉe

← ᖻᕐᕐOᑫAᙁᖻA⟩ᖻᖻ≠ᗯᖻ   ib°o iibᵃa̲n̲ bᵃare̲ii

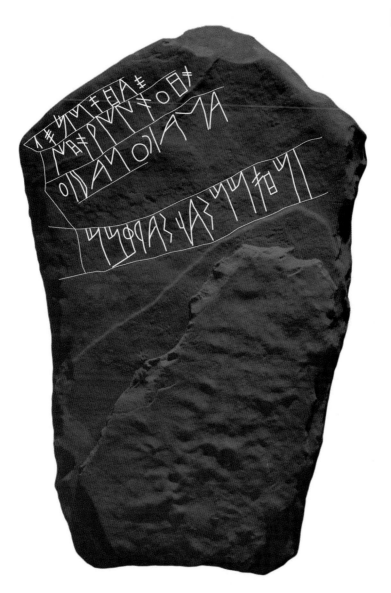

Syntactic analysis

> **sabᵒoi : is̱ṯᵃa̱|ibᵒo rinoebᵒo |anakᵉenak̲ᵉ:e|ibᵒo iibᵃan̲ bᵃare̱ii**
> loc.dat.sg. dat.pl.   dat.pl.   dat.pl.   ?acc.sg. V 3sg.

'In the summer, for these indwelling queens [i.e. goddesses], [this ritual stone] has now borne [offerings] to the ?important place/town.'

or

'[This grave] for Samos (or Sabos) . . . has received [him], invoking those queens of the indigenous people.'

Commentary

The stone is exceptionally large, but not dressed. The inscription is long and complete, but not very neatly laid out, as probably determined by the irregular shape and surface of the stone. The orientation is semi-boustrophedon—right-left, left-right, right-left, right-left.

Of the tentative translations above, the former is probably preferable, in which **sabᵒoi** is an Indo-European locative singular following Untermann's proposal (1997, 167). If so, there would be no personal name (as possibly also in J.1.1 above) and the inscription would be, rather than funerary, a commemoration of a sacrifice or some other kind of offering given the divinities invoked with the co-ordinated triple datives plural: **ist_ᵃa|ibᵒo rino_ebᵒo |anakᵉenak_ᵃ:e|ibᵒo. sabᵒoi** as a reference to the season of the memorialized rite would be the most obvious possibility, i.e. Celtic |*samoi*| 'in the summer' ~ Old Irish *sam*, Old Welsh and Old Breton *ham* < Indo-European **sem-* 'summer'. As John Carey has suggested to me, **sabᵒoi** 'in the summer' might, of course, hold the special metaphysical significance of the Celtic festival whose Old Irish name was *Samain* (cf. the Gaulish month name SAMONI), a time of proximity of the natural and supernatural, mortals and immortals. In favour of reading **sabᵒoi** as |*samoi*|, note that M **m** and W **m** are infrequent in Tartessian inscriptions and the Tartessian character ʒ **b** is derived from Phoenician *mem* /m/, cf. *ŕatubaŕ* in an Iberian inscription from Ensérune, France, for Celtic *Rātumāros*.

More remotely, but not to be overlooked, **sabᵒoi** might be a reference to the Aegean island of Samos, i.e. the large Greek island near Ephesos, with which Tartessos was in contact. Herodotus wrote that Kolaios, a ship's captain from that Samos, received a massive cargo of silver in Tartessos in the mid 7th century BC. Furthermore, objects of Samian type have been found amongst the orientalizing goods of the Tartessian archaeological culture (Chamorro 1987). Therefore, we might consider whether this inscription commemorates a voyage or seeks divine protection for a voyage to Samos, in which case the locative of the destination provides the topic of the inscription.

A third alternative would be to take **sabᵒoi** as the dative singular of the name of the deceased, 'for the man Samos/Sabos'; cf. the Celtiberian family name *Samikum* (K.1.3, III–15) 'of the family of Samos', Gaulish personal names *Sama, Samo, Samus*, &c. (Delamarre 2003, 266). We may also consider the less well paralleled *Sabos* ~ Palaeohispanic place-names *Sabetanum, Sabora*. With these possibilities, **sabᵒoi** would be an o-stem dative singular, with a variant of the same ending otherwise spelled **-ui**, e.g. **aarkᵘui** (J.7.6), **tᵘuŕekᵘui** (J.14.1). If **sabᵒoi** is a dative singular form, it would lend some confirmation to the interpretation of the Huelva graffito ΝΙΕΘΩΙ as 'for Nētos' (Almagro-Gorbea 2002).

J.6.1

'Alagoas 1', Salir, south Portugal [Museu Municipal, Loulé] (Correia no. 16)
6.2–9.0 × 3.6cm

←]ᴎOᑫA𐌄AO[tᵉ-]ea·bᵃare n[a *or* r-]ea·bᵃare n[a *or* ·bᵃaren

← ᴎᴎᴎ[ŕkᵉ[enii

'. . . [this grave] that has carried . . . they remain.'

J.6.2

'Alagoas 2', Salir, Loulé, south Portugal [Museu Nacional de Arqueologia , Lisbon]
(Correia no. 34) 20.5 × 23.5 × 4cm

←] O9A☐ [   ]b̲°ab^e[

J.6.3

'Viameiro', Salir, Loulé, south Portugal (Correia no. 72) 50 × 26 × 6.5cm

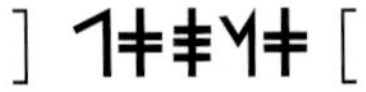

←] ↑‡≢Ϥ‡ [   ]onsol[

J.7.1

Ameixial (Concelho de Loulé) 'Vale dos Vemelhos 3', south Portugal [Museu
Nacional de Arqueologia, Lisbon] (Correia no. 23) 144 × 58 × 12cm

← ϤAϤOϪⅠϪAϤϞϤ↑‡☐A⊟MA
← Ϥ‡↑‡☐AϤA⊟MA

aś⊟a b°o↑ir naŕk^eenai
aś⊟a na·b°olon

Syntactic analysis

aś̲t̲ᵃa   b°o(tⁱ)ir naŕk^eenai | aś̲t̲ᵃa   na·b°olon
?name V 3.pl.pf. V.3.pl. ?middle   ?name neg. V 3.pl.

[Rodríguez Ramos: aśtabobir naŕken-ai / aśtanabolon]
[Correia: abⁱt^eoa b°obⁱirnaŕk^eenai / aśt^eanab°olin]

Commentary

The inscription is complete. It is arranged as two discontinuous, parallel left-to-right lines. A fivefold word division is implied by the repetition of the sequence **aśṃa** in different contexts and **narḱᵉenai** as a recognizable variant of the most common of the Tartessian formula words **narḱᵉentⁱi/narḱᵉenii**. Thus, there are three segmental 'words' in the first line and two in the second. **aśṃa** begins both, thus occupying the position in the inscriptional statement where forms comparable to Palaeohispanic and/or Celtic names most often appear.

narḱᵉenai is therefore in final position in the first line, the usual position for the **narḱᵉe**(-) formula word. The absence of any of the other formula words or a variant of them and the unusual repetition with its phonetically uncertain sign leave the overall interpretation of the text challenging. If not merely a further graphic variant for **narḱᵉentⁱi/narḱᵉenii**, **narḱᵉenai** could represent another member of the paradigm, such as being derived from the mediopassive **-nto-i* contrasting with the primary active **-nt-i*. The diphthongs *ei, ai, āi,* and *oi* of pre-Celtic/Late Indo-European fell together, graphically at least, as Tartessian **e**. The monophthongization of the latter three is post-Proto-Celtic. There are Tartessian examples of the orthography **ae** not yet **e** for this series, as well as some probable inverse spellings (graphic diphthongs written for phonetic simple vowels); see *Tartessian 2,* 134–5. Therefore, **narḱᵉenai** could reflect older **-nto-i*. If **narḱᵉenai** shows present-tense marking (with Indo-European primary *-i*), the present inscription is further evidence for the principle that only one verb per inscription can show present marking with

-*i* (see *Tartessian 2*, 101–12; Appendix C below).

In terms of the basic syntactic structure identified for the statement, **bᵒo↑ir** and **nabᵒolon** are in positions broadly comparable to the place often occupied by the formulaic **tᵉe·ro-bᵃare**. They could therefore be verbs, although **nabᵒolon** might also be an accusative singular comparable to the formulaic **uar(n)bᵃan**, which is also absent from the present text. The occurrence of the signs resembling ↑ in verbal endings, e.g. **lakⁱin↑i**, suggests that these could have the phonetic value of a dental stop before **i**, so **bᵒotⁱir** | *bodir* | 'they are awake(ned)' is possible; cf. Welsh *boddheir* 'one is pleased, willing' < 'is conscious, awake'. **bᵒo↑ir** and **na·bᵒolon** alliterate; perhaps a poetic contrast is intended. As a verb, **na·bᵒolon** would be an Indo-European thematic active 3rd person plural, with the inherited secondary ending *-ont* or an apocopated form of the primary ending *-onti*. **na·** could then be seen as an unaccented variant of the Indo-European negative particle **ne*, probably marking a subordinate clause, hence 'who [does] not'. **bᵒolon** might possibly derive from the Indo-European root **gʷel₁-* 'throw', the source of Old Irish *a-t·baill* 'dies', Early Welsh *ballaf* 'I die', though the particular formation of **bᵒolon** would have to differ from these Insular forms.

If we accept Rodríguez Ramos's identification of the phonetic value of the sign Ħ, we read a repeated name **aśtᵃa**, preceding what are probably plural verbs. As examples of indigenous proper names that might be treated as collectives taking a plural verb, *Hasta (Regia)* near Gadir (Cádiz) and *Astures* in the north-west of the Peninsula may be noted amongst several. A borrowing of the Phoenician goddess Astarte, worshipped as a group like the **lokᵒobᵒo** 'Lugoues' of J.1.1 or **rinoe͟bᵒo** 'queens' of J.5.1, may also be considered. The cult of Astarte was practised at the major Phoenician colony of Gadir and numerous images of the goddess have been found in southern Spain, therefore in and around Tartessos and not far from the land of the Kunētes in south Portugal. She was the consort of Melqart, the leading male god of Tyre and its Hispanic colony Gadir, whose annual spring festival celebrated the god's death and 'awakening'. A bronze statuette of a seated nude Astarte datable to the 7th century BC was found at El Carambolo near Seville, i.e. within the zone of easterly outlying Tartessian inscriptions. We do not know whether the goddess was worshipped with a borrowed form of her Semitic name or syncretized to an indigenous name, or both. A speculative translation derived from the preceding discussion is '[The divinities] ?Aśta(rte) have been awakened. They remain. | [The divinities] ?Aśta(rte) do not die.'

J.7.2

'Vale dos Vemelhos 2', south Portugal [Museu Municipal, Loulé]
(Correia no. 19) 58 x 41 x 9cm

←]٩A⫴‡A‡☐   bᵒotᵒo⫴ar[

← O٩ᴎᴎ‡ᴎ٩OᲳӼAΛAA*[   ]*aa kᵃaŕner-ion ire

Syntactic analysis

bᵒotᵒo⫴ar[|]*aa kᵃaŕner-ion   ire
N   V. ?3.pl. ?rel.acc.sg. N nom.pl.

'Bōdo- (< Boudo-) *or* Boduo- ... whom the men/heroes have entombed.'

J.7.3

'Vale dos Vermelhos 1', Ameixial, Loulé, south Portugal [Museu Municipal, Faro] (Correia no. 19) 12 × 8 × 4cm

←　─ꟼ𐌀✝𐌀ꟾ─　　　]tᵒoar[

J.7.4

Vale dos Vemelhos 4', Ameixial, Loulé, south Portugal [Câmara Municipal, Almodôvar] 97 × 21 × 20cm

←　[ꟈ]△ΜᎩ　　iśtᵘ[u

←　Λ]A̲　　kᵃ[a

'For this man . . .'

J.7.5

'Ameixial 3', Loulé, south Portugal [Museu Nacional de Arqueologia, Lisbon]
(Correia no. 28) 33 × 19 × 5cm

←]ꟽOꟽꟼAꟺ[   ]ꟽꞱ╪◻ꟼAꟺ[

Syntactic analysis

uarbᵒoȘ   i[| **naŕkᵉen**
adj. ?acc.sg.   V 3pl.

[Correia: . . . **uartᵉoli**. . . **naŕkᵉen** . . .]

'. . . to the highest destination. They remain.'

Commentary

If the sign that resembles an oblique Z is correctly construed as a re-orientated variant of ꟽ, then we may understand **uarbᵒoȘ** as **uarbᵒon** |*u̯arₐmon*| < **u(p)erₐmom*, i.e. the masculine accusative singular or nominative/accusative neuter, corresponding to the usual feminine accusative **uarbᵃan** ꟽAꟺꟼAꟺ |*u̯arₐman*| of the formula words, so, once again, 'the highest destination, state, or being' with a masculine or neuter referent in mind. Cf. also **uarbᵒoiir** ꟼꟽꟽ╪ꟺꟼAꟺ (J.22.1) 'lord' < **u(p)erₐmo-u̯iros* 'highest man/hero/husband, i.e. lord'.

J.7.6

'Ameixial 2', Loulé, south Portugal [Museu Nacional de Arqueologia, Lisbon]
(Correia no. 27) 99 × 53 × 4cm

Commentary

Beyond ꓮꓷꓮ the first line is now impossible to read. The initial dative singular man's name **aark**ᵘ**ui** is the most certain aspect of the interpretation. It is likely that the last word should be read [naŕkᵉe]**nii**.

Syntactic analysis

aarkᵘ**ui ori̯ou⟨t**ⁱ**⟩b**ᵉ**a:i   :elurear**[| **u̲ii**   *or* | **n̲ii**
N dat.sg.

'[a grave] for Arku̯ios (?"Archer") . . .'

[Correia: **aart**ᵉ**uiolour**]

J.7.7

'Ameixial 4', Loulé, south Portugal [Museu Nacional de Arqueologia, Lisbon]
(Correia no. 29) 34 × 22 × 3.5cm

←]‡٩𝚾‡Ч٧Ч [   ]ninok°oro[

← 𝚾٩ΑЧ[   ]iark°

Commentary

Both lines of the inscription are well-carved and clearly to be read right-to-left. There is no doubt over the reading of the extant signs. But the text is incomplete, and no formula words, names, or inflexions are obviously recognizable in what survives. The second line appears actually to end oddly with 𝚾 k°, without the expected ‡ o following, as regularly in the first line. k°o-ro- could be a series of the preverbs: Indo-European *ko(m) and *pro. ark° is possibly related to the personal name occurring as dative singular aark^uui on an inscribed stone also from Ameixial (J.7.6).

J.7.8

'Ameixial 1', south Portugal [Museu Municipal, Loulé](Correia no. 26)

34 × 22 × 3.5cm

←]*O)IA44O)I**

← O)IAYO9O3O⊟‡□O[

← A34MAO94Δ44MOY

Syntactic analysis

* *kᵉe≡uuakᵉe*[|]ebᵒo   tᵉe·bᵃere
?nom.acc.dual   dat.abl.pl. pvb V 3sg.

naŕkᵉe|n emun tᵘurea≡iubᵃa
V 3pl.   gen.pl. nom.acc.dual

'[This grave/death] has carried away ... from the group ... **kā and Uuakā, they rest, [and] of them Turos's youngest daughter.' | *Tureā i̯ūₐmā* |

[Correia: ...]etᵉ?tᶜebᵃarenaŕkᵉe / neśun?ureaiobᵃa ...

Commentary

The inscription is arranged in three continuous right-to-left lines. Probably a total of two signs have broken off illegibly at the beginning of the first line. Further along the same line, the surface of the stone has flaked away and several signs have been lost. This obscured section stands above 10 signs on the second line and 7 in the third; therefore, a comparable amount of text has been lost.

kᵉe≡uuakᵉe*[A name would be expected in this position, in which case the two occurrences of **e could possibly be agreeement markers for a feminine co-ordinative comparable to **bᵃane≡ooŕoire** 'wife of Ooŕoire' (J.19.1) **asune≡ uarbᵃan ≡ekᵘuŕine**

'Asuna≡Horse-queen' (J.4.1). For **uuak^ee** < **U(p)-ākāi*, cf. Celtiberian *uarakos*, British VERACVS, Old Breton *Uueroc* < **U(p)er-ākos*.

t^ee·b^aere is significant as a variant of the common and usually very regularly represented formula words **t^ee·b^aare** and **t^ee·ro·b^aare**. The interchange of **a** and **e** after **b^a** is contrary to the basis of the SW orthographic system (the redundancy principle) and not a common variation. Therefore, the **t^ee·b^aere** variant can be seen as confirming that the verb in this recurrent form had a paradigmatic relation with the high-frequency present stem *ber-* 'carry' < Indo-European **bʰer-*, explaining the confusion of the epigrapher.

The well-attested plural **naŕk^ee|n** has in its favour, against singular **naŕk^ee**, the presence of more than one name in the text. Therefore, **emun** is the more probable reading for the text's next segment, which may be understood as a masculine genitive plural pronoun 'their, of these men, of this masculine group'. Genitive plural **emun** would be built on the same stem as the Old Welsh and Old Breton masculine singular independent and affixed pronoun *em*, probably reflecting a paradigm built from the reduplicated accusative **em-em*, cf. Old Latin *em-em*; note also the Gaulish feminine genitive plural pronoun *eianom* (Larzac). In context, the reference is probably to the kindred of the deceased, who are either implicitly known to the community or have been explicitly named in the fragmentary first line, perhaps specifically with the dative/ablative plural that survives only as the ending]eb°o. Incidentally, if we were to adopt Correia's reading **eśun**, more or less the same interpretation could be retained, cf. Umbrian *eisun-k* 'their'. With the alternative segmentation **naŕk^ee nemun**, that would imply a genitive plural group name 'of the Nemoi' for which there are numerous parallels in Celtic, and specifically Hispano-Celtic, onomastics.

As explained in *Tartessian 2* (62–3), **t^uurea≡iub^aa** can be understood as | *Tureā iū_amā* | 'the youngest daughter of Turos'. Grammatically, this is a co-ordinative compound and can take a plural verb. She is possibly the same person named in line 1 or another person of same kin group, as signified by the genitive plural **emun**. Syntactically, **emun t^uurea≡iub^aa** is an amplification of the basic funerary statement, which would have been complete after the final verb **naŕk^ee|n**. It is less likely that **iub^aa** is a non-Indo-European name or name element to be connected with Numidian *Iuba*.

J.7.9

'Azinhal dos Mouros', Loulé, south Portugal [Museu Nacional de Arqueologia, Lisbon] (Correia no. 30)
69.5 x 18 x 7.5cm

(. . . .)

→ 

Syntactic analysis

iru b^{a}arua-ion **b^{a}<u>a</u>[**
N V 1sg. rel.acc.sg.

'the man/hero whom I [this grave] have carried [?so they remain]'

Commentary

It is certain that the end of the text is lost, though it is uncertain how long that remainder might have originally extended beyond the broken edge upwards. It is also likely that an entire line has been lost above the surviving epigraphy. As what survives is a left-to-right line, it can be expected to have followed right-to-left text, as in J.5.1, J.12.1, and MdC. An obvious possibility to be considered is that **b^{a}arua** is a variation on the formula word whose most usual form is **b^{a}are**, i.e. the 1st person singular corresponding to the recurring 3rd person singular. The **u** of **b^{a}arua** is therefore unexpected, but can be explained as incorporating the personal ending of the high-frequency 1st singular thematic present, Celtic **berū* 'I carry', together with that of the preterite *bāra* < perfect **bōra*. Another possibility would be to read **iru≡b^{a}aru** 'the man/hero ⟨and⟩ Barros' with agreement, nominative/accusative dual, cf. **iru≡alk^{u}u** (J.12.1). But that would leave **aionb^{a}<u>a</u>[** as a difficult remaining segment, or **aion** if we anticipate that the text continued to conclude **b^{a}<u>a</u>[naŕk^{e}ent^{i}i]**, like J.16.1, J.16.3, J.18.1. Taking **iru** |*(i̯)iru*| as a case form for 'man' (nominative/accusative dual or, less probably, dative singular), there would be no names.

J.7.10

'Touril', Castro Verde, south Portugal [Museu Nacional de Arqueologia, Lisbon]
(Correia no. 33) 97 × 26 × 9cm

← OۤΑ{ΜΟΜΑ۹ΜΜ۹ΟΚΚΑΥ****[

Syntactic analysis

]****naŕk^eenii raśen   b^aare

]****naŕkᵉenii	raśen	bᵃare
V. 3pl.	pf+pron.	V 3sg.

'. . . they remain; that ?woman whom [this grave/
death] has carried.'

Commentary

The text has the common right-to-left, anti-clockwise orientation. The beginning has broken away.
That lost portion is parallel to six signs on the
opposite side and most probably began the text
with a name, as is most usual.]****naŕk^eenii
raśen b^aare (J.7.10), compared with]uk^e śaen
b^aare naŕk^ee (J.27.1) and the several examples of
ro·b^aare and t^ee(e)·ro·b^aare, suggests that we
interpret raśen b^aare as ro + (?feminine accusative
singular) śaen + b^aare, thus '[death/this grave]
has carried this woman or body or interment' or
the like (see further *Tartessian 2*, 113). The fact that
the more usual order of the formula ro·b^aare
naŕk^eentⁱi is reversed here may account for the
unusual form raśen b^aare. In other words, the
name of the deceased is usually the grammatical
object of ro·b^aare. Here we have naŕk^eenii as
an intervening clause standing between the topic/
object and its verb, so the pronoun object -(a)śen,
also referring to the deceased and suffixed to ro,
fills the gap in the syntax.

J.8.1

Fuzeta (Concelho de Tavira, 'Cerro do Castelo da Fuzeta'),
south Portugal [Departamento de Arqueologia, University
of Lisbon] (Correia no. 62) 141 × 16.5 × 19.5cm

←]*‡□ᎭᐱᑢᎭᏯᎭ***ᎭᏟᎭ*[

*******[

Syntactic analysis

]*aŕi***antᵒonbᵒ<u>o</u> *[

?dat./abl. pl.

J.9.1

Alcoutim, south Portugal [Museu Nacional de Arqueologia, Lisbon]
(Correia no. 32) 97.5 × 52 × 19.5cm

← O⅃] ⅄ / A ⅄O D O ⅄ A ⅃Ᏸ A ⅄ ⅄ A ⅄ A ⅃[→

Syntactic analysis

]kᵃanan	uarbᵃan ebᵉe naŕ[kᵉe . . .	*or*	]aanan
acc.sg.fem.? or V 3pl.	acc.sg.fem. ? V		acc.sg.fem.?

'. . . (and) to the highest destination . . . (?they) remain (. . .).'

Commentary

A portion of one right-to-left line survives, incomplete at both ends. The left-most sign ⅄ ŕ appears to be turned as though the missing line after it veered off up the left-hand side, now broken off. The form of the sign for **r** is unusual, but is confirmed by the context in the formula word **uarbᵃan**. Untermann's proposal (1997, 147–8) is to read D as a variant form of the sign **9 be**, but this is not certain. The parallel of the North-east Iberian scripts suggests that D might stand for **r**, but the different letter form in **uarbᵃan** weighs against that. It is not paralleled to find a second feminine accusative singular in concord with **uar(n)bᵃan** as appears to be the case here. (Although alternatively, it is possible that]*anan is a 3rd person plural active verb in |-an(t)|.) Speculatively, could (-)kanā or (-)Anā (cf. *Anas*, the ancient name of the river Guadiana) be the name of the being identified as the 'highest' |uar̩mā|? Or could the deceased be commended to both the great river Anas and/or (*-kᵘe or *-ue) the great mountain of the south-west Οὐαμα (probably modern Peña Utrera, Badajoz, on which see *Tartessian 2*, 76)? In any event, it is not clear how eDe could be read as an enclitic conjunction to co-ordinate the two accusatives singular. Note the evidence canvassed in *Tartessian 2* (144–5) for Tartessian as a q-Celtic language. Even if we can read eDe as |ekᵉe|, with the labial quality of the consonant assimilated to the following vowel, there is no reason to anticipate a disyllabic reflex of Indo-European *-kᵘe 'and'.

J.10.1

'Mestras' (Martin Longo, Alcoutim), south Portugal [Museu Municipal, Olhão] (Correia no. 32) 128 x 62 x 8.5cm

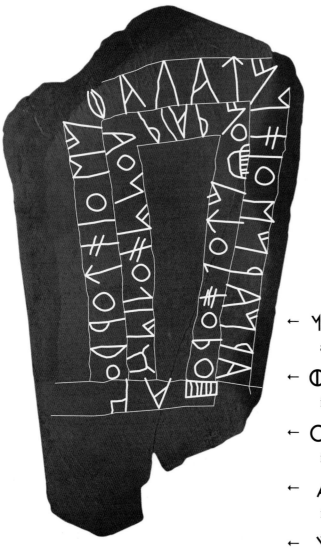

← ꟙ‡ | ΟᙏꟘꟙA ꟘꟙA

ariariś-e : o-n-

← ΦΛΛ↑ꟙ

i-↑akªatⁱ

← ΟↁꟘΟ↑‡ | ΟᙏꟘ

i-śe : o↑er-bᵉe /

← ΛΟꟘꟙ‡Ο⅃ | ꟘX

ŕi : leoine a /

← ꟘꟘAↁꟘ

r-bªari /

← ΟↁΟ‡ꟘΟ↑Ꟙ(?)Ο

e (?n) i↑ensere /

→ ⣿ Aꟛ

(?tª)au

Syntactic analysis

ariariś   -e :   o- n-|i-↑akᵃatⁱ|i-śe :   o↑er-b̠ᵉe|ŕi :
N ?nom.sg. demon. pvb adv.   V 3sg.   demon. pvb?   V?

leoine a|r-bᵃari|e (?n)i↑en sere | t̠ᵃau
?dat.sg. pvb V 3sg.?   V.1sg?

'This man Ariaris (| *Ariaris-se* | < **Ario-ríχs+se*) ?lies down under here. . . ?carries . . . [this grave] has carried onward for ?Līu̯oni̯ā [the goddess]. . . I [this stone monument] stand.'

Commentary

The complete inscription survives and is mostly legible, though with some unusual letter forms. The stone is large and well carved, obviously commemorating someone (or something) important. It is not surprising, therefore, that the text is unusual. But this raises challenges of interpretation. The only apparent direct links to the stock formula words are **ar·bᵃarie**, (probably corresponding to the formulaic **tᵉ·ro-bᵃare** with a different preverb) possibly recurring as the paradigmatic byform of **er-b̠ᵉe|ŕi**. As discussed in *Tartessian 2*, there are significant parallels between J.10.1 and the MdC text in layout, the shape of signs, and vocabulary. The signs are arranged as six continuous right-to-left lines, followed by a short final line of three large signs probably to be read left-to-right. The sign ↑ usually precedes **i** Ꮆ. It apparently has a different value here in **↑akᵃatⁱi**; therefore,⅂ I, which has a similar form and occurs in similar sequences, is considered, i.e. **l̠akᵃatⁱi** (cf. Untermann 1997, 147). It is likely that **er-b̠ᵉeŕi** 'carries ?after' : **ar·bᵃarie** 'has carried onward' are forms of the same verb with different tense/aspect stems and different preverbs. Compare **ar·bᵃarie** with **ar·b̠ᵉieŕitᵘu** (J.12.3), which is probably an imperative, providing further evidence that a compound verb, cognate to Old Welsh *arber* 'use' < **(p)are-ber-*, Greek περιφέρω 'carry around', had existed in Proto-Celtic and Tartessian (see further *Tartessian 2*, 130). The preverb **ar-** alliteratively echoes the name of the honorand, *Ariaris* 'foremost leader', possibly forming an intentional *figura etymologica*, and so can be seen as the keynote of the epitaph. The eccentric representation **bᵃar⟨i⟩e** for the more usual 3rd person singular perfect **bᵃare** could have been influenced by the preceding paradigmatic form of the same verb **b̠ᵉeŕi**, especially if the bard was not the epigrapher. However, **ar·bᵃarie** need not be viewed as an orthographic error, as it would accurately represent the natural phonetic palatalization of **r** before **e**, i.e. | *ar-bār'e* |. Formally **leoine** could be dative singular, thus the indirect object of **er-b̠ᵉeŕi** and/or **ar·bᵃarie**.

J.11.1

Almodôvar, 'Tavilhão 2', south Portugal [Museu da Escrita do Sudoeste,
Almodôvar; Museu Nacional de Arqueologia, Lisbon] (Correia no. 32)
82 × 39 × 13cm

Commentary

The inscription is complete. With the opening name
kⁱielaoe, compare k̲ᵉeilau or k̲ᵉeilauke (Cabeza
del Buey IV) and k̲ᵉeloia (J.57.1). Incidentally,
kⁱielaoe≡bᵃane is unlikely to be an exact forerunner
of Modern Irish *banchéile* 'wife', which is unattested
in the Old Irish period, though it is not impossible
that both elements of the Irish compound correspond
to these Tartessian forms as cognates. robᵃae as
written is most probably | *roₐmāi* | 'foremost woman',
but could be interpreted as a 3rd singular perfect
ro·bᵃae 'she has passed', corresponding to the 3rd
plural present tᵉe·bᵃantⁱi 'they pass away', cf. Old
Irish *dí-bá-*'become extinct' < 'pass on' . However,
as the epigrapher has omitted a sign in nŕkᵉenii
for naŕkᵉenii, ro·bᵃae could stand for the attested
formulaic ro-bᵃare (J.1.1, J.12.1, J.182, MdC).
On the other hand, the representation nŕkᵉenii
might reflect the archaic notion that n by itself
could stand for a syllabic sound; note also nŕkᵉen
(Cabeza del Buey IV; see *Tartessian 2* §§69, 73.2).

← ⊢ΑΜΨ⧻ΙΟ⧻Α⇑ΟΨφ

← ΨΨΨΟ)ΙⵛΨΟΑⳠ⧻ⵀΟⵙΑⳌΑ

Syntactic analysis

kⁱielaoe:≡   oiśaHa ≡bᵃane≡   ≡robᵃae   n(a)ŕkᵉenii
?nom.acc.dual/dat.sg./ nom.   nom.acc.dual nom.acc.dual V.3pl.
    'Kielaos's wife OiśaHā, foremost woman, now rest(s) [here].'

or

kⁱielaoe:≡   oiśaHa ≡bᵃane   ro·bᵃae   n(a)ŕkᵉenii
?nom.acc.dual/dat.sg./ nom.   nom.acc.dual pf V.3sg. V.3pl.
    'Kielaos's wife OiśaHā has passed; (they) now remain.'

[Correia: kⁱielao kᵒorśatᶜabᵃanebᵃaeleŕkᶜenii]

J.11.2

Almodôvar, 'Tavilhão 1', south Portugal [Museu da Escrita do Sudoeste, Almodôvar; Museu Municipal, Faro] (Correia no. 21) 105 × 28 × 10cm

←]AꓱYAOፕ⅄ᛣ□⅄Y1Y‡[

Syntactic analysis

]<u>o</u>n linbᵒoire anbᵃa[| -on Lɪmo(i̯)irē Amba(χ)t- |
     N.nom.pl.   N

'. . . [?the grave] the Lemo-u̯iroi (Elm-men), ?Ambatos. . .'

[Correia:]onlin bᵒoirea bᵃa(?)[ ]

Commentary

The inscription is fragmentary. Signs have been lost at both ends. It is carved skilfully, continuously within an inscribed right-to-left arc. Any conceivable reconstruction would envision a text length at least twice as long as what survives. There are no surviving formula words. The segmentation is established by the 2008 discovery of the MdC inscription, in which **tᵉe·bᵃantⁱi lebᵒoiire** can be recognized as containing a variant graphic representation of the same word as **linbᵒoire**, syntactically positioned as the subject of the preceding compound plural verb, hence | de·bānti Lemo̯iirē | 'the *Lemo-u̯iroi pass away'. Tartessian **lebᵒoiire / linbᵒoire** can be compared with the Callaecian group names, *Lemau̯i* and *Limici*, as well as Gaulish *Lemo-u̯ices* 'Elm-fighters'. **lebᵒoiire /linbᵒoire** could likewise be the formal name of a 'tribe' commemorating their totemic tree. But, if we consider the possibility that a necropolis was thought of as a funerary grove or wood, then 'men/heroes of the elm-wood' might in this context refer generally to the host of the dead. See further *Tartessian 2*, 60–4.

On possibly reading **anbᵃa[** as | Amba(χ)t- |, *Ambatos* is the best-attested of Hispano-Celtic men's names, especially in the western Peninsula. It is the base of the Tartessian adjectival feminine patronym **anbᵃatⁱia[** 'daughter of Amba (χ) tos' (J.16.2).

J.11.3

Almodôvar, 'Cerca do Curralão', south Portugal [Museu da Escrita do Sudoeste, Almodôvar; Museu Municipal, Setúbal] (Correia no. 63) 73 x 38 x 8cm

Commentary

The inscription is unusual in that the extant lines all run left-to-right, including the first line **soloir uarb̲**^{a}**an̲**[. This is possibly a later feature. However, the anti-clockwise spiral orientation is well attested in the corpus. Probably three signs have been entirely lost where the text turns leftwards around the top of the stone. It appears that an entire vertical line, running down the left side, comprising approximately ten signs, has broken away. There would thus have been room for the **t**^{e}**e·ro-b**^{a}**are** formula or a functional equivalent before the usual closing in n] **a̲ŕk**^{e}**enii**. The honorand's name **soloir** is interpreted as Celtic compound of 'sun' and 'man'; see 'Tartessian Linguistic Elements' below for comparanda and etymology. If that's correct, the juxtaposition of **uarb̲**^{a}**an̲** 'to the highest destination' is interesting.

Syntactic analysis

soloir uarb̲^{a}**an̲[ ]in̲a o*[| n]a̲ŕk**^{e}**enii**
nom.sg. acc.sg.fem. V.3pl.

'Soloi̯ir [(who) has gone, has been taken] to the highest destination . . . they remain.'

J.II.4

Almodôvar, 'Vale de Ourique', south Portugal (Correia no. 2)

Commentary

The inscription is known only from the generally excellent drawing in the 'Album' of Frei Manuel do Cenáculo Vilas-Boas, Bishop of Beja 1770–1802. Some letter forms are unparalleled and must be treated with caution.

In the first edition of this book, I suggested that the abstruse final sequence of signs aś*tªa*t̲ª̲a could represent a borrowing of the Phoenician goddess Astarte whose cult is attested in the southern Peninsula during the Orientalizing Period (*c.* 750–500 BC). That remains a possibility, but subsequent progress on the SW corpus has yet to produce confirmed instances of that borrowed divine name. Formally, bªaanon suits Celtic 'of the women', but that interpretation cannot be confirmed by the context.

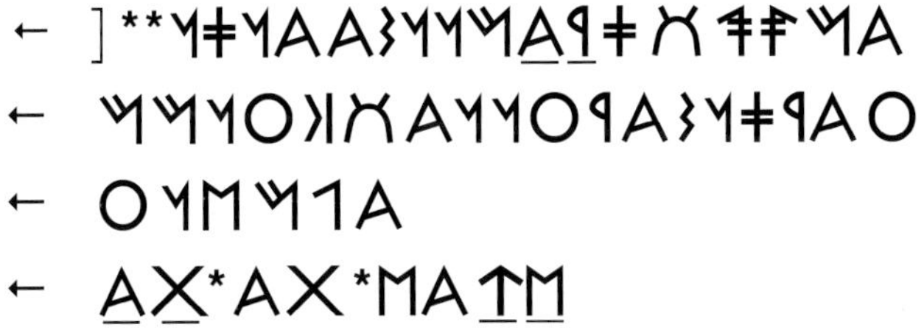

←   ]**Y‡YAA�⋯

←   YYYOKAYYO 9A⸢Y‡9AO

←   OYMY1A

←   AX*AX*MA⏚M

Syntactic analysis

aio̲o̲ŕo̲ra̲inn bªaanon**[| **ea   ro-n   ·bªaren**
            gen.pl.   rel.? pf pron. V 3 pl.

naŕkᵉenii | aliśne | ś̲t̲aś*tªa*t̲ª̲a
V 3 pl.   loc.sg.?

J.11.5

Almodôvar, 'Canafexal', south Portugal [Museu da Escrita do Sudoeste, Almodôvar; Câmara Municipal, Almodôvar] (Correia no. 74) 58 × 54 × 5cm

← ᏢᙏᏟᛘ[a]<u>nb</u>ᵉi<u>k</u>ⁱ[i

←]*ᛘᕵᙏOƸᛡᎱA[   ]arskᵉeir<u>n</u>*[

← ᙏOᛡOᛡᛘAᎩ   naŕkᵉe]<u>nt</u>ⁱi

'. . . they remain.'

Commentary

The inscription is fragmentary. All three surviving lines apparently read right-to-left and are incomplete.

J.12.1

Gomes Aires (Concelho de Almodôvar) 'Abóboda 1', south Portugal
[Museu da Escrita do Sudoeste, Almodôvar; Museu Regional, Beja]
(Correia no. 48) 83 × 51 × 11cm

← ΗΑ𐌔Ϟ𐌜ϞΦϒΟϞΟΚ𐌜ΑϒΙΟ𐌜𐌢ϞΗ𐌢ΑϞϞ𐌜

→ ΟΡ𐌢𐌔ΑΡΟ𐌢ΑΧΑϒΟΑΗΟ

Syntactic analysis

iru꞊alkᵘu	— sie: narkᵉentⁱi	— mubᵃa	tᵉe·ro-bᵃare	𐌢atᵃaneatᵉe
|(i)irū꞊Alkū —	siē narkenti	— Mumā	dĕ· ro- bāre	φataneatē|
nom.acc.dual	demon. V 3 pl.	N nom.sg.	pvb pvb V 3 sg.	N dat. sg.
hero Alkos	these remain	foster	away pf has	winged one
	(men) fixed/still	mother	carried	

'Mumā φataneatē ("the foster-mother to the winged one") has carried away the hero ⟨and⟩ Alkos, these men who now lie [here].'

Commentary

The inscription is complete, comprising three anti-clockwise right-to-left lines beginning at the lower right, a more freely laid out left-to-right line then veers off and up on the left-hand side. The central image of an armed warrior was apparently carved at the same time as the text and can be viewed as a throwback to the Late Bronze Age 'warrior stelae' of the western Peninsula, though this one differs stylistically from those images.

    The overall interpretation of the inscription may be followed in greater detail with the notes on the individual words below and *Tartessian 2* §31.2. The presence of the words **naŕkᵉentⁱi** and **tᵉe·ro-bᵃare** shows that the text is a variant of the Tartessian epigraphic formula (see Appendix C below). It diverges from the basic

pattern in that **naŕkᵉentⁱi** precedes **tᵉe·ro-bᵃare**, ⸝atᵃaneatᵉe follows the last formula word, as an 'amplification', and what is usually the first of the formula words (**uar(n)bᵃan** 'the highest destination' < *u(p)eramām*) is altogether absent. Therefore, **mubᵃa . . . ⸝atᵃaneatᵉe** can be seen as something extra which takes the place and possibly fills the function—logically if not grammatically—of **uar(n)bᵃan**.

These points and the etymologies canvassed in the notes on words lead to the following interpretation. The statement is an epitaph for **iru≡alkᵘu** 'the man/hero

⟨and⟩ Alkos'. The usual closure of Tartessian epitaphs naŕkᵉentⁱi is here centrally inserted in the sentence in a short clause, sie: naŕkᵉentⁱi 'these men (who) now rest here', which modifies iru≡alkᵘu. By referring to the preceding names, iru≡alkᵘu, the formally demonstrative sie: is functionally equivalent to a subordinating relative: 'the men who lie here'. As a compound of Indo-European demonstrative *to- + relative *i̯o-, this might continue an old function of Indo-European *ti̯oi. As usual for the deceased named in a Tartessian inscription's naming phrase, iru≡alkᵘu is the direct object of tᵉe·ro-bᵃare.

Along with the relief carving of the 'guerreiro', the other unusual element here, and the crux of any interpretation of the text, is what appears to be a second, discontinuous noun phrase mubᵃa ... φatᵃaneatᵉe. In the absence of uar(n)bᵃan, mubᵃa ... φatᵃaneatᵉe may tell us where Alkos has gone. The key of the present interpretation is to take mubᵃa as |mumā| ~ Old Irish muim(m)e, mum(m)e 'foster-mother' < *mumm(i)ā under the influence of *mammā 'mother'. Pokorny (1913) related muimme to Greek μύζω 'suck'; Beekes (2010, 975) explains the latter as onomatopoeic, the lips assuming the position of μύ [mu] when sucking. The Irish is clearly also related to Welsh mam, Breton mamm, and numerous other words originating as 'baby-talk' for 'mother, mammie, &c.' in many languages worldwide.

mubᵃa ... φatᵃaneatᵉe |Mumā φataneatē| 'the foster-mother to the winged one' is interpreted as an epithet or kenning for 'the war goddess'. As a commonplace in early Irish heroic literature, such as the Ulster cycle, the war goddess (known by various names including Morrigain '?nightmare-queen' and Bodb 'scald-crow') often assumes the form of the carrion crow on the battlefield. Compare also, more specifically, in the Irish glossary attributed to Cormac mac Cuileannáin (†908), the entry headed Búanand: mumi na·fían .i. bé nAnand ar chosmaile diblínib. Amail ro-bu máthair dēa indí Ánu sic Búanand quasi erat máthair na·fian .i. dag-máthair ... Búanand din .i. dág-máthair oc·forcētal gaiscid do-na·fianaib 'Búanann (búan "constant"): the nurse/foster-mother of

Late Bronze Age throwing spears from the
Ría de Huelva deposition, Museo Provincial
de Huelva (photos: Jane Aaron)

the warband, i.e. bé nAnann ("woman of Ánu"), for the two are alike: she [Ánu] was the mother goddess, as Búanann was the foster-mother of the warband, i.e. the dag-máthair (good mother) . . . [so she was called] "Constant one" (Búanann) for that, i.e. as the "good mother" teaching the warbands feats of arms (lit. "spear and shield")'. So both the bird of prey and the armed hero are 'winged ones' on the battlefield, where their foster-mother nurses them on blood.

The image on this stone shows a warrior in bulky armour with straps crossing his chest. His arms are extended symmetrically with a throwing spear pointing outward from his right hand and another short spear and small shield in his left. This image is reminiscent of an intriguing description of a hero in the *Gododdin* as *aer seirchyawc* | *aer edenawc* 'harnessed [strapped in armour] in battle, winged in battle' < **(p)ataniāko-*. In case this metaphor is otherwise missed, the epigrapher supplies a picture of an armoured warrior with shield and throwing spears extended wing-like. Like the Abóboda warrior, short throwing spears were the principal weapon of the *Gododdin* heroes. Numerous small bronze spear heads and spear butts of the 11th/10th century BC were found as part of the great deposition of Huelva and have been reconstructed as throwing javelins similar to those shown on the Abóboda stone. The kenning for the war goddess is discontinuous in the poetic syntax, but can be isolated as **mub^{a}a ɸat^{a}aneat^{e}e**, 'foster-mother' (nominative singular) + 'to the winged one' (dative singular, probably *i*-stem **(p)ataniatis*). **mub^{a}a ɸat^{a}aneat^{e}e** is a phrasal epithet of Indo-European type, but there are also Semitic and specifically Phoenician parallels; see further pp. 234–5 below.

naŕk^{e}ent^{i}i or a related form usually comes at the end of the funerary statement, but here it is moved forward so that the main sentence artfully wraps around it. 'Hero' and the hero's epithet ('winged' > 'armed') are the first and last words of the statement, with the image of the 'winged'=armed hero in the middle.

J.12.2

Gomes Aires (Concelho de Almodôvar) 'Abóboda 2', south Portugal [Museu da Escrita do Sudoeste, Almodôvar; Museu Nacional de Arqueologia, Lisbon] (Correia no. 49) 38 × 40.5 × 2.5cm

→] O △ ⊕ Ⲙ [   ]et^{u}t^{i}i[

J.12.3

San Sebastião de Gomes Aires (Concelho de Almodôvar) 'Corte do Freixo',
south Portugal [Museu da Escrita do Sudoeste, Almodôvar; Museu Regional,
Beja] (Correia no. 36) 154.5 × 62 × 12cm

←] A ⋀ ⴸ ⋀ ⵕ Ⰽ ⵙ ⵐ Ⴑ Ϙ ⋀ ⋀ Ⴑ Ⴒ Ⴔ ⴵ Ⴔ [

Syntactic analysis

(])uult'ina ar- b^e ieŕit^u u la[k. . .   *or*   (])uult'ina ar-b^e ieŕi t^u u-la[
  N nom.sg. pvb V ?imperative ?V   N nom.sg. pvb V   ?pvb ?V

'Uultina, let her/it carry forward, [? lie down]. . .'

Commentary

The inscription is fragmentary. The layout indicates that about half is missing, assuming that the circle of signs between the ruled lines was once complete. The text
runs in the common right-to-left anti-clockwise orientation. It is not impossible
that **uult'ina**, which appears to be a feminine nominative singular name, originally
began the text with nothing missing ahead of it. It is clearer that **ar·b^e ieŕit^u u** is a
compound of Celtic *(φ)are-ber-* (cf. Old Welsh *arber*), than what the tense and mood
are. Another example of the same compound is the perfect **ar·b^a arie** (J.10.1). As
well as an imperative, a preterite like Gaulish KAPNITOY *karnitu* (Saignon) 'built a

cairn' is possible or a present **ar-b^eieŕi** < Celtic **(φ)are-beret(i)*. If **ar·b^eieŕit^u u** contains Indo-European **bher-*, as the most likely, it may be seen as a variation on the formula word, absent in what survives here, i.e. **t^e·ro-b^aare** 'has carried away'. On the phonology and graphic representation of **ar·b^eieŕit^u u**, see *Tartessian* 2, 129–30, 140, 146, 148, 153.

J.12.4

Gomes Aires (Concelho de Almodôvar) 'Corte Azinheira 1', south Portugal [Museu da Escrita do Sudoeste, Almodôvar; Museu Nacional de Arqueologia, Lisbon] (Correia no. 64) 39 × 31.5 × 6cm

photo: Jane Aaron

→ ‡ΑΓ‡ΑΓ‡ℾↀ[

→]ↇΟↇΑΓΑφℾ𐤉𐤉ↀℾ

Syntactic analysis

salsaloi ↀ^i[	|	]b^ae b^aa lak^inↀ^i i	|*ma laginti*| *or* |*ma lagimi*|
loc/dat.sg.?		cjt. V ?1.sg./3.pl.	

'In/for Salsalo-: . . . so they [the deceased] *or* I [this stone] now lie down.'

Commentary

The inscription is fragmentary. At least one line is missing of some 8–10 signs, possibly more, at the two vertical lines might have continued further upwards before turning and meeting as the missing horizontal line at the top. The orientation is unusual in that the original must be reconstructed as a continuous left-to-right clockwise circuit. As Almagro-Gorbea proposes in connection with the Medellín graffiti (2004; 2008), left-to-right orientation is a relatively late feature, resulting from the influence of alphabetic Greek literacy and post-dating *c.* 625/600 BC, for one local school, at least. The clockwise orientation is most similar to the long Alcalá del Río inscription (J.53.1). Another special link between these two stones is that neither shows any trace of the most common formula word **naŕkᵉentⁱi**, &c., but there occurs, apparently taking the place of **naŕkᵉentⁱi**, **lakᵉentⁱi** in J.53.1 and **lakⁱinᛏⁱi** here in J.12.4. Arguably, we have a new style coming in after *c.* 625/600 BC, marked by both left-to-right orientation and the optional replacement of formulaic **naŕkᵉentⁱi**. Note that **lakᵉentⁱi** appears to be a more intelligible word for us, resembling 'they lie down' or 'they lay down'. Possibly, a formulaic archaism is being replaced by its more common synonym.

J.12.5

south Portugal 18 x 25.5 x 6.5cm

→　]**Δ KO[　　　]** tᵘ kᵉe[

J.14.1

Alcoforado, São Teotonio, Aljezur (Concelho de Odemira), south Portugal [Câmara Municipal, Castro Verde] (Correia no. 71) 102.5 x 39 x 5cm

←]ᛝ⵰ᛝᛞᛒO⋔ᛩΔᛩᛝᛝᛩΑᛝΑX

　　[ ]*[ ]

← Oᛝ⋔ΑᛩOᛩΑᛦOΑXΜᛝᛩ[

　ᛩ

Syntactic analysis

tᵃalainon tᵘuŕekᵘui or[| [ ] i [ ] |]noś tᵃa -e ·bᵃare naŕkᵉe|n

N acc.sg.   N dat.sg.   pvb+?E   V 3 sg. V 3 pl.

'Talauindon (= ?"the country of the blessed headland" *Sacrum promontorium*): [this grave] for Turekos (= "a man of the kindred of Turos") has carried him off to it . . . . . . They remain.'

Commentary

The text is arranged continuously around the sides and top of the stone. An isolated Ⴙ **n** is turned at 90-degrees from the last full line to complete the text at the beginning of the bottom of the field. The signs are easily read, having been carefully carved in right-to-left orientation between two evenly cut lines. The stone is broken at the top where 10 to 15 signs have been lost. It is possible that the formula word **uar(n)bᵃan** | *u̯arₐman* | 'highest destination (place, state, [feminine] being)' has been lost in the missing top of the text field. On the other hand, the initial sequence **tᵃalainon** formally suits an accusative of destination and a compound place-name. This could take the place of **uar(n)bᵃan**, conveying a similar concept, i.e. Tartessian | *Tala(i̯)innon* | < *Tala(u̯)-u̯indom* 'country of the white/blessed headland'. If not merely a poetic allusion to the happy afterlife, this could be the native place-name underlying *Sacrum promontorium*', literally the extreme south-western end of Europe, today Ponta de Sagres, figuratively invoking the land beyond the setting sun, the afterworld. For the meaning of the place-name, compare the Carthaginian foundation Άκρα Λευκα 'white headland', probably Roman-period Lucentum, now Alicante. The position of **tᵃalainon** as an accusative prominently positioned, as topic, at the head of the text could also explain the unusual form **tᵃa-e·bᵃare** as opposed to the more common **tᵉe·bᵃare**. The graphic diphthong **ae** would thus represent a long vowel | *ē* | resulting from the coalescence of the preverb | *de* | and an accusative infix, such as | *e(d)* | or | *en* | or the relative.

J.15.1

São Martinho das Amoreiras (Concelho de Odemira) 'Pardieiro 1', south Portugal [Museu da Escrita do Sudoeste, Almodôvar; Museu Regional, Beja] (Correia no. 67) 104 X 58 X 9.5cm

← Ч[ ]*ＯＡЧＯＡ⸜ //ＯＡＭＯ１ＯΨＡ𝖰ЧＡЧＡ⋈

Syntactic analysis

⸝aitᵘura meleśae≡:	:≡bᵃaenae	*(*)n
nom.sg. nom.acc. dual *or* dat.sg.	nom.acc. dual *or* dat.sg.	

'Φaitura ("lady of the Baeturians"), sweet woman and wife . . .'

Commentary

The text is arranged, partly within inscribed lines, parallel to two edges of the stone. An isolated Ч **n** is turned at 90-degrees at the beginning of a third line and may mark the end, cf. likewise J.14.1. Two to four signs before that Ч **n** are illegible. One orthographic feature of the text is the recurrence of the combination **ae**. As **bᵃaenae** probably corresponds to **bᵃane** 'wife, woman' (J.11.1, J.19.1, J.20.1, J.26.1),

the orthography here appears idiosyncratic, possibly triggered by uncertainty over the *a*-stem nominative/accusative dual or dative singular ending -**e** from earlier -**ai** and/or the paradigmatic changes of the vowel of the root in nominative *b^e**ena**, oblique b^a**ane**. See further *Tartessian 2*, 135–6, on inverse spellings of simple vowels as diphthongs. The three instances of **ae** contrast with **ai** in ⊧**ait**ᵘ**ura**, presumably representing different sounds. The initial position of ⊧**aituura** suggests that it is a name, presumably a feminine *ā*-stem nominative singular. For ⊧ in ⊧**ait**ᵘ**ura**, compare ⧄**at**ᵃ**aneat**ᵉ**e** proposed as | *(φ)ataneatē* | 'to the winged one' < *(p)ataniatei* (J.12.1). As a trace of an earlier *p*, ⊧ in ⊧**at**ᵃ**aneat**ᵉ**e** occurs in absolute initial position, before a vowel (specifically an **a**) in a fully stressed word, thus differing from the preverbs **ro** < *(p)ro* and **ar** < *(p)are* and **uar(n)b**ᵃ**an** < *u(p)er_amām*, where *p* has been fully lost in less favourable environments. As a weakened *p*, the phonetic value of ⊧ could be [φ], [β], [f], or [h], somewhat more probably the first, so tentatively **φait**ᵘ**ura** | *Φaiturā* | or **hait**ᵘ**ura** | *Haiturā* |. Thus, there is a resemblance to *Baeturia*, the name of the adjacent regions of the Turduli and south-western Celtici at the beginning of the Roman Period. *Baeturia*, &c., may have arisen in a language differing from that of the SW inscriptions. Cf. Iberian *banmliŕbaituŕana : kaisanmliŕbaituŕa*, of uncertain meaning, on the lead plaque F.9.5. There are no formula words in the extant text and little room to reconstruct them. Therefore, it is uncertain whether this would be an epitaph for a woman identified for her group and region or a dedication to a territorial goddess, mythological ancestress of the Baeturians.

J.15.2

São Martinho das Amoreiras (Concelho de Odemira) 'Pardieiro 2', south Portugal [Museu Regional, Beja] (Correia no. 68) 112 x 40 x 7cm

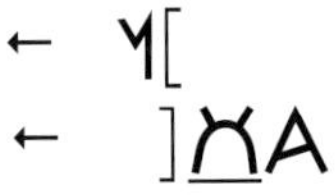

← Y[

←]ᚼA

]n̲ / aŕ[kᵉe(n) . . .

J.15.3

São Martinho das Amoreiras (Concelho de Odemira) 'Pardieiro 3', south Portugal [Museu Regional, Beja] (Correia no. 69) 60 x 32 x 6cm

←]OᚼYᛞOA1AA

aalaein ŕe̲[

← ᛞYO)[ᚼAY

naŕ]k̲ᵉe̲ni

'. . . they remain'

J.16.1

'Nobres', San Salvador, Ourique, south Portugal [Museu da Escrita do Sudoeste, Almodôvar; Museu Nacional de Arqueologia, Lisbon] (Correia no. 47)
110 x 58.5 x 7.5cm

← A3OHYA39A*YAA‡9ᒀᒀ

← ᛞΦYO)ᚼAYA3*9

Syntactic analysis

> **uursaau**   ***arbᵃan**   **tᵉe·bar[e]**   **bᵃa**   **narḱᵉentⁱi**
> ?N   ?nom.sg.   acc.sg.fem.   pvb   V   adv.cjt   V 3pl.

'[This grave/death] has taken away [the man/hero] **uursaau** to the highest destination. Thus they now remain.'

Commentary

The signs are well carved in two right-to-left sequences within inscribed lines. **narḱᵉentⁱi**, the form that often concludes the epigraphic statement, indicates that the text is probably complete. The readings of two signs are unclear and another completely flaked away; however, the restoration of the formula word (**u**)**arbᵃan** is not doubtful. Thus, **uursaau** stands in the position where we look for a name, probably that of the deceased, but that sequence is hard to interpret with two uncertain signs, two double vowels. For two comparable Palaeohispanic men's names, see the note on **uursaau** below. Formally, **uursaau** could be the nominative singular of an *n*-stem or half (standing for the whole) of a masculine nominative/accusative co-ordinative compound in the dual, i.e. to be understand as *iiru≡uursaau 'the man/hero Uursaos' or something similar. The second interpretation is preferable, as it would explain the plural verb **naŕkᵉentⁱi** and also allow transitive **tᵉe·bar[e]** 'has carried away' to have a direct object.

J.16.2

'Fonte Santa 2', San Salvador, Ourique, south Portugal [Museu Nacional de Arqueologia, Lisbon] (Correia no. 55)

→   ‡ MⱵⵋMΛ* [

→   Aⵋ₹AⵔMⱯ M‡ ₹A[

←   A₹O*[

←   *‡Ⴌ‡OⵋOⵋⵋ[

Syntactic analysis

( )omuŕikᵃa[	]anbᵃatⁱia≡	iobᵃa[	]*e bᵃa	na]ŕkᵉe kᵉeo-ion[
N/adj.	nom.acc.dual	nom.acc.dual	?adv./cjt. V	?rel.

'Omurikā (female descendant of the under-sea ancestor). . ., the youngest daughter of Amba(χ)tos . . . remains' *or* 'whom I (this grave) entomb/lay to rest'

Commentary

The stone is broken, leaving four incomplete lines. The interpretation of the text is complicated by an unusual orientation of signs. The two surviving outer lines read left-to-right and the two surviving inner lines right-to-left. It is not clear in which order we should arrange the four segments or how much of the original text is missing. There is a gap in the middle, but it is most likely that this was originally a single text, as the lettering and ruled lines are all closely consistent. The four surviving lines had probably originally been joined by two lines running perpendicular to them.

A secure starting point is provided by]anbᵃatⁱia as a feminine attributive adjective (probably functioning as a patronymic) based on the most common Hispano-Celtic man's name *Ambatos*, so 'daughter of Ambatos'. iobᵃa[is in concord with]anbᵃatⁱia, likewise]omuŕikᵃa[which displays an adjectival suffix common in all the Celtic languages.]omuŕikᵃa[might likewise be construed as a feminine nominative singular in concord with anbᵃatⁱia iobᵃa, thus meaning altogether | Qomurikā *Amba(χ)tiā iō̯ₐmā* | 'the youngest daughter of Ambatos, a woman of the family of Qomurios'. (Alternatively, it is more remotely possible that iobᵃa[and iubᵃa (J.7.8) represent a borrowing of the form attested as the Numidian royal name *Iuba* of the Roman Period; see further below pp. 180–1.)]omuŕikᵃa[of course resembles Gaulish *Aremorica* 'country by/before the sea', so we accordingly consider interpreting it as **u(p)omorikā* 'realm below the sea'. In the present context within a naming phrase, however, the -ikᵃa[suffix more probably conveys the group identity of the dead woman]anbᵃatⁱia.

naŕkᵉe recurs in J.1.1, J.7.8, J.27.1, J.57.1, and S. Martinho. That form can be analysed as a 3rd person singular present active, equivalent to naŕkᵉetⁱi (J.56.1), but having undergone an early apocope of the primary ending *-ti > -t*, i.e. the same development that underlies the formation of the 'conjunct' series of verbal endings found in Old Irish and Early Brittonic. (The SW script was unable to write a final stop consonant as in | *narket* |.) Alternatively, na]ŕkᵉekᵉeo-ion[can be read as a simple dittography for naŕkᵉeo-ion[, which could be read as a 1st person relative 'whom I [this funerary stone] cause to rest, to be buried'.

J.16.3

'Fonte Santa 1', San Salvador, Ourique, south Portugal [Museu Nacional de Arqueologia, Lisbon] (Correia no. 54) 75 X 55 X 10cm

→ �781AD� (inscription line 1)

→ (inscription line 2)

Syntactic analysis

itⁱiabᵉŕebᵉ anakᵃa | ro·bᵃare   bᵃa   naŕkᵉ[e]ntⁱi
                 adj.?nom.sg.fem.   pf V 3sg. adv.cjt. V 3 pl.
or itⁱiarŕer anakᵃa |

'. . . (-)Anākā [this grave/death] has carried. So they remain.'

Commentary

The inscription runs continuously as four sequences of signs forming an approximate square conforming roughly to the shape of the stone. The text is in the less usual orientation—clockwise, left-to-right, beginning at the lower left-hand corner. The conventional closing naŕkᵉentⁱi confirms the arrangement. The writing surface of the stone is badly worn, especially the second of the four lines, the one running across the top, where there may or may not be lost signs following AᛒAᛚᛚA. Therefore, the formula written in the third and fourth lines is relatively clear, but the first and second, presumably containing the names, are not. The reading ro·bᵃa⟨kᵉ⟩e seems to be erroneous: the sign is a damaged ᛒ r, not a ᛕ kᵉ. The symbol D is transcribed here as bᵉ after Untermann, but it is followed by the expected O in neither instance. There is no room for another sign following D in either occurrence. Both examples of D resemble ᛒ r with the stem line worn away.

That **anak^aa** is an *ā*-stem feminine adjective, or final part of a feminine adjective, is likely. A connection with the name of the major river Anas (now the Guadiana at the border of Spain and Portugal) is conceivable, i.e. 'woman of the people of the Anas (Guadiana)', but neither the reading of all the signs nor the segmentation are certain.

J.16.4

'Fonte Santa 3', San Salvador, Ourique, south Portugal [Museu Nacional de Arqueologia, Lisbon] (Correia no. 56) 38 x 8.5 x 7.5cm

→ A𝗠ᴦO‡XAＡ | AXA [

ainest^aa : at^aa[

→ A𝗠ᴦO‡XAＡ | A*[

ainest^aa : a*[

J.16.5

'Penedo', San Salvador, Ourique, south Portugal [Museu Nacional de
Arqueologia, Lisbon] (Correia no. 44) 45 × 21 × 3cm

←]ᴏᴎ | ᴎᴀ§ᴀᴎ

Syntactic analysis

uabᵃan :   ne[
acc.sg.fem.

'to the highest place/state/(feminine) being . . .'

Commentary

uabᵃan as a variant of the formula word **uar(n)bᵃan** | *u̯ar̩man* | < **u(p)eramām*
'highest' corresponds exactly to the place-name Οὐαμα *Uama* 'highest place'
(cf. Luján 2001, 279). *Uama* and the Lepontic personal name UVAMO-KOZIS
(Prestino, *c.* 500 BC) show that there had also been a Celtic superlative without the
r, i.e. **u(p)ₐmo-* < 'Italo-Celtic' **(s)up̩mo-* < notional Indo-European **(s)h₄upm̩ᵐo-*
'highest'. We can understand **uabᵃan**, **uarbᵃan**, and **uarnbᵃan** as feminine singular,
like Οὐαμα. In the funerary formulas, **uarbᵃan**, &c. may convey a purely abstract
or unearthly sublime destination, but a goddess or an ideologically significant
terrestrial height or 'holy mountain' is also possible. Οὐαμα and the Latinized group
name VAMENSI designate a Roman-period settlement (Salvatierra de los Barros,
Badajoz; Falileyev 2010, 228) in the territory of the south-western Celtici, situated
high on the massif within the great bend of the Anas/Guadiana. Οὐαμα probably
originally designated the nearby conspicuous landmark, the highest summit of the
region, Peña Utrera, at 813 metres.

J.16.6

Carapetal, San Salvador, Ourique, south Portugal [Museu Nacional de Arqueologia, Lisbon] (Correia no. 45) 14 × 10.5 × 1.5cm

←]O⍟A[b[ᵃ]<u>are</u>[

'. . .?[this grave/death] has carried . . .'

J.17.1

'Ourique 2', south Portugal (Correia no. 4; on the reading, see also Correa 2006.)

← ( )Ψ**ᛏAΨA‡*AΛϺᒋᙠ

Syntactic analysis

kᵘui kᵃa<u>o</u>sa   **nar[́kᵉe]n(t́i)**
?pron.   V 3pl.

'??who(ever). . . they now remain.'

Commentary

A single line of signs arranged right-to-left runs downwards and is partly illegible at the bottom. **kᵘuikᵃa<u>o</u>sa** (J.17.1) and **kᵘuiarairbᵘbᵘ[u** (J.17.2), both on stones from Ourique, are likely to reflect Proto-Celtic *k^u. Specifically, they resemble forms of the Indo-European interrogative *$k^u ei$ 'who' (cf. Old Irish *cía*, Old Welsh *pui*) or pronominals based on that. The phonological development would conform to sound laws evident elsewhere in the corpus if we assume an original o-grade like that of Old Latin *quoi* 'who'. The o would then have been raised to Tartessian **u** between labial consonant and *i* before the general Tartessian tendency to simplify diphthongs (see *Tartessian 2*, 134–6). Compare **ekᵘu<u>ri</u>ne** |*Ekᵘu-rigₐnē*| (J.4.1) < *$Ek^w o$-rigₐnei*. One can imagine more than one possibility for a commemorative inscription commencing with 'who(ever)' or the like.

J.17.2

'Ourique 4', south Portugal (Correia no. 6)

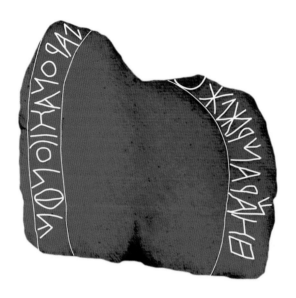

←]*𐤟𐤟𐤟𐤟𐤟𐤟𐤟𐤟𐤟𐤟[←

← 𐤟𐤟𐤟𐤟𐤟𐤟𐤟𐤟𐤟𐤟[←

Syntactic analysis

k^uui arairb^ub^u[u |]b^aare nar̃k^eentⁱi

k̲ᵘu̲i arairbᵘb̲ᵘ[u |]bᵃare nar̃kᵉentⁱi
? pron.   ?superlative   V 3sg. V 3pl.

'?Who(ever) . . . ?most . . . [this grave/death] has carried. They now remain.'

Commentary

We must rely on the drawing in the 18th-century 'Album Cenáculo'. Some letter forms and the sequence 𐤟𐤟 are unparalleled and must be treated with caution. The drawing shows a well-precedented layout with the sequence of signs beginning at the lower right and continuing anti-clockwise within carved lines around the edge of the stone to the conventional ending in **nar̃k^eentⁱi**. Approximately 10 signs were lost where the top of the stone was broken. The opening **k̲ᵘu̲i** indicates a textual relationship with J.17.1 from the same site (see above).

J.17.3

'Ourique 3', south Portugal (Correia no. 5)

←]O)IꓘAꓹO*[

Syntactic analysis

bᵃar]e narˤkᵉe[
V 3sg. V

'... [this grave/death] has carried... remain(s) (...)'

J.17.4

'Ourique 1', south Portugal (Correia no. 3)

← ꓹꓴꟼ⁽*⁾A⅂ꓹꓹOꓘ |

← |Oꓹꟼ| ꓮꓛꓹOꓹꓹL|O9

Syntactic analysis

: kᵉenila⁽*⁾rin≡ | ≡bᵉe:lin enbᵉ·kᵃarne :
acc.sg.   acc.sg. pvb V 3sg.

'[This grave] has ?entombed ?Genilaris, a member of the Beli-group (*or* the strong one, hero).'

Commentary

The drawing is from the 18th-century 'Album Cenáculo'. The reading of some signs is insecure. Two sequences—probably but not certainly to be read one after the other—run right-to-left, between carved lines. The stone appears to have been broken at the top, but there is no indication of partial or missing signs; the two series stop well before the edge of the stone. The text apparently begins conventionally at the lower right with what may be understood as names in concord: **: kᵉenila⁽*⁾rin≡ | ≡bᵉe:lin**. It is unusual in that there are no formula words, and those probable names appear to be in the accusative singular. **enbᵉ·kᵃarne :** is interpreted as a past tense verb functionally equivalent to the missing formula word **tᵉe·ro-bᵃare**.

J.18.1

'Mealha Nova 1', Aldeia de Palheiros (Concelho de Ourique), south Portugal
[Museu Regional, Beja] (Correia no. 38) 107 × 45 × 7cm

← ੧‡ᐱ੧Ο)(ᗄ੪ᗄ☼ᗆΦ‡◻

← [ʒ]Οᚻᗄʒ‡

← ੪Ο)(ᚻᗄ੪ᗄʒΟ੧ᗄ

← ᗆΦ

Syntactic analysis

bᵒotⁱieana≡ kᵉertᵒo =robᵃa tᵉe· bᵃare bᵃa   naŕkᵉentⁱi
N fem.   gen.sg.   fem. pvb V 3 sg. adv/cjt V 3pl.
| *Bōd´eanā≡ kerdo =ro_ₐmā de· bāre; ma narkenti* |

'[this grave/death] has carried away Bōdⁱeanā ⟨and⟩ the first-born daughter of the artisan; so "they" now remain [here]'.

Commentary

Although the stone has broken at the top, the text is complete and easily read. It follows the most conventional layout, i.e. right-to-left, anti-clockwise, beginning with the naming phrase at the lower righthand corner. Ruling lines carved above and below the signs remain visible flanking the righ-thand sequence.

For **bᵒotⁱieana**, note that Hispano-Celtic names in both *Boudi-* and *Bouti-* are very common in Celtic-speaking parts of the Peninsula during the earlier Roman Period, and both stems occur with spellings showing the simplification of the diphthong to *o* (see the note on the name below and *Tartessian 2*, 134–6).

For **robᵃa** | *ro_ₐmā* | < Indo-European *pro-meh₂, cf. Middle Irish *rom* 'early, too soon' < Indo-European **pro-mo-* (*Lexique* R-41–2) possibly also *róm-* 'pre-eminent', Homeric πρόμος 'foremost man', Gothic *fruma*, Old English *forma* 'first, earliest' < Indo-European **pr̥-mo-*. For **(p)romo-* 'first offspring', compare the formation of ordinals like Latin *decimus* as well as Western Indo-European superlatives.

See further *Tartessian 2*, 102–4.

J.18.2

'Mealha Nova 2', Aldeia de Palheiros (Concelho de Ourique), south Portugal [Museu
Regional, Beja] (Correia no. 39) 67 × 38 × 9cm

←‥| AⱵOⰛⰋ᛫᛭ⰐOOHⰋA |‥

Syntactic analysis

>]an   tᵉe(-)e· ro-bᵃare na[ŕkᵉe(. . .)
> ?acc.sg. pvb ?E pf   V 3sg. V

' . . . [this grave/death] has carried (him/it) away (?to the highest destination);
remain(s).'

Commentary

On this very clearly carved fragment, in the more conventional right-to-left orientation, only a portion of the formula **uar(n)bᵃan tᵉe(e)·ro-bᵃare (bᵃa) naŕkᵉentⁱi**
survives. It is possible that the double **ee** in **tᵉee·ro-bᵃare** signifies an accusative
infixed pronoun or elided relative after the first preverb.

J.18.3

'Mealha Nova 3', Aldeia de Palheiros (Concelho de Ourique), south Portugal
[Museu Regional, Beja] (Correia no. 40) 73 × 39 × 6cm

← ···]ᚼ‡*↲ᛉ

← ···]ᛉᐱᐱᚼᛔᚼ

k^{e}eŕk^{a}aŕ[

i↲*oŕ[

Commentary

A badly broken stone with two fragmentary lines reading right-to-left, both complete at the beginning. If something has been lost before —k^{e}eŕk^{a}aŕ[, it could have been a prefixed element and be compared with **uuŕerk^{a}ar** and/or **ark^{a}are** from the recently discovered Monte Gordo stela. But note that the *r*-signs are used differently (cf. *Tartessian 2* §114).

J.19.1

Herdade do Pêgo, Santana da Serra (Concelho de Ourique), 'Pêgo 1', south
Portugal [Museu Regional, Beja] (Correia no. 41) 37 × 45 × 5cm

← <u>A</u>⏐ƐO⑁M‡⋏‡‡O⑁AƐ⑁4ᗺAX‡O⑁⑁⑁⑁₁
← ⑁⑁⑁Oⵊ....

Syntactic analysis

]liirnest^aak^uun b^aane ≡		oořoire	b^aa[re nař]k^eenii
gen.pl.	fem.nom.acc.dual	fem.nom.acc.dual	?V V 3 pl.

[Rodríguez Ramos:]iirnest^aa b^uun-b^aane...]

'[This grave/death] has carried a woman of the Lir(a)nestoi ("people near the
sea")] ⟨and⟩ wife of Oořoir (< *U(p)er-u̯iros). "They" now remain [here]'.

Commentary

The signs are carved legibly but somewhat freely within lines as an inward
turning spiral with squared angles in the more usual right-to-left, anti-clockwise
orientation. The stone is broken at the bottom, where what is lost forms part of

the reconstructable formula b^a<u>a</u>[re naŕ]k^eenii.

This is the epitaph of the wife (nominative/accusative dual or dative singular b^aane) of the man commemorated in J.19.2, the epigraphy and orthography of which are very similar.

ooŕoire | Qoŗoir(ẹ)ē | is interpreted as a nominative/accusative feminine dual (less probably a dative singular) of a *iā*-stem adjective designating a female relative of Ooŕoir, from a notional Proto-Celtic *U(p)er-ụiriāi. On the phonological development, see the note on **ooŕoir** and **ooŕoire** below and *Tartessian 2*, 61–3.

J.19.2

Herdade do Pêgo, Santana da Serra (Concelho de Ourique), 'Pêgo 2', south Portugal
[Museu da Escrita do Sudoeste, Almodôvar; Museu Nacional de Arqueologia, Lisbon] (Correia no. 42) 39 X 36.5 X 5cm

← ᛎ↑ᛉΟ)ᛉΑᛉ9ᛉ‡ᛉ‡‡

Syntactic analysis

ooŕoir   naŕkᵉen↑ⁱi
N nom.sg.   V 3 pl.

'Ooŕoir (*U(p)eruiros): I (*or* they) now remain here.'

[Rodríguez Ramos: . . . **naŕkᶜenbⁱi**]

Commentary

The inscription survives complete, and all 14 signs are easily legible. They are arranged approximately as a rounded square, conforming to the shape of the stone.
They follow the more conventional orientation, right-to-left, anti-clockwise, beginning at the lower right with a name and closing with **naŕkᶜentⁱi**. Inscribed lines
enclose the text on the top and left-hand sides. This example may be viewed as a
highly compressed form of the standard formula, with only the final formula word
and minimal naming passage. This is interpreted as the epitaph of the husband of
the woman commemorated in J.19.1, a stone from the same site. If we accept the
transliteration of Rodríguez Ramos **naŕkᶜenbⁱi**, we can then interpret the text
as | *Ooŕoir naŕkemi* | with a 1st person singular athematic, present-tense verb, thus
meaning something like 'I, Ooŕoir, now rest [here]'. On the phonology of **ooŕoir**
< **U(p)er-uiros*, see the note on **ooŕoir** and **ooŕoire** below and *Tartessian 2*, 61–2,
117, 129, 137, 140, 152, 162.

J.19.3

Herdade do Pêgo, Santana da Serra (Concelho de Ourique), 'Pêgo 3',
south Portugal [Museu Nacional de Arqueologia, Lisbon]
(Correia no. 43) 12 × 14 × 9.5cm

]* ‡1‡ [   ]olo*[

J.20.1

Bastos, Santa Luzia (Concelho de Ourique), south Portugal [Museu Regional, Beja] (Correia no. 37) 15 × 32 × 15cm

← ꟼ9ᗣ44⧺ᛗᗄ1O𝖯ᗄᗄ𝖷ᗄ[

←]ᗄO)𝖪ᗄᗄᗄ9ᗣꙅ*Oᗄᗣꙅ

Syntactic analysis

]**uŕni bᵉelisón uarn|bᵃan e̠* bᵃar(e)n naŕkᵉen̠[..**
|... *Belisón* *u̯ar̯aman* ... *bāren* *naŕken*[|
N? N gen.pl. acc.sg. V ?3pl. V 3pl.

'[The group?] have carried]urnī of the Beli- group (or of the strong ones) to the highest destination. They remain.'

Commentary

The inscription is arranged as a continuous series of signs in two right-to-left vertical lines (down then up) with an incised line between them. A sign has apparently been lost at the beginning, probably the opening of the naming phrase in its usual position. The second line is more badly worn, but clearly ends with **naŕkᵉen̠[**, a form of the conventional closing formula. Two notable features in the formula words are **uarn|bᵃan** rather than the usual **uarbᵃan**, thus confirming the phonetic form |*u̯ar̯aman*|, and the apparent plural marking of **bᵃar(e)n**, as opposed to the more usual **bᵃare**. In the naming phrase,]**uŕni** probably represents a name of the deceased. The genitive plural **bᵉelisón**, corresponding to dative plural **bᵉelibᵒo** (J.1.2) and accusative singular **bᵉe:lin** (J.17.4), probably expresses a tribal or kinship affiliation. Whatever the exact meaning, genitive plural **bᵉelisón**, may refer to the group that is the logical subject of plural **bᵃar(e)n**.

J.21.1

Arzil, Garvão (Concelho de Ourique), south Portugal [Museu da Escrita do Sudoeste, Almodôvar; Museu Regional, Beja] (Correia no. 61) 109.5 × 46.5 × 11cm

Commentary

The inscription is carefully carved between two lines along three sides of the large stone. It follows the conventional arrangement— right-to-left, anti-clockwise, beginning in the lower right-hand corner, and closing with the formula word **narkᵉenii**. Signs have been lost at the beginning (removing the entire naming phrase, which cannot have been longer than eight signs) and also in the middle, where the formula **t̲ᵉe̲[(e)· ro-bᵃ]a̲re** can be restored with confidence.

← ᛒᛁᛁᛟᛝᛉᚪᛉᛟᏓᚪ[   ]ᛟᚼᛁᚪᛝᚪᛁ[

Syntactic analysis

 ...]u̲arbᵃan t̲ᵉe̲[(e)· ro- bᵃ]a̲re narkᵉenii
| ... u̲arₐman de (e)· .. ro- bāre; narḱenji |
  acc.sg. pvb ?E pf V 3sg. V 3pl.

'[This grave/death] has carried away... to the highest destination. They now remain.'

J.22.1

'Cerro dos Enforcados 1', Panóias (Concelho de Ourique), south Portugal
[Museu da Escrita do Sudoeste, Almodôvar; Museu Nacional de Arqueologia,
Lisbon] (Correia no. 17) 144 × 67 × 13cm

Syntactic analysis

uarbᵒoiir	sarune	ea	bᵃa|re nafˊ|kᵉenii
| Uarₐmo-iir	Sarunē	eā	bāre; nafˊkenji |
cpd.N nom.sg.	dat.attribute	?rel.	V 3sg. V 3pl.

'Uarₐmo-iir Sarunē ("Noble Consort to the ?Star goddess"), she who has carried [him] [away]. They now remain.'

Commentary

The inscription is arranged along three sides of a rectangular carved field. With the signs set within incised lines, it exhibits the most common arrangement—right-to-left, anti-clockwise, beginning in the lower right-hand corner with a name, and closing with the formula word **nafˊ\|kᵉenii**. All signs are legible, and none seem to be missing. The syntax differs somewhat from the standard formula. I believe that this departure has been determined by the circumstance that the name or epithet of the deceased (**uarbᵒoiir sarune**) is related by form and meaning to one of the usual formula words (**uarbᵃan**). The former I understand as 'highest man/hero' *U(p)erₐmo-uiros* 'to the star goddess', dative *Stₐrunāi*. The formula word **uarbᵃan** is a feminine accusative of destination < *u(p)erₐmām* 'highest place, sate, being'. In other words, the divine namesake of **uarbᵒoiir sarune** might be the same afterlife destination implied in the standard formula, or one such possibility within the belief system. Note that the pre-eminent Phoenician goddess Astarte, whose cult spread widely within the southern Peninsula during the orientalization of the Early Iron Age, was a star goddess, similar in this aspect to Aphrodite/Venus. **uarbᵒoiir sarune** may be compared with the Phoenician/Punic name *Abd-Astart* 'Servant of Astarte' (see further note on **uarbᵒoiir sarune** below). The segment **ea** is consistent with the regular phonological outcome for the feminine nominative singular relative from Proto-Celtic *ịā* with characteristic Tartessian lowering of *i* to e before a (see *Tartessian 2* §78). In other words, in this interpretation it would not be death, the unspoken pre-eminence of the grave, or some nameless deity that 'has carried away' the deceased, but the personal eponymous goddess of **uarbᵒoiir sarune** himself. Similarly, in J.12.1, I propose that it is the feminine supernatural being invoked as **mubᵃa ⊨atᵃaneatᵉe** 'foster-mother to the winged one'—again a goddess in the sky—who has carried the dead hero to the afterlife.

J.22.2

'Cerro dos Enforcados 2', Panóias (Concelho de Ourique), south Portugal
[Museu Nacional de Arqueologia, Lisbon] (Correia no. 18) 69 × 60 × 5cm

←]ꟼAᐱAOOᎽꟺꟼAⴲ[→

Syntactic analysis

]sarune ea   oar[

dat.sg.   ?rel.

'. . . to Sarunā (?the star goddess) . . .'

Commentary

The stone is broken, and what survives of the inscription is the middle sequence
of a text inscribed within a ruled rectangle. The signs are in the conventional right-
to-left, anti-clockwise orientation. The text is clearly related to that of J.21.1. The
fragmentary **oar**[could commence an unusual orthographic representation for
uar(n)bᵒo- or **bᵃare**, if not a different word or words.

J.23.1

Monte Nova do Visconde, Casével (Concelho de Castro Verde), south Portugal
[Câmara Municipal, Ourique] 95 X 34 X 22cm

←   4Ⴗﾑ ⅄ ⅄ Ⴔ Ⴑ Ⴑ Ⴑ Ⴑ

← | ⅄ | Ⴑ ⅄ Ⴑ

←   Ⴑ Ⴑ ⅄ ⅄ ⅄

Syntactic analysis

bᵉ**et**ⁱ**isai t**ᵉ**e(-)e· b**ᵃ**arent**ⁱ**i iru≡| (u)arb**ᵘ**u   i   el**
dat./loc.sg. pvb+?E   V 3pl.   nom.acc.dual? nom.acc.dual ?   ??

naŕrkᵉ**e:n: | uśn**ee
V 3pl.   dat./loc.sg.?

'[A grave] for Betisa, the one who the lord (VIROS VERAMOS) ??god has now carried away. They remain in the highest place (Uxamā).'

Commentary

The stone is an unimproved irregular shape. There is no ruling flanking the signs, which consequently vary greatly in size. However, none appear to have been lost and all are legible. The layout is typical, a loose approximation of a three-sided anti-clockwise spiral with right-to-left orientation. It begins, as most commonly, at the lower right.

The text departs from the usual pattern in several interesting respects. **naŕrk**ᵉ**e:n:** does not close the statement, but is penultimate. Orthographically **naŕrk**ᵉ**e:n:** is a unique variant and clearly carries the significant implication that the sounds represented by 𝗬 ŕ and 𝟵 r were similar and easily confused, if they continued to differ at all in the sound system of the Tartessian language at this period. The two verbs of the formula are present, but their morphology partly reversed, so that there is present marking on **t**ᵉ**e(-)e·b**ᵃ**arent**ⁱ**i** but not on **naŕrk**ᵉ**e:n:.** There are no **ro** forms. **t**ᵉ**e(-)e·b**ᵃ**arent**ⁱ**i**, unlike the recurrent **t**ᵉ**e(e)·ro·b**ᵃ**are** 'has carried away', is marked as plural, probably because what has carried the deceased away is not left unnamed as usual, but here named with the co-ordinative dual **iru≡(u)arb**ᵘ**u i-el**, which I interpret as a divine name. The formula word **uar(n)b**ᵃ**an** 'to the highest place, state, being' (feminine) is absent, perhaps avoided because the form is already

present in **uarb^uu(i)** 'highest one' (masculine), but we probably have a closely similar idea expressed in the final word **uśnee** (which could also be read **uśnb^ee**) 'in' or 'to the highest place, state, being' (feminine), cf. the recurrent Hispano-Celtic place-name *Uxama*.

J.24.1

Neves, Castro Verde, south Portugal [Mining Museum, Neves-Corvo]
(Correia no. 70) 25 × 39 × 2.5cm

←]ᔓ***A1[	]la***bᵃ[
← AM[...]ᙏ≢٩≢☐1AO*[	]*e a̲b°oroi[*or*]*ea̲nb°oroi[
←]ᛒΧAO≢AΛA≢ᙏ	isakᵃaoeaŕt̲ᶜ[
← O٩≢AA[	]at°ore/
←]O̲AAΛ[	]kᵃaae̲[

Commentary

The stone is broken. No line is complete, and the layout is hard to reconstruct from what survives. There are no evident formula words and little basis for word division. The reading follows Untermann. **alb°oroi**[resembles a known Hispano-Celtic personal name (see Notes below). **isakᵃa** could be a feminine adjective.

J.26.1

Herdade do Gavião, Aljustrel, south Portugal [Museu da Escrita do Sudoeste, Almodôvar; Museu Regional, Beja] (Correia no. 59) 115 × 46 × 12cm

← OYAℰ ዣዣ ⅄HO ዣዣ A X [

→] ⁎ ℥A P O ⴹ A ⴽⴽ [

Syntactic analysis

...]tᵃarnekᵘ⟨k̲ᵘ⟩un	≡bᵃane		ro-]bᵃare naŕkᵉ[e ...
|...Tarₐnekūn	≡bₐnē	ro- bāre naŕke-|	
gen.pl.	fem.nom.acc.dual/dat.sg.	pf V 3sg. V	

'[This grave/death] has carried the wife ... ⟨and⟩ woman of the Tar(a)nekoi (group/family of Tar(a)nus); they/she remain(s).'

Commentary

Two well-carved series of signs run right-to-left between three carefully ruled lines on a relatively smooth surface. The stone is broken, and both lines are incomplete at both ends. The signs are legible, but there is one unusual sign (which looks like an incomplete repetition of ⴹ kᵘ) standing between ⴹ kᵘ and ⅄ u, which is thus to be excluded from the romanization (following Untermann), in order to accord with the principle of redundancy. The partial vertical stroke before bᵃare indicates that the missing formula word could be ro, but not tᵉe(e). We anticipate that what is gone at the beginning of the first line would be the first element of the naming phrase, probably a woman's own name or gamonym in the nominative/accusative dual.

J.27.1

Góis, São Miguel do Pinheiro (Concelho de Mértola), south Portugal

← O)ꓘAꟈO9AꟛꟈOAꟈO)I4[

→ 9OM**ꟈ*[

Syntactic analysis

]uk^ee śaen   b^aare nańk^ee* [ ] b^eeś**n*[
          ?demon.acc.sg. V 3sg. V

'. . . -uka, [this grave/death] has carried ?to this place; he/she remains . . .'

Commentary

The inscription is known only from the 18th-century 'Album Cenáculo'. At that time it was already fragmentary with three or four signs illegible in the second line. The orientation is boustrophedon (alternating right-to-left/left-to-right). The first line ends with b^aare nańk^ee, as a concise version of the formula. The difficult b^eeś**n* is thus an amplification. If we take śaen as a demonstrative with feminine accusative singular marking, it might be taking the place of the formula word uar(n)b^aan, expressing the destination to which the deceased has been carried.]uk^ee are thus the final signs of the opening naming phrase.

J.28.1

Mértola (Marques de Faria), south Portugal [Museu Municipal, Mértola]
79 X 39 X 8–12cm

]✶✶[

→   ]AOＥAＬ‡✶[

←   ]ＹＹ‡ＹＩ9‡Ｙ[

←   ‡ＬＹA[

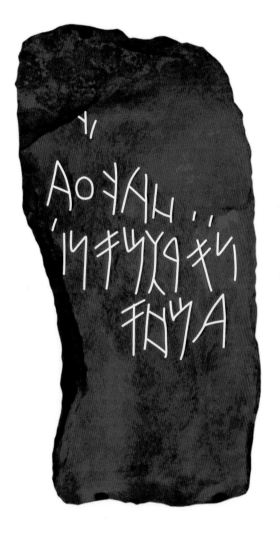

Syntactic analysis

]✶✶[

]ae<u>t</u>ᵉa<u>b</u>ᵒo✶[

dat./abl.pl

]<u>n</u>or↑ioni[

]aibᵒo

dat./abl.pl

Commentary

All the lines are incomplete. Readings of some signs are doubtful. There are no evident formula words or recognizable names on which to base an interpretation.

J.51.1

Los Castellares, Puente Genil, Córdoba, Spain [Museo Arqueológico Provincial, Málaga] (Correia no. 76) 96 ✗ 48 ✗ 15cm

]k̠ⁱu

]**bᵃa

]t̠ᵘurkᵃaio[

Commentary

The principle of redundancy is apparently not adhered to in the first line, although the expected rule is followed in the second with]**bᵃa and twice in the third in the sequence]t̠ᵘurkᵃaio[. De Hoz (2010, 401) rejects the alternative reading tᵘuraaio. As this inscription was found near the extreme south-eastern edge of the geographic distribution of the corpus, it would be significant if we were able to confirm that it was written in the same language as that attested in the Algarve, but this is not altogether certain from the extant text. bᵃa may be part of a formula word, e.g. bᵃare or uarbᵃan. If]t̠ᵘurkᵃaio[is not a name, a 1st person singular perfect verb with suffixed relative, *u̯ou̯rga + *i̯o- 'that I have made/done', is another possibility.

J.52.1

Villamanrique de la Condesa, Sevilla, Spain [Museo Arqueológico, Sevilla]
(Correia no. 79) 61 × 61 × 28cm

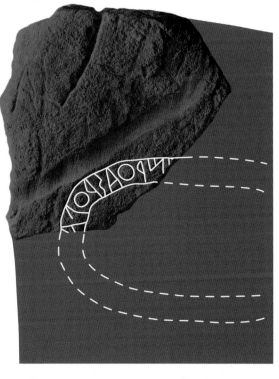

←]A109³AO9Ϻ[→

Syntactic analysis

]ire abᵃre la[

read]ire bᵃare la[k-
?nom.pl. V 3sg. ?V

'. . . ?men . . . [this grave/death] has carried;
?lie/lay down. . .'

Commentary

The arc of text occurs on a fragment of very thick stone, which had probably been part of a large stela with a long inscription over a complete circuit. **abᵃre** for the common formula word **bᵃare** is an obvious error and—since Tartessian could also be written left-to-right—easily explained. **lakᵉentⁱi** ?'they are lain down' is found instead of **naŕkᵉentⁱi** in J.53.1, and is merely raised as a possibility here.

J.53.1

Alcalá del Río, Sevilla, Spain (Correia no. 75; on the reading,
see further Correa 2005, 138.)

→   ⋈ ΔͰΑΡΑΗΟΔͰ↑ͰΗ⧧ͻΑͰ⧣ΡͻΑ⧦ΟΧΑ

→   ΓΑΚΟͰΦͰΡΑⰘΑΛΑΜΟΧΑͰΑ

←   ΗΟⰓⰓΑ⅂⧧ΡͰⰍ⧧⋈

Syntactic analysis

kᵒ-	tᵘ- ua-ratᵉe	tᵘn↑ⁱitᵉsbᵃan	orbᵃa	setᵃa
| Ko(n)·tu	-ụa -rāte	tumitesₐman	(o)orₐmā	sedā
pvb	pvb pvb V 3sg.	acc.sg.fem.superlative	nom.sg.?superlative	nom.sg.
			or |... orba-sedā..|	

lakᵉentⁱi raⰘa		≡kᵃaśetᵃana
Lāgenti	*RaHa*	*≡kassedannā* |
V 3pl.	fem.(?nom.acc. dual)	fem.(?nom.acc. dual)

bᵒbᵉ kᵒoŕbᵉo	bᵃarleⰨ
?	gen.sg.masc. ?

'The highest throne/sublime place of repose (*or* inherited resting place) has safely
delivered (< has run under) to the greatest tumulus: Raφa ⟨and⟩ the bronze minister are now lain down [here] — (?daughter) of Korbeos (?"charioteer, chariot-
maker") ...'

Commentary

The stone was lost during the Spanish Civil War, and we rely on the only available
drawing, which leaves little doubt about most signs. The orientation of the main text
is the more unusual left-to-right, clockwise. There are six violations of redundancy.

For possible interpretations, see *Celtic from the West* 251–2; *Tartessian 2*, 82–7. Two
new suggestions are offered now. First, if we follow Correa and romanize the sign
↑ in tᵘn↑ⁱitᵉsbᵃan as bⁱ, then | tumitesₐman | can be taken as a feminine singular
superlative 'what has grown greatest', cf. Welsh *tyfu* 'grow', *twf* 'growth', and from the
same root Old Irish *túaim* 'hillock, mound', Middle Welsh *tomm-en* 'heap, mound',
also Latin *tumulus*, Greek τύμβος 'tomb, burial mound', all from Indo-European
*teu-m- 'swell' (Pokorny 2002, 1082). Therefore, tᵘnbⁱitᵉsbᵃan could mean 'the
greatest/best tumulus'. (On | tumitesₐman | < **tumetisₐmām*, cf. *Tartessian 2*, 126, 129
on the phonology.) Secondly, kᵒoŕbᵉo as well as possibly being the genitive singular
of a man's name *Korbeos* or *Korbos* (cf. Old Irish *Corbb*) could be a common noun,
pertaining to a wheeled vehicle (~ Old Irish glossary word *corbb* 'chariot [frame]',

British *karbanto-* 'chariot' = Old Irish *carpat*) as anticipated by the verb **ua-rat^e e** < **u(p)o-rāte* 'has run under, has conveyed to safety'. None of the formula words appear here, but the underlying ideas of the formula are represented. Thus, **t^e(e)·ro-b^aare** 'has carried away' is absent, but **ua-rat^e e** 'has delivered' has a similar meaning and grammatical form. The absent formula word **uar(n)b^aan** 'to the highest destination' has arguably split in two. These could refer literally to different aspects of the funerary structure and rite: subject **orb^aa set^aa** 'most sublime place of repose' meaning the carriage or bier on which the deceased has been carried, accusative of destination **t^unⵝit^e sb^aan** meaning 'greatest/best tumulus'. On the other hand, **orb^aa set^aa** and **t^unⵝit^e sb^aan** could be religious metaphors: 'highest throne' for god the ruler and 'greatest tumulus' for the heavenly mountain and happy afterlife. Instead of **nark^e ent^i i**, there is a different verb, but it is also 3rd person marked for the present tense, **lak^e ent^i i** 'they now lie down, are lain down'.

It is noteworthy that this inscription, from the core area of the Tartessos polity, is unusual in several respects: clockwise orientation, omissions of redundancy, verb-initial syntax, no formula words, and a woman identified by her office. The Alcalá del Río inscription is not the only evidence for women of important social and economic rank in Tartessian society. The famous wealthy orientalizing burial of Aliseda, Cáceres (*c.* 625 BC), was that of a woman who has been interpreted as a priestess.

Alcalá del Río was also the find spot of a Late Bronze Age sword of a type with parallel sides and an elongated point.

J.54.1

Capote, Higuera la Real, Badajoz ('La losa de Capote'), Spain [Museo
Arqueológico Provincial, Badajoz] (Correia no. 80) 95 x 60 x 16cm

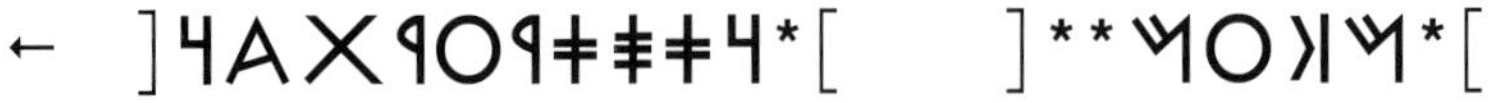

←]�५ᗅ✕ᑫOᑫ⧻⧻�५*[   ]**ᗰOᛁᛈ*[

Syntactic analysis

]*ikᵉei**[   ]*uosor ertᵃau[ne
                    ?VN

Commentary

The stone is a reused Late Bronze
Age 'warrior stela', which is orientated
downwards from the perspective of
the inscription, like the reused warrior stela of Cabeza del Buey IV below.
Díaz-Guardamino (2010, 19) proposes a
date in the 8th century BC with reuse in
the 7th–6th. The earlier carving includes
most prominently schematic images of
a chariot with two horses and what appears to be a large lyre at the bottom
(originally the top). The evident interest
in songs and poetry might be significant.
The signs are carved in a right-to-left arc,
beginning in the lower right. The stone
surface has broken so that approximately
8–10 signs have been lost in the middle of
the text. Signs have also been lost at both
ends. There are no recognizable formula
words, but ertᵃau[ne may be the same
word as eertaune in J.55.1, cf. Celtiberian
u]ertaunei (K.1.1) which is probably a verbal
noun (Wodtko 2000, 120).

J.55.1

near Siruela, Badajoz, Spain [Museo Arqueológico Provincial de Badajoz]
(Correia no. 78) 120 X 52 X 25cm

← Oᕼ𐌰Xᑭ0Οᕼ‡ᕼ1‡Ͷ‡የ

→ X𐌰ᑭᕼΟᒋᕼ‡ᕼ|ᒋᕼ�XᕼᕼΟᕼΟᕼ𐌰ᕼᕼΟᕼ𐌰ᕼ

Syntactic analysis

ro- kᵒoli̱o̱n eertᵃaune (*or* ao kᵒoli̱o̱n . . .)
prep. acc.sg. VN dat.sg.   prep.

tᵃarielnon : li̱r̓niene naŕkᵉenai
acc.sg.   V 3pl. middle

[Rodríguez Ramos: **aokᵒolion . . .**]

'To ??exchange Darielnos for Kolios. . . They remain.'

Commentary

A right-to-left series of signs, beginning at the bottom right of the writing field, followed by a much straighter left-to-right series arranged between two ruled lines. The only formula word is recognizable as a version of the conventional closing, but its specific form **naŕkᵉenai** is not so common, but does occur also in J.7.1, another unusual text. This form's paradigmatic function is possibly 3rd plural middle < *-nto-i*. If so, meaning could be something like 'cause themselves to rest'. **ro-kᵒoli̱o̱n** could be a 3rd plural verb + preverb. But perhaps it is more plausible to interpret it and **tᵃarielnon** as *o*-stem accusatives singular in syntactic co-ordination. If **eertᵃaune** like Celtiberian u]*ertaunei* (K.1.1) is a dative infinitive/verbal noun (Wodtko 2000, 120), Proto-Celtic **u̯ert-* 'turn, exchange, sell' may be considered, if so 'to exchange Darielnos for Kolios'. If the name is *Aokolios*, that could be the same name and even the same man as the **akᵒoli̱oś** whose funerary monument (J.56.1) was not far away. Note also **kᵒoloion** (Monte Novo do Castelinho). For the meaning of *Kolios* or *A(o)kolios*, Old Irish *buachail* and Old Welsh *buceil*, like Greek βουκόλος, go back to

Indo-European *g^wou-k^wolos 'cowherd'. The simplex would therefore mean 'guide, leader, helmsman'. This same Indo-European root *k^wel- 'turn' also gives Old Irish *cul* 'chariot' and the word for 'wheel' in several languages, including English. So, could Tartessian **k⁰o(l)ioś**, &c., mean essentially 'charioteer' or 'chariot warrior', thus translating into words one of the recurrent images of the Late Bronze Age warrior stelae of the south-western Peninsula? If we read the initial preposition either as **ro** or **ao**, it would entail the characteristically Celtic loss of Indo-European *p* in original *pro or h_2epo.

J.56.1

Madroñera, Cáceres, Spain [Museo Arqueológico Provincial, Cáceres]
(Correia no. 77) 160 × 65cm

← ᛘⵌⵔⵔⵕⵀ**ᛐⴼⵔⵀⵖⵉⵖ(ꓤ)ⵕⵕⴻⵕ**   *Syntactic analysis*

ak⁰o(l)ioś naŕkᵉetⁱi
N nom.sg.   V 3sg.

'Ákolios now lies/rests [here].'

[Rodríguez Ramos: **ak⁰olion:** ...
But, see De Hoz 2010, 394 n. 517.]

Commentary

A single complete series of 14 signs running right-to-left in the middle of a smooth surface. The stem line of **ꓤl** is obscured where the stone is cracked. This short inscription is significant in obviously illustrating an Indo-European funerary formula at its most basic: one nominative singular name + a 3rd person singular verb with present marking **ak⁰o(l)ioś naŕkᵉetⁱi**. This minimal statement must convey, pragmatically at least, something very much like 'Ákolios now lies, rests, remains [here]'.

J.57.1 (T1 86H/En12–1)

Medellín, Badajoz, Spain (on the reading, see Almagro-Gorbea 2004; 2008 752–4; Correa 2006, 297.)

← O])ᛈAᛉAᛑᛗᛒ1O))ᛗᛒᛈᛒ1[

←]ᛗ1

←]A}

Syntactic analysis

]lok°on ḵᵉeloia nar̂kᵉ[e .. | li[| bᵃa[re
  acc.sg. nom.sg. V   ?V

'. . . the burial/funerary urn . . . the daughter of Kelaos remains . . .'

Commentary

A fragment of a stela of *c.* 650–*c.* 625 BC reused in a burial of *c.* 550–*c.* 500 BC where it was found with other 7th-century fill material. There are three broken fragmentary lines of text, two very short (two signs each). The surviving portion of the long line ends with a form of the formula word that usually closes the epitaph—**nar̂kᵉ**[e. The word **lok°on** (probably 'burial, urn') occurs also in J.1.1. Forms resembling ḵᵉ**eloia** occur in J.11.1 (**kⁱielaoe**) and Cabeza del Buey IV (**kᵉeilau**). These are presumably names, but possibly terms of rank or kinship, cf. Old Irish *céile* 'fellow, client'.

    As discussed in *Tartessian 2*, 126–7, there are several examples in which Proto-Celtic *i* and *i̯* are found lowered to O **e** when preceding an A **a** either directly or with an intervening consonant: for example, **meleśae** (J.15.1) ~ Gaulish *Meliððus*, **tᵘurea** < **Turi̯ā* (J.7.8), and **kᵃaśetᵃana** 'female bronze minister' (J.53.1) ~ Gaulish *cas(s)idan(n)os*. There are also some counter-examples, such as **anbᵃatia̱** (J.16.2), which might be considered more archaic, representing the state of the language before the lowering assimilation (*i* > **e**) had occurred. ḵᵉ**eloia**

represents another such counter-example, and in this case we have a relatively early absolute date *c.* 650–*c.* 625 BC based on archaeological criteria. Alcalá del Río (J.53.1), which is also from Spain, presents a thorough contrast: (1) the main text is written left-to-right, (2) there are six violations of the principle of redundancy, (3) new diction replaces the old formula words, and (4) there is kᵃaśetᵃana with e from Proto-Celtic *i. The first two of these developments can be ascribed to the influence of Greek alphabetic (as opposed Cypriot) literacy, which would have occurred from the mid 7th century BC and more strongly after *c.* 600. It is not impossible that the third development might also have something to do with Hellenization, as this might also have encouraged new cultural concepts and ceremonial practices.

T2 86H/13–1

Medellín, Badajoz, Spain (Almagro-Gorbea 2004; 2008 754–8)

← **ΟΑΥΔᗺ**   tetunae

→ **ᛗᛉᚠᗡᚠᛈ** *or* **ᛗᛉᚠᚾᛈ**
śnelkar, śneler, śnorkar, *or* śnoror

Commentary

Two non-consecutive lines of graffiti scratched post-firing on a wheel-turned dish or shallow bowl, datable *c.* 625–*c.* 600 BC. The first reads **tetunae** right-to-left orientation. That form has possible Celtic affinities, cf. Gaulish *Tettus, Tettonis,* Cisalpine TETVMVS (Delamarre 2007, 180–1). It can be understood as a mark of ownership in the dative singular '[belonging] to Tetunā'. The second reads left-to-right. That reading is uncertain, but none of the range of possibilities appears Celtic. Therefore, it looks as though there were two systems of writing, and possibly two languages, in use in Medellín in the late 7th century BC. Neither line shows redundancy, and in this respect they are inconsistent with the writing system used on the inscriptions on stone, but instead anticipate the 'Meridional' or SE Iberian writing system. As well as these two brief inscriptions, a double zigzag has been scratched on the bowl, which is probably not writing. There are also two images of owls. These resemble Greek relief images of owls of the Archaic Period, but somewhat more closely the Egyptian hieroglyph that has the phonetic value 'M'.

T3 86/TP–1

Medellín, Badajoz, Spain (Almagro-Gorbea 2004; 2008 758–9)

→ ⲄⲆⲄⲆⲄ *or* ⲄⲆⲄⲆA

erere, ororo, erera, *or* **ererka**

Commentary

A single line of five signs, orientated left-to-right, scratched post-firing on a wheel-turned dish or shallow bowl, datable *c.* 550–*c.* 500 BC. The sign forms are unusual and, consequently, the reading uncertain. There is an inexact similarity between the last of the possible transliterations above and the opening sequence of the Monte Gordo inscription (below), i.e. **uuŕerkᵃarua****, for which the segmentation is uncertain.

Monte Novo do Castelinho [J.105]

Concelho de Almodôvar, south Portugal [Museu da Escrita do Sudoeste, Almodôvar] (Guerra et al. 1999; Correa 2002, 409)

← ⲘⲪⲨⲔ[ ]‡Ⲓ⋏[ ]ⲄA‡↑‡⋈ : Ⲩ‡Ⲙ‡↑‡⋈[

Syntactic analysis

]**k̲ᵒoloion : k̲ᵒoloar**[ ]**ŕ**[.]**s**[ʔkᵉ]**ntⁱi**

    acc.sg.   V 3 pl.

Commentary

The inscription appears to end in a present-tense 3rd person plural verb, and what survives of the text appears to begin with an accusative singular noun or nominative/accusative neuter, or possibly]**k̲ᵒolo-**, of whatever meaning, followed by the accusative relative particle -**ion**.

Corte do Freixo 2 [J.107]

Concelho de Almodôvar, south Portugal [Museu da Escrita do Sudoeste, Almodôvar] (text from Guerra 2002, cf. Correa 2004)

←]ꟼꟼO)|ᛕAꟼ[

Syntactic analysis

]narkᵉeuu[
V ?1 sg.

'. . . ?I [this stone monument] rest unmoving . . .'

S. Martinho [J.106]

south Portugal [Museu da Escrita do Sudoeste, Almodôvar]
(text from Guerra 2002; cf. Correa 2004) 133 × 95 × 11–13cm

←]O?ᚠ‡ꟺAꟼꟼ‡ꟺ‡ᛕꟼ᙭Oᚠ‡A⟩

← ‡ꟺꟺ*ꟼAꟺOꟼ*‡[ ]ꟺ[

← *A⟩O)|ᛕAꟼA?▢ᛕꟺꟺꟺꟼA1Aꟺ᙭O

[The main text is in a continuous anti-clockwise circle printed here as three lines.]

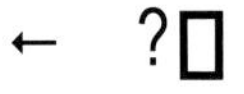

← AꟼAⳝꟵAO

← ?▢

Syntactic analysis

bᵃastᵉebᵘurͅoi onunaio tᵉ?e
cpd.N loc.sg.
[...]i[...]o*reiar*nio ebᵘu alakⁱimurͅbᵒ? a
                     ?adj.   dat./abl.pl.
narͅkᵉe bᵃa̲* | ea̲n̲   bᵃara | bᵒ?
V 3sg.   rel.? acc.sg.fem. V 1sg.

'In Bast-eburo- ("the yew wood of ??death") . . . ?to/from the seas . . . remains. . .'
'?she whom I [this grave] have carried.'

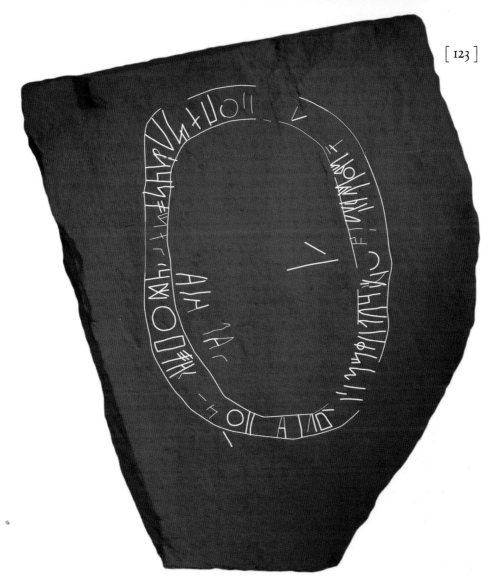

Commentary

Though the inscription survives complete and is skilfully arranged, the carving is shallow and hard to read in places. The main text forms a complete anti-clockwise circuit, within a double inscribed oval. A shorter sequence, also reading right-to-left, is inside the oval, where it probably continues the text. The main text begins with **bᵃasteᵉbᵘuŕoi**, which looks like it comprises familiar Palaeohispanic place-name elements, the second of which is Celtic *eburo-* 'yew'. This identification supports interpreting the ending as locative singular. 'The yew grove (of ??death)' can be understood as figurative for the necropolis. The form **alakⁱi** could be an adjective with a velar suffix and **muŕbᵒ** a dative/ablative plural written without redundancy. **naŕkᵉe**, a form of the recurrent closing formula, occurs near the end of the main text. **ean bᵃara**, 'she whom I have carried', can be read as a displaced variant of the formulaic **tᵉe·ro-bᵃare** '[this grave/death] has carried away.'

Cabeza del Buey IV [J.110]

Museo Arqueológico Provincial de Badajoz (De Hoz et al. undated, 52–4;
Correa 2008) 100 X 40 X 20cm

←] ⵏⵓⵊⵅⵏⵢⴰⵎⵎⵓⵊⵅⴷⴰⵜⵎⵓⵊ[ ]⁕ⴼⵎⵏ[

Syntactic analysis

]ḵⁱiu [---] ḵᵉeilau ḵᵉe iśa̱ n[a]ŕkᵉen   '. . . they remain . . .'
      name   V 3pl.

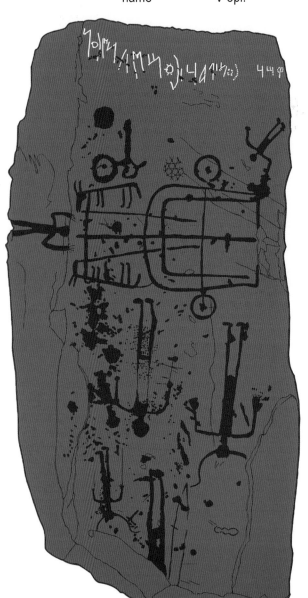

Commentary

A Late Bronze Age 'warrior stela'
with several figures and a prominent chariot with a conventionally
stylized two-horse team has had
a single right-to-left line of signs
added to the bottom, so that the
top and bottom of the stone have
been reversed from the earlier
to the later carving. The text
ends with **n[a]ŕkᵉn**, a form of
the recurrent formulaic closing.
]ḵⁱiu [---] ḵᵉeilau may represent
the co-ordinated masculine names
of the deceased ~ ḵᵉeloia (J.57.1).

image redrawn after Tera, S.L. L.

Mesas do Castelinho

Museu da Escrita do Sudoeste, Almodôvar (Fabião & Guerra 2008; 2010; Guerra 2009; 2010; *Tartessian 2*, 43–81)

1a	←	ΛX‡ΑΛϞΑЧ日ϞЧ日Ο1ᴎⵔ/
1b	←	ΑϟΟ日Ϥ𝚼
1c	←	ΧΑᴎΟϞΑϟ‡ϞΟϞᴎᴎ‡□Ο1ᴎⵔᴎ
1d	←	ЧЧᴎΦΑ1*****|)ι
2	←	ΛXᴎᴎᴎΑᴎΟ**ᴎᴎ1
3	←	‡ΛXΟ日1ΑΛΑϞᴎᴎΑΟ
4	→	ϬΟ‡ΑΡⴼ☼Αᴎ

Romanized transcription

1a :tⁱilekᵘurkᵘuarkᵃastᵃa

1b mutᵉebᵃa

1c ntⁱilebᵒoiirerobᵃarenaŕ

1d kᵉ[e(n)----o̱]lakⁱiuu

2 lii*eianiitᵃa

3 eanirakᵃaltᵉetᵃao

4 bᵉesaru[?n]an

Proposed word division

₁ₐ:tⁱilekᵘu̱ṟkᵘu≡arkᵃastᵃa ₁ᵦmu tᵉe·bᵃa ₁꜀ntⁱi lebᵒo-iire ·ro-bᵃare naŕ ₁d̲kᵉ[en--- -o̱·]lakⁱiuu ₂lii*eianiitᵃa ₃ea nira-kᵃaltᵉe tᵃao- ₄ -bᵉe saru[?n]an

Syntactic analysis

The interpretation here is a synopsis of that reached in *Tartessian 2*. The text is understood as a complex continuous statement, thus broadly parallel in structure to the continuous layout of the signs on the stone. It opens with the names of the deceased and closes with a feminine accusative singular, understood as a theonym and destination for one or both of the preceding verbs of motion. There are five nouns, most or all of them names, including two close compounds. Two of these five substantives form a co-ordinative *dvandva* compound. There are four, possibly five, finite verbs, two of these with preverbs, and possibly a third preverb (partially illegible). There is one possible personal pronoun and one possible relative pronoun. Underlying the syntax, we can recognize three or, more probably, four logical actors: the deceased referred to in the dual and 3rd person plural, the divinity Saru[n]ā as the destination of the verbs of motion, the funerary monument itself speaking in the 1st person singular, and probably the subterranean grave as a distinct element from the inscribed stone and acting in the 3rd person singular. The case form of **nira-kᵃaltᵉe** is uncertain; it could thus be another masculine plural (with **-e** < *-oi*) referring to the deceased or a locative singular referring to the place of the burial.

tⁱilekᵘur̲kᵘu͇arkᵃastᵃa̲m̲u̲ 'Tillekurkos and the man greatest in silver', nominative/ accusative dual, direct object of **ro·bᵃare** 'has carried (away)' and/or **o·]l̲a̲kⁱiuu** 'I [this stone memorial] conceal/entomb' and/or subject of **tᵉe·bᵃantⁱi** 'they pass away' and/or **nar̲kᵉ[en---** 'they remain in place [here]'.

lebᵒo-iire 'Lemauian (elm) men', nominative plural, subject of **tᵉe·bᵃantⁱi** and/ or **nar̲kᵉ[en---**.

nira-kᵃaltᵉe 'man/chieftain+?', possibly locative singular or dative singular or nominative plural; if the last, subject of **tᵉe·bᵃantⁱi** and/or **nar̲kᵉ[en---**.

saru[?n]an 'Sarunā (?star goddess)', accusative of destination for **ro·bᵃare** and/ or **tᵉe·bᵃantⁱi**.

tᵉe·bᵃantⁱi compound verb, 3rd person plural, present active, expressing action of the deceased.

ro·bᵃare perfectivized verb, 3rd sperson ingular, preterite/perfect, expressing the completed action of the grave and/or the divinity.

nar̲kᵉ[en---- uncompounded verb, present, probably 3rd person plural present active (*Tartessian 2* §37), expressing present state of the deceased, possibly with the divinity, possibly also the grave.

o·]l̲a̲kⁱiuu verb, probably compound, 1st person singular, present active, causative, expressing action of the inscribed stone.

tᵃao possibly a verb, 1st singular, present active, 'I [this memorial stone] stand', expressing action/state of the inscribed stone.

bᵉe possibly a personal pronoun 'I/me [this memorial stone]'.

ea possibly a relative pronoun, nominative feminine singular or nominative/ accusative neuter.

Proposed edition

|*Tillekurkū≡arga(n)stamū de·bānti Lemo-ịirē, -ro-bāre, naŕke[n(ti) ---
(ọ)o·]lagiụū . . . . ea nīra-kaldē tāō-me Saru(n)an.*|

A possible translation is provided to make the syntactic analysis and discussion of individual elements easier to follow. However, the full range of alternatives canvassed in *Tartessian 2*, and no doubt others as well, should be considered.

> [The divinity and/or this grave] has carried away—
> [and] I, who stand [here] in the grove of men/leaders, conceal in burial—
> Tillekurkos ⟨and⟩ the man greatest in silver;
> the Lemauian ('elm-')men/heroes pass on to Sarunā (the star-goddess);
> [here] they now rest.

Castelo de Moura

←]A⟨↑‡⟨AɣˑΓ   ]*nabᵃorạ[*or*

→]A⟨↑‡⟨AɣˑΓ   ]ạ robᵃa n*[*or*]ạ robᵃan *[

Commentary

The site is on the mid Guadiana. A fragment of a well-executed post-firing scratched graffito on a shard of Iron Age wheel-thrown red slip ware (recently unearthed in excavations led by José Gonçalo Valente) is possibly either a mark of ownership for a domestic vessel or identification of cremated remains. According to Guerra (pers. com.), the range of possible dates remains wide; nonetheless, the first half of the 4th century BC is suggested at http://avenidadasaluquia34.blogspot.com/2011/02/

moura-e-escrita-do-sudoeste.html. The shape of the signs suggests right-to-left orientation and a violation of redundancy; so a left-to-right reading with redundancy is also offered. In the latter case the fragmentary text would probably be part of a naming formula for a woman (cf. J.18.1). Had the original included a patronym, **robᵃa** | *roₐmā* | < *(p)roₐmā* would probably mean 'first-born daughter of', otherwise 'foremost woman'. The segmentation **robᵃan** would be the accusative. The find is also published in Portuguese *National Geographic* n° 118, Janeiro 2011.

Corte Pinheiro, Loulé

Museu da Escrita do Sudoeste, Almodôvar (transliteration and image after Guerra 2009; 2010)

←ᕵᕁO⊃I⋔O⋔⊃*OA[   ]*ᕵO9

b^{e}eu*[   ]ae*b^{a}reŕk^{e}eni

Syntactic analysis

b^{e}eu*[   ]ae* b^a[a]re [na]ŕk^{e}eni
?name   ?pvb   V 3 sg.   V 3pl.

Commentary

The beginning and ending of the text are intact. But as many as 10 signs could easily have been lost in the long gap between **b^{e}eu*[** and **]ae* b^a[a]re [na] ŕk^{e}eni**. The usual formulaic ending is clearly apparent, but truncated and perhaps unintentionally garbled.

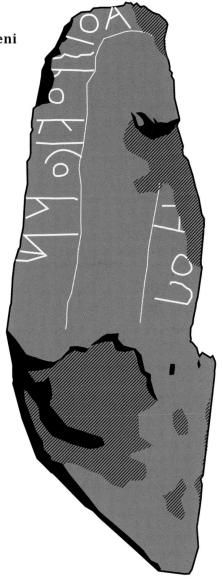

Vale de Águia, São Bartolomeu de Messines, Silves

Museu Municipal, Silves (transliteration and drawing after Guerra
2009; 2010)

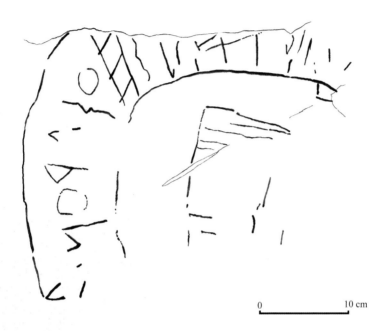

0   10 cm

←   ]AꟼOꟼAƷOⱻ}*******[

]*******bᵃtᵉebᵃarena[ŕkᵉe---]

Syntactic analysis

    ]*******bᵃ tᵉe· bᵃare na[ŕkᵉe---]
      ?pvb V 3 sg. V

Commentary

The text reads right-to-left, anti-clockwise. What survives is well carved between two arcing ruled lines. There are approximately seven unreadable signs before the first legible one **}** **bᵃ**. This is not the only loss. Most of the stela and more than half of the text have broken away. **tᵉe·bᵃare na[** is clear and undoubtedly an example of the 'Formula' (on which see Appendix C).

Monte Gordo

←   ****ᐱᐱᐤᐱᛘᛝᗝ᙭ᛉᛉ**

←   **ᐱᛘᗝᛝᗝᐱᛉᛞ∔ᛝᗝᛝᐱᛝᛝᐱᗝ᙭ᛘᛝᛝᐱ**

←   **ᛝ∔ᛘ᙭∔ᛝᐱᗝᛝᐱ᙭ᛝᗝᛝ᙭**

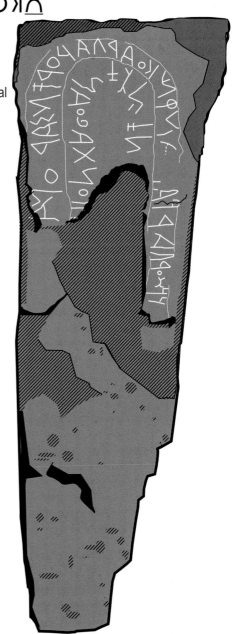

Syntactic analysis

uuŕerkᵃar	**ua***n**	**kⁱikᵉe**	**≡arkᵃare**
?nom.sg.	?acc.sg.	nom.acc.dual	nom.acc.dual

ro‑n·bᵃare	**na[ŕ]kᵉen**	**tᵃa‑bᵉe**	**anoŕion**
pf E V 3sg.	V 3pl.	?V ?pron	?rel

'Uuŕerkar [?and] Kikā Arkareā (K. daughter of Arkar(os)) whom [this grave/death] has carried to the highest destination remain [here]. ?I [this stone] stand . . .'

Commentary

This recent discovery shows conventional layout and orientation, beginning in the lower right, reading from right-to-left throughout, along two inscribed arcing lines. The text is relatively long, and there is an amplification beyond the formulaic closing **na[ŕ]kᵉen**.

Following Guerra's suggestion, **ua***n** is understood as the formula word **uarbᵃan** |*uarₐman*|. That implies that the opening sequence, where a name is expected, is **uuŕerkᵃar**, which looks vaguely Iberian. Note, however, that *r*-stem nominative singular *kar* (probably 'hospitalitas') is well attested in Celtiberian (Jordán 2005, 172–4). After **ua[rbᵃa]n** the next sequence is **kⁱikᵉe≡arkᵃare**, which can be understood as a feminine nominative/accusative co-ordinative compound 'Kikā and Arkar(e)ā', though the reference is probably to one

Drawing and transliteration of signs after Guerra

woman or girl. On the name *Kikā*, compare the Gaulish woman's name *Cicena* at Larzac, which may mean precisely 'daughter of Kikā' < **Kíkiknā*. Old Irish *cích* 'breast' probably goes with these. The second member of the **kⁱikᵉe≡arkᵃare** compound resembles the inscription's first name **uuŕerkᵃar**, but they are not exactly the same. Could they refer to members of the same family? That possibility might mean that the names **arkᵃare** and **uuŕerkᵃar** were actually etymologically linked, the latter reflecting notional Proto-Celtic **U(p)er-(p)are-kar*, but they may merely have sounded alike, though being of distinct origin. I take **arkᵃare** as a feminine adjective of relationship, like **bᵃane≡ooŕoire** 'wife of **U(p)er-uiros*' (J.19.1) < **bₐnai U(p)er-u̯iri̯āi*. Here, Kikā is the kinswoman of Arkar(os) < **(P)are-kar(os)* ~ Latinized Gaulish ARECARORVM (Delamarre 2007, 25). However, Kikā is not explicitly the wife of Arkar(os), perhaps then his daughter, the default relationship. If so, the apparently related names **arkᵃar-e** and **uuŕerkᵃar** might refer to father and son. In other words, **kⁱikᵉe≡arkᵃare** and **uuŕerkᵃar** could be sister and brother, the children of Arkar(os), in any event close relatives.

ro-n·bᵃare occurs rather than the more common **tᵉe(e)·ro-bᵃare**. I take the **n** to be an elided masculine accusative singular pronoun *en* or masculine accusative relative **ion** infixed, according to rule, after the first preverb, which is in this case the perfect marker **ro** < Indo-European **pro*. Cf. likewise **ro-n·bᵃaren** (J.11.4). The infix would refer back to **uuŕerkᵃar**, the head of the family, if this is a group burial as proposed. Alternatively, an elided form of the feminine relative particle **ean** is possible, referring back to **uarbᵃan**.

With **tᵃa-bᵉe**, compare **tᵃao-bᵉe** similarly placed in the MdC inscription, near the end of the text and after all the formula words. I hold to the suggestion offered in *Tartessian 2* (72–3), though this remains no less tentative presently, owing to the graphic variation. Thus, possibly the stone itself is made to say | *tāō-me* | or | *tāā-me* | 'I myself stand' < **(s)tā(i̯)ō+me-*. The differences in the representation (**tᵃa-bᵉe** versus **tᵃao-bᵉe**) can be understood as diachronic phonology. In the first, the regular development of Pre-Celtic *ō* > Proto-Celtic *ū* in final syllables has been inhibited by the appended pronoun *-bᵉe* | *-me* |, by consequence of which the long vowel is not fully word final. With Monte Gordo **tᵃa-bᵉe** | *tāā-me* | the long vowel has gone on to share the fate of fully internal Pre-Celtic *ō* to become Proto-Celtic **ā* > Tartessian **a**, as in for example **-ratᵉe** | *-rāte* | 'has run' (J.53.1) < earlier **-rôte*.

Folha do Ranjão (Baleizão, Beja) [J.102]

(Faria & Soares 1998)

←]ЧＨO[   ]ekᵘu[

Abul

Alcácer do Sal, Setúbal, Portugal (Correa 2011)

←   ]ЧＥ٩Ч△

Romanized transcription

t̲ᵘur∃n[

Commentary

The right-to-left text is a fragmentary grafito on two contiguous shards of wheel-turned grey ceramic. The finds were stratified within an archaeological layer of *c.* 650–*c.* 550 BC. The beginning is complete and the reading not in doubt. **t̲ᵘur∃n[** is probably a Palaeohispanic personal name as a mark of ownership. There are numerous specifically Hispano-Celtic parallels: see notes on **t̲ᵘurea** and **t̲ᵘuŕekᵘui** below.

Salacia

Coin legend of Alcácer do Sal, Setúbal, Portugal (Correa 2011)

←   ꓩ口ꛦꓩ彐Ɋ

Romanized transcription

b^eeuibon

Commentary

The coinage of Salacia is of a much later period than all or most of the SW inscribed stones. If we could be certain that this was actually the same writing system and language it would reflect a major chronological extension of the corpus. Taking the Abul grafito (previous item) into consideration, the indigenous coinage would not by themselves extend the geographical distribution. The phonetic values of the first and second signs remain uncertain. The sixth and seventh signs ꓩ口 violate the principle of redundancy; therefore, it is doubtful whether these numismatic texts really can be said to continue a late form of the SW writing system. If it were instead a form of SE/Meridional, the final five signs would be transcribed -uibun. In either event, it is tempting to see here the common pre-Roman Palaeo-Hispanic place-name element *-ip(p)o-* in a mint mark. This name element must mean, or at least function as meaning, something like 'town'. Whether the ending is read -**on** or -**un**, a Celtic interpretation would be possible: accusative singular or nominative/accusative neuter singular (for the first) or genitive plural (for the second). With the last, the significance of the mint mark could be 'of the people of the town . . .'.

Tartessian Linguistic Elements

A. An Updated Provisional List of Segmental Tartessian 'Words' in Transliterated SW Texts

As explained in *Tartessian 2* (§§20, 44), the MdC discovery sets the challenge of determining word divisions in the SW corpus on a more secure basis. Furthermore incremental advances with segmentation have subsequently been possible in the work embodied in the present edition of the present book. Therefore, it is useful again to provide a full list of the sequences of signs segmented as words updated to the current level of understanding. It is to be stressed once more that at this stage all of this must remain open to revision as work progresses. Many sequences are still profoundly uncertain. These lack any identifiable stem, prefix, or termination; neither do they form a plausible unit occurring after an identifiable termination and before an identifiable word beginning and/or bounded at one end by the obvious and undamaged beginning or end of the inscribed text, and their identification as a unit cannot be confirmed by its repetition in the corpus. The sequences of signs below for which the segmentation remains most uncertain are marked with a preceding long dash —. To distinguish distinct SW signs used for Tartessian | *m* |, Ⰳ is transcribed below as **m** and the less common Ⱳ as sans-serif **m**; however, there is no evidence to suggest that the sounds differed.

— aalaeinŕe[(J.15.3)

— a(a/m)<u>musok</u>ᵉeonii (J.1.5)

aarkᵘui (J.7.6)

—]<u>ae</u>Ⱶ<u>aeol</u>eaala[(J.1.4)

—]aetᵉabᵒo (J.28.1)

—]aibᵒo (J.28.1)

aibᵘuris[(J.3.1)

<u>ainest</u>ᵃa : a*[(J.16.4)

ainestᵃa : at<u>ᵃa</u>[(J.16.4)

akᵒo(l)ioś (J.56.1)

— alakⁱi (S. Martinho)

— alakⁱimuŕbᵒ? (S. Martinho)

<u>alb</u>ᵒoroi[(J.24.1)

aliśne (J.11.4)

alkᵘu (J.12.1)

ana<u>k</u>ᵃa (J.16.3)

anakᵉenakᵉ:eibᵒo (J.5.1)

anbᵃa[(J.11.2)

anbᵃatⁱ<u>ia</u> (J.16.2)

a]nbᵉi<u>k</u>ⁱ[i (J.11.5)

ane (J.1.1)

***antᵒonbᵒo (J.8.1)

<u>ao</u>- (J.55.1)

<u>ao</u>- kᵒol<u>ion</u> *or* <u>ro</u>- kᵒol<u>ion</u> (J.55.1)

aŕai<u>ai</u> (J.1.1)

*arbᵃan (J.16.1)

ar·bᵃarie (J.10.1)

— ar·bᵉieŕitᵘu *or* ar·bᵉieŕi (J.12.3)

—-u)arb^{u}u i (J.23.1)

—-u)arb^{u}u i el (J.23.1)

]are[(J.16.6)

'Αργανθωνιος

]*aŕi*** (J.8.1)

ariaríśe (J.10.1) = ariaris-se

ark^{a}are (Monte Gordo)

ark^{a}ast^{a}amu (MdC)

—]arsk^{e}eirn*[(J.11.5)

aśt^{a}a (J.7.1 twice)

asune (J.4.1)

—at^{a}a[(J.16.4)

—]at^{o}ore/ (J.24.1)

]b^a (Vale de Águia)

b^{a}a (J.1.2, J.12.4, J.16.1, J/16.2, J.16.3, J.18.1), b^{a}a[(J.7.9), b^{a}a[(J.57.1),]**b^{a}a (J.51.1), b^{a}a* (S. Martinho)

b^{a}aanon**[(J.11.4)

—-b^{a}ae (J.11.1)

b^{a}aenae*(*) (J.15.1)

b^{a}ane (J.11.1, J.19.1, J.20.1??, J.26.1)

-b^{a}ant^{i}i (MdC)

b^{a}ara**[(J.4.1)

(-)b^{a}are (J.1.1, J.1.3, J.14.1, J.22.1, J.26.1, J.27.1, Vale de Águia, MdC, Monte Gordo), b^{a}a(r)e (J.11.1), b^a]are[(J.16.6),]b^{a}are (J.17.2), b^{a}ar[e] (J.20.1), ab^{a}re (J.52.1) = b^{a}are, b^{a}re (Corte Pinheiro)

b^{a}areii (J.5.1)

b^{a}aren (J.11.4)

b^{a}arent^{i}i (J.23.1)

— b^{a}arle⊣ (J.53.1)

b^{a}arua (J.7.9)

b^{a}arua-ion (J.7.9)

b^{a}ast^e- (S. Martinho)

b^{a}ast^{e}eb^{u}uŕoi (S. Martinho)

b^{e}e (MdC, Monte Gordo)

(b^e)e (J.1.1)

b^{e}elib^{o}o (J.1.2)

b^{e}e:lin (J.17.4)

b^{e}eliśon (J.20.1)

— b^{e}eś**n*[(J.27.1)

b^{e}et^{i}isai (J.23.1)

— b^{e}eu*[ ]ae* (Corte Pinheiro)

b^{e}euibon (Salacia)

— b^{e}ieŕit^{u}u or b^{e}ieŕi (J.12.3)

—]b^{o}ab^{e}e[(J.6.2)

]b^{o}oara (J.2.1)

— b^{o}b^{e}e (J.53.1)

b^{o}ot^{i}i✵ana (J.18.1) = b^{o}ot^{i}ieana

b^{o}o↑^{i}ir (J.7.1)

b^{o}ot^{o}o⧖ar (J.7.2)

ean (S. Martinho)

eanb^{a}ara (S. Martinho)

— eb^{e}e (J.16.3)

eb^{e}e (J.9.1)

]eb^{o}o (J.7.8)

— eb^{u}u (S. Martinho)

-eb^{u}uŕoi (S. Martinho)

eert^{a}aune (J.55.1)

ek^{u}u- (J.4.1)

]ek^{u}u[(Folha do Ranjão)

— -ek^{u}ui (J.14.1)

ek^{u}uŕine (J.4.1)

— elu (J.7.6)

— elurear[(J.7.6)

enb^{e}e (J.17.4)

— enb^{e}ek^{a}arne (J.17.4)

— er·b^{e}eŕi (J.10.1)

ert^{a}au[ne (J.54.1)

]eśi*[(J.4.2)

—]et^{u}ut^{i}i[(J.12.2)

⧖ait^{u}ura (J.15.1) = hait^{u}ura or φait^{u}ura

⧖at^{a}aneat^{e}e (J.12.1) = hat^{a}aneat^{e}e or φat^{a}aneat^{e}e

Gargoris

—]iarkᵒ[o (J.7.7)
ib̲ᵒo-iion (J.4.1)
— ii (J.1.1)
iibᵃa̲n (J.5.1)
-iion (J.4.1)
-iire (MdC)
—]*ikᵉei**[(J.54.1)
-inon (J.14.1)
—]i↙*oŕ[(J.18.3)
iobᵃa[(J.16.2)
-ion (J.1.3, J.7.2, J.7.9)
— iraśen (J.7.10) *or* raśen
ire (J.7.2, J.11.2, J.52.1)
iru (J.7.9, J.12.1, J.23.1)
— iruarbᵘu i-el (J.23.1) ?=
 iru≡{u}arbᵘu i el
iśa̲ (Cabeza del Buey IV)
— isakᵃaoeaŕt̲ᵉ[e (J.24.1)
iśiinkᵒolobᵒo (J.1.1)
ist̲ᵃa̲|ibᵒo (J.5.1)
iśtᵘ[u (J.7.4)
— (?)i↑ensere (J.10.1)
— it̲ⁱiabeŕebᵉ anak̲ᵃa (J.16.3)
iubᵃa (J.7.8)

kᵃ[a (J.7.4)
—]kᵃaae̲[(J.24.1)
kᵃakⁱi- (J.1.1)
kᵃaltᵉe (J.1.1, MdC)
]k̲ᵃanan (J.9.1)
k̲ᵃarne (J.17.4)
kᵃaŕner (J.7.2)
kᵃaŕner-ion (J.7.2)
— kᵃa[ŕn]ir (J.1.3)
— kᵃa[ŕn]ir-ion (J.1.3)
kᵃaśetᵃana (J.53.1)
— k̲ᵉeilau-kᵉe (Cabeza del Buey IV)
k̲ᵉeloia (J.57.1)
— kᵉenila(*)rin (J.17.4)

— kᵉeŕkᵃaŕ[(J.18.3)
kᵉertᵒo (J.18.1)
——**kᵉe≡uuakᵉe*[(J.7.8)
kⁱielaoe (J.11.1)
kⁱikᵉe (Monte Gordo)
kⁱinbᵃai↑ⁱi (J.3.1)
]kⁱiu (Cabeza del Buey IV)
—]k̲ⁱu (J.51.1)
kᵒ- (J.53.1)
kᵒo- (J.1.2)
kᵒoli̲o̲n (J.55.1)
— kᵒoloar[(Monte Novo do
 Castelinho)
]k̲ᵒoloion (Monte Novo do
 Castelinho)
kᵒoŕb̲ᵉo (J.53.1)
kᵒtᵘuaratᵉe (J.53.1)
 Κυνητες
— k̲ᵘu̲iarairbᵘbᵘ[u (J.17.2)
— kᵘuikᵃa̲o̲sa (J.17.1)

la[(J.12.3, J.52.1)
—]la***bᵃ[a (J.24.1)
-la⪜ (J.3.1) = -lak̲ᵘa
[l]akᵃat̲ⁱi (J.10.1)
— [l]akᵃat̲ⁱi-śe (J.10.1)
lakᵉent̲ⁱi (J.53.1)
lakⁱin↑i (J.12.4)
l̲akⁱiuu (MdC)
lebᵒo- (MdC)
lebᵒo-iire (MdC)
leoine (J.10.1)
— li[(J.57.1)
— lii*eianiitᵃaea (MdC)
l̲iirnestᵃakᵘun (J.19.1)
linbᵒo-ire (J.11.2)
liŕniene (J.55.1)
lokᵒobᵒo (J.1.1)
lokᵒon (J.1.1), lo̲kᵒon (J.57.1)

meleśae (J.15.1)

mubᵃa (J.12.1)

— muŕbᵒʔa (S. Martinho)

——mutᵘuirea (J.1.5)

na (J.1.2, J.7.1)

nabᵒolon (J.7.1) = na·bᵒolon

— nakⁱibᵘu (J.1.2) = na-kⁱibᵘu

naŕkᵉe (J.1.1, J.7.8, J.27.1, J.57.1, S. Mar-
    tinho), naŕ[kᵉe . . (J.17.1), naŕkᵉe[
    (J.17.3), naŕkᵉ[e.. (J.26.1, J.57.1),
    na[ŕkᵉe---] (Vale de Águia)

naŕkᵉen (J.7.5, J.14.1), naŕkᵉen[..
    (J.20.1), naŕkᵉ[en.. (MdC),
    n[a]ŕkᵉen (Cabeza del Buey IV),
    na[ŕ]kᵉen (Monte Gordo)

naŕkᵉenai (J.7.1, J.55.1)

naŕkᵉeni (J.1.2, J.1.3),
    [na]ŕkᵉeni (Corte Pinheiro)

naŕkᵉenii (J.2.1, J.21.1),
    n(a)ŕkᵉenii (J.11.1), [naŕ]kᵉenii
    (J.19.1)

naŕkᵉentⁱi (J.12.1, J.16.1, J.17.2,
    J.18.1, J.19.2), [n]aŕkᵉentⁱi (J.1.5),
    na]ŕkᵉentⁱi (J.4.3)

na]ŕkᵉe⟨kᵉe⟩o-io* (J.16.2)

naŕkᵉetⁱi (J.56.1)

]naŕkᵉeuu[(Corte do Freixo 2)

naŕrkᵉe:n: (J.23.1)

ne[(J.16.5)

ne-bᵃa (J.1.2)

— nemun (J.7.8) or emun

niirabᵒo (J.1.1)

—]ninokᵒoro[(J.7.7)

nira- (MdC)

nira-kᵃaltᵉe (MdC)

—]nor↑ioni[(J.28.1)

]noś (J.14.1)

oar[(J.22.2)

obᵃar (J.4.1)

oira (J.1.2)

oira-uarbᵃa(n) (J.1.2)

——oiśaHa (J.11.1)

o·]lakⁱiuu (MdC)

—]olo*[(J.19.3)

( )omuŕikᵃa[(J.16.2)

— onunaio (S. Martinho)

— o-ni-[l]akᵃatⁱi-śe (J.10.1)

—]on (J.11.2)

—]onsol[(J.6.3)

ooŕoir (J.19.2)

ooŕoire (J.19.1)

orbᵃa (J.53.1)

—]o*reiar*nioebᵘu (S. Martinho)

oretᵒo (J.4.1)

— oriou⟨tⁱ⟩bᵉa:i (J.7.6)

—]*uosor (J.54.1)

— otᵉerkᵃa (J.1.4)

— o↑erbᵉeŕi (J.10.1)

raⱡa (J.53.1)

—]ŕakᵘurś (J.1.3)

— raśen (J.7.10) or iraśen

-ratᵉe (J.53.1)

—]*reonuu[(J.4.4)

-ŕine (J.4.1)

rinoebᵒo (J.5.1)

ŕkᵉeni (Corte Pinheiro)

ro (J.1.1, J.3.1, J.11.1, J.11.4, J.16.3, J.18.1,
    MdC, Monte Gordo), ro (J.55.1)

robᵃa (J.18.1), robᵃa or robᵃan
    ?? doubtful orientation (Moura)

robᵃae (J.11.1) ?= ro·bᵃae

ro·bᵃare (J.1.1, J.12.1, J.18.2, MdC),
    ro·bᵃare (J.16.3)

ro- kᵒolion or ao- kᵒolion (J.55.1)

ro·laⱡa ?= ro·lakᵘa (J.3.1)

ro-n·bᵃare (Monte Gordo)

ro-n·bᵃaren (J.11.4)

]ŕ[.]s[ʔkᵉ]ntⁱi (Monte Novo do
    Castelinho)

sabᵒoi (J.5.1)

——śaen (J.27.1)

salsaloi ↑[(J.12.4)

saru[ˀn]an (MdC)

sarune (J.22.1), s̲arune (J.22.2) *or*
  saruneea (J.22.1), s̲aruneea
  (J.22.2)

-śe (J.10.1)

-s̲]ekᵘui (J.1.4)

setᵃa (J.53.1)

sie̲: (J.12.1)

soloir (J.11.3)

s̲utᵘuirea (J.1.5)

tᵃa (Monte Gordo)

]**tᵃa (J.4.1)

— tᵃab̲ᵃa* (J.1.6)

tᵃa-bᵉe (Monte Gordo)

tᵃae (J.14.1)

tᵃae·bᵃare (J.14.1)

tᵃala- (J.14.1)

tᵃalainon (J.14.1)

tᵃao (MdC)

tᵃao-bᵉe (MdC)

tᵃarielnon (J.55.1)

]tᵃarnekᵘ⟨k̲ᵘ⟩un (J.26.1)

t̲ᵃau (J.10.1)

— tᵉasiioonii (J.1.1)

tᵉe- (J.1.1, J.1.3, J.12.1, J.16.1, J.21.1, MdC,
  Vale de Águia), tᵉˀe (S. Martinho)

tᵉeaion(kᵃ)a[(J.4.3)

tᵉe·bᵃantⁱi (MdC)

tᵉe·bᵃar[e] (J.16.1)

tᵉe·bᵃare (J.1.3, Vale de Águia)

t̲ᵉe·b̲ᵃare (J.18.1)

tᵉe·bᵃere (J.7.8)

tᵉee (J.18.2, J.23.1)

tᵉee·bᵃarentⁱi (J.23.1)

tᵉee·ro-bᵃare (J.18.2)

tᵉe[(e)-ro·bᵃ]are (J.21.1)

tᵉe·ro-bᵃare (J.1.1, J.12.1)

tⁱilekᵘu- (MdC)

tⁱilekᵘur̲kᵘu (MdC)

tⁱirtᵒos (J.1.2)

tᵒo (J.1.1)

—]tᵒoar[(J.7.3)

tᵘu (J.53.1)

— tᵘula[(J.12.3)

tᵘn↑ⁱitᵉsbᵃan (J.53.1) = tᵘnbⁱitᵉsbᵃan

t̲ᵘur⋛n[(Abul)

tᵘurea (J.7.8)

tᵘur̆ekᵘui (J.14.1)

——]t̲ᵘurkᵃaio[(J.51.1)

ua (J.53.1)

uabᵃan (J.16.5)

ua-ratᵉe (J.53.1)

uarbᵃan (J.3.1, J.4.1, J.21.1), uar̲bᵃan
  (J.9.1), uar̲b̲ᵃan̲ (J.11.3),]uarbᵃan
  (J.21.1), uarbᵃa(n) (J.1.2), ua***n
  (Monte Gordo)

uarbᵒoiir (J.22.1)

uarbᵒoiir sarune (J.22.1) *or* uarbᵒoiir
  saruneea

— uarbᵒo⸙i[(J.7.5)

— uarbᵘu i (J.23.1)

uarn|bᵃan (J.20.1)

u̲ii (J.7.6)

—]ukᵉe (J.27.1)

—]ukᵉeśaen (J.27.1)

— ur (J.1.6)

-ur̲kᵘu (MdC)

]ur̆ni (J.20.1)

uśne̲e (J.23.1) ?*or* uśnϱe = uśnbᵉe

(])uultⁱina (J.12.3)

uur̆erkᵃar (Monte Gordo)

uurkᵉe (J.1.4)

——uur̲saau̲ (J.16.1)

Tartessian Linguistic Elements

B. Itemized Segmentable Forms with Notes on their Syntactic Contexts, Probable or Possible Grammatical Functions and Etymologies

¶ NOTE. The term 'Hispano-Celtic' is used in the citations and compared forms below for more than one degree of Celticity. (1) For forms which have recognized Celtic parallels outside the Iberian Peninsula, or where there is a distinctively Celtic sound change, such as loss of Indo-European *p* or $*g^u > b$, then Celticity is more certain. The relevant comparanda and/or sound changes are set out in the entries below. (2) Other forms labelled 'Hispano-Celtic' are probably but not certainly Celtic. These occur in the zone of Celtic names in the north, west, and centre of the Peninsula. They appear to be Indo-European (rather than Iberian or Basque) but are not Latin. They do not show preserved Indo-European *p*. The label 'Lusitanian' is applied only to forms from the five Lusitanian inscriptions discussed by Wodtko (2010). No attempt has been made to identify Celtic borrowings in the Lusitanian inscriptions and thus distinguish more and less 'properly Lusitanian' vocabulary in these five texts. The sequences of signs below, the segmentation of which remain most uncertain, are marked with a preceding long dash ——.

—— **aalaein** ᚣᛗOA1AA (J.15.3) possibly shows the same root as in Celtiberian *alaboi* and/or the family name *Alaskum* (K.1.3; Wodtko 2000, 17). Untermann (1997, 168) cites *Alainus* and *Alaius* from Yecla de Yeltes, Spain.

—— **a(a/m)<u>mus</u>ok^eeonii** A*MH‡‡ΚO‡ᚱSᛗᛗ (J.1.5)   The reading and interpretation are uncertain. It is not surely a name and is possibly to be segmented differently. It may be a *i̯o*-stem with the same suffix found in Ἀργανθωνιος and/ or t^e**asiioonii** (J.1.1), although only the former comparandum is surely a name. Another possibility is to take (-)**sok^eeonii** as a 3rd plural present-tense verb of the Indo-European type with *o*-grade in the root and the suffix and -*ei̯e/o*- as occurs in the formation of causatives.

aarkᵘui ᙏ𐌇𐌇𐌘𐌀𐌀 (J.7.6) appears to begin the statement (although the inscribed stone is not in perfect condition) and thus is expected to be a personal or divine name. The ending looks like the dative singular, *o*-stem or *u*-stem. The form is probably | *Arkᵘuūi* | < *Arkᵘiūi 'for Archer' with assimilation of the glide to the following *ū* (see *Tartessian 2* §96.2) or 'for Arg(i)os', cf. ARCO · MANCI F · commemorated at Oliveira do Hospital, Coimbra, Portugal (Búa 2000, 481), ARC[O] | NI AMB | ATI F at Villar Pedroso, Cáceres, Spain (Sánchez Moreno 1996, 124), ARCIVS EPEICI BRACARVS on an altar from Vila da Feira, Aveiro, Portugal (Búa 2007, 26), ARCVIVS at Barcelos, Braga, Portugal (Búa 2000, 359), ARQVIVS VIRATI F. also Braga (Luján 2008, 77), the Western Hispano-Celtic divine epithets in NAVIAE ARCONNVNIECAE (*L'Année épigraphique* 1955, 78, Lugo) and LVGVBO ARQVIENOBO (Sober, Lugo), LVCOVBV[?s] ARQVIENI[s] (Outeiro do Rei, Lugo; Búa 2000, 266–7). Untermann (1997, 168) cites the personal name *Arquius* attested in Celtiberia, Lusitania, and southern Extremadura (e.g. CAMALA ARQVI F. TALABRIGENSIS [*L'Année épigraphique* 1952, 27, Viano do Castelo]). A different root is probably involved in Celtiberian *Arkailikos*, genitive singular place-name ARGAILO (Untermann, 1997, 407), Gaulish personal name *Com-argus*, Old Irish *arg* 'warrior, hero', Greek ἀρχός 'guide, leader'. Note also the Hispano-Celtic place-name *Arcobriga*. **i arkᵒ[o-**] 𐌗𐌘𐌀ᙏ (J.7.7), also from Ameixial, is possibly the nominative or accusative of this same name.

abᵃre 𐌏𐌘𐌙𐌀 (J.52.1) is clearly for **bᵃare** (which see) with two signs transposed as demanded by the system redundancy, i.e. **bᵃ** before **a**.

]aet̲ᵉabᵒo*[ ]𐌀𐌏𐍈𐌀𐌇 𐍈*[(J.28.1) ?dative/ablative plural.

aibᵘuris[ ]𐍈ᙏ𐌘𐌘𐌭ᙏ𐌀 (J.3.1) begins the epigraphic statement and thus is probably a name, specifically a name in *-ris* from Celtic *-rīχs* (< Indo-European **h₃rēg̑-s* showing characteristically Celtic *ī* < *ē*; see *Tartessian 2* §81). For the first element, compare Western Hispano-Celtic AEB(VRVS) (*Hispania epigraphica* 1994, 133–4, A Coruña) and CRISSVS TALABVRI F. AEBOSOCELENSIS (*L'Année épigraphique* 1952, 42–3, Cáceres). *Aebarus* and *Aebicus* occur as personal names in Lusitania (Untermann 1992, 392). One place named *Aipora/Ebora* near Gadir/Cádiz was the find site of a spectacularly wealthy hoard or burial of the Tartessian culture, which included 93 manufactured gold items and 43 carnelians (Cunliffe 2001, 271). Another *Aebura* is known at the important Early Iron Age silver mining site at Ríotinto, Huelva. Note the preservation of the diphthong in the first syllable of **aibᵘuris[**, possibly implying accented initial syllables, similarly 𐌄ait̲ᵘura ?= φait̲ᵘura or **hait̲ᵘura** (J.15.1), **ainestᵃa** (J.16.4).

akᵒolioś M‡Ϻ(⌐)‡⋈A (J.56.1)	The complete text **akᵒo(l)ioś naŕkᵉet'i** clearly appears to be a nominative singular subject followed by its 3rd person singular present-tense verb. **akᵒo(l)ioś** is therefore a nominative singular masculine *o*-stem, possibly the same individual named in (J.55.1) **kᵒolion** or his relative (see below), if they are not merely graphic variants of the same name—the latter with elision following **ro-**. -**akᵒolioś** might include the preposition **ad** prefixed to **kᵒolioś**. Cf. Celtiberian and North-west Hispano-Celtic personal name ACCA (Albertos 1985, 261). On the meaning of **kᵒolioś**, see Commentary on J.55.1 above. In **t'irtᵒos** (J.1.2) a nominative singular masculine *o*-stem ends with the other sibilant sign, **s ‡**. In both examples, the following sign is **n Ϥ**. However, **ne** following **t'irtᵒos** is interpreted as the negative particle, with original Indo-European *n*-, whereas the tentatively proposed etymology for **naŕkᵉet'i** involves an Indo-European **sner-k´-* 'bind', so **ś M** possibly signifies the reflex of a strong or double |*-s (s~)*| at the word boundary. Cf. *Tartessian 2* 154–5, on the possible phonetic value(s) and interchange of **s ‡** and **ś M**.

albᵒoroi[ ]Ϻ‡ϥ‡□1A (J.24.1)	The inscription is fragmentary and its layout confusing. This is the clearest form in it. So we must go on the form alone without clues from syntax, thus probably dative singular 'to Alburos' |*Alburūi*| < |*Alburōi*|, alternatively locative singular 'in Alburo-' or nominative plural group name 'the Alburoi' (cf. Untermann 1997, 327) ~ North-west Hispano-Celtic ALBVRVS, ALBVRA (Albertos 1985, 263; Luján 2007, 248; 2008 77). Note that the grapheme **u Ϥ** does not occur in J.24.1, so the signs possibly represent |*Alburūi*|.

aliśne OϤϺϺ1A (J.11.4) follows **ro-n-bᵃaren naŕkᵉenii** near the end of the text. These are clearly variants of the usual penultimate and closing elements of the Tartessian epigraphic formula (on which see Appendix C). Thus **aliśne** can be seen as part of a syntactic amplification after the usual ending. The formula word **uar(n)bᵃan** 'highest destination' is absent. Therefore, **aliśne** possibly fills a logical gap of the expressed destination, as a locative singular place-name, | *Al-isₐnē*| 'in Alisₐno-, Alisₐnā', from **Alisₐnoi* or **Alisₐnāi* with simplification of the diphthong (on which see *Tartessian 2* §94). For the etymology, compare Latin *alnus* 'alder' < **alisnos*, Celtiberian *alizos* (K.0.2), and the family name *Alizokum* (K.0.1, genitive plural), Northern Hispano-Celtic ALISSIEGINI (genitive, Latinized?) (Untermann 1980b, 376), Gaulish place-names *Alesia*, IN ALISIIA, IN ALIXIE, *Alisicum*, also ALISANV 'to the god of Alesia': Indo-European **h₂éliso-* 'alder'. On Gaulish *an* corresponding to Tartessian **n**, written as a non-syllabic, see *Tartessian 2* §69. **aliśne** would mean 'in the alder wood' or 'in the place of the alder god', or similar, perhaps in a transferred sense of sacred grove as necropolis.

alk^{u}u ᛋHᛚA (J.12.1) The syntax and inflexion of the inscription's initial naming phrase is identical to that of MdC: **iru≡alk^{u}u** ~ **t^{i}ilek^{u}ur̲k^{u}u≡ ark^{a}ast^{a}am̲u.** **alk^{u}u** is probably *o*-stem masculine nominative/accusative dual |*Alkū*| '(the hero) and Alkos', less probably dative singular |*Alkūi*| 'for Alkos'. Cf. Lepontic *Alko-uinos* (end of the 2nd century BC), Gaulish *Alco-uindos, Alcus, Alcius,* and the place-names *Alcena, Alciacum,* 'Αλκι-μονις, Hispano-Celtic *Alce* (Delamarre 2003, 38). Tacitus (*Germania* 43) mentions central-European divine twins called *Alci,* worshipped by the Naharvali, a subtribe of the extensive Lugii (whose name is probably related to the divine name **lok^{o}ob^{o}o** in J.1.1). That the deceased was a warrior is implied by the stela which shows an armed man brandishing weapons—short throwing spears and a shield—surrounded by the inscribed text. Rodríguez Ramos's reading **alb^{u}u** could also be paralleled in Celtic.

anak^{e}enak̲^{e}:eib^{o}o ǂHᛖO | ⟩IAᛖO⟩IAᛖA (J.5.1) The naming phrase consists of three dative/ablative plural forms in agreement: **ist̲^{a}a̲|ib^{o}o rinoe̲b^{o}o | anak^{e}enak̲^{e}:e|ib^{o}o.** The interpretation offered for **anak^{e}enak̲^{e}:e|ib^{o}o** is |*an(d)agenākəbo*| < **andogenākabo(s)* dative/ablative plural group adjective 'indwelling, indigenous', cf. Gaulish forms from Larzac *andogna[* 'indigenous', feminine accusative singular *andognam,* negatived *anandognam,* Middle Welsh *annyan* 'nature, inborn quality' < **andoganā,* Latin *indigena* 'native, &c.' < Indo-European **(e)ndo-g´enh$_{1}$* 'born inside' (Delamarre 2003, 48), possibly also the comparable British *andagin-* if this can be understood as an invocation of an unnamed local goddess on the Bath pendant ADIXOVI | DEV̲INA | DEV̲EDA | ANDAGIN | VINDIORIX | CVAMI̲I̲N | AI 'Vindiorix ardently entreats the indwelling holy goddess for Cuamena (the dear woman)' (for the initial verb, cf. Welsh *dihew-yd* 'ardent desire', but other meanings are possible, for example, if this pendant is another Bath curse inscription, 'Vindiorix ardently entreats the holy goddess: something bad (**an-+daga-*) for Cuamena' (published interpretations vary: Tomlin 1988, 133; Lambert 1994, 174; Schrijver 2004, 16–17; 2005, 57–9; Sims-Williams 2007, 16–17).

The composition vowel of **ando-* reduced to **a** as in **ana-** is a regular Tartessian development; compare **ariariśe** (J.10.1) < **Ari̯o-rīχs+se* (*Tartessian 2* §81), **oirauarb^{a}an** (J.1.2) |*o̯ira-uar$_{a}$man*| < **u̯iro-u(p)er$_{a}$mām* 'to the heroic summit' (*Tartessian 2* §73.1). The series of double vowels preceding the recurrent dative/ablative plural ending **-b^{o}o** in the co-ordinated series **ist̲^{a}a̲ib^{o}o rinoe̲b^{o}o anak^{e}enak̲^{e}:eib^{o}o** can be understood as hesitation over unaccented stem vowels with indistinct quality, |*istəbo rīg$_{a}$nəbo an(d)agenākəbo*|, as opposed to phonetic diphthongs (*Tartessian 2* §73.1).

To invoke the 'indigenous queens', probably means chthonic deities or local goddesses of the particular place. There could also have been an intended contrast with influential foreign cults, such as that of the Phoenician goddess Astarte, which flourished in the south-western Iberian Peninsula during the Orientalizing Period (*c.* 750–*c.* 550 BC). In these terms, **ekᵘuŕine** 'Horse-queen' would likewise have been one such native 'queen' competing with Astarte.

Anas is the ancient name of a great river of the south-western Iberian Peninsula, which reaches the Atlantic at the modern border of Portugal and Spain. It is now called *Guadiana* (with Arabic *wadi* 'river' prefixed). *Anas* is likely to be related to Gaulish *anam* glossed 'paludem' ('swamp') in Endlicher's Glossary, cf. also Old Irish *an* 'water, urine'. If this is the correct etymology, the name shows loss of Indo-European *p* in the root **pen-* 'swamp, dirty water', cf. Sanskrit *pánka-* 'swamp', Prussian *pannean* 'swamp', English *fen* (Delamarre 2003, 43–4). Citing archaic sources, Avienus (*Ora Maritima*, line 202) wrote that the Anas flowed through the land of Cynetes.

anbᵃa[ ]A꞉ꟼA (J.11.2)　　Although the reading of this fragmentary form is less certain, it is not unlikely that this form is another instance of the name or, less probably, the common noun occurring as the next item, thus | *Amba(χ)t-* |.

anbᵃat'ia A꞉AꟼA (J.16.2) | *Amba(χ)tia* | occurs in the text's opening naming phrase ( )**omuŕikᵃa**[≡]**anbᵃat'ia≡iobᵃa**[, which appears to comprise three feminine forms in agreement. In this context, **anbᵃat'ia** can most easily be construed as a feminine singular nominative of a *ia*–stem meaning 'female relative of Amba(χ)tos'. The preceding ( )**omuŕikᵃa**[looks like a typical Hispano-Celtic kindred name formed with a suffix *-ko-/kā-*. **iobᵃa** is marked as a feminine superlative adjective. Thus ( )**omuŕikᵃa**[≡]**anbᵃat'ia≡iobᵃa**[is interpreted as | *Qomurikā Amba(χ)tiā iȏₐmā* | 'woman of the kindred of Qomurįos and youngest daughter of Amba(χ)tos'. As in]**liirnestᵃakᵘun bᵃane≡ooŕoire** 'woman of the kindred of Lir(a)nestos and wife of Ooŕoir' (J.19.1) and **ɮait"ura meleśae≡::≡bᵃaenae** 'Lady of the Baeturians, sweet woman and wife' (J.15.1), the form expressing group identification comes first.

　　In the earlier Roman Period *Ambatus* 'Aμβατος is the most widely attested man's name over a wide area comprising the centre-west and north of the Peninsula including northern Celtiberia, in other words, across the greater part of 'Hispania Celtica' on the Celtic/Indo-European side of the *-brigā*-line. The appearance of **anbᵃat'ia** in the SW corpus is one further detail reinforcing the cumulative impression that the language of Tartessian inscriptions and the people who made them were the same as the Peninsular Celts encountered by the Romans four or five centuries later. The following list, which includes the feminine form *Ambata*, is based on Vallejo 2005, 134–40 (cf. Albertos 1985, 264): BOVTIVS [AM]BATI, MODESTVS AMBATI F. COBEL(CVS), AMBATVS, AMBATVS, AMBAT[O],

[A]MBATO RIVEI FILIO, MENTINA AMB(ATI), CORIA AMBATI F.,
IANVA AMBATI, CLOVTI(A) AMBATI FILIA, AMBATVS DIV⟨I⟩LI F.,
ΑΜΒΑΤΟΣ ΔΟΚΟΥΡΙΟΥ, A[N]DERCIA AMBATI, IRINEVS AMBATI F.,
AMBATVS PE[L]LI, AMBATVS MALGEINI F., AMBATVS, [AM]BATO,
REBVRRVS AM[BA]TI, AMBATVS PINTOVI, TANCINVS AMBATI F.
/ AMBATVS TANCINILI F., FLACCVS AMBA[TI], CAMIRA [A]MBATI
F., ARCONI AMBATI F., CAVRVNIVS AMBATI CAVRINICVM, AMBATI
BVRILI TVROLI F., AMBATO, SECONTIO EBVREN[I]Q(VM) AMBATI F.,
[A]MBATO ALEBBIO [B]ODANI F., CABEDVS SEGGVES AMBATI F., MACER
OBISOQ(VM) AMBATI F. TOLETANVS, AMBATVS F., ACCETI CARIQO(N)
AMBATI F., DOID[ER]O AMB(ATI) FIL., AMBATVS VECTVS, AMBA[T]VS
SERM., FVSCVS CABEDVS AMBATI F. VADINIENSIS, AMBA[T]VS PLEND[I]
F., TILLEGVS AMBATI F. SVSARRVS, AMBA[TO] PACI[DO AM]BATI,
AMBATVS, TALARIVS CAESARI AMBATI, ELANVS TVRAESAMICIO(N)
AMBATI F., AMBATA PAESICA ARGAMONICA AMBATI VXOR, MADICENVS
CALAETVS AMBATI F., ... AMBATI F., ARCEA ... M(ARCI) AMBATI F.,
AMBATA BETVCA AMBATI F., ...S. AMBA[, AMBATVS VEMENVS ATI F.,
AMBATVS, AMBATO PARAMONIS F., AMBATI PENTOVIECI AMBATIQ(VM)
PENTOVI F. / AMBATVS, DOITERV[S ...] AMBATI F., DOITENA AMBATI
CELTI F., AMBA[TO], [T]OVTONI ARGANTIOQ(VM) AMBATI F.,
[A]MBATUS [A]RAUI F., AMBATI, AVELCO AMBATI F., PINTOVIO AMBATI,
AMBATO ARQVI F., L. POSTVMIVS AMBATVS, AMBATVS, AMBATI,
AM ¦ BAT MAR., AMBATA APPAE F., IVNIA AMBATA VIRO[NI] F., AMBATA
SEGONTI, AMBATA, AMBATA, AMBATA ALB...AVCA SEGOVETIS F.,
AMBATA CAELICA CAI F., [CA]LPVRNIAE AMBATAE LOVGEI F., AMBATA,
AMBATAE AIONCAE LOVGEI F., [AM]BATA [AI]ONCA [CAE]NIVETIS,
AMBATA BETVCA AMBATI F., AMBATAE [D]ESSICAE RVFI, AMBATE
MEDICAE PLACIDI F., AMBATA PAESICA ARGAMONICA AMBATI F.,
AMBA[TA AL]TICA, AMBATAE PLANDIDAE, C(AIAE) AMBATAE ...SEGEI
F., SEMPRONIAE AMBATAE CELTIBERI, AMBATAE TERENTIAE SEVERI
F., AMBATAE VENIAENAE VELERI CRESCENTI F., A[MBAT]A MATIGENI,
AMBADVS PALARI, AMBAD(VS) AL(IVS?) NEGA[LI?], VIVATIA AMBADA,
CORNELIAE AMBADAE, VALERIA AMBADAE, FLA(VIVS) AMBATIO,
VERNACVLVS AMBATIC(VM) MODEST(I).

What is probably the Celtic common noun behind this Hispano-Celtic name occurs in Gaulish, meaning 'a man sent in service of a chief': *ambactus* (e.g. Caesar, *De Bello Gallico* 6.15), *ambaxtus* 'servant of high rank, envoy, representative' (De Hoz 2007b, 191), based on the past passive particle of a Celtic compound verb *ambi-ag-tó-s* 'one sent around', Indo-European *h_2entb^hi- 'around' + *h_2eg'- 'drive, send'. Note also Gaulish *ambascia* 'embassy' < *ambi-aχtia* (De Hoz 2007b, 191).

AMBACTHIVS and AMBAXIVS occur as names in Latin inscriptions of the Roman Period from the Netherlands and Germany respectively, and AMBACTVS is found as a name in Germany and Serbia (Raybould & Sims-Williams 2007, 34).

——a]n͟b^ei͟kⁱ *or* a]n͟b^ei͟tⁱ ꟼ Ϻ ꟼ Ͷ [(J.11.5)   The inscription is fragmentary and has lost several signs. The transliteration is uncertain. a]n͟b^ei͟kⁱ shows an apparent violation of the principle of redundancy. ?Cf. Gaulish *ambito* (Lezoux) of uncertain meaning (Delamarre 2003, 42) based on the Celtic preposition *ambi* 'around' < Indo-European *$h_2entbʰi$-, Celtiberian and Gaulish *ambi*, Old Irish *imb, imm*.

ane ᴏͶA (J.1.1)   Not certain. Possibly compare the Gaulish and British preposition *ande*. With the sequence **lok°on ane nar´k^ee**, one might consider the Gaulish compound preserved in the 9th-century *Andelagum monasterium* (De Hoz 2007b, 195), possibly with a basic sense of 'lying down within'; if so, 'the burial/urn rests inside' for **lok°on ane nar͟k^ee** | *logon an(d)e narket* | An intensive force is often attributed to Gaulish and British compounds with initial *ande-*, e.g. *Ande-roudos* 'very red', similarly Welsh *annwyl* 'dear' : *gŵyl* 'humble', cf. also Sanskrit *adhi-deva-* 'greatest god', *adhi-rāj-a-* 'over-king' (Búa 2005, 119–20). For other possible examples of Proto-Celtic *-nd-* to Tartessian **n** Ͷ; see **anak^eenak͟^e:eib°o** (J.5.1) and **t^aalainon** (J.14.1). There are no counter examples. The fact that | *-nti* | is found alternating with | *-n(n)i* | or | *-nji* |, in e.g. **nar͟k^eentⁱi** versus **nar͟k^een(i)i**, makes it very likely that Proto-Celtic **-nd-* had become or was becoming | *-n(n)-* | in Tartessian. A case form of the river-name *Anas* (above) is another possibility for **ane**, unrelated to Gaulish/British *ande-*.

——]ant°onb°o͟ ‡ꟼϺ‡ΑͶA[(J.8.1)   A fragmentary form possibly preserving the case ending of a dative/ablative plural | *-antonbo* |, but the orthography could also represent | *-antombo(-)* | or | *-antomo(-)* |.

ar ꟼA appears as a prefix (preverb or compounding preposition) in the following forms in the corpus: **ar·b^aarie** (J.10.1) interpreted as a compound verb 'has carried forward', **ar·b^eieŕit^uu** (J.12.3) interpreted as another tense and mood of the same compound verb, such as an imperative 'let her/it/him carry forward', **ark^aare** (Monte Gordo) explained as a name 'female relative of Ar'kar(os)'. **ar** in these examples is probably derived from the compounding preposition **(p)are* < **(p)ari* 'forward, in front of' < Indo-European **peri* 'over, &c.' The same phonological development (*ar-* < **(p)are* < **peri*) is found in a Western Hispano-Celtic name ABRVNVS ARCELTI F. (Coria, Cáceres; Vallejo 2005, 183) explained as **(p)ar(i)+Celtius* ~ *Conceltius* by Prósper (2002, 422): *i* is lost in the compounding preposition **ar-** < **(p)ari-*. Gaulish *Armorica* alongside *Aremorica* suggests that the tendency to lose this syllable was old, occurring in more than one Ancient Celtic language.

aŕaiai ꓷꓮꓴꓮꓦꓮ |araiāi| or less probably aŕaiui ꓷꓴꓦꓮꓦꓮ |araiūi| (J.1.1). The context lok°ob°o≡niirab°o t°o aŕaia̠i is obviously similar to the Celtiberian TO LVGVEI ARAIANOM, reflecting related languages and cognate traditions of formulaic diction. From this comparison, it appears that Hispano-Celtic *to* is a preposition which governs the dative case. Etymologically aŕaiai could have to do with 'ploughland', as could ARAIANOM (Schwerteck 1979; cf. Wodtko 2000, 29–30; Jordán 2006). Alternatively, aŕaiai could be a dative singular personal name '(to) Aŕaia (*or* Aŕaius, Aŕaios)', corresponding exactly to the Celtiberian genitive plural family name *Araiokum* 'of the people of Araios'. Note also the possibly distinct Western Hispano-Celtic personal name and family name occurring in an inscription from Ávila ARAV(VS) | ARAV | IAQ(VM) TVRANI F(ILIVS) (Sánchez Moreno 1996, 121) and the theonym ARABO̱ COROBE|LICOBO TALVSICO·ḆO (Arroyomolinas de la Vera, Cáceres, Spain [Búa 2000, 526]). If both the Tartessian and Celtiberian reflect a development of an epenthetic vowel in an older *ar̥o-* 'one who is in front' (alternatively 'man of the native people', Indo-European *h₄er̥i̯ós* [cf. ariaríśe below]), that would be a significant shared innovation betokening a close relationship between Tartessian and Celtiberian. Note also that the *Ora Maritima* of Avienus mentions a promontory called *Aryium* (line 157) a few days' journey by sea beyond Tartessos. That name, deriving from sources as old as the 5th or 6th century BC, could mean simply 'promontory, projecting point' in the Celtic of western Hispania. In other words, this would be typically Celtic in both the semantic development from the Indo-European preposition *peri* and in the loss of *p*.

ar·b°arie ꓳꓦꓯꓮꓱꓯꓮ (J.10.1) occurs in an unusual inscription, a long and complete text, which uses some sign forms of uncertain value and lacks the familiar formula words. Therefore, we consider that ar·b°arie may be a variant of the recurrent ro·b°are (J.1.1, J.12.1, J.18.2, MdC), ro·b°ar°e (J.16.3); t°e·b°ar[e] (J.16.1), t°e·b°are (J.1.3, Vale de Águia), t̠°e·b̠°are (J.18.1); t°ee·ro-b°are (J.18.2), t°e[(e)-ro·b°]are (J.21.1), t°e·ro-b°are (J.1.1, J.12.1). The stem would be the same as in these more numerous examples, but the prefix different, more precisely, the same verb with a different preverb: | ar-bắr'e | 'has carried onward' probably from *(p)ari-bắre*, cf. Old Welsh *arber* 'use', Greek περιφέρω 'carry around'. The next item, Tartessian ar·b°ieŕit°u or ar·b°ieŕi (J.12.3), is identified as the same compound verb with different vowel gradation reflecting a different tense/mood stem. As to the i ꓦ in b°arie contrasting with the frequent b°are, in both this item and the next, it is possible that the lost *i* of *(p)ari* manifests itself or is recollected elsewhere in the word graphically, written following a consonant which preceded a front vowel and would thus have been phonetically palatalized. In the present example, it is probable however that within the context er·b^eieŕi : leoine ar·b^aarie the epigrapher has simply been influenced by the i ⋎ of the preceding form, which looks like a different tense form of the same compound verb. On the phonology, see further *Tartessian 2* §99. On the stem, see b^aare below.

——ar·b^eieŕit^uu ⋎Δⵋ⋌Oⵋ⊲ⵑA or ar·b^eieŕi ⋎⋌Oⵋ⊲ⵑA (J.12.3)   In the context of the surviving fragment (]uult^iinaarb^eieŕit^uula[, uult^iina can be recognized and isolated as a personal name. For what follows, the segmentation ar·b^eieŕit^uu la[is somewhat more likely. In either case it is understandable as a form of the same compound verb as ar·b^aarie OⵋⵑAⵑⵑA (J.10.1) with a different vowel grade in the root; see above. ar·b^eieŕit^uu can be explained as a 3rd singular imperative | ar-b´eritū(d) | 'let her/it/him carry onward' < *(p)ari-beretūd (on the phonology, see *Tartessian 2* §§83.1, 85). The alternative possibility, with the segmentation ar·b^eieŕi, could be interpreted as a present tense | ar´b´erit | < *(p)are-beret(i) 'carries forward' with early apocope of the primary -i or possibly the imperfect 'used to carry forward'.

Ἀργανθώνιος (Herodotus 1.163–5) is interpreted as masculine o-stem | Argantonios |, 'pertaining to *Argantonos, -ā ?"god of silver" *arganton' ~ Celtiberian arkanta, Arganda, Old Irish arggat, airget 'silver', Middle Welsh aryant 'silver', Breton arc'hant, argant 'silver', Latin argentum, Sanskrit rajatám 'silver' < Indo-European *h₂erǵ´ntom 'silver' (< *h₂erǵ- 'white'; cf. Falileyev 2010, 55–6). Compare the Western Hispano-Celtic ARGANTO MEDVTICA MELMANIQ[VM] (Riba de Saelices [Vallejo 2005, 186–7]), the divine epithet in LVGGONI ARGANTICAENI (Villaviciosa, Oviedo [Búa 2000, 274]), the family name of [T]OVTONI ARGANTIOQ[VM] AMBATI F[ILIVS] (Palencia [(González Rodríguez 1986, 123; Vallejo 2005, 186–7]) ~ Cisalpine Gaulish (Vercelli) ARKATOKO⟨K⟩MATEREKOS/ ARGANTOCOMATERECVS. On the Celticity of the name Ἀργανθώνιος, see further Ballester 2004, 119; De Bernardo Stempel 2006, 47; Almagro-Gorbea et al. 2008, 1050–2. The value of the io-stem suffix of | Argantonios | could be specifically an expression of child-to-parent relationship, i.e. 'son of *Argantonos' or '*Argantonā', cf. Gallo-Greek BIMMOC LITOYMAREOC 'Bimmos son of Litumāros' (Saint-Rémy-de-Provence; a usage of Indo-European date, cf. Vedic túgrya 'son of Tugra'). *Argantonos or *Argantonā are intelligible as Ancient Celtic names for the deity of silver. In the mythological tales of the Welsh Mabinogi, the son of Aryanrot (meaning 'Silver-wheel') is Lleu, i.e. the regular Welsh manifestation of the pan-Celtic Lugus, cf. inscription J.1.1.

The historical figure Ἀργανθώνιος was the beneficent philo-Greek king of the silver-based polity of Ταρτησσος Tartessos, whose phenomenal 80-year reign was notionally *c.* 625–*c.* 545 BC. He hosted a party of Phokaian Greeks *c.* 550 BC and gave them 30 talents of silver (about 780 kg) with which they paid for a defensive wall to protect their home city against the Medes. Ἀργανθώνιος is the only Celtic personal appellation in the Histories of Herodotus. The scarcely believable details of the story—that Arganthonios ruled for 80 years and died at the age of 120, soon after the visit of the Phokaians—are explicable if we understand that the king of Tartessos who welcomed the ship's captain Kolaios of Samos in the period 650 × 638 BC (Herodotus 4.152) was also called Ἀργανθώνιος and was assumed to be the same ruler (cf. Harrison 1988, 54). Writing about a century before Herodotus, the poet Anakreon, a contemporary of Arganthonios, also mentioned a fabulously long-lived ruler of Tartessos, surely the same man or men. Given his function, which included making massive diplomatic exchanges of silver, it is likely that 'Arganthonios' designated the office of the most powerful man of Tartessos (understood as βασιλεύς 'king' and τύραννος 'absolute ruler' by the Greeks), rather than being the man's name. Compare Gaulish ARGANTODANNOS / ARCANTODANNOS 'moneyer, magistrate of silver and/or coinage' on the coins of the Lexovii and Meldi (De Hoz 2007b, 192–3), Tartessian kᵃaśetᵃana 'tin-/bronze minister' (J.53.1).

As well as the episodes recorded by Herodotus, Greek contacts with Tartessos are indicated by an abundance of Greek material, mostly pottery, recovered from Tartessian sites and datable to the Orientalizing Period (*c.* 750–*c.* 550 BC), including material from Cyprus and Attica, also Samos and Phokaia. An Attic krater found at Huelva dates to 800–760 (Harrison 1988, 69). This Greek material is explicable partly as redistribution by the Phoenicians, but also probably as the result of direct contact.

A gravestone for FLACCVS | ARGANTONI [filius] | MAGILANICVM | MIROBRIG | ENSIS in Vettonian territory (Alconétar, Cáceres) shows *Argantonios* in use as a personal name during the Roman Period (Sánchez Moreno 1996, 127; Vallejo 2005, 186–7, cf. Luján 2007, 253), in or near what had been the territory of Tartessos in the Early Iron Age. It is possible that this later individual was named after the famous Tartessian king as known through classical literature; however, continuous survival as a Hispano-Celtic name in the western Peninsula is the inherently more economical explanation, especially in view of the manifest Celticity of the naming milieu including *Magilo-* and *Mirobrigā*. During the Hellenistic period, a similar name, Ἀργανθώνειον *Arganthoneion*, was in use for a mountain on the north-west coast of Asia Minor near Byzantium. It is not impossible that that name was old and known to Herodotus and thus might have influenced how he wrote the king's name (cf. Moret 2006), such as the θ for the expected τ. Nonetheless, Herodotus would hardly have thought in this connection of the name of a Bithynian mountain (which just happened to be homophonous with the Celtic word for the principal export of Tartessos, which was a key detail of the story), unless the king of Tartessos had been known by a very similar name or title. The references to mount Arganthoneion by Apollonius of Rhodes and Strabo post-date Herodotus by centuries, so any hypothetical assimilation more probably ran in the opposite direction, from the famous king to the landmark. It is also worth noting that the Celtic Aigosages were settled in the Troad very near the mountain during the 3rd century BC. On the Greek spelling, note also that the earlier Greek alphabets did not yet distinguish o and ω.

ariariśe ΟΜΨᖾᗋΜᖾᗋ (J.10.1)   As recognized by Untermann (1997, 257), there is apparent congruence in the endings of two sequences of signs near the opening of this inscription: **ariariśe : oni↑ak^{a}at^i|iśe**. The provisional interpretation here is that **śe** is a demonstrative suffixed to both the name that is the subject of the statement and its 3rd person singular verb: **ariariś-e : o-n-|i-(l)ak^{a}at^i|i-śe** ?= | *Ariaris+se ǫo-ni-lãgati-se* | 'this man Ariorīχs ("Foremost leader") now lies down under here', nominative singular + demonstrative, with **ś** M representing the double sibilant | *-s s-* |. On the first element of the name, compare North-west Hispano-Celtic ARIOVNIS MINCOSEGAEIGIS (A Porqueira, Ourense [Búa 2000, 303–4]); Gaulish *Ario-manus* (attested five times in Roman inscriptions from Austria [Raybould & Sims-Williams 2007, 37]), *Ario-uistus, Ario-gaisus*, simplex *Ariíos* (St-Germaine-Source-Seine), *Arius, Ariola*, the coin legend ARIVOS SANTONOS, the central-European *Harii* named as a subgroup of the Lugii (Tacitus, *Germania* §43), Old Irish nominative singular *aire* 'lord, freeman, noble', genitive *airech* < **arik-s, -os* (De Hoz 2007b, 192). On Tartessian **a** from the composition vowel **o*, see *Tartessian 2* §73.1. If Tartessian **aria-** is based on Indo-European **peri* 'over', it shows characteristically Celtic loss of Indo-European *p*. Alternatively, Indo-European **h₄eriós* 'member of one's own group' has been reconstructed as the now infamous Indo-European source of the Indo-Iranian self-designation *árya-* 'Aryan' (Pokorny 2002, 1.67; Mayrhofer 1992–2001, vol 1.3, 174–5; Mallory & Adams 2006, 266). The second element is explained as *-ris* from Celtic *-rīχs* < Indo-European **h₃rēg-s* showing characteristically Celtic *ī* < *ē*; see *Tartessian 2* §81.

ark^{a}are ΟᖾΛᖾᗋ (Monte Gordo)   In context, a plausible explanation of the case form is a co-ordinated feminine nominative/accusative dual **k^{i}ik^{e}e≡ark^{a}are** | *Kīkē≡Ar'kareē* | 'Kīkā ⟨and⟩ the daughter of Ar'kar(os)' < . . . **(P)are-kariāi*, alternatively dative singular (nominative singular 'Arkareā' < **(P)are-kariā*) ~ Gaulish ARECAR[I]ORVM (Delamarre 2007, 25). It is not certain whether the co-ordinative pair **k^{i}ik^{e}e≡ark^{a}are** is in apposition to **uuŕerk^{a}ar** at the beginning of the inscription, amplifying that name, or whether it identifies a second individual (or possibly two).

arkᵃastᵃamu ꓩꙨꓮ✕✝ꓠꓥꟻꓯ (MdC)   Of the alternatives weighed in *Tartessian 2* §§31.10–33.6, the one preferred is a name or epithet |*arga(n)stamū*| 'man greatest in silver' < **argant(o)(-isto)-tamū*, a superlative in a nominative/accusative dual case form, as the second element of the statement-initial co-ordinative naming phrase **tⁱilekᵘurkᵘu=arkᵃastᵃam̲u̲** |*Tillekurkū̲=arga(n)stamu*|. See further **tⁱilekᵘurkᵘu** below.

a̲ŕtᵉ[ ] ꟻ⋀ꓯ (J.24.1)   In the context of a fragmentary line reading **isakᵃaoeaŕtᵉ[**, the segmentation and interpretation remain uncertain. Compare possibly Cisalpine Gaulish ᴀʀᴛᴠᴀ́ꟶ (accusative plural) used for the stones of a funerary monument at Todi, Old Irish *art* 'stone'.

aśtᵃa ꓯꟼꓟꓯ (J.7.1, twice)   The transliteration (especially for ꟼ), etymology, and meaning are uncertain. Palaeohispanic *ast-* occurs in the major group name *Astures* in the north-west (from which the personal names *Asturus, Astur, Asturius,* and *Asturia* are derived). Note also the place-names *Astapa, Astigi, Asta, Astia/Hastia,* all south of the *-brigā* line. This apparent series is likely to be of multiple origin (Vallejo 2005, 188). A borrowing of the Phoenician Astarte is not impossible, but more likely with **aś*tᵃa*t̲ᵃa** ꓯ✕*ꓯ✕*ꓟꓯ (J.11.4). The Astarte cult was strong among the Tyrians and was established in their colony at Cádiz/Gadir near Tartessos, and images of the goddess have been found within the orientalizing zone of the Peninsula; see further under **sarune, bᵒo↑ir,** and **bᵒolon** below.

asune Oꓩꓩ✝ꓯ (J.4.1)   **asune≡ uarbᵃan ≡ekᵘurine** appears as a discontinuous naming phrase with marked syntactic agreement; the formula word **uarbᵃan** (a feminine accusative superlative) intervenes. Within this syntax, **asune** is a nominative/accusative dual or dative singular of a feminine *ā*-stem divine or personal name *As(s)unā*, cf. Gaulish *Assuna, Assonius*. To suggest a general meaning for the broader context on the basis of etymology, **asune≡ uarbᵃan ≡ekᵘurine ...** **bᵃara ... oretᵒo** 'As(s)un(n)ā and Ekurīgₐnī ("Horse Queen") ... I [this burial] have carried in deliverance (< running under) to the highest destination'. If the text does indeed contain words meaning 'Horse-Queen' and 'running under' (< **u(p)o-reto-*) as proposed, an obvious suggestion is that **asune** means 'divine mare' or 'she-ass', as the byname or partner of the Tartessian equivalent of the Gaulish Epona Regina. A difficulty or, at any rate, complication with this explanation is that Gaulish *Assuna* is not usually grouped with Old Irish *asan*, Old Cornish *asen* 'ass', &c. These medieval Celtic forms are explained as borrowed from Latin *asinus*, which is itself not usually regarded as native Indo-European vocabulary, but a loanword from the east ~ Sumerian *anšu* 'ass' (Vendryes, *Lexique* A-93). It is, however, not unlikely that this word spread widely in later prehistory with knowledge of the equine breeding and vehicle technology.

bᵃa A⟩ (J.1.2, J.12.4, J.16.1, J.16.2, J.18.1)   In the syntactic contexts **tᵉe·bᵃar[e] bᵃa naŕkᵉentⁱi** (J.16.1), **ro·bᵃa͟re bᵃa naŕkᵉ[e]ntⁱi** (J.16.3), and **tᵉe·bᵃare bᵃa naŕkᵉentⁱi** (J.18.1), the short segment **bᵃa** is plainly the same word in each instance and an extension of the basic epigraphic formula **uar(n)bᵃan tᵉe·ro-bᵃare naŕkᵉent·i**. A simple affirmation of the basic sense is thus inherently likely. In this light, statement-final **bᵃa lakⁱin↑ⁱi** (J.12.4) may be seen as a variant wording of the basic formula, with **lakⁱin↑ⁱi** as a synonym or functional equivalent of **naŕkᵉent·i**. Prefixed to the recurrent final verb and with a graphic representation that could stand phonetically for |ma|, **bᵃa** can be compared with Old Irish *ma* 'if', later *má*. The syntactic usage of Tartessian **bᵃa** shares with Old Irish *ma* placement preceding the verb at the head of its clause. Old Irish *ma* has been seen as of common derivation with the Vedic affirmative enclitic *sma*, *smā* 'indeed, ever after', Homeric μήν 'truly, really' in oaths, also the functionally identical μά, e.g. ναὶ μὰ τόδε σκῆπτρον 'yea by this sceptre!' < Indo-European **sm(e)h₂* (*Lexique* M-1, where an original meaning 'ainsi' is proposed for Old Irish *ma*; see also Pokorny 2002, 966; Beekes 2010, 888, 944–5). A sense 'so ever after' suits the three Tartessian examples above. In view of the affirmative meaning of the comparanda and use in Greek oaths, **bᵃa** |ma| preceding **naŕkᵉent·i** can be seen as adding the force of an injunction to a basic statement functionally equivalent to 'rest in peace'.

In light of the foregoing, we should probably understand statement-final **ne-bᵃa naŕkᵉeni** (J.1.2) as the negation of the usual closing formula, meaning 'so indeed not, by no means, do they now rest/remain', containing the cognate of Vedic *ná-sma* 'indeed not, by no means'. If we take **na-kⁱi·bᵘu** at the beginning of J.1.2 as containing another negative particle, then the sense of the standard formula is not incongruously reversed, but creatively intensified with a double negation: provisional translation, 'By no means does Tirtos now rest [here] in the company of the strong ones as one who has not been to the heroic summit', in other words, 'indeed he has, so now he does'.

——**bᵃaanon Y╪YAA⟩** (J.11.4)   These signs are clear enough in the extant 18th-century drawing, but the context **aioo͟ro͟rainn bᵃaanon****[is not helpful and contains doubtful readings as well as a break. Falling back on etymology, **bᵃaanon** corresponds precisely to the paradigmatic form implied by the identification of the recurrent **bᵃane** (J.11.1, J.19.1, J.20.1, J.26.1) as |bₐnē| < **bₐnai* 'woman, female, wife' nominative/accusative dual or dative singular ~ Old Irish *mnaí* (see below). Thus **bᵃaanon** < Proto-Celtic genitive plural **banom* ~ Old Irish *ban*; Gaulish genitive plural *bnanom* (Larzac) is probably a reformation based on the oblique cases of the singular. If this is the correct interpretation for **bᵃaanon**, that would suggest that **bᵃane** is a monosyllable |bₐnē| rather than **|banē|, i.e. the epigrapher has written the vowel double in **bᵃaanon** to make it clear that this means |banon| with a full syllable before the first nasal.

bᵃane OⴹA⧕ (J.19.1)

bᵃaenae OAⴹOA⧕ (J.15.1) occurs in the statement-initial feminine naming phrase ⱻaitᵘura meleśae≡∷≡bᵃaenae and is interpreted as an orthographic variant of bᵃane (J.11.1, J.19.1, J.20.1, J.26.1), i.e. as |bₐnḗ| < *bₐnai 'woman, female, wife' nominative/accusative dual or dative singular ~ Old Irish *mnaí* (see below). The repetition of the graphic diphthong **ae OA** is a peculiarity of this text. The three-term naming phrase as a whole is structured as a singular nominative *ā*-stem followed by two co-ordinated feminine forms in the nominative/accusative dual, with the provisional gloss 'Lady of Baeturia, sweet woman and wife'.

bᵃane OⴹA⧕ (J.11.1, J.19.1, J.26.1) is too frequent in the SW corpus to be a name. However, it always occurs within the naming phrases of the inscriptional texts, attested in the following contexts: kⁱielaoe:≡ oiśaHa ≡bᵃane≡robᵃae,]liirnestᵃakᵘun bᵃane≡ooŕoire,]tᵃarnekᵘun ≡bᵃane; similarly also the probable variant orthography in ⱻaitᵘura meleśae≡∷≡bᵃaenae (J.15.1). In three of these four examples, there is an overt congruence of endings in **-e** (or, in the last, **-ae** as a more archaic graphic variant of **-e**), which can be interpreted as forming feminine co-ordinative compounds in the nominative/accusative dual. In two of the examples, there are typical Hispano-Celtic genitive plural kindred names immediately preceding bᵃane, thus]liirnestᵃakᵘun 'of the kindred of Lir(a)nestos' and]tᵃarnekᵘun 'of the kindred of Tar(a)nus'. Two of the phrases include forms resembling feminine *ā*-stem nominatives singular: oiśaHa and ⱻaitᵘura. These may be taken as nominatives singular in apposition to the co-ordinative duals. In J.19.1,]liirnestᵃakᵘun bᵃane≡ooŕoire appears to be identified with an attributive

form derived from the name **ooŕoir** (J.19.2) borne by an individual commemorated in the same necropolis.

In the light of the foregoing points, the explanation offered is that these
relatively long and complex naming phrases identify women. As in many early
societies in Europe (and indeed elsewhere), these Tartessian women depend for
their social status and personal identification upon their male relatives and their
group affiliation. Therefore, **bªane** is interpreted as a case form of Celtic *bena*
< Indo-European *$g^u énh_2$* 'woman' (Wodtko et al. 2008, 177–85), most probably
nominative/accusative dual *b_anai*, alternative dative singular, both becoming
Old Irish *mnaí*. Accordingly, translations may be suggested for the examples:
kⁱielaoe:≡ oiśaHa ≡bªane≡robªae 'Kēlauos's first/foremost wife Oiśa?a',
]liirnestªakᵘun bªane≡ooŕoire 'Ooŕoir's wife, woman of the Lir(a)nestoi
people (of the kindred of Lir(a)nestos)', **]tªarnekᵘun ≡bªane** 'woman of the
kindred of Tar(a)nus'; **ɮaitᵘura meleśae≡::≡bªaenae** 'Lady of the Baeturians,
sweet woman and wife'. Tartessian **bªane** 'and the woman/wife' shows characteristically Celtic *b* < Indo-European voiced labio-velar *g^u*. **bªaanon Ч⧧ЧΛΛꓨ**
(J.11.4) is possibly the genitive plural from the same paradigm showing inherited
vowel gradation found also in Old Irish.

Compare Gaulish ?accusative singular *beni* (Châteaubleau), genitive plural
bnanom (Larzac), accusative plural *mnas* (Larzac) < Celtic *bnam-s* (see further
Delamarre 2003, 72), personal names *Seno-bena, Uitu-bena*, Old Irish nominative
singular *ben* 'woman, wife' < Celtic *bena* < Indo-European *$g^u énh_2$*, dative singular
archaic *bein* < Celtic *bene*, later Old Irish *mnái*, genitive plural *ban* < Celtic *banom*,
compositional form *ban-* < Celtic *bano-*.

-bªantⁱi Ч⬭ЧΛꓨ (MdC) occurs once in the SW corpus. Formally, it resembles an
Indo-European 3rd person plural active verb with present-tense marking, i.e.
the primary ending. This basic identification is consistent with the fact that
it is preceded by a prefix as **tᵉe·bªantⁱi** and **tᵉe(e)** occurs repeatedly in the
corpus prefixed to forms inflected as verbs or showing other preverbal prefixes:
tᵉee·bªarentⁱi (J.23.1) and the recurrent formulaic **tᵉe·bªare** (J.1.3, Vale de Águia),
tᵉe·bªar[e] (J.16.1), **tᵉe·bªare** (J.18.1) and **tᵉee·ro-bªare** (J.18.2), **tᵉe·ro-bªare**
(J.1.1, J.12.1). For the simplex **-bªantⁱi** a suitable form and meaning (for a funerary inscription) occurs in Old Irish *baïd* 'dies', *bath* 'died' < *$g^u h_2$-tó-*, *bath* 'death'
< Indo-European *$g^u eh_2$-* 'goes, steps away' (cf. Greek βιβάντι 'they stride'; Rix
2001, 205; Schumacher 2004, 214–16). **-bªantⁱi** could represent either |*bānti*|
from the Indo-European *e*-grade of the root or |*banti*| from the zero-grade.
The proposed etymology implies the characteristically Celtic sound change
of *b* < Indo-European *g^u*. As discussed previously (Koch 2010, 261), it is possible that the verbal noun of this root (corresponding to Old Irish *bás* 'death')
occurs in Tartessian **bªastᵉebᵘuŕoi** (S. Martinho), which would thus mean 'in

the yew-wood of ?passing/death' = 'funerary grove, necropolis' (see further *Tartessian 2* §§101, 117).

bᵃara A˥A˧ (S. Martinho), bᵃara** **A˥A˧ (J.4.1) can be understood as a distinct grammatical item belonging to the same paradigm as the formula word -bᵃare (see next item), occurring in the compound forms tᵉe·bᵃare (J.1.3, Vale de Águia), tᵉe·bᵃar[e] (J.16.1), t̲ᵉe·b̲ᵃare (J.18.1) and tᵉee·ro-bᵃare (J.18.2), tᵉe·ro-bᵃare (J.1.1, J.12.1), ro·bᵃare (J.1.1, J.12.1, J.18.2, MdC), ro·bᵃar̲ᵉe (J.16.3), ro-n·bᵃare (Monte Gordo). These comparanda have prefixes and endings making them analysable as compound verbs. Note likewise the inflexional ending of tᵉee·bᵃarentⁱi (J.23.1). bᵃare is interpreted as the 3rd singular perfect of *ber- 'carry'. On the basis of the form, then, bᵃara would be the corresponding 1st person singular 'I have carried'. In S. Martinho, the sequence ea̲n̲ bᵃara comes near the end of the complete text, where it can be appropriately understood as following a feminine singular relative and meaning 'she whom I [this grave] have carried', referring back to the deceased (see ean below). In J.4.1, the context is less helpful: bᵃara follows the opaque hapax obᵃar and is followed immediately by a long break. bᵃarua (J.7.9) and]bᵒoara (J.2.1) are explained as significant byforms of bᵃara (see both below). On the Indo-European comparanda, see bᵃare.

bᵃare O˥A˧ occurs as a simplex in J.27.1 and probably again as (J.1.5) bᵃar[e]. bᵃare is frequently found with the recurrent prefixes tᵉe(e) or ro or both, in which case they are invariably in the order tᵉe(e)·ro-, see bᵃara above for the citations. Taking ar·bᵃarie (J.10.1) to be an orthographic variant of the same stem and ending, ar can be added to the list as a third prefix occurring with -bᵃare. With ar·bᵉieŕitᵘu or ar·bᵉieŕi (J.12.3) and possibly also er-bᵉeŕi (J.10.1), the same compound occurs with another vowel grade of the root. In J.17.2]b̲ᵃare naŕkᵉentⁱi it could be compound or simplex, as there is room for several signs in the preceding gap.

  -bᵃare is an essential element in the formula, which in the fullest form of its many variants comprises, # NAMING PHRASE uar(n)bᵃan tᵉe(e)·ro-bᵃare (bᵃa) naŕkᵉentⁱi (AMPLIFICATION) #. The hypothetical interpretation for this formula is |... u̯arₐman de·ro-bāre, ma narkenti (...)| '[this grave/death] has carried the deceased away to the highest destination, so they now rest/remain/ lie [here] ...' (See further Appendix C.)

  For the examples cited above, -bᵃare and its prefixes are interpreted as forms of *ber- < Indo-European *bʰer- 'carry' and the well-attested Celtic preverbs *de 'away from', *(p)ro (which has many functions, including the formation of perfective verbs, as here), and *(p)are 'in front of'. -bᵃare itself would be the 3rd person singular perfect of *ber-. A further indication of this pattern of vowel gradation in the root is tᵉe·bᵃere 'has carried away' (J.7.8) where the second e has probably been influenced by the high-frequency present-stem ber-, though the consonant grapheme **bᵃ** anticipates the usual vowel of the perfect *bāre*. Possibly **tᵉeˑbᵃere** can be read as imperfect (with the present stem and ending -*e* < Indo-European **bʰeret*) rather than perfect.

A perfect of **bʰer-* cannot be reconstructed from comparative Indo-European evidence (e.g. Rix 2001, 77; cf. Wodtko et al. 2008, 15–30), arguably none existed in Proto-Indo-European. Though possibly generated independently by analogy, similar perfect forms came about early in some of the branches of Indo-European: e.g., Vedic *jabhára* 'has brought', *babhára* 'has carried' (the long vowel in these is not original), Gothic strong preterite 1st singular and 3rd singular -*bar* 'carried' (cf. New English *bore*). Old Irish and Early Welsh do not derive their preterites of this verb from the Indo-European perfect, but rather have *t*-preterites that probably derive from an *s*-aorist: e.g. Old Irish -*ruˑbart* < **roˑbir-s-t* or **roˑber-s-t*, Middle Welsh *kymmyrth* < **kom-bir-s-t* or **-ber-s-t*. **roˑbᵃare**, &c., therefore implies either that the Indo-European perfect and aorist had not yet merged in Tartessian (and therefore had not yet merged in its Proto-Celtic ancestor) or that the merger had taken place, but the process had once given more scope to formations derived from the perfect, a tendency that prevailed fully in Germanic (cf. Schumacher 2005). Unless and until a similar form turns up in another Celtic language, there is no certainty that a form like **roˑbᵃare** had existed in Proto-Celtic (as **(p)ro bāre*) as opposed to being a Tartessian innovation.

It should be remembered that, although the verb **ber-* was extremely common in all the Celtic languages, as an inheritance from Indo-European, the sense required here was unusual: 'this grave, whose inscription you now read, is presently in a state resulting from having previously carried away the person or persons named who now rest here.' Within the SW corpus there is an inherited Common Celtic compound verb with a 3rd person perfect formed in exactly the same way as **tᵉe(e)ˑroˑbᵃare**, &c. That form is **kᵒtᵘuaratᵉe** (J.53.1) 'has rescued, delivered' ~ Old Irish *fuˑráith*, Old Welsh *guo-raut* < **u(p)o-rāte* < older **-rōte* with long *ō* (on the derivation of the Insular Celtic *ā*-preterites from the Indo-European perfect, see Schumacher 2004, 75–6; cf. 2005). Old Irish and Early Welsh evidence furthermore supports the reconstruction of the double-preverb compound **to-u(p)o-ret-* 'deliver to' < 'run under towards' as a common inheritance (*Tartessian 2* §50.1). -**tᵘ-ua-ratᵉe** apparently functioned pragmatically the same way in its epitaph, as the formulaic **tᵉe(e)ˑroˑbᵃare**, expressing conveyance of the deceased in the funerary rite and probably also the metaphysical conveyance of the spirit. That inherited basis could have been the analogical pivot leading to **tᵉe(e)ˑroˑbᵃare** as an innovation. In the surviving Goidelic and Brittonic material, there are no examples of verbs with the root shape *Cer-* forming an *ā*-preterite. However, these patterns could be due either to a Tartessian or an Insular innovation, or a mere accident of survival, as the category is not numerous.

The possibility of an older inherited basis for tᵉe(e)·ro-bᵃare, though it is surely an innovation from the Indo-European standpoint, cannot be easily excluded, and there is also some indication that the form was old, at least within the dialect background of Tartessian. First, it is highly unlikely that Early Welsh *ri guanaid* and *guoreu* (both 'has done, has made' < *(p)ro wreχ(s)t, *wowrāge) and *amwyth* and *amuc* (both 'fought for, fought about' < *ambi wiχ(s)t, *ambi woike) reflect the only two Proto-Celtic verbs that had both aorist and perfect forms, or that these pairs had lacked any distinction of meaning or function, and were thus used totally interchangeably, for many centuries. (Early Welsh *goruc*, which also means 'did, made', belongs historically to the perfect form of a different verb *u(p)er woike 'has vanquished'.) Second, Tartessian]bᵒoara (J.2.1) can be explained as a variant of bᵃara 'I [this grave] have carried' (the 1st person singular of bᵃare), in which the orthography]bᵒoara recollects the vowel of the Pre-Celtic stage *bʰōra; see]bᵒoara below.

bᵃare͟ii ⴹⵎ◯ⵕА⎬ (J.5.1)   In the complete and unusual text, sabᵒoi : ist̲ᵃa̲|ibᵒo rinoeb̲ᵒo |anakᵉenak̲ᵉ:e|ibᵒo iibᵃa̲n bᵃare͟ii, there are slight traces of the formula ... uar(n)bᵃan tᵉe(e)·ro-bᵃare (bᵃa) naŕkᵉent̲ⁱi. Thus iibᵃa̲n ?'to the important place' (with *ippa-* possibly as a non-Indo-European synonym of *brigā* 'hill, hillfort' or the superlatives *Uama* and *Uxama*) could be the feminine singular accusative of destination taking the place of uar(n)bᵃan 'highest one'. bᵃare occurs, but without either of its preverbs. It is in the usual position of the missing naŕkᵉent̲ⁱi, where it strikingly appears to have the final -i(i) which is usual for the other verb. More than one explanation is possible, but as a marker of the present tense and in the absence of ro marking completed action, bᵃare͟ii can be understood as conveying present perfect sense through adding the primary -i to the perfect ending: 'this burial is *now* in a state of having carried . . .' That would be an innovation from the Indo-European perspective. See further Appendix C below.

bᵃar(e)n ⴹⵕА⎬ (J.20.1) simplex and ro-n·bᵃaren ◯ⵕА⎬Ⲩ≠ⵕ (J.11.4), are explained as 3rd plural forms of bᵃare, as is -bᵃarent̲ⁱi (next item), where the longer ending reflects present marking. In ro-n·bᵃaren, like ro-n·bᵃare (Monte Gordo), the unusual -n· is explained as an accusative object pronoun or relative infixed into the perfective preverb. This interpretation of this -n· is supported by the circumstantial detail that ro-n- never follows the preverb tᵉe(e)·; in other words, the -n· is always in the so-called 'Wackernagel's position', where it is expected from the Indo-European and comparative Celtic parallels. In the SW writing system bᵃaren could represent |bārent|. In Indo-European, the personal endings in the perfect paradigms did not resemble those of the present/

aorist tenses. In the plural that continued the Indo-European perfect in the Insular Celtic pretrites, these inherited anomalous forms had been replaced by endings that clearly resembled the plural personal endings of other paradigms. So, for example, in the Old Welsh 'Surexit Memorandum' one finds the preterite < perfect verbs *am·gucant* 'they fought about' < **ambi-woik-+-ant(i)* and *im·guodant* 'they besought one another' < **embi-gʷād-+-ant(i)*. In both cases, an easily recognized, high-frequency 3rd plural personal ending has been attached to a suffixless preterite stem derived from the Indo-European perfect, whereas the corresponding singulars have the zero ending, which had developed regularly from the inherited Indo-European **-e*. bᵃaren and -bᵃarentⁱi are in any event clearly 3rd person plural. They are also likely to be perfects, having undergone analogical replacement of the inherited perfect ending as suggested. The vowel of the ending in bᵃaren and -bᵃarentⁱi may simply be the e of bᵃare, i.e. the 3rd singular ending of the Indo-European perfect. However, it is alternatively possible that this vowel too has been extracted analogically from a present paradigmatic form, such as naŕkᵉentⁱi which usually occurs alongside bᵃare in the basic formula.

-bᵃarentⁱi ᛉ⊕ᛉO⁹A⦃ (J.23.1) occurs only once in the corpus, in the complete text: bᵉetⁱisai tᵉe(-)e·bᵃarentⁱi iru≡{u}arbᵘu i el naŕkᵉe:n: | uśn̲e̲e̲. The text is remarkable in that all the formula words are present, but not in the most usual order and each one is inflected in a unique way. Taken together these details seem to indicate sweeping and intentional (creative?) innovation, rather than incremental or evolutionary change. They are also valuable in confirming grammatical functions. Thus, for example, {u}arbᵘu (inflected for a different case and gender) confirms the identification of the recurrent uar(n)bᵃan as an o/ā-stem superlative |uarₐman| < **u(p)erₐmām*. Likewise bᵃarentⁱi overtly inflected as a verb (with 3rd plural active present marking) confirms that the less unambiguous form -bᵃare is also correctly identified as a verb. As explained in Appendix C below and *Tartessian 2* 101–13, the preverb ro (< Indo-European **pro*) is a marker of completed action and thus mutually exclusive with the 'primary' endings -(n)tⁱi, which mark actions and states continuing to the present. However, the agreement in vowels between bᵃarentⁱi and -bᵃare raises the possibility that bᵃarentⁱi might represent an innovative 'present perfect', rather than a simple present tense. Note, for example, the Old Welsh *am·gucant* and *im·guodant* as discussed in the previous note. As the naming phrase opening the inscription bᵉetⁱisai formally suits a dative singular and the 3rd plural verb tᵉe(-)e·bᵃarentⁱi precedes the complex noun phrase iru≡|{u}arbᵘu i el, which can be construed as the verb's subject, cf. lakᵉentⁱi ra⦀a≡kᵃaśetᵃana (J.53.1).

bᵃarua-ion ⦃A�srᵖᛃAᛉ⧺ᛌ (J.7.9) The inscription apparently begins iru bᵃarua-ion, but it is not impossible that an entire line has been lost before this. The

text is definitely imcomplete at the end. As discussed in the Commentary on
the inscription above, two interpretations can be considered, i.e. 'the man/hero
whom I [this grave] have carried' or 'the man/hero ⟨and⟩ Barros. . .' (segment as
iru≡bᵃaru. . .). Though ,of course, it could be neither of these.

bᵃastᵉ-⊢‡Λ⟩ (S. Martinho) opens the long inscription, where it appears to be the
first element of a compound, plausibly a place-name in the locative singular case;
see next item. In the pre-Roman toponomy and group names of the southern
Iberian Peninsula, there are several forms commencing with *Bast-* or *Mast-* (elements that are probably related to one another if not identical): for example,
Bastetani near Granada, *Bastuli* near Gibraltar, and *Mastia* near Cartagena. The
geographic distribution suggests that this is a non-Indo-European element, the
fluctuation of *b-* and *m-* also fits Iberian phonology. On the other hand, in the
present context further west and beginning what is probably a funerary inscription, another possibility is worth considering, namely the meaning 'death' ~
Old Irish *bás* < **bāsto-m* < **gᵘōsto-m* : Indo-European **gᵘes-* 'extinguish' (*Lexique*
B–21) showing the characteristically Celtic treatment of Indo-European *gᵘ* and *ō*.
Cf. Celtiberian *bastoniam* (though explained differently by Prósper 2007, 26–7).

bᵃastᵉebᵘuŕoi ᴎ‡ᴎᴻᴌᴑ⊢‡Λ⟩ (S. Martinho) 'in the yew-wood (?of death)'
locative singular of an *o*-stem compound name, probably referring to the place of
the interment, thus possibly a term for 'necropolis'. As explained above, the first
element might be a non-Indo-European place-name element or the cognate of Old
Irish *bás* 'death'. The second element is the common Ancient Celtic name element
Eburo-, *Ebura* 'yew wood', see **ebᵘuŕoi** below. The positioning of a locative at or
near the beginning of the text agrees with the placement of **sabᵒoi** |*samoi*| 'in
the summer' in J.5.1.

bᵉe ᴑ9 (J.1.1, Monte Gordo) 6ᴑ(MdC).   In the three examples, **bᵉe** occurs near
the end, probably as the second-to-last word in long or fairly long texts. In each
case, **bᵉe** occurs after the last of the formula words and thus forms part of the
'amplification' or non-essential continuation of the statement. However, there
is no certainty that this short sequence must be the same word or particle in all
three. MdC **tᵃaobᵉe** and Monte Gordo **tᵃabᵉe** are more similar to each other, and
thus more likely to be the same or related forms, than is J.1.1 (**bᵉ**)**etᵉa**|**siioonii**.
    In the SW writing system, **bᵉe** can stand for |*me*| as well as for |*be*| (with
a long or short vowel in either case). Therefore, one possibility is that some or
all of these examples correspond to Old Irish *mé*, Old Welsh *mi*, Old Breton *me*,
mi, which are independent pronouns meaning 'I, me', and can be employed, for
example, as the predicate focus of the copula. Cf. also the Gaulish suffixed 1st
singular subject pronoun *-mi* 'I' used following 1st person singular verbal end-

ings (*Tartessian* 2 §41). In numerous ancient languages, 1st singular pronouns occur in 'talking' inscriptions, e.g. Venetic nominative *ego* and accusative *mego*, Etruscan *mi*. In such a talking inscription on a stela standing over a burial, the cognate of Old Irish *táu*(+ *mé*) 'I exist' < 'I stand' (Indo-European **steb₂-*) may be considered; see **tᵃao-bᵉe** below. If that is the correct analysis, then it is a form of the 1st person singular pronoun beginning in *m-* in the nominative, contrasting, for example, with the type of Latin *ego* or German *ich* (and numerous other Indo-European languages). The disparity is often regarded as a Celtic innovation, comparable to the spread of initial *s-* at the expense of *t-* forms through the originally heteroclite Indo-European demonstrative paradigm. However, Jordán (1993) argues for Celtic nominative **me* as an archaic survival of an Indo-European 1st singular **me*, originally functioning as subject, agent, and patient, as reflected also in Tocharian. The vowel in the Celtic form of this pronoun was probably originally short *e* as in the accusative **me(d)*, which can be seen preserved without lengthening in Old Irish *meisse* 'I (myself)' with the (demonstrative) emphasizing particle. However, *mi* in Gaulish and Welsh indicate that the long-vowel byform **mī* < **mē* was probably at least as old as the common ancestor of those two languages.

bᵉelibᵒo ✝□ᴎ⁊O9 (J.1.2) , **bᵉe:lin ᴎᴎ⁊| O9** (J.17.4) **bᵉelis̱on ᴎ✝ᴍᴎ⁊O9** (J.20.1)   These forms lend themselves to interpretation as items within a single nominal paradigm—*i*-stem dative/ablative plural, accusative singular, and genitive plural, respectively. The three contexts are consistent with taking | *Belēs* |, singular | *Belis* |, (in theory these could also be | *Melēs* |, | *Melis* |) as naming a group or a common noun referring to a group. In each case, this would be the group to which the named deceased belongs: **kᵒo-bᵉelibᵒo . . . tⁱirtᵒos** 'Tirtos in the company of the Belēs', **kᵉenila⁽'⁾rin≡bᵉe:lin** 'Genilaris the Belis', **]uŕni bᵉelis̱on** '( )Uŕni of the Belēs'.

For the form, compare the Western Hispano-Celtic dative plural divine name COROBELICOBO (?'to the deities of the host of the Beles', Arroyomolinos de la Vera, Cáceres), Celtiberian group names *Belisonae*, *Belloi*, the accusative personal name *Belikiom*, the genitive plural family name *Belaiocum*, Gaulish and British divine names *Belisama*, *Belenos*. If **bᵉe:lin**, **bᵉelibᵒo**, **bᵉelis̱on** represent a common noun in these examples, the meaning is possibly 'the strong one(s)' or similar, as is sometimes proposed for the Celtic comparanda. For the root, a possible cognate is the second element of Welsh *rhyfel*, Latin *proelium* 'war'. Alternatively, John Carey reminds me that, in the absence of a certain Celtic etymology, the Phoenician theonym *Baal* should not be overlooked as a possible source. Another Punic/Phoenician possibility is the word *b'l* 'citizen' (e.g. of Carthage), plural *b'lm*, probably to be vocalized *balim*. Though merely an intriguing possibility, that last possibility would have historical implications: would these SW epitaphs then be claiming citizenship of a Phoenician colony? Or had the concept and institution of citizenship been borrowed, say, by the indigenous state of Tartessos and/or the polity of the Kunētes as part of the cultural transformations of the Orientalizing Period?

I have tentatively interpreted **kᵒobᵉelibᵒo** (J.1.2) with **kᵒo-** as the separate preposition | *ko(m)* | assigning dative case, but cf. MODESTVS AMBATI F. COBEL(CVS) (Aldea-Nova, Guarda; Vallejo 2005, 134). For the inflexion of genitive plural **bᵉeliśon**, compare Celtiberian *kentisum* 'of the children' < **gentissūm* (Jordán 2005, 108). Note that the voiceless /s/ of Celtiberian *kentisum* corresponds to the Tartessian sign that was at least sometimes used for strong or double sibilants in **bᵉeliśon**. To judge from the cognate languages, **bᵉeliśon** and *kentisum* do not reflect the inherited Indo-European or Proto-Celtic *i*-stem genitive plural form, but a significant innovation shared by Tartessian and Celtiberian, implying an especially close relationship and/or continuing contact, suggesting that the category 'Hispano-Celtic' is valid linguistically as well as geographically.

bᵉetⁱisai ᙏA‡ⱷO9 (J.23.1)   The form begins a complete inscription and immediately precedes an unusual variant of the one of the formula words, followed by a further two examples: **bᵉetⁱisai tᵉe(-)e·bᵃarentⁱi iru≡|{u}arbᵘu i el naŕkᵉe:n:** …Thus **bᵉetⁱisai** represents the naming phrase in its usual position, comprising a single item. As **bᵉetⁱisai** appears to be inflected as an *ā*-stem dative singular, thus meaning '[a grave] for Betisa', it would therefore not be the subject of the verb. On the other hand, a nominative/accusative dual is possible, in which an elided '⟨and⟩ woman, daughter, wife' is understood. For the form, compare the Celtiberian family name *Betikum*, also BETACI from the Évora region and the family name BEDAQ[VM] from Soria (Vallejo 2005, 210, with further examples).

]bᵒoara]▯/‡A٩A (J.2.1)   The inscription is fragmentary. Only the ending survives: **]bᵒoara naŕkᵉenii.** That provides a standard form of the recurrent formulaic closing, which strongly implies that **]bᵒoara** is a variant of the formula word that usually comes before this, i.e. **-bᵃare.** However, **bᵒoara** and **-bᵃare** differ formally. In keeping with the working hypothesis that **-bᵃare** is the 3rd singular perfect of **ber-* 'carry', thus 'has carried', **bᵒoara** conforms to the predicted form of 1st person singular: 'I have carried' **bāra* < **bŏra*. So in this variant of the formula, the grave would be speaking as itself in the inscription, rather than the inscription speaking about the grave in the 3rd person as in the usual formula. The form **bᵒoara** is an archaism. The paradigmatic forms show that the 1st singular had mostly become **bᵃara** (S. Martinho). **bᵒoara**, probably for labialized | *bᵒāra* |, shows a trace of the earlier *ō* vocalism < Pre-Celtic **bᵇŏra* < notional Indo-European **(bᵇe)bᵇorh₂e* (see further *Tartessian 2* §99.3).

bᵒo↑ir ٩ᴎ↑≠□ (J.7.1)   The text is exceptional and difficult, owing to its unusual sign forms and deviation from the recurrent syntactic patterns of the corpus: **aś🄷a bᵒo↑ir naŕkᵉenai | aś🄷a na·bᵒolon**. Accordingly, the interpretation is highly tentative. A starting point is provided by **naŕkᵉenai**, recognizable as a variant of the formulaic closing **naŕkᵉentⁱi**, at the end of the first line, in other words, in syntactic position something like the usual placement of **naŕkᵉentⁱi**, &c. The value of the sign 🄷 is uncertain. It could stand for a phoneme, but an iconographic ideogram is also possible. ↑ could stand for **bⁱ**, as one would expect from the sign's value in the SE or Meridional script, but some of the examples in verbal endings in the SW corpus suggest the transliteration **tⁱ**. Furthermore, the sign does formally resemble ⊣ l, which in light of the symmetry of **aś🄷a bᵒo↑ir ... aś🄷a na·bᵒolon** could be decisive. That repetitive structure is unparalleled elsewhere in the corpus, but may be helpful. **bᵒo↑ir** and **bᵒolon** look similar and also occur in the same position in their respective lines. And the endings of both forms can be understood as verbal; see **bᵒolon** below. As such, the ending **-ir** could be either 3rd plural perfect on Indo-European parallels or anticipate Insular Celtic passive/impersonal forms. **bᵒo↑ir** transliterated as | *bobīr* | might suit a form of the verb 'to be' (? 'they have been'). Transliterated as | *bōdīr* |, **bᵒo↑ir** could be understood as the reflex of **boudīr*, meaning 'they are awakened', cf. Old Irish *ro-bud*, Middle Welsh *ry-buð* 'warning', *boð* 'awareness, free will, &c.' < Celtic **budā*, Sanskrit *bōdhati* 'is awake, is aware of' (Lewis & Pedersen 347), Indo-European **bʰeu̯dʰ-* 'make aware, pay attention, be observant' (Rix 2001, 82–3).

bᵒolon ᴎ≠⊣≠□ (J.7.1)   Following the discussion of the previous item, **na·bᵒolon** resembles a negatived 3rd plural active verb, used in syntactic parallelism, contrasting with the affirmative verb **bᵒo↑ir** with which **bᵒolon** also alliterates, further drawing attention to the parallelism. As a verb, **bᵒolon** could reflect either the Indo-European thematic secondary ending **-ont* (past tense) or the thematic primary ending **-onti* (present tense) having undergone an early apocope of final *-i*. It is less obvious as to which particular Celtic and Indo-European verbal root **bᵒolon** belongs. One possible set of comparisons is Old Irish *at·baill* 'dies', Early Welsh *aballaf* 'I (shall) perish' (Marwnad Cunedda), Sanskrit *galati* 'drops, disappears', Old English *cwelan* 'to die' (Lewis & Pedersen §502), Lithuanian *gãlas* 'end, death': Indo-European **gʷelH-* (Rix 2001, 207–8). If this is the relevant root, Tartessian **bᵒolon** shows diagnostically Celtic *b* from Indo-European *gʷ*.

bᵒotⁱi ✸ana ᴧY̌ᴧ ✸ᴎ⬭≠□ (J.18.1) occurs at the beginning of the statement-initial naming phrase **bᵒotⁱieana≡ kᵉertᵒo ≡robᵃa**. In the proposed interpretation as 'B. first-born daughter of the craftsman', | *Bōdⁱeanā* | or | *Bōtⁱeanā* | is a feminine *ā*-stem woman's name. The name BOVTIVS (genitive BOVTI) and similar forms

bᵒot'i ☼ana ᐱᎭᐱ ☼Ꭽ⊕╫☐ (J.18.1)

were extremely common in the western and northern Peninsula in earlier Roman times, often collocated with a second Celtic-looking name, such as BOVTIA TANCINI F twice from the Cáceres region and many further examples, including (but not listing exhaustively): TONGIVS BOVTI F., BOVTI TRITI, [T] VREVS BOVTI F., TONGETA BOVTI F., CILIVS BOVTE, CILO BOVTI F., CALAETVS BOVTI F., BOVTIVS CAMALI F. F., TANGINVS L(VCII) BOVTI, LUBACVS BOV[TI] F., BOVTIO TANCINI F., MAELO BOVTI F., TRITIVS BOVTI, ERGVENA BOVTI F. AMMARICVM, CLOVTIO BOVTI F., AVSCVS BOVTIVS VIRONI F., BOVTIO SEGONTI F. CL(VNIENSIS), MVNIGALIGI ABANI BOVTI F., BOVTIO MATVGINI F., CAMALA BOVTI F., BOVTIA TANCINI F., BOVTIA TANGINI F., BOVTIAE CLOVTI F., BOVTIA CAMALI F., BOVTIAE SAELGI F., BOVTIA BOVTII F., BOVTIAE MANTAI F., BOVTIA MANDI F., BOVTIA BOVTI F., BOVTIA CADARI F., TALAVS TONCETAMI F. BOVTIE(CVM) (Sánchez Moreno 1996, 122; Vallejo 2005, 214–22). The simple vowel is found for the diphthong in BOTILLA from the same area as BOVTILA (or BOVTIIA [Búa 2000, 564]). These forms are probably based on Indo-European *gᵘou- 'cow', thus showing characteristically Celtic b < *gᵘ. There are also numerous Hispano-Celtic forms related to the common Celtic word boudo-, boudi- 'victory, benefit, &c.', Old Irish búaid, Early Welsh bub: BODIVS, BOVDICA, BODECIVS, BOVDENNA CARAI, BOVDELVS CONCELTI F, TVRENNO BODEGGV[N] BODDI F. VAD[INIENSI] (Albertos 1985, 271; Vallejo 2005, 222–4). The symbol ☼ is explained by Untermann as a variant letter form for e O. The orthography bᵒot'ieana reflects the regular Tartessian sound changes in which an earlier i̱ is lowered to e when preceding the vowel a or ā directly or following an intervening consonant (Tartessian 2 §78) and the resulting phonemicization of the 'i-quality' or strongly palatalized consonant t' as a consequence of the phonetic conditioning by i̱ from the original Proto-Celtic *Boudi̱anā or *Bouti̱anā (Tartessian 2 §§99.1–4), also the regular simplification of the Proto-Celtic diphthong *ou in Tartessian (Tartessian 2 §94).

bᵒotᵒo⩘ar[ ]⑂A⩘‡Δ‡□
(J.7.2)

bᵒotᵒo⩘ar[ ]⑂A⩘‡Δ‡□ (J.7.2)   By its positioning at the beginning of the text, this form, which breaks off after the seventh sign, is expected to be a personal name. Formally, **bᵒotᵒo⩘ar[** resembles a compound. If so, the first element could go etymologically with the base of **bᵒot'ieana** above. A second possibility, Proto-Celtic **bodu̯o-* would suit the form as written better and explain why the composition vowel was retained as **o** after a labial sound, rather than being reduced to **a**, cf. similarly **lebᵒoiire** (MdC) < **Lemo-u̯iroi* (*Tartessian 2* §73.1). Compare the Gaulish personal names *Boduos, Boduus, Bodua, Boduacius, Boduia, Boduisso, Boduo-genus, Boduo-gnatus, Maro-boduus*, probably *Bodorix*, &c., British ʙᴏᴅᴠᴏᴄ, Old Irish *bodb*, later also *badb* 'crow, war goddess', Old Breton *Boduuan*, &c., Old Welsh *Bodug*. The Hispano-Celtic place-name *Budua* (south-west Spain) possibly also belongs to this root, with the vowel of the first syllable assimilated to the labial glide. The phonetic value of ⩘, which appears to be the initial sound of the second element is uncertain; a labial and/or aspirate is possible.

——**bᵘu(o)‡⑁⋈** (J.1.2)   In the context -**bᵉelibᵒo na-kⁱi·bᵘu oira-uarbᵃan**, the segment -**bᵉelibᵒo** can be considered relatively securely identified as a dative/abla-tive plural (see above). **oira-uarbᵃan** or **ira-uarbᵃan** has one of the Tartessian formula words as its second element, and the first has several parallels within the corpus, as well as the parallelism of the collocation as a whole with Celtiberian VIROS VERAMOS 'supreme man' (K.3.18). That leaves the sequence of six signs in the middle **nakⁱibᵘu**. Comparison with the medieval Insular Celtic languages suggests the segmentation **na-kⁱi·bᵘu** meaning approximately 'that was not'. The standard etymology of the Old Irish substantive verb *boí* 'there was', Old Welsh *bu* 'was' drives it from a formally perfect **bou(e)* 'has been' corresponding to the Indo-European root **bʰueh₂-* 'be' (Rix 2001, 98–101; Wodtko et al. 2008, 46–58). In some respects, this remains preferable to Schumacher's proposal of a Proto-Insular Celtic **bube* (2004, 252–5), which would be expected to have produced some traces of a byform ***byf-* (alongside *bu-*) in Welsh. The development of the vowel in **bᵘu(o)** < **bou(e)* is like that seen in **iubᵃa** (J.7.8) < **iou_ₐmā* 'youngest female' (*Tartessian 2* §94). The absence of a final *-e* in **bᵘu(o)** could be a result of early apocope of **bou(e)*.

ea ΛO, ean ꟼΛO   There are several examples in the SW corpus showing regular phonetic lowering of Proto-Celtic **(-)iā̆(-)* and **(-)iCā̆(-)* to Tartessian (-)**ea**(-) and (-)**eCa**(-) (see *Tartessian 2* §78). Note the similar development in Celtiberian *sekobirikea* (K.0.3; Wodtko 2003, §4). Therefore, the predicted outcomes of the relative pronouns **iā* (feminine nominative singular and nominative accusative neuter plural, Celtiberian *ia* [Wodtko 2000, 133]) and **iām* (feminine accusative singular) would be Tartessian **ea** and **ean** respectively. Such short segments do occur in the corpus in contexts which allow this possibility to be considered, albeit at a relatively speculative level. Thus, **eanb̲ᵃara** ꓮꟼΛꓘꟼΛO, occurring near the end of the lengthy S. Martinho inscription could be interpreted as **ean·b̲ᵃara** 'whom I [this grave] have carried', referring back to the deceased. I now think that the most promising segmentation and analysis for J.22.1 **uarᵇºoiirsaruneeabᵃa | renaŕ | kᵉenii** is | *Uar_ₐmo-iir Sarun(n)ē eā bāre; naŕkenji* | 'Uar(a)moiir Sarun(n)ē ("Noble Consort to the Star Goddess"), she who has carried [him]; they now rest', in other words the deceased has been redeemed by his eponymous goddess. Note also the similar but fragmentary]**sarune ea oar**[(J.22.2) from the same site. J.1.5 **mutᵘuireabᵃar**[. . .]**aŕkᵉentⁱi** could be read as **mutᵘui r'-ea·bᵃar**[e n]**aŕkᵉentⁱi** '[a grave] for Mutuos, that has carried [him]; they now remain [here]', but the more likely segmentation is **mutᵘuirea bᵃar**[e n]**aŕkᵉentⁱi** '[this grave] has carried X daughter of Muturos; they now remain [here]'. The fragmentary J.6.1]**ea·bᵃare** n̲[a could mean '[this grave] that has carried [the deceased]'. If J.11.4 **ea ro-n·bᵃaren naŕkᵉenii** is introduced by a subject relative, **ea** would have to be neuter plural, as the following verbs both show plural marking, so something like '[these stones] that have carried him. . .' (?). In the last three lines of the long MdC text **lii*eianiitᵃa | eanirakᵃaltᵉetᵃao | bᵉesaru**[?n]**an**, the third to last line remains opaque, but the segmentation of the last two lines as **ea nira-kᵃalteᵉe tᵃao-bᵉe saru[?n]an** is more straight-forward, revealing another probable example of a segment **ea**, though difficult to construe without an interpretation of the preceding line.

eb̲ᵉe OꝺO (J.9.1)   The sense of **eb̲ᵉe** remains unclear, but can be limited by the analysable context of the fragmentary]**kᵃanan uarb̲ᵃan eb̲ᵉe naŕ[kᵉe . . .** or]**a̲anan. . . .** There are the two formula words in their usual sequence, and **-anan** apparently agrees with **uarb̲ᵃan**, if so, accusative feminine singular. Possibilities for **eb̲ᵉe** include a pronoun | *eme(n)* | referring either to the deceased or burial or some part of it (see **emun** below), or an enclitic conjunction co-ordinating the two accusatives. The similar segment **ebᵉ Oꝺ** (J.16.3) involves a more problematic reading and context.

]**ebᵘo ⧾☐O**[(J.7.8) is an incomplete form preceded by a long illegible section and can be taken as a dative/ablative plural ending of a divine name, social group name, or personal pronoun 'to/from them', similarly]**aibᵒo ⧾☐ᴟA**[(J.28.1).

ebᵘuŕoi ᴟ⧾ʌᴧᴟᴋO (S. Martinho)   **bᵃasteᵉebᵘuŕoi** opens the long and complete inscription and is thus comparable to **sabᵒoi** opening J.5.1. The latter has obvious and abundant comparanda as a place-name and the second as the familiar Celtic < Indo-European name of a season. The ending **-oi** suits an inherited Indo-European *o*-stem locative singular, which would be appropriate for both lexical categories: **ebᵘuŕoi** 'in the yew-wood' ?= 'funerary grove, necropolis', **sabᵒoi** | *samoi* | 'in the summer'. The orthographies either predate monothonization of the final syllable or conservatively preserve that representation; see *Tartessian 2* §94. There was an *Ebora* near Cádiz, also *Ebora* now *Évora* and *Eburobrittium* on the Atlantic coast north of Lisbon; cf. also the North-west Hispano-Celtic personal names EBVRA, EBVRVS, and related forms (Albertos 1985, 283): EBVRVS [A]VRI F., C(AIVS) ARIVS EBVRI F. APILOCVS, APANA EBVRI F., AMANA EBVRI F., FABIA EBVRI F. LEMAVA ERITAECO, CASIA EBVRI F., LVCILA EBVRA, EBVRIA CALVENI F. CELTICA SVP(ERTAMARCA) Ɔ LVBRI, [T] VRAIOS EBVRENIVS CALA[E]TI, CAENOBIVS EBVREINI, EBVREINIVS CVRVNDI F. CARAECIQ(VM), SECONTIO EBVREN[I]Q(VM) AMBATI F., EBVRINVS, L(VCIVS) IVLIVS C(AI) F. GAL. EBVRA[N]CVS, L(VCIO) TERENTIO PATERNO EBVRANCO(N) TITI F. QVIRINA, ANT(ONIVS) ADDIO EBVRANCO(N) AM(ALI) FI., EBVRIANVS, CAENOBIVS EBVREINI, EBVREINIVS CVRVNDI F. CARAECIQ(VM), SECONTIO EBVREN[I]Q(VM) AMBATI F., EBVRINVS (Vallejo 2005, 313–15); MANTAIVS EBVRIAE (MdC, see *Tartessian 2* §2). Amongst numerous Gaulish examples are the Gallo-Roman divinities MATRIS AVG(VSTIS) EBVRICIS (Jufer & Luginbühl 2001, 38). The Old Irish cognate *ibar* has strong mythological associations, especially with death and the otherworld. Catuvolcus, chief of the Eburones of Gaul, committed suicide, by means of the poisonous yew (Caesar, *De Bello Gallico* 6.31), that is, his tribe's totemic tree. *Eburianus* is attested as a Hispano-Celtic divine name on a tombstone from Duratón, Segovia (Marco Simón 2005, 297); its exact cognate is Galatian EBOYPIANOΣ (Freeman 2001, 53). As Welsh *efwr* means 'cow parsnip' and Breton *evor* 'hellebore', it is possible that Proto-Celtic **eburo-* could refer to a variety of plants.

eertᵃaune OᎩᎩAX⑨OO (J.55.1), **ertᵃau[ne]ᎩAX⑨O** (J.54.1)   The first example belongs to a better preserved text, with relatively clearcut word divisions: **ṛo- kᵒoli̲o̲n eertᵃaune tᵃarielnon lir̃niene nar̃kᵉenai**. As well as the formula word **nar̃kᵉenai** in its usual closing position, there is recurrent prefix **ṛo-** and apparent congruence of case endings between **kᵒoli̲o̲n** and **tᵃarielnon**, also probably **eertᵃaune** and **lir̃niene**. **]*ikᵉei**[ ]*uosor ertᵃau[ne** is more difficult, so the similarity of the final fragmentary **ertᵃau[** to **eertᵃaune** is merely noted. That more difficult and damaged text, from Capote, Badajoz, is a (reused) Late Bronze Age warrior stela with a prominent chariot and an oversize lyre orientated upside-down from the perspective of inscription. **eertᵃaune** |*eertaunē*| represents an exact phonetic equivalence to Celtiberian *uertaunei* (Botorrita; cf. Ballester 2004, 119): the Tartessian showing that dialect's characteristic phonetic assimilation of *u̯* to the following vowel (on which see *Tartessian 2* §§97.1–3) and also regular simplification of the diphthong *ei* as **e** (see *Tartessian 2* §94). Celtiberian *uertaunei* is usually interpreted as the dative of a verbal noun, though various meanings and etymologies have been proposed (see Untermann, MLH 4.529). A suitable meaning here would be 'to exchange, sell', Welsh *gwerthu* < Indo-European **u̯ert-* 'turn' (Rix 2001, 691–2), which could explain the construction with the double accusative and **ro——** 'to exchange Dari(e̲)elnos for Kolios'. It is noteworthy that both find sites for the texts with these forms were in Spain, east of the Guadiana. J.55.1 is at the north-eastern edge of the distribution of the SW inscriptions. Therefore, the close correspondence with Celtiberian may have a basis in dialect geography, reflecting the Celtic of the central Peninsula.

ekᵘu- ᎤᎦO ᎤᎦO appears as the first element of a compound name **ekᵘur̲i̲ne OᎩᎩᛕᎤᎦO** (J.4.1), for which a meaning 'horse(-queen)' < Indo-European **h₁ek̑'u̯os* is proposed; see below. 'Horse' could also occur as an *o*-stem dative singular in the fragmentary **-sek̲ᵘui ᎩᎩᎭO*[** (J.1.4). It is possible that the dative singular of 'horse' also occurs as the second element of a compound name in **tᵘur̃ekᵘui ᎩᎩᎦOᛕᎩΔ** (J.14.1), but that form is more probably the dative singular of the group name 'for a man of the clan of Turos' ~ Celtiberian *turikum* 'of the family of Turos (?"Fourth")' (K.1.3). The first of these three is the strongest example of Tartessian **ekᵘu-** 'horse' and indicates that Tartessian was not a *p*-Celtic language, but preserved the Indo-European palatal consonant in

*$h_1ek\,'uos$ as a velar or labio-velar.

ek^{u}uŕine OᙗMᚁ𐤷ᛘＯ (J.4.1)   The first relevant point of context is that the same site also yielded stone J.4.2, of the same thickness and geological type as J.4.1. On J.4.2 a fragmentary line of Tartessian signs was accompanied by the relief image of a woman, viewed from the back, wearing what appears to be a Greek helmet and riding a large horse side-saddle. In other words, what looks like the word 'horse' **ek^{u}u-** is confirmed by the iconography.

See the note on **asune** above for the verbal context and proposed interpretation: **asune≡ uarb^{a}an ≡ek^{u}uŕine . . . b^{a}ara . . . oret^{o}o** 'As(s)un(n)ā and Ekurīg$_a$nī ("Horse Queen") . . . I [this burial] have carried in deliverance (< running under) to the highest destination'. **ek^{u}uŕine** is explained as a nominative/ accusative dual in co-ordination with **asune** (see above) or as the dative singular of a feminine divine name, probably ī-stem |Ek^{u}urīg$_a$nī|. This compound has an initial element *ek^uo-* 'horse' (Indo-European *$h_1ek\,'uos$ [Wodtko et al. 2008, 230–3]), cf. the consecration to DEIS EQVEVNV(BO(S)) 'equine gods' on a tombstone of the Roman period from north-west Spain and most significantly the epithet of the goddess Arentia at Sabugal (Guarda) EQVOTVLLAICENSI (Marco Simón 2005, 299–300). In Vettonian territory in the western Peninsula, Luján (2007, 255ff.) lists two names apparently based on 'horse': EQVAESVS, with the velar retained, and EPONEILVS, with *p* < Indo-European *k'u*. Cf. also Celtiberian *ekualakoś, ekualaku?* (Wodtko 2000, 104–5), possibly meaning 'warrior, knight' < 'horseman' (De Hoz 2007b, 200), cf. Middle Welsh *ebawl* 'foal'.

The second element of **ek^{u}uŕine** is probably Celtic *$*rīg_anī$* 'queen' (suiting the iconography of J,4.2), a reflex of Indo-European *$*h_3rēg\,'nih_2$* ∼ Sanskrit *rājñī* 'queen', Gaulish *rigani*, Cisalpine genitive *rikanas*, Old Irish *rígain*. The same element probably occurs also as a simplex dative/ablative plural **rinoeb^{o}o** ᚠᚾ𐤷Ｏ𐌇𐌖 (J.5.1). The complete compound name **ek^{u}uŕine** is reminiscent of the Gaulish and British divine name *Epona* 'Horse goddess', and note again EPONEILVS from Roman Vettonia, which appears to be a man's name based on *Epona*. The *Rhiannon* of the Welsh Mabinogi has often been interpreted as the functional equivalent of Epona in the light of her numerous equine associations. The accompanying image on stone J.4.2 is comparable to representations of Epona of the Roman Period. In the Roman dedications, the recurrent collocation EPONAE REGINAE 'to queen Epona [Horse Goddess]' (Jufer & Luginbühl 2001, 39–40) suggests that Eponā and the equestrian Rhiannon < *Rīgantonā might both continue the function and myth of an earlier *Ekuo-rīg(a)nī. It is possible that Tartessian **rin-** 'queen' recurs in J.17.4 as instrumental plural in a compound **k^{e}enila-(*)rinb^{e}e** ＯᚱᙗMᑋ(*)ΛᚁᙗᚊＯ)ᛁ 'with/by the queens of the kindred'. Welsh *Rhiannon* and PIᚱANTIK on Gaulish coin legends point to the existence of a form *$*rigant-$* in both Gaulish and British.

Three regular linguistic factors explain why a notional Proto-Celtic *$Ek^{u}o$-$ríg_an\bar{i}$ should appear as Tartessian ek^{u}uŕine. (1) The Indo-European syllabic nasals *$\underset{.}{n}$ and *$\underset{.}{m}$ continued to be represented as single nasal phonemes in Tartessian, rather than an and am as in the other early Celtic languages, wherever this was permitted by phonotactic constraints. This treatment of the syllabic nasals is an archaism, one of the few in which Tartessian evidence carries implications for the reconstruction of Proto-Celtic. Therefore, Proto-Celtic *$ríg_an\bar{i}$ contained only two syllables, continuing Proto-Indo-European *$h_3r\bar{e}g\,'nih_2$. It is possible that this archaism was a matter of traditional representation and a system of linguistic learning based on an inherited quantitative metrics, rather than the survival of the syllabic nasals as such. See *Tartessian 2* §§69, 74, 107–8. (2) Following a labial consonant and preceding an r followed by ĭ, Proto-Celtic *o became Tartessian u, for example omuŕik̲ᵃa[(J.16.2) < *$U(p)o$-$morik\bar{a}$, thus likewise ek^{u}uŕine < *$Ek^{u}o$-$ríg_an\bar{e}i$. See *Tartessian 2* §91. (3) The SW writing system could not represent a stop consonant followed by another consonant. Therefore, as |$_an$| in |-$ríg_an\bar{e}$| was not counted as containing a phonemic a, the writing system had no way to represent |g| before |$_an$|. It would be a common phonetic development if Celtic *$ríg\bar{n}i$ had developed as Tartessian /$r\bar{i}n\bar{i}$/ with loss of g before n. However, such an explanation is not necessary. The SW writing system does not allow us to see whether such a vocalization had happened or not.

Ἐλιβύργη, πόλις Ταρτησσοῦ 'Eliburgē, a city of Tartessos' is attributed to Hekataios (c. 500 BC) by Stephanus of Byzantium (see Freeman 2010, 313). The place-name appears to combine the well-attested Iberian word for town, il(l)i, ilti with a second element. Untermann (forthcoming) proposes that -βύργη is an Iberianization (explaining b < m) of the Tartessian element -murga as found in the ancient place-name *Lacimurga* near Badajoz. An alternative possibility is the tautological Celtic *brigā* 'hillfort, town' < earlier *$b^b rg\,^{'b}\bar{a}$, common in Ancient Celtic place-names, most especially in the Atlantic zone and interior of the Iberian Peninsula (see Parsons 2010). In this connection, it is worth considering the possibility that the place-names *Lacimurga* and *Lacobriga* reflect dialect variants of the same compound, or the former an Iberianization, both attested within the zone of the Tartessian inscriptions.

——elu-ꟼꓳ (J.7.6)   There is little basis for suggesting word divisions in this portion of the inscription: :elurear[, which is worn and fragmentary. Therefore, it is merely noted that the three signs elu resemble a widespread Celtic root, meaning 'many, numerous', common in the formation of Ancient Celtic names: for example, Celtiberian *Elu* (Botorrita), family name *Elokum*, Gaulish personal names *Eluontiu*, *Eluadius*, *Eluo-rix*, group names *Elu-sates*, *Helvetii*, *Helve-cones* (a subtribe of the Lugii in central Europe), Old Irish *il-* 'many, poly-', Welsh *elw-* 'profit, gain' (Delamarre 2003, 162): Indo-European *$*p\acute{e}lh_1us$* 'much'. If this identification is correct, Tartessian **elu-** would show characteristically Celtic loss of Indo-European *p-*.

—— ?emun ᗅᕼᗅO (J.7.8)   The latter half of this partially illegible inscription reads:]ebᵒo tᵉe·bᵃere naŕkᵉe|n emun tᵘurea≡iubᵃa. For this, the segmentation **naŕkᵉe nemun** is also possible. The formula word, clearly an Indo-European verb, is attested as both singular **naŕkᵉe** plural **naŕkᵉen**. In favour of the segmentation **naŕkᵉen emun**, see the Commentary on the inscription. At the end of the text, **tᵘurea≡iubᵃa** | *Tureā i̯ṵₐmā* | 'youngest daughter of Turos' is unproblematical. What comes after the usual formulaic closing, here **naŕkᵉe** or **naŕkᵉen**, would structurally be an amplification of what would already have been a complete formulaic epitaph. **tᵘurea≡iubᵃa** would therefore be either an elaboration on the identification of the deceased (the naming phrase at the beginning of the text is largely obliterated) or perhaps the naming of another person, of lower status, commemorated on the same stone. What is clearest about the segment **(n)emun** is that it shows an ending attested elsewhere in the corpus as genitive plural. **(n)emun** is therefore saying something further about the identity of **tᵘurea≡iubᵃa**, specifically the group to which she belongs. As there is no velar suffix -*Vkᵘun*, **(n)emun** is not a Hispano-Celtic kindred name. Turos's youngest daughter either belongs to a group called the **Nemoi* (see **nemun** below) or perhaps just 'of them' or 'of these men', taking **emun** as a genitive plural pronoun or demonstrative, the significance of which would have been clear had the beginning of the inscription survived and/or further cultural context was known to us. Possibly, 'of them' refers to nothing more than the name forms partially obliterated at the beginning of the inscription, so that the amplification offers more specificity about who is commemorated, which one 'of them'. 'Youngest daughter of Turos' identifies the deceased through her male kindred, and **emun** would be a masculine genitive plural pronoun; see Commentary on the inscription for comparanda.

—— en ᗅO (J.27.1)   See **śaen** below.

enb̲ᵉ ᑫᗅO (J.17.4)   The context : kᵉenilaꜛ⁽*⁾ꜛr̲in≡|≡b̲ᵉe:lin enb̲ᵉ·kᵃarne : presents several difficulties. We are relying on the 18th-century 'Album Cenáculo', and the drawing shows some unusual sign forms. None of the formula words occur. The text, however, appears to be complete, and the apparent naming phrase at the beginning shows useful congruence of the case ending in -**in**. It is, nevertheless, unusual that these forms appear to be accusatives singular. With **enb̲ᵉ** there is an obvious anomaly in that the third sign as read anticipates a following **e** O which is absent. The easiest remedies would be either to insert the missing vowel, i.e.

enbᵉe, or to assign ⟨ a syllabic value, i.e. **enbe**. Either way, the phonetics would be | *embe* |. If we take **enbᵉe·kᵃarne** as a word or close compound, the regular Tartessian lowering rule of Proto-Celtic *i before *ă* should apply (*Tartessian 2* §78); therefore, an earlier *embi is possible. Celtiberian and Gaulish have a preverb and preposition *ambi-*, with a basic meaning 'around, on both sides of'. It corresponds to Old Irish *imb·*, *imm·*, Welsh *am-* and reflexive *ym-* < Indo-European *h₂ent-bʰi, *h₂nt-bʰi. If **enbᵉ** can go back to an earlier *embi, as explained, could that reflect the Proto-Celtic preverb and preposition *ambi? We have no examples in the corpus of a**NT**ⁱi, i.e. **a** followed by a nasal, followed by a stop, followed by an **i**. But there are forms like **lakᵉentⁱi** (J.53.1) and **lakⁱin↑i** (J.12.4) with **e** or **i** in that position. If [l]**akᵃatⁱi** (J.10.1) belongs to the same paradigm as either or both of **lakᵉentⁱi** and **lakⁱin↑i**, then Proto-Celtic *ăNTi became Tartessian e**NT**ⁱi or i**NT**ⁱi, which is not at all an unusual phonetic change, cf. Old Irish *imb·*, *imm·* < *ambi. The byforms **lebᵒo-iire** (MdC) and **linbᵒo-ire** (J.11.2) for | *Lɪmo-ịịrē* | indicate that *e* and *i* fell together before | *m* |, which again is not an unusual phonetic development. The likelihood of such sound changes in Tartessian opens possibilities for the interpretation of the form **kⁱinbᵃai↑ⁱi** (J.3.1) and the south-western names *Cimbii* in Livy (28.37) and *Cempsi* in the *Ora Maritima* of Avienus. In summary, then, it is not impossible that Tartessian **enbᵉ** stands for | *ɪmbe* | < *ₐmbi. This provisional proposal entails a sequence of sound changes: first *ₐmbi > *embi, then *embi-karne > *embe-karne. *em > * *ɪm* could occur either after the first change (so *embi > * *ɪmbi*) or the second (*embe-karne > * *ɪmbe-karne*).

enbᵉ·kᵃa|rne Ο⅄ꟼ| ⋀⋀◁⅄Ο (J.17.4) General features of the context were discussed for the previous item **enbᵉ**. In the final sequence of a good-sized complete inscription, a verb would be expected more than a name. From that starting point, **enbᵉ·kᵃa|rne** looks more like the past tense formula word *-bᵃare* than the present-marked formulaic closing **naŕkᵉentⁱi**. **tᵉe·ro-bᵃare** explained as 'has carried away' has to do with what has happened to the deceased and the resulting present state of the remains in the grave. If **enbᵉ·kᵃa|rne** is expected to fill a similar syntactic and logical slot in the statement, then etymology suggests that **enbᵉ·kᵃa|rne** conveys something like '[this burial] has put a stone cairn around Genilaris Belis'. See further **kᵃa|rne** below.

——**-er-** ꟼΟ, **er-bᵉeŕi** ⅄ꟼΟ◁ꟼΟ (J.10.1) This sequence in the middle of this long and complete inscription has few close parallels in the corpus: **o↑erbᵉe|ŕi : leoinea|rbᵃari|e**. What is closest is **ar·bᵉieŕitᵘu** *or* **ar·bᵉieŕi** (J.12.3), on which see above, suggesting that a segmentable **er·bᵉeŕi** should be isolated here. That looks like a preverb + verb, as does the example from J.12.3. The usual formula words are absent from J.10.1, but **ar·bᵃarie** (on which see above) does look like the recurrent **tᵉe·ro-bᵃare** '[this grave/death] has carried away' with a different preverb. : **leoine** as a probable name is thus isolatable in the middle. From there, note that **ar·bᵉieŕitᵘu** or **ar·bᵉieŕi**, **er·b̲ᵉeŕi**, and **ar·bᵃarie** could all be forms of the same compound verb ~ Old Welsh *arber* 'use', Greek περιφέρω 'carry around'. However, **er·b̲ᵉeŕi** differs in the vowel of the preverb. One possibility is that it is in fact a different preverb, going with Old Irish *íar, er* 'after(wards)', rather than *air, ar, er* 'before, in front of', in which case there may be an intended contrast of direction as well as tense between **er·b̲ᵉeŕi** and **ar·bᵃarie**, something like 'carries afterwards; has carried forwards'. On the other hand, if the contrast is only tense and this is expressed primarily by a vowel change in the root of the verb, a preverb with a weak or variable quality (**er/ar** < Indo-European **peri*) might have tended to vowel harmony with the verb stem to clarify the contrast. **b̲ᵉeŕi** |*berit*| could continue Indo-European **bʰereti* 'carries'. Other probable examples of Proto-Celtic *e* preceding *i* raised to Tartessian **i** include **iśiinkᵒolobᵒo** (J.1.1) < **eχskingolobo(s)* and **tᵘn↑ⁱitᵉsbᵃan** (J.53.1) < **tumetisₐmām* (cf. *Tartessian 2* §83.1).

≋aitᵘura Α٩ᚺ⋀ᛩΑ≋ (J.15.1)   The basic structure of the naming phrase **ᚦaitᵘura meleśae≡::≡bᵃaenae** appears to be a feminine *ā*-stem nominative singular name amplified by a feminine *ā*-stem nominative/accusative dual co-ordinative or *dvandva* compound. The phonetic value of the initial sign of **ᚦaitᵘura** is uncertain: probably |*Φaiturā*| or |*Haiturā*|; see Commentary on the inscription above. The Phoenician letter ≋ 'hē' was pronounced [h]. In SE script (Meridional) ≋ possibly represented *be*. In Iberian and Celtiberian script the value is usually *e*, probably reflecting the influence of Greek E. In the interpretation of the following example **ᚦatᵃaneat̲ᵉe** (which is in left-to-right orientation), **ᚦ** is in the position of Indo-European *p-*. If that interpretation is correct, ≋ would stand for a weak and unstable sound, which has already disappeared completely from most positions, thus in accord with standard defining criterion of the Celtic languages. Following this analysis, we expect that, had the name **≋aitᵘura** survived, it might be found in more recent Hispano-Celtic materials with the ≋- < **p-* completely gone. This prediction seems to be borne out. Inscriptions of the Roman Period from the western Peninsula are likely to represent forms of the same name: AETVRA ARQVI F., AETVRA ALVQI F., also the corresponding masculine form C(AIVS) IVLIVS AETVRVS SOLICVM, MARCVS A[E]TVRI, and probably a genitive plural family name in AEM(ILIO) ELAVO ETVRICO(N). Note also AETARA (examples from the collection of Vallejo 2005).

A further possibility is that **≋aitᵘura** is related to the ancient district name *Baeturia* (and numerous related forms). Note the analogous derivation of Palaeo-hispanic personal names based on the district name *Asturia* and group name *Astures*: ASTVR⟨V⟩S TVREI F., ASTVRI, ATILIVS ASTVR, ASTVRIO LOGEI

F., ASTVRIO TRITI F., [AS]TVRIO CL[OVTI], ASTVRIAE CAPITONIS F.
MATERNAE (Vallejo 2005, 188). Iberian -baitura (of unknown meaning) also
possibly goes with Romanized Baeturia, Aetura, &c., as well as Tartessian ᴚaitᵘura.
Such a pattern would be comparable to that of the Palaeohispanic place-name
Bletisama (modern Ledesma) and Celtiberian Letaisama all from *(p)letisₐmā 'broadest'. In other words, the pattern could be one of languages in close contact,
losing p from their sound systems and accommodating in various ways inherited
names with p shared between more than one linguistic community. Following
this argument, ᴚaitᵘura would mean something like 'Lady of the Baeturians'
and commences either with the phonetically weakened reflex of an original p-, or
the initial sound of a borrowed name in which the Proto-Celtic reflex of p- has
been substituted for a similar foreign sound, appearing as B- in Latin Baeturia,
&c. A tentative translation for ᴚaitᵘura meleśae≡::≡bᵃaenae is accordingly:
'Lady of the Baeturians, sweet woman and wife'.

   A second possibility, but one that does not explain ᴚ or the suffix, is that
ᴚaitᵘura goes with the numerous examples of the Western Hispano-Celtic or
Lusitanian type of AVITVS from Montehermoso, Cáceres (Búa 2000, 552–3),
AVITVS ARCONIS F. from Conimbriga, genitive AVITI from Ávila (Sánchez
Moreno 1996, 133), feminine BINAREAE TRITI F. AVITAE from Idanha-a-Velha,
Castelo Branco, the genitive plural group name AVITA[E]CON from Cantabria
(Untermann 1980b, 375). See Vallejo 2005, 201–5, for many more examples. These
Hispanic forms are probably related to ogam Irish AUITTORIGES, Late Romano-
British AVITORIA on the stone from Eglwys Gymyn, Carmarthenshire. Note that
-ORIGES and -ORIA represent the second element (ríχs 'king') of a compound
name and are not equivalent to the suffix in Baeturia. Proto-Celtic *u̯ is regularly
assimilated to a following i in Tartessian, for example (i)ire | i̯irē | 'men, heroes'
< *u̯iroi (J.7.2, J.11.2, J.52.1, MdC; see Tartessian 2 §§97.1–3); therefore, Tartessian
aitᵘ- might stand for earlier *au̯it-.

ᴚatᵃaneatᵉe ᴚAXAᴦOAHO (J.12.1) | φataneatē | or | hataneatē | 'to the winged
   one ((p)ataniatis)', interpreted as the qualifying second element of a two-word
   epithet mubᵃa...ᴚatᵃaneatᵉe; see the Commentary on the inscription above.
   Compare Old Breton attanoc 'winged creature', plural atanocion, Old Welsh hataned
   'wings', Early Welsh edein, plural adaneb 'wings' < Indo-European *ptn̥- : *pet(e)r-
   'wing, feather', with characteristically Celtic loss of Indo-European p, and Celtic
   agent suffix -i̯atis. On the sign ᴚ and its possible phonetic values, see the previous
   item. See further Tartessian 2 §§18, 98, 103.

Gargoris 'Savage king': in an excellent example of a myth of cultural origins, Justin's
   epitome of the Philippic Histories of Trogus Pompeius (44.4) tells of the pre-
   agricultural honey collector Gargoris, first king of the Cu[n]etes (see Κυνητες

below) who dwelt in the forest of the Tartessians (*saltus uero Tartessiorum, in quibus Titanas bellum aduersus deos gessisse proditur, incoluere Cu[n]etes, quorum rex uetustissimus Gargoris mellis colligendi usum primus inuenit*). For a full text and translation of the tale, see Freeman 2010, 316–18. It is widely recognized that *Gargoris* reflects Celtic *Gargo-ríχs*. For the first element, cf. Old Irish *garg* 'fierce, savage' and the Gallo-Roman place-name *Gargarius* (Delamarre 2003, 175–6). Compare also the woman's name *Gargenna/Gergenna* from Abertura, Cáceres (Luján 2007, 256), but probably not the form **kᵉeŕkᵃaŕ**[ ]i↑ in J.18.3. **aibᵘuris**[(J.3.1) and **ariariśe** (J.10.1) = **ariaris-se** are probably Celtic *ríχs* names, but due to the limitations of the SW script, it is not possible to tell whether they preserve [χ] before [s] or not. Similarly, with **anbᵃatⁱia** (J.16.2), the orthography could represent either |*Ambaχtiā*| or |*Ambatiā*| anticipating later Hispano-Celtic AMBATVS. The place-name Οὐξαμα *Uxama* (< *U(p)sₐmā* 'Highest') as spelled in Greek and Roman letters indicates that Proto-Celtic [χ] was not simply lost from all positions in all Hispano-Celtic languages. On the other hand, Justin's spelling *Gargoris*, which would presumably reflect the Greek of Trogus Pompeius on this point, indicates that Tartessian lost χ before *s*. As to the quality of the composition vowel, **lebᵒoiire** (MdC) < *Lemo-u̯iroi* shows is preserved between a labial consonant and a lost Proto-Celtic *u̯. **aibᵘuris**[possibly shows *o* raised to **u** between a labial conosnant and -*ríχs*. **ariariśe** < *Ario-ríχs+se* shows the composition vowel reduced, or at any rate unrounded, to **a**. We might therefore expect *kᵃaŕkᵃaris in native script (see *Tartessian 2* §73.1). However, given the difference of date, medium, and transmission factors, one would not expect the dialect features of Justin's Hispano-Celtic names to agree exactly with those reflected in the SW corpus.

——(?)**ibᵒoiion** ↰‡↳↳‡🗎↳∫ or (?)**ibᵒonion** (J.4.1)   This sequence of signs begins this long inscription. The sign of uncertain value at the beginning could alternatively belong to the end of the text, which forms a complete circuit. It is possible that that unusual sign merely marks the beginning and ending of the text and has no phonetic value, though it would be a unique example for such a practice. A further uncertainty in the reading is whether the fifth sign is **i** ↳ or **n** ↳. A range of segmentations and grammatical analyses are possible: (?)**ibᵒo iion** with the first element resembling a dative/ablative plural, (?)**ibᵒoi ion** with the first element possibly a locative singular (?'in Ippo- [the town]'), or (?)**ibᵒon ion** in which the first element could be an accusative singular or nominative/accusative neuter. The following segment, **iion** or **ion**, conforms to the expected form of the accusative singular masculine relative pronoun in Tartessian, but since the statement is incomplete it is impossible to say with certainty whether (**i**)**ion** can be construed in this way. In any event, (?)**ibᵒoiion** does not suggest any obvious comparison with known Palaeohispanic or Celtic names apart from the -*ip(p)o*-place-names of the south-western Peninsula. If that meaning for this form could be confirmed, it would be significant to find this typically 'Tartessian' name type (in the historical sense) within the SW corpus, thus demonstrating the correctness of calling the language of the inscriptions 'Tartessian'. iibᵃan̲ (J.5.1, see below) is a somewhat more likely example of -ip(p)o- in a SW text. Be that as it may, the majority of the lost inscription J.4.1, as is known from the surviving photograph, is unusual enough, and of such extraordinarily high quality, as to raise uncertainty over assigning it to the most common funerary category. The formula word **uarbᵃan** is present. And **bᵃara** 'I [this monument] have carried' may be seen as taking the place of the usual **tᵉe·ro-bᵃare** '[this grave] has carried away'. But unless **naŕkᵉentⁱi** has completely and cleanly disappeared into the gap before the end, the usual closing is wholly absent. The text closes instead with **oretºo** (probably 'of deliverance' < *u(p)o-retosi̯o).

An alternative possibility is that **ibºo** is a dative/ablative plural personal pronoun or demonstrative; cf. the Gaulish personal pronouns of the Larzac inscription: 3rd feminine genitive plural *eianom*, 3rd singular nominative feminine *eia*, 3rd plural feminine instrumental plural *eiabi*, possibly genitive singular *esias* (Delamarre 2003, 161).

ii ꓩꓩ (J.1.1)   In the context **lokºobºo꞊niirabºo . . . kᵃakⁱiśiinkºolobºo ii tᵉe·ro-bᵃare**, the segment **ii** can be isolated between an ablative/dative plural ending, in concord with the two datives/ablatives plural that open the inscription, and the recurrent formula word **tᵉe·ro-bᵃare**. On the other hand, in the case of **naŕkᵉenii** (J.2.1, J.21.1), **n(a)ŕkᵉenii** (J.11.1), **[naŕ]kᵉenii** (J.19.1), this two-sign sequence is clearly a variant of **naŕkᵉentⁱi** (J.12.1, J.16.1, J.17.2, J.18.1, J.19.2) and therefore **-ii** is part of the verbal ending, as is also probably the case with **bᵃareii** (J.5.1). Standing before **tᵉe·ro-bᵃare**, which is probably a compound verb, **ii** could possibly be another prepositional preverb (? < Indo-European *hᵢepi) or a case form of the relative pronoun *i̯o- or a demonstrative. Definite conclusions about such a minimal segment would require more evidence, such as further examples in clearly parallel contexts.

iibᵃan̲ ꓩꓩꓯꓤ or **iibᵃau̲** ꓩꓩꓯꓤ (J.5.1)   The form occurs as the penultimate word of a complete, and mostly readable, but unusual text: **sabºoi : ist̲ᵃa|ibºo rinoebºo |anakᵉenak̲ᵉ:e|ibºo iibᵃan̲ bᵃareii**. The bulk is taken up with a sequence of three datives/ablatives plural. The initial sequence **sabºoi** is more easily paralleled and etymologized as a season name in the locative singular ('in summer') than as a personal name. If so, there is no named deceased at the opening of the text, or anywhere else, as would indicate that this is another of the funerary inscriptions. Arguably, there is a highly compressed variant of the usual closing formula. So, in the place of **tᵉe·ro-bᵃare naŕkᵉentⁱi**, there is **bᵃareii**, i.e. the first verb shorn of its preverbs, but with the primary ending (**-ii**) of the verb that usually closes the statement. **iibᵃa̲n̲** is inflected like the formula word **uar(n)bᵃan** 'to the highest destination', so probably it likewise signifies where the commemorated ritual 'has taken' (**bᵃare**) someone or something. By sense, the Hispano-Celtic place-names Ούαμα, *Uxama*, and the extremely common *-brigā* would all mean something very much like Tartessian **uar(n)bᵃan**, to which the first two are etymologically related. The *-ip(p)o-* (also *-ipa*) names of the south-western Peninsula function like *-brigā* in identifying major towns. So **iibᵃan** here could mean 'to the town, the high or important place, the community'. The whole inscription might then commemorate a seasonal civic offering: **sabᵒoi : ist̲ᵃa̲|ibᵒo rinoeb̲ᵒo |anak̲ᵉenak̲ᵉ:e|ibᵒo iibᵃa̲n̲ bᵃare̲ii** 'In the summer, for these indwelling queens [i.e. goddesses], [this ritual stone] has now borne [offerings] to the ?important place/town.'

The distribution of the *-ip(p)o-* names is densest in the region south of the SW inscriptions, and *-ip(p)o-* is not found compounded with Celtic elements. They also appear to be non-Indo-European, and surely non-Celtic, phonologically. As the language of the Iberian inscriptions also lacks *p*, it is not at all clear which pre-Roman language was the source of this place-name element. The geographic distribution of the *-ip(p)o-*-names has been regarded, not implausibly, as reflecting the extent of the political power of Tartessos (e.g. Almagro-Gorbea & Torres 2009; Almagro-Gorbea 2010). But as linguistic evidence their import is unclear. The form lacks an etymology and does not coincide with the distribution of the place-names, personal names, or inscriptions of any known language. **iibᵃa̲n̲** might therefore be viewed as a loanword within the language of the SW inscriptions. Another possibility is that **iibᵃan** is native vocabulary, a feminine singular pronoun |*iman*|. But a borrowing of non-Indo-European *-ip(p)o-* might be seen as more likely, because the regular Tartessian lowering rule (*Tartessian 2* §78) would be expected to give ****ebᵃan** |*eman*| < *imām in inherited vocabulary. With *-ip(p)o-*, on the other hand, the lowering might not have operated across the double *pp* or simply have taken place previously and ceased to operate by the time of the borrowing. However, this may not be a valid consideration. The byforms **lebᵒo-iire**(MdC), **linbᵒo-ire** (J.11.2, *Tartessian 2* §108) indicate that the distinction between /*e*/ and /*i*/ could be lost before /*m*/, which is a common phonetic development. If so, the effect of the following nasal would have obscured the output of the lowering rule. In other words, **iibᵃan** |*ɪman*| <* |*eman*| < *imām is possible.

ion   This sequence of three signs occurs in contexts where it might stand for the relative pronoun accusative singular 'that, which, whom', cf. Celtiberian *iom*. But syntactically it would be functioning as an enclitic in these examples, like the Gaulish uninflected *io*, e.g. DVGIIONTIIO 'who serve' (3rd plural). Thus, ?relative 1st singular perfect **bᵃarua-ion** {ΛΡΉΛΝᵛ≠Ν |*bār(ū)a-i̯on*| 'whom I [this

grave] have received' (J.7.9); ?suffixed relative in **kªaŕner-ion** 'whom they have
entombed in a stone monument' or 'who is entombed' (J.7.2), then possibly once
again in **kªa[ŕn]ir-ion** (J.1.3). Note also **ibᵒoiion** (J.4.1) above.

-ir ⟨⟩ (J.11.3), **-iir ⟨⟩** (J.22.1) probably stands for |*iir*| 'man, hero' nominative
singular as the second element of the compounds **ooŕoir ⟨⟩** (J.19.2),
soloir (J.11.3) and **uarbᵒoiir ⟨⟩** (J.22.1) < **uiros* ~ Celtiberian VIROS,
Old Irish *fer*, Old Welsh *gur*. Examples of Lusitanian and/or Hispano-Celtic
personal names probably or possibly based on **uiros* are extremely numerous.
Unlike the Tartessian examples, they consistently preserve the initial labial sound,
mostly written V- with one example of -B, indicating a pronunciation [-β].
The following are from the collection of Vallejo (2005): VIRIVS ALLV[QVI]
F., VIRIO TANGINI, VIRIVS COPORVS CEL(TI) F., F. VIRIVS *or* XIRIVS
CALATIVS, VIRIVS CAESSAI F. LEMAVS EODEM (ERITAECO), L. VIRIVS
RVFINVS, [---]VIRIO, VIRIVS... FVSCO, C. VIRIV FRONTONI FLAM EX
LVCENS, C. VIRI FRONTONIS FLAMINIS, C. VIRIVS C. F. GAL. NEPOS,
... VIRIAE, VI.RI.AMO, VIRIAE M. F. SEVERAE, VIRIA FLAVIN[A] FIL.
C. VIRI FRONTONIS FLAMINIS, VIRIAE ACTE, VIRIA ACTE, VIRRIA
M[-]N[-], VIRRIA *or* VIBBIA SE[---], VIRIATVS, VIRIATI LOVESI F.,
VIRIATVS, VIRIATV(S), VIRIATVS, BASSVS VIRIATI F., VIRIATVS TANCINI
F., RVTILIVS VI[RIA?]TVS, ARQVIVS VIRIAT[I], [C]ATVRO VIRIATI,
BVTVRRA BIRIATI FILIA, VIRIATIS LIBERTVS, VIRIATIS SEVERI F.,
[LOB]ESAE VIRIATIS (VIRIATVS), REBVRRVS VIRIATIS INTERAMICVS,
C. VIRIACIVS VETTO, [---]VIE VIRILLIO, ARANTA VIRANI FI., VIRINIVS,
VIR(ONVS), [V]IRON[I], CASIA VIRONI F., AMAENIA VIRONI F.
TRITECV(M), TRITIANVS, VIRONI SERV., CAVELIA VI[R]ONI, VIRONVVS
TOVTONI F., VIRONO TAVR[IN]OR(VM) DOIDERI F., VIRON(O) CAES?
F.?, BLOENAE VIRONI, [FL]ACCVS VIRON[I], IVLIA AMBATA? VIRO[NI]
F., SEGIVS VIRONO MATIENI F., AVSCVS BOVTIVS VIRONI F., AIA
ORIGENA VIRONI F., VIRONO CAELENI, VIRONO CAELENI, VIRON[ ],
VIRONO SEGISAMI F. VADINIENSIS, VIRONO TA[---], VIRONO TVRONI
F., M. VIRONIO SEMONI VAL. MIROBRIGENO, CILLI VIRONIGI ARENNI
F., [PEN]TIO VIR[ONI]CVN CA[DI F.], NEGALO VIRONIGORV(M),
OCULATIO CANGILI F. SEGISAMO(NENSI) GENTE VIROMENIGORVM,
TVROLIVS VIROTI?, TONGIVS VIROTI, CANTABER VIROTI F. NATIONE...,
Uiriaskum, Uiroku, [AE]CIVS VEROBLI. I. F. / MILES CORTI(S) TERTIA(E)
LVCE(N)S(IVM), ADRONO VEROTI F. Further probable forms of this word
in the SW corpus include: **ooŕoire** (J.19.1), **ire** (J.7.2, J.52.1), **iru** (J.7.9, J.12.1,
J.23.1), **lebᵒo-iire** (MdC), **linbᵒo-ire** (J.11.2), **oira-uarbªa(n)** (J.1.2), which see.
All of the attested forms are invariably written with **r** rather than **ŕ**.

The loss of the final syllable in the nominative singular would of course be reminiscent of Latin *uir* < Old Latin VIROS and may reflect a common tendency across a wide dialect area of western Indo-European. A possible analogical factor favouring such a development was the currency of the synonymous inherited *r*-stem **ni(i)ra-** 'man, leader'; see below.

ire O𐤉𐤌 (J.7.2, J.52.1) probably occurs as an isolatable word on its own, rather than as the second element of a compound, only once where this segmentation is relatively clear, at the end of the nearly complete text **bᵒotᵒo§ar**[|]***aa kᵃaŕner-ion ire**. It occurs possibly, but not certainly, as a separate word a second time in the fragment]**ire abᵃre la**[, which had probably originally been part of a long text. If we take **kᵃaŕner-ion** as related to the Cisalpine Gaulish preterite KARNITU 'entombed, made a cairn/grave (mound)', this would of course suit what is most probably a funerary context. Therefore, the ending and suffix of **kᵃaŕner-ion** may be construed as the Indo-European 3rd plural active perfect: 'they have entombed, they have made a burial mound/cairn'. **-ion** would then be the masculine singular accusative of the relative pronoun, Celtiberian *iom*: thus, '[the man] whom they have entombed'. Regular Tartessian sound laws allow **ire** to stand for nominative plural |i̦irḗ| derived from **u̯iroi* 'men, heroes'. The initial glide of **u̯i-* regularly assimilated its articulation to the following palatal vowel to become |i̦i-|. On Proto-Celtic **u̯* in Tartessian, see *Tartessian 2* §§97.1–3. The SW corpus reflects extensive simplification of Proto-Celtic diphthongs, including examples of **oi* > **e**; see *Tartessian 2* §94. Thus, a general interpretation for the epitaph can be offered: '**bᵒotᵒo§ar**[. . . [the man] whom the men/heroes have entombed [here]'.

The same word **i(i)re** 'men, heroes' probably recurs as the second element of a compound in **linbᵒoire** (J.11.2) and **lebᵒoiire** (MdC), both |Lɪmo-i̦irḗ| < **Lemo-u̯iroi* 'elm+men'; see below. The signs **ire** also occur on a fragment of a vessel from the 5th or 4th century BC from Córdoba (De Hoz 1989, 555), though this may be coincidental.

iru 𐤉𐤉𐤌 (J.7.9, J.12.1, J.23.1) occurs in the latter two instances immediately preceding an element with which it is evidently in marked inflexional agreement: **iru≡alkᵘu** and **iru≡{u}arbᵘu**. And both contexts appear to be naming phrases; see below. In these, **iru** is interpreted as the phonological outcome of **u̯irū* 'man, hero' (nominative/accusative dual, although dative singular would also be possible), showing the regular Tartessian sound change in which the glide **u̯* assimilates to the articulation of the following front vowel, to become |i̦irū|; see *Tartessian 2* §§97.1–3. J.7.9 is incomplete.

iru≡alkᵘu 𐤉𐤌𐤀��H𐤉𐤉𐤌 |i̦irū≡Alkū| (J.12.1) begins a complete and legible inscription. The text contains two elements of the recurrent formula in their usual forms, **naŕk^eent^ii** and **t^ee·ro·b^aare** (see Appendix C). Therefore, it is expected, in this context, that **iru≡alk^uu** names the deceased in an epitaph. As a matter of the phonological derivation of the repeated case ending **-u**, the nominative/accusative dual of an *o*-stem would regularly provide Proto-Celtic **-ū* < Later Indo-European **-ō*. Syntactically, this would imply a co-ordinative or *dvandva* compound in the dual, like Vedic *mitrā̆≡varuṇā* 'Mitra and Varuna', an example which also implies the sense of one god in two aspects. Thus, **iru≡alk^uu** would be grammatically 'the hero and Alkos', though probably logically and factually singular 'the hero Alkos'. This co-ordinative could function either as the object of **t^ee·ro·b^aare** 'has carried away the hero Alkos' and/or as the subject of **naŕk^eent^ii** 'the hero ⟨and⟩ Alkos now lie here'. The 3rd plural **naŕk^eent^ii** has an expressed subject, the nominative plural demonstrative **sie:**. **t^ee·ro·b^aare** 'has carried away' is transitive, but lacks any overt direct object (except possibly a concealed accusative pronoun **e(d)* 'it' or **e(n)* 'him' infixed into **t^ee·** (cf. *Tartessian 2* §§34.4, 93)). Therefore, I take **iru≡alk^uu** as the accusative object of **t^ee·ro·b^aare**: 'she has carried the hero ⟨and⟩ Alkos away', making the statement one complete sentence with a second brief sentence from the formulaic language (**sie: naŕk^eent^ii**) embedded between the *dvandva* compound naming the deceased, as a preposed direct object, and the rest.

iru≡{u}arb^uu i el ⌐O⋎4⋈⋈9A[ ]49⋎ | *i̯irū̆≡u̯ar_amū̆ iel* | (J.23.1). If one takes the third sign **u 4** as doing 'double duty', that gives a reading with two forms recurring elsewhere in the corpus: **iru** also in J.12.1 and **uarb^uu** or **uarb^uui** as a masculine case form of the superlative adjective that recurs as a feminine singular accusative **uar(n)b^aan** 'to the highest destination' in the formula (see Appendix C). On balance, exact formal agreement is more likely, thus segmenting as **iru≡{u}arb^uu** rather than **iru≡{u}arb^uui**. The latter would seem to involve an incongruous variation in the representation of the *o*-stem dative singular ending. **iru≡{u}arb^uu** | *i̯irū̆≡u̯ar_amū̆* | < **u̯irū̆≡u(p)er_amū̆* can be interpreted as a co-ordinative compound in the nominative/accusative dual, like **iru≡alk^uu** above. These same two elements recur, with presumably the same sense 'supreme man' i.e. 'lord, chief', in Celtiberian VIROS VERAMOS (Peñalba de Villastar). They recur in the SW corpus, in what is probably a close compound, as **uarb^oiir** | *u̯ar_amo-i̯ir* | (J.22.1) < **u(p)er_amo-u̯iros*. These collocations evidently reflect a common inheritance of Hispano-Celtic honorific diction. They probably convey a special ideological and/or sociological significance, i.e. a specific and well understood status within the social order and legal system.

The segment **-iel** follows, which is unparalleled within the SW corpus. A borrowing of the Western Semitic *el* signifying the highest god would make sense in the context (in which the co-ordinative subject takes a plural verb): **b^eet^iisai t^ee(-)e· b^aarent^ii iru≡{u}arb^uu i el naŕrk^ee:n: uśnee** '[A grave] for Betisa, whom the lord (VIROS VERAMOS) god has now carried away. They remain in the highest place (Uxamā)'. In this interpretation the i- of -iel would be a non-etymological glide. It is not unlikely that the distinction between the dative singular ending -ui and nominative/accusative dual -u was neutralized before e- as a simple matter of phonetics.

——isakᵃaoe O‡ΛΛA‡Ϻ (J.24.1)   Because of the uneven arrangement of the lines of text and poor state of survival of the inscribed portion of the stone, it is not possible to establish the context or confirm the segmentation of this form. A name or a common noun with an adjectival suffix -āko- would be consistent with the possibility that this is a Celtic name. A connection with the British and Primitive Irish TOVISACI 'leader, prince' (genitive) is not impossible. However, in a Tartessian cognate of TOVISACI we would expect lowering of short i to e in a syllable before a as well, perhaps, as the sign ś which can occur for strong sibilants. If the form ends as -akᵃaoe, |-ākaoē| that is probably an adjectival formation in the feminine, dative or locative singular or nominative/accusative dual.

istᵃa̲|ibᵒo ←Χ‡Ϻ | →Ν̃Θ‡ (J.5.1) occurs as the first of three datives/ablatives plural istᵃa̲|ibᵒo rinoeb̲ᵒo |anak̲ᵉenak̲ᵉ:e|ibᵒo, which determines the word division and supports taking this form as a demonstrative modifying the following noun phrase 'for these indwelling queens'. Compare the Celtiberian demonstrative pronoun accusative singular feminine stam, also iste (for which there are various interpretations, see Untermann 1997, 506), Lepontic iśos, Latin iste.

   iśtᵘ[u[Ⴟ]ΔϺϺ (J.7.4) is possibly a further instance of this demonstrative, meaning 'for this (man)' |istūi|. However, the inscription is extremely short and fragmentary, so a secure interpretation is impossible. Note also śtᶦaś*tᵃa*t̲ᵃa̲ ΑΧ*ΑΧ*ϺΑⵜϺ (J.11.4), but the reading and segmentation of this sequence are also uncertain, and they might alternatively be Romanized as śb̲ᶦaś*tᵃa*t̲ᵃa̲.

iubᵃa Α⸮ЧϺ (J.7.8), iobᵃa[Ν̃‡⸮Α[(J.16.2)   On the context ( )omuŕikᵃa[≡]anbᵃatᶦia≡iobᵃa[and its interpretation as |Q̟omurikā Amba(χ)tiā iȭₐmā| 'woman of the kindred of Q̟omurios and youngest daughter of Amba(χ)tos', see]anbᵃatᶦia above. In the light of the close parallelism of the collocations tᵘurea iubᵃa and anbᵃatᶦia iobᵃa[, the most likely interpretation is that iubᵃa and iobᵃa[are feminine singular ā-stem adjectives in agreement with feminine singular i̲ā-stem adjectives of relationship, meaning 'female relative of Turos' and 'female relative of Amba(χ)tos', thus based on two well-attested Hispano-Celtic men's names, probably specifically patronymics with 'daughter of' being the default relationship in the absence of any indication otherwise. In this context, iubᵃa and iobᵃa[are most easily interpreted as |i̲ū̲ₐmā| < |i̲ȭₐmā|, the cognate of Old Irish *oam* and Middle Welsh *ieu(h)af* 'youngest' < *$\ast \bar{\imath}ou_a m\bar{a}$*. On the phonology of these forms, see *Tartessian 2* §94. As the youngest daughters of Turos and Amba(χ)tos, their identification formulas contrast with **robᵃa** | *ro$_a$mā* | (J.18.1, Moura) 'foremost woman' = 'first-born daughter of'. The difficult form **iou⟨tⁱ⟩bᵉa:i** ᛦ|ᚨᚲ(Ⓓ)ᛇ╫ᛦ (J.7.6) possibly goes with these.

A different—and I now think less likely—possibility was previously proposed. There were two well-known native Numidian kings, father and son, named *Iuba* (Ιόβας, Ιουβας in Greek sources) in the period *c.* 60 BC–AD 23. The younger king was relocated westward to Mauretania as a Roman client. Their name is therefore presumably Numidian (Palaeo-Berber) and suited an aristocratic male. Tartessian **iubᵃa** and **iobᵃa**[could reflect a borrowing of this name. Iuba I's kingdom was not far from Utica and Carthage.

——(kᵃakⁱ)iśiinkᵒolobᵒo ╪☐╪1╪⊠ᛦᛦᛦᛗᛦᛩᚠᚠᚨᛚ (J.1.1)   What is most certain about this form is that it is inflected as a dative/ablative plural. Therefore, it syntactically refers back to, or is at least parallel to, the first two words of the inscription **lokᵒobᵒo niirabᵒo** 'for the divine Lugoues [and] the chief men'. What precedes that case ending resembles the Gaulish personal name ΕΣΚΕΓΓΟΛΑΤΙ (genitive, Les Pennes-Mirabeau), also ESCENCOLATIS in Roman script (Aubagne) for EXCINGOLATIS /*e(χ)skiŋgolatis*/ (Raybould & Sims-Williams 2007, 59), EXCINGOMARVS (Raybould & Sims-Williams 2007, 59), feminine dative ΕΣΚΕΓΓΑΙ /*e(χ)skiŋgāi*/ (Gargas), and Iberianized Gaulish *eśkinke* (Untermann 1980a, 47). The basic sense of Celtic *$\ast e\chi skingos$* is 'hero, champion', thus a plausible amplification to a list commencing with gods and chief men. The preceding element might represent Celtic pronominal *$\ast k^u \bar{a} k^u o$-* 'all, everyone, whosoever' < *$\ast k^w \bar{o} k^w o$-* ~ Gaulish inflected forms *papon, papi, pape, papu*, Old Irish *cách*, Old Welsh *paup*, Old Breton *pop*, hence 'invoking all the heroes'. On the phonology, Tartessian ᛦ **i** is found for Proto-Celtic short *e* preceding a high vowel also in **ar·bᵉieŕituu** | *ar-bⁱeritū(d)* | 'let her carry on' (J.12.3) < *$\ast (p)ari$-beretūd* ~ Avestan *barətū* 'let him carry'. It can be seen from the Gaulish spellings that the Proto-Celtic -χsk- had been unstable and prone to simplification. Tartessian ᛗ **ś** can be used to represent a heavy or geminate *s*. The evidence of the Hispano-Celtic languages suggests that there was a deep-seated tendency to lose χ.

With such a long form and with few close parallels in the SW corpus, apart from the case ending, an alternative segmentation as **kᵃakⁱiśiin kᵒolobᵒo** may be considered. With such a word division, the first part would have some inexact Iberian parallels. The latter, again a dative/ablative plural, might be related to **kᵒoli̯on** (J.55.1) and/or]**k̲ᵒoloion** (Monte Novo do Castelinho).

kᵃaltᵉe ᚩᛟ1ᚨᛚ (J.1.1), **nira-kᵃaltᵉe** ᚩᛟ1ᚨᛚᚨᛩᛦᛦ (MdC)   The first, and I now think strongest, possibility is to understand these as locatives singular

|kaldē| 'in the grove, i.e. in the necropolis' and |nira-kaldē| 'in the grove of men/leaders' < *-kaldei ~ Old Irish caill 'wood, forest', Old Welsh celli, Old Cornish kelli, Gaulish place-names Caldis, Caldeniacum < Celtic *kaldi (Lexique, s.n. caill), Old English and Old Norse holt 'wood'. The Palaeohispanic group name Callaec(i)i may also belong here, as 'forest(-country) people', suiting Galicia, as suggested to me by Juan Luis García Alonso. That etymology is supported by the Callaecian personal name CALDAECVS, if that form is recognized as an archaic variant of the ethnonymic Callaecus (cf. Prósper 2011, 227), in which the original ld cluster has not yet been simplified. For possible examples of further forms with a similar sense in the SW corpus, note also **aliśne** 'in the place of alders' (J.11.4; see above) and especially **bᵃastᵉebᵘuŕoi** 'in the yew-wood of ?death/passing' (São Martinho), once again as part of a long and skilfully carved funerary statement. If we now read the Celtiberian family name kaltaikikos on a tessera from Osma, Soria (González Rodríguez 1986, 126) as kaldaikikos (Prósper 2011), that might also belong here.

A second possibility is to take **kᵃaltᵉe** and **nira-kᵃaltᵉe** as datives singular of an ā-stem group name with a notional nominative singular *kᵃaltᵃa or *kᵃaltᵃas. It could thus correspond to the ā-stem plural group names Greek Γαλάται Galátai and/or Latin Celtae. Note that some modern writers consider these often interchangeable Greek and Latin names to be of common origin (cf. Sims-Williams 1998, 22). McCone (2006) rejects this possibility. However, he suggests that another Latin synonym Gallus comes immediately from Etruscan *Kalde—thus similar phonetically to Celta and any possible Etruscan version of that—though ultimately, and plausibly, he derives both Gallus and Γαλάτης from a Celtic *galatis, meaning essentially 'fighter'. During the Roman Period, Celtius occurred frequently as a personal name in the western Iberian Peninsula and mostly in context with other Hispano-Celtic names, making the possibility of a learned borrowing from Latin less likely. Strabo (4.1.14) considered Κέλται, rather than Herodotus's Κελτοί, to be the oldest form of the name, agreeing with the Latin Celtae and Tartessian **kᵃaltᵉe** (if dative singular); he used the form Γαλάται himself. Herodotus locates the Κελτοί Keltoí 'Celts' beyond the Pillars of Hercules as neighbours of the Kunētes and writers of the Roman Period name peoples in the western Iberian Peninsula as belonging to the Κελτικοί Celtici. Following this possibility **nira-kᵃaltᵉe** (MdC) is possibly a compound, ?'for the Nerian Celt', in which the group names **nira-** and **kᵃaltᵉe** are again juxtaposed as in J.1.1.

Comparison made in this book's first edition between **kᵃaltᵉe** and the Lepontic kalite (probably a past-tense verb) is now effectively ruled out by the discovery of **nira-kᵃaltᵉe** at MdC, which appears clearly to be a nominal compound within a text otherwise well supplied with verbs.

]ḵᵃanan ᴎAᴎA(Λ)[|-ganan| or |-kanan| or]aanan ᴎAᴎA(A)[|Anan|
(J.9.1)   Short and fragmentary and with an uncertain reading, the form
nonetheless does resemble a feminine ā-stem accusative singular. Possibilities
include a name ending with the common Ancient Celtic element -ganā 'born of'
(Indo-European *ǵ′enh₁- 'beget a child, be born' [Wodtko et al. 2008, 136–9]).
For the second reading, a connection with the river name Anas (now Guadiana)
is possible. The feminine name Anna and masculine n-stem Anno are common in
Hispano-Celtic contexts in inscriptions of the earlier Roman Period: for example,
ANNA MADVGENA F., ANNAE CALEDIGE, VALERIO ANNONI LVGVADICI
F. VXAMENSIS (Vallejo 2005, 141–9).

ḵᵃa | rne Oᴎꟼ | A)l occurs in enḇᵉ·ḵᵃa | rne Oᴎꟼ | A)lᑰᴎO (J.17.4), on which there
is a note above. The reading is doubtful, but the form and its position in the
statement favour interpreting ḵᵃarne as a 3rd person perfect verb, taking the place
of the formulaic bᵃare and having to do with the disposition of the deceased.
Therefore, an etymological connection may be considered with Cisalpine Gaulish
KARNITU (Todi) 'built a stone funerary monument', plural KARNITUS 'they
built a stone funerary monument' (Briona). Thus one may consider enḇᵉ·ḵᵃa | rne
as a compound verb |embi karne| 'has entombed'. See further next entry.

——ḵᵃarner-ion ΛАꟼᴎOꟼᴎⴲᴎ (J.7.2)   The context is discussed in the
note on the form ire above. There is possibly a recurrence as akᵃa**ir-ion
Λ**ᴎꟼᴎⴲᴎA[(J.1.3), that is, if read a kᵃa[ŕn]ir-ion. This latter form also
occurs near the end of its text. Inscription J.7.2 is nearly complete and contains
no formula words. akᵃa**ir-ion follows the formula words tᵉ·bᵃare naŕkᵉeni.
The initial form of J.7.2 bᵒotᵒoᴚar[can be construed as a name according
to both its placement in the text and comparanda for the form. Conversely,
the position and form of ḵᵃarner-ion suggest a verb. Note Cisalpine Gaulish
KARNITU, &c.; see previous entry. It is widely thought that KARNITU, &c., are
verbs derived from a noun, *karnom 'stone funerary monument' with reflexes in
most of the Celtic languages. However, in the light of the early attestation of the
verbal forms, the reverse development is worth considering, that is, Celtic *karn-
in the first instance being a verb ('to build a stone funerary monument') and the
noun being derived from that. As explained in the note on ire, Indo-European
and Celtic parallels suggest that ḵᵃarner-ion is a 3rd plural perfect with a suffixed
accusative relative pronoun, so 'whom they have entombed', referring back to the
name of the deceased at the head of the inscription. Another possibility can be
found in the Insular Celtic languages, in which a verbal desinence -Vr can be added
directly to the stem of the verb to create a passive or impersonal form; in other
words, ḵᵃarner-ion might mean 'whom is entombed', though that would leave
the following segment ire unexplained.

k^{a}aśet^{a}ana ΛΑΜΟΧΑΥΑ (J.53.1) appears in this long and complete, but now lost, inscription as the last of three segmentable words that conclude the long anti-clockwise series of signs: **lak^{e}ent^{i}i ra⊭a≡k^{a}aśet^{a}ana**. These words are evidently a 3rd plural verb, taking the place of the usual formulaic closing **naŕk^{e}ent^{i}i**, but showing the usual personal form and present-tense marking, and two feminine *ā*-stem nouns in overt agreement. An Indo-European verb appearing to mean something very much like 'they now lie down' suits the phonetic form and probable funerary context. The paired nouns would be the subject, identifying the deceased. The second noun **k^{a}aśet^{a}ana** corresponds exactly to the Gaulish masculine *casidani, casidan(n)o*, &c., repeatedly in the graffiti of La Graufesenque, translated once as Latin 'flamen' and directly comparable to the Gaulish term ARGANTODANNOS 'moneyer' (< 'silver minister') occurring on Gaulish coinage (Delamarre 2003, 108, citing De Bernardo Stempel 1998; cf. Gorrochategui 1984, 182), also *platiodanni* 'overseers of metal' or 'overseers of streets' (De Hoz 2007b, 193, 196). As De Bernardo Stempel has proposed, Gaulish *cassidannos* meant 'tin' or 'bronze officer', and that likewise was the most probable meaning of Tartessian **k^{a}aśet^{a}ana**, the office of the dead woman **ra⊭a**, an office of significance in the metal-based economy of Tartessos in the Early Iron Age. **k^{a}aśet^{a}ana** | *kassedannā* | shows the regular phonological development in which Proto-Celtic short **i* was lowered to Tartessian **e** | *e* | when preceding *ă* either immediately or in the following syllable after a consonant. Compare also the personal names Celtiberian *Kasilos*, Gaulish *Cassi-talos*, British *Cassi-vellaunos* ('Excelling in [feats of] bronze'), &c. Greek κασσίτερος 'tin' is of uncertain origin and probably a trade word going back to the Bronze Age. The name Κασσιτερίδες 'tin islands', mentioned repeatedly in the Greek sources (e.g. Herodotus 3.115), is of course related. Modern writers have located these islands variously in Galicia, Armorica, Scilly, and Cornwall, perhaps all of these.

k^{e}enila(*)r̲i̲n̲ ΥΜϤ(*)Α1ΜΥΟ)Ι (J.17.4) occurs at the beginning of the inscription, thus where the naming phrase is expected. It is also consistent with this point that the form appears to show overt agreement with the case ending of the following form: **k^{e}enila(*)r̲i̲n̲≡b^{e}e:lin**. However, the reading from the surviving 18th-century drawing is not trustworthy. It is not clear whether there is a sign between **a** and **r̲**. And there are no certain parallels for the two-element compound name **k^{e}enila(*)r̲i̲n̲**, if that's what it is, or as a single root + suffixes. Like the following word **b^{e}e:lin**, **k^{e}enila(*)r̲i̲n̲** appears to be an *i*-stem accusative singular. For the name of the deceased to be in accusative singular form is unusual. However, it can be construed syntactically if we take the noun phrase to be the direct object of what is possibly a compound verb at the end of the statement: **enb̲^{e}·k̲^{a}a̲ | rne** ?'has entombed'. Possibly the nominative/accusative dual had died out in the *i*-stems and only survived in the *ā*- and *o*-stems, requiring

a different number and case for this naming phrase. Analysing k^{e}enila(*)rin as
a compound, the initial element could be Indo-European *$\acute{g}$'enh₃- 'to be born'
~ Celtiberian *kenis, kentis, eśkeninum* (Botorrita). Indo-European *ken- 'fresh' is
another possibility. Gaulish *Cenillo* and *Genetli* (genitive) are attested as potters'
names at Lezoux. If the second element corresponds to Old Irish *lár*, Welsh
llawr 'floor, flat open area' < Indo-European *$pleh_2ro$-, that would show characteristically Celtic loss of Indo-European *p*, but is hardly a likely element in a
personal name, better suiting a place-name. In the second syllable, one would
have expected *i* lowered to **e** before $\breve{a}$, unless the vowel had been a long *ī* (which
would not help at all with the comparanda and etymology) or k^{e}enila(*)**rin** is
archaic, predating *i* > **e** _/(C)$\breve{a}$.

k^{e}ert^{o}o ⧧Δ٩O)| (J.18.1), in the context of the statement-initial naming phrase
b^{o}ot^{i}ieana≡ **k^{e}ert^{o}o** ≡rob^{a}a, intervenes between two co-ordinated substantives
in overt concord. Formally, **k^{e}ert^{o}o** can be identified with the *o*-stem genitive
singular as found in Celtiberian. As a masculine genitive singular in the middle of
a two-term feminine naming formula, **k^{e}ert^{o}o** can be interpreted as designating
the father of the dead woman: | *Bōd^{i}eanā*≡ *kerdo* ≡*ro$_a$mā* | 'Bōd^{i}eanā, first-born
daughter of *kerdos*'. Compare the Gaulish personal name *Cerdo*, Old Irish *cerd*
'artisan' or specifically 'bronze smith', Early Welsh *kerδawr* 'artisan' or specifically
'musician, poet': Indo-European **kérdos* 'craft' ~ Greek κέρδος 'gain, advantage;
tricks', thus 'Bōd^{i}eanā first-born daughter of the artisan'.

———**k^{e}e≡uuak^{e}e*[ ] *O)|Δ 44O)|*** (J.7.8) is a possible feminine naming phrase,
with nominative/accusative dual or dative singular case marking; see Commentary
on the inscription.

k^{i}ielaoe: |O⧧Δ1OⵙႲ (J.11.1), **k^{e}eloia Δⵙ⧧1O)|** (J.57.1), **k^{e}eilau ႻΔ1ⵙO)|**
(Cabeza del Buey IV)   The three are similar enough to be interpreted as the
same form with different case endings. It may be significant that the latter two
of these similar forms occur on inscribed stones recovered from sites in Spain,
the basin of the upper Guadiana, about 200 kilometres to the north-east of the
main concentration of the SW corpus in south Portugal. In the context of the
complete **k^{i}ielaoe:**≡ **oiśaHa** ≡b^{a}ane rob^{a}ae n(a)ŕk^{e}enii, the usual formulaic
closing appears in its most common location with no amplification. **k^{i}ielaoe:**
opens the naming phrase and is followed by one and possibly two forms in
marked case agreement. **k^{i}ielaoe:** in this context suits a 'gamonym', i.e. a feminine
adjective of relationship based on the husband's name: 'Kielaos's wife OiśaHā',
cf. b^{a}ane≡ooŕoire 'wife of Ooŕoir' (J.19.1). **k^{i}ielaoe** and **b^{a}ane** are probably
in the nominative/accusative dual, forming a co-ordinative compound, literally
'female relative of Kielaos and woman/wife'. **rob^{a}ae** could be a perfect verb

ro·bᵃae 'she has passed, i.e. died' or a further element of the naming phrase
| roₐmẽ | < *(p)roₐmāi 'foremost woman, first-born daughter, first wife'. Text
J.57.1 (= Medellín T1 86H/En12–1) is fragmentary —]lokᵒon kᵉeloia naŕkᵉ[e
. . — but includes the recognizable lokᵒon (also in J.1.1, probably 'interment,
funerary urn') as well as the most common of the formula words. Cabeza
del Buey IV is fragmentary and hard to read, but the end is intact showing
a form of the formulaic closing:]kⁱiu [---] kᵉeilau kᵉe iśa n[a]ŕkᵉn. It is
possible that]kⁱiu [---] kᵉeilau are co-ordinated masculine appellations of the
deceased in agreement. There are several comparable Western Hispano-Celtic
(and/or Lusitanian) forms, including CILEA, CILEIOVI, CILIVS, CILO,
CILSVS, and the interesting compound with 'sea' MORICILO̱ (Albertos 1985,
278; Vallejo 2005, 278ff.; cf. Búa 2000, 530–6), also the group name *Cileni*, all
attested in the north-west of the Peninsula in earlier Roman times. If these are
valid comparanda, they imply a base for the Tartessian series *Kilau̯o-. There
are three evident phonological developments, all paralleled elsewhere within
the corpus: (1) Proto-Celtic *i* (if this is short) is lowered to Tartessian **e** by
affection with *a* in the second syllable; (2) this vowel change phonemicized the
strongly palatal or '*i*-quality' of the initial *K*-. Thus, *Kilau̯o- > | Kⁱelao̱- |. A
third change is that, as pervasively in Tartessian, the labial glide *u̯* assimilated to
the quality of the following vowel, thus varying depending on the case ending.
Comparable changes are found in the feminine nominative singular **bᵒotⁱieana**
| Bôdⁱeanā | (J.18.1) < *Boud̯ianā. That what appears to be the same form occurs
three times in the SW corpus allows the possibility that **kⁱielaoe**, &c., express a
relationship of kinship or social rank rather than a personal name. It is not clear
whether Tartessian **kⁱielaoe**, &c., and/or Hispano-Celtic CILEA, CILIVS, &c.,
also go with Old Irish *céile* 'fellow, client, spouse', cf. Gaulish *cele* '?companion,
spouse' (Châteaubleau; Delamarre 2003, 112). Old Breton *i kiled* and Middle
Welsh *kilyδ* show a different vowel, which cannot be fully explained by assuming
a Pre-Celtic form with a movable accent, *kéilii̯o- and *kilii̯o-, as the Brittonic
forms imply an earlier long *ī (see *Lexique* C.–52-3).

kⁱikᵉe〇)|ᛉꟼ | Kikē | (Monte Gordo) < *Kīkāi   In the context . . . kⁱikᵉe⹀arkᵃare
ro-n·bᵃare na[ŕ]kᵉen. . . , this appears to be part of the naming phrase, a
woman's name, ā-stem, nominative/accusative dual, in co-ordination, 'Kīkā ⟨and⟩
the daughter of Ar'kar(os)', or dative singular. As explained in the Commentary
on the inscription, **kⁱikᵉe** has parallels in Gaulish personal names.

kⁱinbᵃai↑ⁱi ᛉ↑ᛉАﬤᛉᛉꟼ (J.3.1)   This note follows from the Commentary on
the inscription. If the correct etymology is **kⁱinbᵃai↑ⁱi** = Cempsi/Cimbii ~
Old Irish *i*-stem *cimbid* 'captive' < 'giver of tribute' (< Celtic *kimbiatis*: Old Irish
cimb 'tribute'), the names could refer to a specific local client group and their

k^{i}inb^{a}ai↑^{i}i ᛘ↑ᛘΑ≷ᛘᛘφ (J.3.1)

hinterland territories or mean that the deceased **aib^{u}uris** was buried by or with his subjects. **k^{i}inb^{a}ai↑^{i}i** could be an instrumental plural |*Kimbab'i*| 'with/by the Cempsi /Cimbii and/or tributaries, subjects' or |*Kimbat'i(-)*| ?'a man of the Cempsi/Cimbii/', ?*i*-stem nominative singular. It is a well-carved stone, consistent with the commemoration of a high-status burial.

k^{o}o ǂ⧗ (J.1.2), **k^{o}** ⧗ (J.53.1) The two examples in the corpus suit reflexes of Indo-European **kom* ~ Latin *cum* as a preposition with ablative, *com-* in compounds; Old Irish *co* nasalizing with dative 'with', *com-* in compounds, *con·* as a pretonic preverb. **k^{o}o-b^{e}elib^{o}o** can be most easily interpreted as a preposition governing a dative/ablative plural form, although the independent case form of a compound, i.e. |*komelibo*|, is not impossible. In the statement-initial **k^{o}t^{u}uarat^{e}e** ⋈ΔΓΑΡΑΗΟ, **k^{o}** appears to precede a compound verb, meaning 'has delivered to, has run under towards' |*ko^{n} tu-u̯a-rāte*| < **kom+to-u(p)o-rāte*. If **k^{o}** functioned to mark completed action here, as is often the function of Old Irish *com* in its various positional variants, the comparanda would not lead us to expect it as the first preverb. In other words, we would look instead for a placement like that of **ro** in **t^{e}e·ro-b^{a}are**. This pattern also holds true for Cisalpine Gaulish TOŠOKOTE (Vercelli) = *to-śo(s)·ko(n)-de* 'has given these' (Koch 1983, 187–8). However, if the tendency to mark the perfective preterite with an 'augment' in this way is itself a Celtic innovation, the associated syntactic structures may have become more regular over time, rather than less so. On the other hand, **k^{o}** in **k^{o}t^{u}uarat^{e}e** might be a lexical preverb, to express the idea that the burial vehicle or litter had run under and *together with* the deceased towards the destination.

Another possibility is that **k°** functions here as a conjunction: 'and so' or 'so *because* the most sublime place of repose has delivered her to the finest tumulus, Ra᷉a the bronze minister now lies [here]'.

k°olion ᴎ⧺ᴎ⏉⧺ᴈ (J.55.1)   The inscription is complete, and the reading is mostly unproblematical: **ro- k°olion eert͏ᵃaune | t͏ᵃarielnon : lirniene nark͏ᵉenai.** However, it is an unusual text without obvious syntactic parallels within the corpus, apart from the closing with a form of **nark͏ᵉe-**, which does not however occur here with that verb's most common ending. For an epigraphic statement to begin with **ro** is unparalleled, but that reading has been disputed (the photograph nonetheless looks like **ro**). **k°olion** appears to show overt agreement with **t͏ᵃarielnon**, possibly two masculine names in the accusative singular. A similar form, possibly a variant representation of exactly the same name (?) and case form, occurs as **k°oloion** (Monte Novo do Castelinho, which possibly shows an epenthetic vowel developing before the glide i), cf. Celtiberian *Kueliokos* (probably an adjective derived from a proper name). | *Kolios* | or | *K°olios* | could mean 'chariot-' or 'cart-driver, -warrior', as a *io*-stem agent noun corresponding to Old Irish *cul* 'chariot' < Proto-Celtic *k^uol- : Indo-European *k^uel- 'turn'. If **eert͏ᵃaune** contains Indo-European *$uert$-, also 'turn', then that could confirm the semantic field in a statement having to do with chariots. Alternatively, *K°olios* could correspond to the second element of Old Irish *búachaill*, Old Welsh *buceil* 'cowherd' < Indo-European *g^uou-k^uolios, hence *Kolios* 'leader, guide, protector' (ultimately also Indo-European *k^uel- 'turn'). During the Roman Period, masculine *Coelius*, feminine *Coelia*, and related forms are well attested in the Indo-European zone of the Peninsula, which are possibly, but not surely, connected with **k°olion**. *Coelius*, &c., would thus derive from earlier *k^uolio- (note QVOELIA below) in which the diphthong in the first syllable has come about from a palatalized *l* and epenthesis. It is notable, however, that these forms do not show a general pattern of co-occurring with clearly Celtic name elements as part of the same naming phrase: for example, NI[G]ER COELAE LIBERTVS, IVSO Q. COILI Q(VAESTORIS), ELAESVS COELONIS F. EQVES ALA ASTVRVM, Q. COELIVS AQVILA, Q. COELIVS CASSIANVS, Q. COELIVM CASSIANVM II VIR, M. COELI[VS] CEL[S]VS, C. COELIVS C. PAP(IRIA) VALENS, Q. COE[LIVS---], COELIO PATIENTI PATIENTIS, COELIVS SEXTANVS, COELIVM, COELII TESPHOROS ET FESTA ET TELESINVS, COELIE MATERNE QVOELI F., QVOELIA, COELIA ROMVLA, COELIA MANI F., FAVSTA COELIA, COELIE MATERNE QVOELI F., COELIA, COELEA MANI F., COELEA MAELONIS F., COELEAS VACANI F., . INSTEIVS M. F. PAL. COELENVS (ALAE I HISPANORVM AVRIANAE) (Vallejo 2005), but note the typically Hispano-Celtic family name COILIONICV[M] from Yecla de Yeltes, Salamanca (Sánchez Moreno 1996, 124).

]kᵒoloion: | Ϥ⧧Ϥ⧧⏋⧧⋈[(Monte Novo do Castelinho) In the context]
kᵒoloion : kᵒoloar[ ]ŕ[.]s[ʔkᵉ]ntⁱi,]kᵒoloion: could be part of the naming phrase.
If this form refers to the deceased in the accusative singular, it is presumably
the object of a verb meaning 'has carried away', 'has buried', or the like, either
merely implicit or in the lost portion of the inscription. See further the previous item **kᵒolion** and the Commentary on the inscription. The similarity of the
name of Κωλαῖος, belonging to the ship's captain from Samos who, according
to Herodotus (4.152), profitably visited silver-producing Tartessos in the period
650 x 638 BC, is intriguing in this connection, though probably coincidental.

kᵒoŕbᵉo ⧧⟨⋋⧧⋈ (J.53.1) This portion of this lost inscription is detached
from the rest, reads in the opposite orientation (right-to-left), and is generally
difficult to read. **kᵒoŕbᵉo** is the clearest segmental series of signs within this
portion of the text. Note that there are six further violations of the principle of redundancy within the main text. Therefore, an edited transliteration
| koŕbeo | is indicated. Compare the Old Irish man's name *Corb*, ogam genitives
CORBBI, CORBAGNI, also the very common Old Irish men's names *Cormac*
< older *Corb-macc* and *Coirpre*. Alternatively, 'of the wheeled vehicle' | koŕbo- |.
Formally, **kᵒoŕbᵉo** resembles a Hispano-Celtic genitive singular, *o*- or *i̯o*-stem.
Phonetically, | koŕbeo | could be a development of **korbi̯o-* 'chariot-man', but
there is no exact parallel for this sound change in the corpus. It could also
have an *e*-grade of that agent suffix | koŕbēo | < **korbei̯o-*. Because this part of
the text is detached and its immediate context difficult to interpret, it is not immediately apparent what 'of koŕbeos' would refer to. The father of the deceased
is a likely possibility in the absence of any other indication or any other name
of a male relative close to the name of the deceased ra⧧a≡kᵃaśetᵃana. However, with **kᵒtᵘuaratᵉe**, probably 'has run under towards', in the main text, it is
alternatively possible that **kᵒoŕbᵉo** refers to a vehicle or driver. One is reminded
of **oretᵒo** near the end of inscription J.4.1., probably the genitive of the verbal
noun 'running under, rescuing' | ϱo-reto |. See further the Commentary on the
inscription. A connection with **kurm-* 'beer' is less likely, as the grapheme u Ϥ is
used in this inscription and there is no precedent in the SW corpus for Proto-
Celtic **u* to be lowered to o in this context, at least not systematically as opposed
to graphic variations.

kᵒtᵘuaratᵉe ⋈△ᕼᎪᏢᎪℍᎾ (J.53.1) This note follows from the discussion of **kᵒo**
above. The form begins the main left-to-right, clockwise circuit of a complete and
lengthy inscription: kᵒ-tᵘ-ua-ratᵉe tᵘn↑ⁱitᵉsbᵃan... Within this sequence, which
may be intentionally alliterative, kᵒ-tᵘ-ua-ratᵉe is interpreted as a 3rd person
singular perfect verb of motion with multiple preverbs, thus broadly equivalent
to the missing formula word **tᵉe•ro•bᵃare** 'has carried away'. **tᵘn↑ⁱitᵉsbᵃan** is
interpreted as a feminine singular superlative accusative of destination (with

the ending *-is_amām*), thus filling the syntactic role of another of the missing formula words **uar(n)bᵃan** < **u(p)er_amām* 'to the highest place/state/(feminine) being'. An appropriate meaning for **-tᵘ-ua-ratᵉe** can be proposed on the basis of etymology: Old Irish *fu·rráith* = Old Welsh *guo-raut* 'he saved, helped' < 'has run under' < Celtic **u(p)u̯o-rāte* < older **-rōte* with long ō (on the derivation of the Insular Celtic ā-preterites from the Indo-European perfect, see Schumacher 2004, 75–6; cf. 2005). Note that these Insular Celtic ā-preterites agree exactly with the attested Tartessian perfect. Early Welsh also has a related compound with two preverbs *dywaret* < **to-u(p)o-ret-*. This compound also means basically 'rescue, save' and can be assigned to Proto-Celtic on the basis of Tartessian **-tᵘ-ua-ratᵉe** | *tu-u̯a-rāte* | 'has delivered, has conveyed to safety' < **to-u(p)o-rāte*. As De Bernardo Stempel (2008) has argued, the basic sense of the preposition and preverb **to* is 'to, towards' with implied motion. Therefore, the original difference between **u(p)o-ret-* and **to-u(p)o-ret-* would have been 'run under > rescue', taking a direct object, as against 'run under towards > deliver to', with a direct object and a destination. In the context **kᵒ-tᵘ-ua-ratᵉe tᵘn↑ⁱitᵉsbᵃan orbᵃa setᵃa . . . ra⊭a≡kᵃaśetᵃana**, with a proposed meaning along the lines of 'the sublime throne has delivered [the deceased =] Raϕa the bronze minister to the best tumulus', **tᵘnbⁱitᵉsbᵃan** (probably 'tumulus'+superlative) is the destination. Allowing for more figurative and abstract thought, the message could be essentially 'god has carried Raϕa the bronze minister to heaven', thus tempering any expectation of a spectacular burial with funeral carriage in the neighbourhood.

   There is a possible connection between the facts that there is no comparative Celtic cognate for **kom+to-u(p)o-ret*——in Old Irish reflexes of **kom* do not usually occur first in a chain of preverbs like this—and that we have two unusual verb-initial clauses in this text. In other words, the epigrapher is open to innovations in the syntax as likewise in the left-to-right, clockwise order of the writing.

   On the phonological developments, see *Tartessian 2* §§70.1–2, 94.

Κυνητες *Kunētes*, Κυνησιοι *Kunēsioi*, Κονιοι *Conii*   Speaking of his own time (the mid 5th century BC), Herodotus (4.48) calls the Kunētes—as likewise when he writes their name *Kunēsioi* (2.34)—the westernmost people of Europe (i.e. in what is now southern Portugal, the area of densest concentration of Tartessian inscriptions) with the Κελτοί as their immediate neighbours to the east. With these forms, compare the Romano-British place-name *Cunētio* and Old Welsh *Cinuit*, the eponym of the *Kynwydyon* < Brittonic **Cunētiones* (probably a recharacterized plural from older *Kunētes*). The Kynwydyon were the principal dynasty of Dumbarton in the early Middle Ages. Note also the Old Welsh place-name *arx Cynuit* in Asser's Life of Alfred. These Brittonic names are based on Celtic **kuno-* 'hound, wolf', forms of which were commonly used in the metaphoric extension 'warrior, hero': Indo-European **ḱ´(u)u̯ōn* 'dog'

(Wodtko et al. 2008, 436–40). In the 12th-century Welsh genealogical source *Bonedd Gwŷr y Gogledd* ('Pedigree of the Men of the North'), the *Kyn[n]wydyon* figure specifically as a warband (cf. Charles-Edwards 1978, 66–8), so it may be that the ancestor *Cinuit* was a legendary eponym extracted from a name that was primarily a plural group name. The name *Kunētes* is glossed by De Bernardo Stempel (2008b, 103) as 'the tribe of the hound' and likewise implies a society of warriors.

According to the myth preserved by Trogus/Justin, the first king of Tartessos ruled the Cunetes (as usually restored for *curetes* in the extant text [e.g. Almagro-Gorbea et al. 2008b, 1035–42]), and it implies that the wooded territory inhabited by the Cunetes was an integral part of Tartessos (see further *Gargoris* above). In the *Ora Maritima* of Avienus, the Cynetes are mentioned five times, they figure there as neighbours of the Tartessians, and the river Anas (Guadiana) was their common boundary. *Conii* occurs for a people in the south-west in sources of the Roman period (e.g. Polybius 10.7.5: Κονιοι *Konioi*). Strabo (3.2.2) says that *Konistorgis*, a place-name which probably means 'Town of the Konioi', was the most famous city of the south-western Keltikoi. As now shown convincingly by Almagro-Gorbea et al. (2008b, 1033–60), the location of Konisturgis was Medellín on the upper Guadiana, site of the important Early Iron Age necropolis of the orientalizing Tartessian culture, findspot of J.57.1, &c. *Konioi* is probably also based on Celtic 'dog', meaning 'hound-like men' or 'descendants of the [mythic] hound'. The pre-Roman place-name *Conimbrigā*, modern Coimbra on the central Portuguese coast north of Lisbon, can be understood as standing for a Celtic noun phrase, rather than a close compound of the more usual type, i.e. **Koniiūm brigā* 'hillfort of the Konioi'.

Most historians have regarded *Kunētes*, *Konioi*, &c., as variant names for the same group. They were thus an extensive group. The group name Κονισκοι *Koniskoi* occurs in an area of thick Ancient Celtic place-names in the north-central Peninsula and probably represents another 'Hound Tribe' or even an offshoot of the south-western Kunētes/Konioi (as per De Bernardo Stempel 2008b, 113).

That the SW inscriptions are most heavily concentrated where this group name is found indicates that the shared name is meaningful, and that the same cultural practices and language were vigorously in use in these areas. Neighbouring groups apparently differed, at least as far as the practice of writing the vernacular extensively on non-perishable media. However, future discoveries from other regions of greater Tartessos might alter this picture. It is not certain whether the Kunētes, their name, and their language had equally deep roots across this widespread region or whether they had spread from a particular core area relatively recently. The arguments based in the archaeological chronology of Arruda (2011) might favour west-to-east spread in the Early Iron Age. Almagro-Gorbea et al. 2008b and Almagro-Gorbea personal communication emphasize the Atlantic Bronze Age background of the population of the Medellín necropolis. However, this argument is also linked to a case for a Tartessian colonization of Portugal, spreading westward from the core area around Huelva, in the Early Iron Age (Almagro-Gorbea & Torres 2009; Almagro-Gorbea 2010). For archaeologists today, these are complex and often controversial issues. They now take on special significance for philologists because of the close connections between the SW inscriptions and people(s) called Kunētes/Konioi.

—— k͟ᵘuiarairbᵘb͟ᵘ[u]*⋈⋈⫫ᛘΑᛉΑᛉΗ⊟ (J.17.2)   The two opening signs have unusual forms (Untermann, MLH 4.298). It is not certain that this is a name. The initial phonetic sequence suggests a pronominal (interrogative). In the extant drawing, it looks as if k͟ᵘuiarairbᵘb͟ᵘ[u is the beginning of the text. Some message broadly along the lines of 'whoever honours this grave will be blessed' and/or 'whoever dishonours it will be cursed' could be paralleled in many examples from various cultures and periods, but is merely noted for consideration here. A personal name is another possibility. The next item k͟ᵘuikᵃa͟o͟sa comes from near the present example's find site and begins its text with the same three signs, which could therefore be either a similar interrogative formula or a related name. Though the etymologies of k͟ᵘuiarairbᵘb͟ᵘ[u and k͟ᵘuikᵃa͟o͟sa remain uncertain, they are harder to explain if *k^w had developed to p in Tartessian as in Gaulish and Brittonic and Osco-Umbrian. In other words, this evidence is consistent with Tartessian being a Q-Celtic language (see further *Tartessian 2* §100). Double bᵘbᵘ is unusual and more probably represnts | -bŭ(-) |, | -bū(-) |, | -mŭ(-) |, or | -mū(-) | than a dative/ablative plural in | -bo |.

—— k͟ᵘuikᵃa͟o͟sa Α⧧*ΑΛᛘ⫪⊟ (J.17.1)   See the note on the comparable k͟ᵘuiarairbᵘb͟ᵘ[u above. Opening a fragmentary and badly worn inscription (Untermann, MLH 4.295–6), k͟ᵘuikᵃa͟o͟sa could be an interrogative pronoun < *k^woi or the name of the deceased, resembling a nominative singular feminine ā-stem. If Celtiberian *kuekuetikui* does mean 'to whomever' (Wodtko 2000 s.n.), that or a similar sense would suit the opening of an inscription. A name built on the Celtic number '5' *kᵘinkᵘe (Indo-European *pénkᵘe), Old Irish *cóic*, is another possibility, in which case, compare Celtiberian *Kuintitaku* (an adjective from a man's name *Kuintitos). Note also the Gaulish personal names *Peccia, Peccio*, ogamic Primitive Irish (genitive) QECIA, QECEA (Delamarre 2003, 247).

lak-   The following segmentable forms appear, within their respective contexts, most probably to be paradigmatic forms of the same verb, sometimes appearing as a compound with one or more preverbs, sometimes as a simplex. Their grammatical functions can be proposed as follows on the basis of well-known comparanda: 1st singular perfect **ro-la⊟a** Α⊟Α⇑⧧ᛉ (J.3.1) ?= **ro-laφᵃa** *or* ro-lak^{u}a, 3rd singular present o-ni-[l]ak^{a}at^i-śe ⟨OMMΦΛΛΑↃMↄ⟩ (J.10.1), 3rd plural present lak^{e}ent^{i}i ⟨ΓΛΚΟΝΦΝ⟩ (J.53.1), lak^{i}in⟨Ϯ⟩i ⟨ΓΑΝΝↃΝ⟩ (J.12.4) ?= 1st singular athematic present lak^{i}inb^{i}i | *lăgimi* | or 3rd plural present lak^i-int^{i}i, 1st singular thematic present (o-)lak^{i}iuu ⟨ЧЧMЧΑↃ⟩ (MdC). The final segment of the fragmentary]ire ab^{a}re la[to be read]ire b^{a}are la[might belong here as well. Apart from the long MdC text, lak- does not occur together with the most ubiquitous of the formula words, i.e. the verb nark^{e}ent^{i}i and its variants. The equivalence is especially evident with J.12.4 b^{a}a lak^{i}in⟨Ϯ⟩i ~ when compared with b^{a}a nark^{e}ent^{i}i (J.16.1), b^{a}a nark^e[e]nt^{i}i (J.16.3), and b^{a}a nark^{e}ent^{i}i (J.18.1), all of which close their respective texts. Therefore, it seems very probable that the verb lak- can take the place of nark^{e}ent^{i}i and that it must mean the same thing or something similar, at least that the two can be functionally and logically equivalent. The obvious Indo-European root to which to assign the Tartessian epitaph words in lak- is **leg^b-* 'lie down.' The noun lok^{o}on ⟨Мↄ✕ↄↃ⟩ (J.1.1, J.57.1), probably 'interment, funerary urn', would also belong to this root. As Dagmar Wodtko suggests to me, [l]ak^{a}at^{i}i, lak^{e}ent^{i}i, and lak^{i}in⟨Ϯ⟩i may reflect an *ā*-stem formation, with raising of *ā* before nasals + *-i*. The same root is reflected in Old Irish *laigid* 'lies down', which possibly shows that the stem **lag-* existed in Common Celtic, but *laigid* more probably reflects **legeti*. The fact that there is an ancient place-name *Saguntia* near Cádiz and Huelva, contrasting with *Segontia* elsewhere in Spain and *Segontium* in Wales, suggests a sound change *eg > ag* in the neighbourhood of Tartessos. The prevalence of a-vocalism in the Tartessian verb may have a different, or more than one, explanation. The Gaulish verbs LEGASIT (Bourges) and LOGITOE (Néris-les-Bains) also belong to this root. In context, both require a past tense transitive meaning, 'caused to lie down, placed, offered'. LEGASIT appears to be based on an Indo-European *s*-aorist. It is less clear what historical tense LOGITOE belongs to, but the ending is reminiscent of Cisalpine KARNITU 'built a stone funerary monument', also clearly past tense. Following the explanation given for b^{a}a in the note above, b^{a}a lak^{i}in⟨Ϯ⟩i can be interpreted as meaning something like | *ma lăgimi* | 'so I [this stone] now lie down' or | *ma lăginti* | 'so they [the deceased] now lie down'. In the light of the graphic variants leb^{o}o-iire (MdC) and linb^{o}o-ire ⟨ΟↃMↄↃΠMↄↃ⟩ (J.11.2) (see below), it likely that Proto-Celtic short *e* and *i* fell together before nasals in Tartessian. Therefore, lak^{i}in⟨Ϯ⟩i and lak^{e}ent^{i}i might represent the same vowel in the seond syllable or precisely the same form | *lăginti* | .

leb^{o}o-iire ⟨ΟↃMↄↃΠΟↃ⟩ (MdC), linb^{o}o-ire ⟨ΟↃMↄↃΠMↄↃ⟩ (J.11.2), see *Tartessian 2* §108. In the context t^{e}e·b^{a}ant^{i}i leb^{o}o-iire ·ro-b^{a}are, we have leb^{o}o-iire between two verbs. ·ro-b^{a}are is a variant of the formula word, the more usual form of which is t^{e}e·ro-b^{a}are, which does not usually have an overt subject. Therefore, t^{e}e·b^{a}ant^{i}i

lebᵒo-iire is interpreted as a plural verb + plural subject with -iire | -i̯irē | < *-u̯iroi 'men, heroes'. **linbᵒo-ire** (J.11.2) occurs as part of a relatively small fragment of what had been a longer inscription. Therefore, its textual context is not very helpful. However, as variant graphic representations, **lebᵒo-iire** alongside **linbᵒo-ire** indicate that the orthographies mean | Lɪmo-i̯irē |, which can be understood as reflexes of *Lemo-u̯iroi. The variant representations **le-bᵒo-** ~ **linbᵒo-** reflect the raising of e to i before | m | or neutralization of the distinction in that environment (see *Tartessian 2* §83.2), rather than the zero-grade equivalent (*limo- < IE *l̥mo-). Celtic parallels suggest a basic meaning 'elm-men'. That could be either a formal group name, like those cited below, or a figurative reference. Within the long MdC epitaph, the sense of **tᵉe·bᵃant'i lebᵒo-iire** could suitably be along the lines of 'the heroes of the [funerary] grove pass on'. On the first element, compare the Gaulish group name *Lemouices* also attested as *Limouices*, also the *Lemaui* and the *Limici*, neighbouring groups in south-central Callaecia. The Callaecian groups are attested in inscriptions of the Roman Period confirming their Celticity: for example, FABIA EBVRI F LEMAVA ... VIRIVS CAESSI F LEMAVS ... (from Astorga, León; Búa 2004, 387), ANCEITUS VACCEI F. LIMICVS Ɔ TALABRIGA (from near Huelva), CAMALVS M[EL]O[N]IS LIMI[C]VS (from north Portugal) (Vallejo 2005). On the second element -(i)ire, explained as nominative plural 'men' < *u̯iroi, see above. See further *Tartessian 2* §§35.1–3.

leoine ΟꞰꟿ‡Οꟼ (J.10.1)   More than one segmentation of **erbᶜe|ŕi:leoine a|rbᵃari|e** is possible. Nonetheless, **erbᶜe|ŕi:** and **a|rbᵃari|e** look like forms of the same verb, related to the formula word **tᵉe·ro-bᵃare** (which does not occur in this complete text) with a different preverb; see further the Commentary on J.10.1. Thus, we may consider the series of signs **leoine** as an isolatable word or name. There is an inexact resemblance to the Gaulish divine name *Liona*, *Liuoni* (in Noricum), *Lioni*. That name probably signifies the goddess of beauty. Compare the byforms *Llion* and *Lliwan* in south Wales as river names; also Gaulish *Lio-mari* (genitive), Welsh *lliw*, Old Cornish *liu* 'colour', Old Irish *lí* 'colour, beauty', Latin *liuidus* 'livid' (Delamarre 2003, 205). As a possible example of the suffix -on- in Tartessian names, compare **leoine** with Ἀργανθωνιος and **tᵉeaiona**[(J.4.3). The proposed derivation would entail a phonetic development from Proto-Celtic *[liːuwoni̯aːi] > [leːo̯on′e̯eː] in which not only the semivowel [w] assimilated to the height of the following [o]—the usual outcome of the semivowel in this environment in Tartessian—but the entire diphthong of the first syllable was lowered to mid height (see further *Tartessian 2* §§81, 86). It is common for languages to have the diphthongs [iu] and [eo], but not high-to-mid [io̯]. The **i** in **leoine** looks like an epenthesis, similarly **mutᵘuirea** (J.1.5). The representation **leoine** is easier to explain if we begin with the preform with [-ni̯-], thus | *Le̯oon 'e̯e* | < **Liu̯oni̯āi* 'the female pertaining to, or the female relative of, or the woman like, the goddess of beauty', dative singular or nominative/accusative dual. Lusitanian may also show the diphthong *oi* arising through palatalization and epenthesis in the name LOIMINNA/LOEMINA.

Ligustinus lacus (Avienus, *Ora Maritima*, lines 284–5; see Freeman 2010, 384) is the ancient name for the broad shallow estuary of the Guadalquivir, the river Avienus apparently called 'Tartessus'. This body of water, between the city of Seville and the Atlantic, is today low and marshy land. De Bernardo Stempel (2006, 47, 49) takes *Ligustinus* to be a Celtic name, based on the population name *Ligues* 'the strikers' < Indo-European **pleh₂g-*, thus showing characteristic Celtic loss of Indo-European **p* and Celtic *ī* < Late Indo-European **ē*. Even if we accept this etymology and the implication that *Ligustinus* is a Celtic name, it would not necessarily follow that groups called 'Ligurians' and the like in ancient sources spoke Celtic. There is, however, an early and recurrent connection between the names: Stephanus of Byzantium quotes Hekataios of Miletos (*c.* 500 BC) calling Massalia a 'Ligurian city' (πόλις τῆς Λιγυστικῆς) near Keltikē.

l̲iirnestᵃakᵘun ᒍᕼ𐌱ᗅ᙭‡ᴑ᙮᙮ᒎᒎᒐ (J.19.1)   Having examined the stone, I think it likely that there was originally no sign preceding the chipped l̲ ᒐ. What is most certain about this form is that it is a characteristic Hispano-Celtic 'gentilic' or group name (using an adjectival *k*-suffix) in the genitive plural with Tartessian **-un** < Indo-European *-ōm* (Untermann, MLH 4, 166). For group names of this type, cf. Tartessian]tᵃarnekᵘun (J.26.1), Celtiberian *Alizokum* 'of the descendants of Alizos', *Tirtanikum* 'of the descendants of Tirtanos', *Turikum* 'of the descendants of Turos' (Wodtko 2003, 26), and from Cantabria AVITA | [E]CON (Untermann 1980b). In inscriptions of the Roman Period, endings with *-on* and *-um* are well attested, but also *-velar+un* (as found in Tartessian): ALONGVN, AVLGIGVN, BALATVSCVN, BODDEGVN 'of the clan of Bōdios', CA | DDECVN, CANTABREQVN, CELTIGVN 'of the clan of Celtius', VIR[ONI]CVN (González Rodríguez 1986, 145–6). It is likely in any event that the articulation of the final nasal assimilated to the following consonant.

Interestingly, within the last centuries BC and first AD, the gentilic names of this type are not attested in the old region of the SW inscriptions, nor in the westernmost Peninsula at all. In other words, it appears as though the Kunētes of the Early Iron Age had a linguistic feature found in subsequent centuries amongst the Celtiberians and other central Hispano-Celts, but not among the Callaecians or western Celtici. That point would imply that the Kunētes had once possessed a feature characteristic of central Hispano-Celtic social organization that, by early Roman times, was absent in the west. It is noteworthy that the most comparable form in the corpus, another genitive plural group name, occurs in the parallel naming phrase]tᵃarnekᵘun bᵃane (J.26.1). bᵃane (see above) is interpreted as a case form of the word for 'woman, wife'. A woman called bᵃane is thus identified mostly with relationship to others, and specifically her group of origin (and there is a regular syntax in which the genitive plural gentilic name immediately precedes bᵃane). Though perhaps an accident of survival, there is no comparable example with a man's name in the corpus. This practice makes most sense if we assume that wives were leaving their birth kindred for their husband's. It would not make much sense to identify a woman as belonging to the kindred of the Lir(a)nestākoi, if everyone she lived with and was buried with also belonged to that group. But if we assume that the wives were moving, l̲iirnestᵃakᵘun not only effectively identified the deceased woman, but also advertised the value of a marriage alliance for her husband's kindred, in whose territory the burial and inscribed stone were probably located.]l̲iirnestᵃakᵘun bᵃane=ooŕoire thus means something like 'woman of the group of Lir(a)nest- and female relative (probably wife) of Ooŕoir [i.e. the man commemorated in J.19.2, an inscribed stone from the same site]'.

A tentative proposal is offered for the sense of the base name *Lir(a)nest-*. It looks like a two-element compound. For the first element, examination of the stone supports the reading with l̲-. Compare Old Irish *ler*, Middle Welsh *llyr* 'sea' < Celtic **lir-o-*, perhaps related to Latin *plērus* < **pleiro-* 'very many' (Indo-European **pelh₁-* 'fill'), if so, showing characteristically Celtic loss of Indo-European *p*. Cf. also the 'family name' LER | AN[I]QV | M on a funerary inscription of the Roman Period from Segovia (González Rodríguez 1994, 172), also the place-name *Lerabriga* in west-central Portugal, overlooking the Tagus estuary, though the variant *Ierabriga* is probable. However, note that a sequence *-liř-*, of uncertain meaning, occurs in Iberian inscriptions, e.g. *taśkaliřs* (C.2.3). For the second element, compare Gaulish *neδδamon* 'of the nearest ones', Old Irish *nessam*, Welsh *nesaf* 'nearest' < **ned-smHo-*. As Wodtko notes (2003, 26), the *-ako-* suffix in Celtiberian is best attested in expressing a relationship to a place: e.g. *Kontebakom* 'pertaining to Contrebia', *Sekaiδakom* 'pertaining to Sekaiδa'. That might also hold for the Tartessian evidence in this example. So the **Liranestākoi* would be the 'people of the maritime district' (**Liranestā*) if not 'descendants of the man nearer the sea' (**Lironestos*). The Celtiberian family name *kounesikum* (K.1.1) has a double relevance here: first, as showing the cognate adjectival velar suffix and genitive plural case ending in the same functions and, second, by identifying a group by an eponymous ancestor **Kom-ne'sos* 'neighbour, man living nearby'. Celtiberian and Tartessian are once more seen to be closely related. On the phonology and orthographic representation, Proto-Celtic *-o-* as a composition vowel tended to be unrounded or reduced to Tartessian a (*Tartessian 2* §73.1). Therefore,

*(P)liro-nestākūm would become **liranest^aak^uun**. However, because Tartessian tended conservatively to represent the reflex of Indo-European syllabic *ṇ simply as **n**, although it had probably already come to be pronounced *an* as in the other Celtic languages, inverse spellings of **n** for | *an* | from other sources became possible (see *Tartessian 2* §73.2).

líṙniene ⌐ᒥ∖ ᗅᒥ∖ ᗞᒥᗞ (J.55.1) resembles the previous item **liirnest^aak^uun** and thus could be a form of the same compound. If so, one possible interpretation of the form is as a locative singular meaning 'in the land near the sea' = *lir-(o-)ned-nā-i.

lok°ob°o ‡□‡⋈‡⊣ (J.1.1)   This long, well-carved, and complete inscription opens with a dative/ablative plural, which is closely co-ordinated with a second and more loosely with a third: **lok°ob°o⹀niirab°o . . . k^aak^iśiin|k°olob°|o.** Compare J.5.1: **ist̲^a̲a̲|ib°o rinoe̲b°o | anak^eenak̲^e̲:e|ib°o.** (One might consider the possibility that in both cases the threefold structure of the phrases were intentional parallelisms with invocations of triadic deities.) **lok°ob°o** is probably for | *Lugubo* |, as the grapheme **u** ᕼ apparently does not occur amongst the 72 signs of this inscription, dative plural divine name, 'to/for/in the name of the divine Lugoues'. This interpretation is by now widely accepted; see, for example, Villar 2004; Jordán 2006. There is a close and obvious correspondence for both this form and its syntactic context to four North-west Hispano-Celtic examples of the dative plural theonym from the earlier Roman Period: LVCVBO ARQVIENOBO (Sober, Lugo), LVCOVBV[s] ARQVIENI[s] (Outeiro do Rei, Lugo; Búa 2000, 266–7), DIBVS M[.] LVCVBO from Peña Amaya, north of Burgos (Búa 2003, 153–4; Marco Simón 2005, 301), and LVCOBO AROVSA[-] (Lugo). For the dative plural ending -BO used similarly in dedications, note also DEIBAB̲O̲ NEMVCEL̲AIGAB̲O̲ (Vila Real, north Portugal), ARAB̲O̲ COROBE|LICOBO TALVSICO·B̲O̲ (Arroyomolinas de la Vera, Cáceres, Spain [Búa 2000, 526]). -*bo* is also the form of Gaulish case endings, where examples of similar dedicatory formulas are well attested: ΜΑΤΡΕΒΟ ΓΛΑΝΕΙΚΑΒΟ 'for the mothers of Glanum' (Saint-Rémy G-64), ΡΟΚΛΟΙΣΙΑΒΟ 'for the listeners' (Saint-Rémy G-65), ΑΤΕΡΕΒΟ 'for the fathers/ancestors' (Plumergad, Morbihan). By contrast, the Celtiberian ending is -*bos* (Untermann 1985, 358). If both Gaulish and Tartessian have lost -*s* in this ending, though both languages retain Proto-Celtic final -*s* in other contexts, that would be a significant shared innovation. However, it is possible that -*bo* is the older form and that -*s* has spread analogically as a plural marker from the nominative and accusative.

For the divine name, note Celtiberian dative singular LVGVEI 'to [the god] Lugus' (Peñalba de Villastar, K.3.3). A Latin inscription from Uxama in Celtiberia records a dedication to LVGOVIBVS 'to the divine Lugoues' by a guild of shoemakers, which is intriguing in view of the shoemaking episode in the story of Lleu (< Celtic Lugus) in the Mabinogi. Cf. Gaulish *Lugoues* (nominative plural) from Avenches, Switzerland, Old Irish *Lug*, Welsh *Lleu*. Hispano-Celtic LVGVA CA | DDEGVN is a personal name (inscription from La Remolina, León; Untermann 1980b, 386), like Gaulish ΛΟΥΓΟΥΣ; also commonly as an element in compound personal and place-names as in Hispano-Celtic and in Gaulish (e.g. LVGVSELVA [Raybould & Sims-Williams 2007, 65]), Goidelic (e.g. ogamic LUGUQRIT, LUGUVECCA, LUGUDECCAS, &c., ~ Hispano-Celtic VALERIO ANNONI LVGVADICI F. VXAMENSIS from Segovia), Brittonic (e.g. Late British *Louocatus*, Old Breton and Old Welsh *Loumarch* > *Llywarch*), as well as the simplex Λυγοι group name of north Britain, the extensive *Lugii* of central Europe, also LVGGONI ARGA<u>N</u>TICAENI in Asturias, northern Spain (Villaviciosa, Oviedo, Búa 2000, 274); that collocation is interesting in the light of the Welsh tradition of *Lleu fab Aryanrot*. *Lugunae* are attested as a group of goddesses at Atapuerca (Burgos) (Marco 2005, 302).

lokᵒon ꓬ‡Ⴟ‡ꓭ (J.1.1), **lo̱kᵒon** ꓬ‡ꓮ‡ꓭ[(J.57.1)   With no overt agreement and appearing to stand apart from the naming phrase, the context of neither is very helpful. As **uar(n)bᵃan** is absent from both texts, **lokᵒon** is arguably taking its place as an accusative of destination (see Appendix C on 'The Formula'). From the standpoint of form and etymology, there is a close match with Cisalpine LOKAN /*logan*/ 'burial, funerary urn' (= Latin V<u>RN</u>VM, Todi), Early Welsh *golo* 'burial' (< *uo-log-): Indo-European root *$legʰ$- 'lie down'. As an *o*-stem neuter, **lokᵒon** | *logon* | 'burial, funerary urn' is probably an older gender than the Cisalpine feminine *ā*-stem. But a masculine accusative singular is also possible. Both stones come from necropolises, which is of course also consistent with the interpretation 'burial, funerary urn', especially as **lokᵒon** is neither evidently a personal name nor one of the Tartessian formula words.

meleśae ꓳꓮꙠꓳꓛꟿꟿ (J.15.1)   On the syntactic stucture of the naming phrase ₱ait"ura **meleśae**≡::=**bᵃaenae**, which is at the beginning of the text, see ₱ait"ura above. **meleśae** is interpreted as | *mele'sē* | < *$meli'sāi$, *ā*-stem nominative/accusative dual or dative singular 'sweet woman' or '(woman named) Meleśā' ~ Gaulish masculine personal name *Meliððus*, Old Irish *milis*, Welsh *melys* 'sweet' (< 'honey-flavoured', an epithet of mead) < Indo-European *$melit$-ti-. ꟿ is a common form for /m/ in Phoenician scripts. In this inscription **meleśae** agrees, and forms a co-ordinative compound, with **bᵃaenae** | *bₐnē* | < *$bnai$ 'woman, wife'. The lowering of Proto-Celtic *i* in **meleśae** | *mele'sē* | < *$meli'sāi$ is a regular phonological development in Tartessian (see *Tartessian 2* §78). It is less likely for phonetic reasons that **meleśae**≡::=**bᵃaenae** could mean 'wife of *Meleśos (Sweet man)', as that would imply a preform *$Meli'siāi$, in which the lowering of the vowel would probably not occur before an original palatal glide.

mubᵃa A{4M (J.12.1)   In other examples of the basic epigraphic formula
uar(n)bᵃan tᵉe(e)·ro-bᵃare (bᵃa) naŕkᵉentⁱi (on which see Appendix C),
tᵉe(e)·ro-bᵃare 'has carried away' lacks an overt subject. But here, in **mubᵃa
tᵉe·ro-bᵃare**, a form unproblematically resembling a feminine *ā*-stem nominative singular precedes the 3rd person singular compound verb. Thus, ʿ**mubᵃa**
has carried (him) away'. **mubᵃa** is possibly a superlative in ~ₐmā, but a simple
derivation yielding strong sense is │*mumā*│ ~ Old Irish *muim(m)e, mum(m)e*
'foster-mother' < **mumm(i)ā*. See the note on **ꝑatᵃaneatᵉe** and the Commentary
on the inscription above.

mubᵃa . . . ꝑatᵃaneatᵉe A{4M . . . ꝑAXArOAHO (J.12.1)   The gloss 'to
the winged one', dative singular of a Celtic agent noun, is suggested by both
the form and the accompanying image of a spear-brandishing warrior. For the
interpretation of **mubᵃa . . . ꝑatᵃaneatᵉe** as │*Mumā ꝯ̔ataneatē*│ 'the foster-
mother to the winged one', as a discontinuous nominative+dative phrasal epithet
or kenning for the war goddess, see the Commentary on the inscription and the
notes on **mubᵃa** and **ꝑatᵃaneatᵉe** above.

——**mutᵘuirea** AOꝗꝟ4Δ4M (J.1.5)   This form begins a complete inscription and appears to be all there is to the naming phrase. Compare the Celtiberian personal names *Muturiskum* (family name meaning 'of the descendants
of *Muturos'), *Muturrae, Mutorke*. The first is the closest and would lead to
interpreting **mutᵘuirea** as 'female relative of *Muturos', feminine *i̯ā*-stem,
nominative singular. An alternative segmentation is possible: dative singular
mutᵘui. śutᵘuirea is a possible reading, or dative singular **śutᵘui**. With the
most probable reading as **mutᵘuirea**, the **i** before the **r** would not represent a
historical diphthong, but apparently phonetic epenthesis or palatalization of
the consonant reminiscent of the varying consonant qualities of Goidelic. To
have a feature resembling the medieval and modern Gaelic opposition of *caol
agus leathan* in evidence at such an early date—over a millennium before its appearance in Old Irish—might seem startling or simply implausible. However,
as a phonetic feature, varying quality of consonant phonemes anticipating the
articulation of the following vowel is a linguistic commonplace, a near universal.
So it should not be inherently surprising that two languages of the same family might phonologize such commonly inherited and hardly unusual phonetic
tendencies independently, at widely differing dates. Intensifying contacts with
foreign languages and the adoption of literacy may have similarly contributed
to reanalyses of the sound systems of both Tartessian during the Orientalizing Period and Goidelic in Early Christian times. See also **leoine** above and
Tartessian 2 §99.3.

na· ꓯꓴ (J.1.2, J.7.1), **ne·** Oꓴ (J.1.2)   These three are possible instances of the negation 'not' corresponding to Celtiberian *ne* (Wodtko 2000, 269), Gaulish *ne* (Delamarre 2003, 233) < Indo-European **ne* 'not' (Mallory & Adams 2006, 62): kᵒo-bᵉelibᵒo na-kⁱi·bᵘu oira uarbᵃan tⁱirtᵒos ne-bᵃa and aśᴴa bᵒo↑ir narᵏᵉenai | aśᴴa na·bᵒolon. In the first example the tentative interpretation (on which see the Commentary on the inscription above) is that the first negative **na** forms part of the negation of a relative clause (see next item **na-kⁱi**) and the second with the form **ne** negates the main clause. In the main, this conclusion is based on the syntax of the very common formula word **narᵏᵉentⁱi** (and its variants), which shows almost no trace of possible relative morphology or syntax in any of its many instances, especially so when appearing in statement-final position, as this example. Unproblematically, such examples conform to the basic structure of a verb-final language. In the Insular Celtic languages, *na(-)* and *ni* show this basic distinction, subordinate/relative negation versus main-clause negation. It is likely that this contrast arose due to the accent, that is, that the *na(-)* forms represent a reduction of the vowel from **ne* > **nə* where the particle was proclitic upon an accented verb, as would have been the case in Indo-European subordinate clauses. Owing to the same factors, the unreduced **ne** remained, where the following verb itself lost its accent in the final position in main clauses (cf. Appendix C below; *Tartessian 2* §74; Koch 1987; Hock 2005). The examples are too few to work out the system of negation in Tartessian even if these interpretations can be confirmed.

na-kⁱi ꓴꟼꓯꓴ (J.1.2) is interpreted as a compound of the negative particle (< Indo-European **ne*; see previous item) plus a second element of uncertain derivation. Possibilities include the second element found in the Gaulish conjunction *duci* 'together with', the Indo-European interrogative pronoun neuter **kʷid* or masculine **kʷis* (these came also to function as relative pronouns in more than one branch of Indo-European ~ Vedic *ná-kis* 'not any one'), or as a graphic representation |*nakʷe*| 'and not' corresponding to Celtiberian *ne-kue* 'and not', Old Irish *na·*, *nach·*, Welsh *na*, *nac* 'that not, and not, than' < Indo-European **ne-kʷe* 'and not'. In the second possibility, one would expect **kʷi-* to develop to **kⁱi** | *kⁱi-* | by the same regular palatal assimilation that produced Tartessian **iir** | *iir* | < **u̯iros* 'man, hero' (see *Tartessian 2* §§97.1–3). Overall in context, **na-kⁱi** is interpreted as a subordinate or relative negation, contrasting with the negation of the statement's main verb with **ne**.

narᵏᵉe(-) Oꓡꓤꓯꓴ   For a full list of the forms and suggested etymology, see p. 4 above. On the syntactic function and possible meaning of **narᵏᵉe(-)**, see also the note on **lak-** above. For its role in the epigraphic Formula, see Appendix C. **narᵏᵉe(-)** is the most common of the formula words. It is inflected as an

Indo-European verb. Some of the numerous variant forms of naŕkᵉe(-) can be interpreted as displaying meaningful paradigmatic contrasts. However, the stem vowel e of naŕkᵉe(-) is invariable, as is the consistent absence of the usual prefixes (preverbs) ro < *(p)ro, tᵉe(e) < *dĕ, ar < *(p)are, and o/ua < *u(p)o. Only bᵃa, interpreted as |ma| 'so, indeed', is found immediately preceding the formulaic closing naŕkᵉentⁱi ⋎ⵏⵄⵎⵄ)ⵏⵄⴰ⋎ in J.16.1, J.16.3, J.18.1. As with the other formula words, the orthography is very consistent. However, the graphic representation naŕrkᵉe:n: |⋎ ⵔ ⵔ)ⵏⵄ ⴰ ⋎ (J.23.1) provides a clear indication that ŕ ⴽ and r ⵔ were phonetically very similar, possibly allophones. naŕkᵉentⁱi and naŕkᵉenii, naŕkᵉeni, the best attested of the forms, can be interpreted as 3rd person plural, present, active. The latter two forms are probably secondary phonological developments of the first. naŕkᵉen and variants, without final -i, are too well attested to be considered purely graphic variants or abbreviations, especially given the orthographic consistency already noted. Therefore, it is possible that these variants show an early apocope of the Indo-European 'primary -i' marking the present tense (see Appendix C). naŕkᵉetⁱi ⋎ⵄⵔ)ⵏⴰ⋎ (J.56.1) is clearly 3rd person singular. As the carving is very clear, neatly arranged, and uncrowded on the dressed surface of the stone, an error for naŕkᵉentⁱi ⋎ⵄⵎⵄ)ⵏⴰ⋎ is unlikely (despite De Hoz 2010, 391). Instances of naŕkᵉe (where the relevant portion of the inscription is clearly intact) can be provisionally understood as showing an apocopated form of the 3rd singular. There are no syntactic examples to indicate that naŕkᵉentⁱi, &c., are transitive, taking an accusative argument. Rather, as the most common verb in a funerary formula, it probably means something like 'now rest, lie down, remain unmoving'. Therefore, naŕkᵉenai ⋎ⴰⵎⵄ)ⵏⴰ⋎ (J.7.1, J.55.1), the form of which suggests an Indo-European 3rd plural middle (expressing a state or action internal to the subject), might not have a very different meaning from the corresponding 3rd plural active naŕkᵉentⁱi. However, both examples of naŕkᵉenai belong to texts that are unusual in other respects, and it is not certain that either is an epitaph.

Within the epigraphic statement, naŕkᵉentⁱi, &c., is often the closing segment, certainly where the endings of the texts survive undamaged and as a likelihood in other examples: (J.1.2) #...uarbᵃan tⁱirtᵒos ne-bᵃa naŕkᵉeni#, (J.1.2) ...]bᵒoara naŕkᵉenii#, (J.11.1) #...n(a)ŕkᵉenii#, (J.11.3) #soloir uarbᵃa͟n[ ]i͟na o*[| n]a͟ŕkᵉenii#, (J.14.1) #...tᵃa-e·bᵃare naŕkᵉen#, (J.16.1) #... *arbᵃantᵉe·bar[e]bᵃa naŕkᵉentⁱi#, (J.16.3) #...ro·b͟a͟re bᵃa naŕkᵉ[e]ntⁱi#, (J.17.2) #...]bᵃare naŕkᵉentⁱi#, (J.18.1) #...tᵉe·bᵃare bᵃa naŕkᵉentⁱi#, (J.19.1) #... bᵃa͟[re naŕ]kᵉenii#, (J.19.2) #ooŕoir naŕkᵉenⵀⁱi#, (J.20.1) #... bᵃar(e)n naŕkᵉen[. .#, (J.21.1) #...]uarbᵃan tᵉe[(e)·ro-bᵃ]are naŕkᵉenii#, (J.22.1) #...bᵃare naŕkᵉenii#, (J.26.1) #...ro-]bᵃare naŕkᵉ[e...#,

(J.55.1) #...naŕkᵉenai#, (J.56.1) #akᵒo(l)ioś naŕkᵉetⁱi#, (Cabeza del Buey IV) #... n[a]ŕkᵉen#, (Corte Pinheiro) #...bᵃ[a]re [na]ŕkᵉeni#.

In other examples, the naming phrase and formula is completed in their usual order, ending with a form of the verb naŕkᵉe(-), but the statement continues. These may be categorized as 'amplifications' of the basic pattern: (J.1.3) #... tᵉe·bᵃare naŕkᵉeni...#, (J.1.5) #...bᵃar[e n]aŕkᵉentⁱi...#, (J.7.1) #aśᚻa bᵒo↑ir naŕkᵉenai | aśᚻa na·bᵒolon#, (J.7.8) #...tᵉe·bᵃere naŕkᵉe|n emun tᵘurea≡iubᵃa#, (J.11.4) #...ea ro-n·bᵃaren naŕkᵉenii | aliśne | śtⁱaś*tᵃa*tᵃa#, (J.27.1) #... bᵃare naŕkᵉe | bᵉeś**n*[. .#, (Monte Gordo) #... ro-n·bᵃare na[ŕ]kᵉen tᵃa-bᵉe anoŕion#. Occasionally in this category, naŕkᵉe(-) stands at the end of a carved line.

In other examples naŕkᵉe(-) is not in its usual position, i.e. the naming phrase or a form of tᵉe·ro-bᵃare or of uar(n)bᵃan follows it. These can be categorized as 'rearrangements' of the basic pattern. Often these are the longer and more elaborate texts: (J.1.1) #... naŕkᵉe kᵃakⁱiśiinkᵒolobᵒo ii tᵉe·ro-bᵃare. ..#, (J.7.10) #]****naŕkᵉenii raśen bᵃare#, (J.12.1) #iru≡alkᵘu—sie: naŕkᵉentⁱi—mubᵃa tᵉe·ro-bᵃare ᚽatᵃaneatᵗe#, (J.23.1) #bᵉetⁱisai tᵉe(-)e·bᵃarentⁱi iru≡{u}arbᵘu i el naŕrkᵉe:n: uśnee#.

The syntax of naŕkᵉe(-), mostly at the end of the statement, might be largely due merely to Tartessian having verb-final basic order, as was the case with many early Indo-European languages. But its placement may also have to do with the frequent occurrence of present-tense marking with this verb, so it articulates the present state, subsequent to the completed action expressed by the perfect tᵉe·ro-bᵃare, which it follows in the usual order of the statement. If, as tentatively proposed, naŕkᵉe(-) is the cognate of Greek ναρκάω 'grow stiff, numb, dead' < Indo-European *(s)ner- 'bind, fasten with thread or cord', the verb may have the force of the 'binding' of a final injunction, carrying the notion of 'so may they remain permanently (amen)'. The most usual orientation of the inscriptions, as an anti-clockwise circle or spiral, may likewise be meant to affect the closing or binding of the inscriptional statement, perhaps magically.

There is more than one possible derivation for a paradigm with 3rd person singular naŕkᵉetⁱi and 3rd plural naŕkᵉentⁱi. A spread of athematic -entⁱi forms into the paradigms of thematic verbs, as in Oscan and Umbrian, was suggested to me be Peter Schrijver. An original Indo-European -$ei̯e$/o- stem is possible, as Dagmar Wodtko has suggested, thus a development broadly comparable to that of Latin *moneo, monet, monent*. Either development could explain why -e- occurs in all attested forms of the paradigm, thus contrasting with bᵒolon (J.7.1), assuming that bᵒolon is a verb, which would thus show that the *o* of the Indo-European thematic 3rd plural -*ont* had survived in Tartessian.

——?nemun ᕴᕴᙏO ᕴ (J.7.8)   There are two possible segmentations of the text: naŕkᵉe|n emun or naŕkᵉe| nemun. The former is somewhat more probable, despite the position of the line break; see ——?emun above. In either case, the ending -un indicates that the form is a Hispano-Celtic genitive plural ~ Celtiberian -um < *-ōm. Thus, interpret the naming of the deceased -un tᵘurea≡iubᵃa, 'of them, the youngest daughter of Turos'. If the segmentation is naŕkᵉe nemun, the form would mean 'of the Nemoi', a group name comparable to the Hispano-Celtic group name Νεμετατοι Nemetatoi, situated in what is now coastal northern Portugal. Compare also Western Hispano-Celtic dative plural goddess name DEIBABO NEMVCELAIGABO (Aguas Frías, Chaves, Vila Real, Portugal [Búa 2000, 396]), the Celtiberian personal name (?) NEMAIOS, Cisalpine NEMETALUI (Davesco 4th/3rd century BC [Morandi 2004, 530–40]), NEMUŚUS (Zignago, end of the 4th century BC [Morandi 2004, 696–7]), Gaulish, British, and Galatian nemeton 'sacred place', Old Irish nemeth 'thing or person of special privilege', Early Welsh niuet (Gododdin), also Old Irish nem 'heaven', genitive nime, Welsh nef, plural nefoedd < Celtic *nemos, *nemesos. nemun might also be a common noun, meaning broadly the same as Proto-Celtic *nemeto- 'of the privileged persons, of the sacred things'.

—— -ni- ᕴᕴ is interpreted as an adverbial particle meaning 'down' as it occurs in o-ni-[l]akᵃatⁱi-śe OᕴᙏⴱΛΛΛ↑ᕴᕴ‡ (J.10.1) 'lies down under here': Indo-European *ni ~ Vedic ni, ny- 'down(wards)', Old Welsh ni-tanam 'down under me [this memorial stone]' (Tywyn inscription).

ΝΙΕΘΩΙ occurs as a graffito in archaic Ionic Greek script on a Greek bowl (probably Milesian) found at Huelva and dated by Almagro-Gorbea (2005, 55) to 590–560 BC. He identifies this linguistic form with the name of the Hispano-Celtic divinity Nētos (accusative Nēton), who is described by Macrobius (Saturnalia I.19.5) as a solar, ray-adorned manifestation of the war god, i.e. Mars. Incidentally, Macrobius's description of Netos as simulacrum Martiis radiis ornatum may illuminate the enigmatic imagery of the numerous so-called 'diademed' Bronze Age stelae of the western peninsula. Harrison (2004) lists four 'diademadas', which are likely to predate significantly the stelae with weapons. Note also the probable etymological connection with Old Irish níam 'radiance, beauty' (Lexique N-16). For the name, Marco (2005, 292) compares Nēton with Celtiberian Neito (Botorrita), though it is now doubtful that neito could be a theonym, and the Hispano-Celtic divine epithets of the Roman period—Cossue Nedoledio, Nidanlua-, Reva Nitaecus, and the Netaci Veilebricae named on an altar from Padrón. Cf. also NETONI DEO on an altar, now lost, from Trujillo, Cáceres (Búa 2000, 571–2). F. Beltrán (2002) has registered doubts about this reading, as well as some of the other evidence which has been adduced in support of a Hispano-Celtic god Neito-/Nēto-. Almagro-Gorbea compares ΝΙΕΘΩΙ and *Neton* with Irish forms such as Old Irish *nía*, genitive *níath*, ogam NETTA, NETA 'champion, hero': e.g. NETTASLOGI, NETASEGAMONAS, NET(T)ACUNAS. That word could also be related to Old Irish *nioth* (genitive), ogam NIOTA 'nephew, sister's son' < Indo-European **nepot-s*, genitive **nepotos* (McManus 1991, 109–10). ΝΙΕΘΩΙ and *Neton* would imply a Hispano-Celtic *o*-stem, dative and accusative respectively. If ΝΙΕΘΩΙ is indeed derived from Indo-European **nepot-*, it shows that characteristic Celtic loss of Indo-European *p* between vowels was complete in Tartessian by the earlier 6th-century BC. However, the sequence ιε more probably represents an attempt to write a palatal consonant and long close vowel in |*N´ētūi*| (from an earlier **Neitōi*, with a diphthong) and thus unconnected with 'nephew' and Indo-European *p*.

niirabᵒo ‡□𐤀𐤔𐤌𐤔𐤌 (J.1.1) is the second word in this unusual and high-quality inscription, where it is also the second of three datives/ablatives plural in agreement: **lokᵒobᵒo=niirabᵒo . . . kᵃakⁱiśiin|kᵒolobᵒ|o**. The first and surely the most important in this series is **lokᵒobᵒo** 'for the [divine] Lugoues'. The syntactic sense is probably one of co-ordination without a conjunction: 'to the Lugoues and for the **nira-**.' **nira-** 𐤀𐤔𐤌𐤔 in **nira-kᵃaltᶜe** in the MdC text is surely the same word. **kᵃaltᶜe** also occurs in J.1.1 (see note above), so these two texts share diction and ideas.

It has been recognized for some time that **niirabᵒo** might have something to do with the Callaecian group name attested as *Neri* and Νέριοι *Nerii* and the place-name *promontorium Nerium* (e.g. Villar 2004). These names are based on an important Indo-European noun: **h₂nér-* 'man, hero' ~ Vedic *nárya-* 'masculine, virile, heroic'. Thus, with the second element as a common noun, **lokᵒobᵒo=niirabᵒo** (J.1.1) could mean something more like 'for gods and for men/heroes' (cf. Cisalpine Gaulish ΤΕΥΟΧΤΟΝΙ()ΟΝ at Vercelli), rather than 'for the Nerian Lugoues'. In a Roman-period inscription from Briteiros, north Portugal—CORONERI CAMALI DOMVS 'a casa de Coronerus Camali' (Búa 2007, 28)—NERO- occurs in a compound name, where it could signify either 'of the (Callaecian group) Ner(i)i' or 'man, chief (of the warband)' or both. Like Welsh *ner* 'lord', Callaecian *Ner(i)o-* preserves the *e*-grade of Indo-European **h₂nér-* 'man, hero' (Búa 2004, 382; Wodtko et al. 2008, 332–8).

The equation of **niirabᵒo** with these forms has become more interestingly complex as a result of the discovery of the MdC stela in 2008, which includes the form **nira-kᵃaltᶜe**. The vowels i and a have thus been confirmed and must be accounted for as correctly carved. This can be done if we recognize that the *e*-grade in Callaecian and Welsh represents a relatively recent simplification of the paradigm. The Indo-European paradigm had ablaut: **h₂nér, *h₂nér-, *h₂nr̥-´*; e.g. Homeric nominative singular ἀνήρ, dative ἀνδρί, accusative ἄνδρα (Homeric and Attic ἀνέρα), nominative plural ἄνδρες, dative ἀνδράσι, accusative ἄνδρας; Avestan nominative singular nā (< Indo-European *h₂nēr), genitive nərəš, dative narōi, accusative narəm, nominative plural narō, genitive plural narąm-ca; Oscan nominative singular niir 'leader, magistrate', Umbrian nír < Italic *nēr.

In Celtic, as indeed in Latin, this complicated paradigm was in trouble, contributing to this word's replacement by the synonymous *u̯iros. However, the forms niirabᵒo and nira-kᵃalteᵉe indicate that Indo-European nominative singular *h₂nēr had survived as Proto-Celtic *nīr. niirabᵒo and nira-kᵃalteᵉe show characteristically Celtic ī < ē. Within Tartessian, this i evidently spread through the anomalous inherited paradigm.

There is more than one possible explanation for the -a- in niirabᵒo and nira-kᵃalteᵉe. It had possibly spread from the inherited accusative forms *(ə)neram(s) < Indo-European *h₂nérm̥: replacing the problematical reflex of Indo-European *h₂n̥rbʰo(s). For niirabᵒo, note also the dative/ablative plural demonstrative-noun-adjective phrase istᵗᵃaibᵒo rinoebᵒo anakᵉenakᵉ:eibᵒo (J.5.1) 'for these indwelling queens (=goddesses)', where what appear to be incongruous diphthongs before each instance of the desinence more probably reflect hesitation over an indistinct vowel in this position /istəbo rignəbo an(d)agenākəbo/. Finally, we may consider the possibility that the divine lokᵒobᵒo are feminine in J.1.1 and so have a feminine ā-stem epithet. Whatever the actual motivation, these particular developments were probably not confined to Tartessian: the genitive singular of the first name in Primitive Irish DUBONIRRAS MAQQI TENAC[I] (McManus 1991, 65) could equally go back to *-nīros or *-nīras. Whether -NIRRAS shows the innovative a or not, the ī is seen to have spread from the nominative to the genitive singular.

Given the difference in the vowels, it is less likely that niirabᵒo and nira-kᵃalteᵉe refer to the group inhabiting Galicia some centuries later. Nonetheless, the form is relevant as a cognate. The fact that Strabo (3.3.5) and Pliny (*Naturalis Historia* 4.111) classed the Νέριοι Neri of Galicia as Κελτικοί Celtici, an over-arching group name also used in south-west Hispania, is certainly relevant to this problem and points towards a general shared 'Celtic' identity across the western Peninsula (cf. Villar 2004, 247).

nira-kᵃalteᵉe ΟΒ1ΑΛΑ9ᵜᵜ (MdC) is interpreted as a two-element compound noun; see *Tartessian 2* §§40.1–2. For the etymology, meaning, and phonology of the first element, see the note on niirabᵒo above. For the second element, see the note on kᵃalteᵉe above. An explanation is offered above for the a of nira-. For this particular form, a second factor would also have favoured this development. Where not flanked by labial sounds, the Proto-Celtic composition vowel -o- gives Tartessian -a-: for example, ariariś-e (J.10.1) < *Ari̯o-rīχs+se and oira-uarbᵃa(n) (J.1.2) < *u̯iro-u(p)erₐmam; see further *Tartessian 2* §73.1.

Therefore, *n̥īro- in composition would have become Tartessian **nira-** if other factors had not already produced the same outcome.

Νωραξ   According to mythology recorded by Solinus (§4.1, cf. Pausanias, *Description of Greece* 10.17.5; Freeman 2010, 320), Nōrax of Tartessos was the founder of the town Nora, near modern Pula, in southern Sardinia, the site of a Phoenician presence of the 9th/8th century BC. It is worth noting in this connection that 'Tartessos' is probably the meaning of Phoenician *tršš* in the first surviving line of the stela from Nora, Sardinia, *c.* 850/775 BC. The names Νωραξ and *Nora* are probably linked with the Sardinian term *nuraghe* for the prominent Late Bronze Age tower-like fortifications of the island, Palaeo-Sardinian *nurake*. The ending of the latter resembles the Celtic adjectival suffix *-āko-/ā*.

The Νυραξ *Nurax* (or Νυρακη) mentioned by Hekataios of Meletos, writing *c.* 500 BC (Fragment 54), as a *polis* of the *Keltoí* is more often identified with Noreia in Noricum, the historical kingdom of the last centuries BC in the eastern Alps, but the fragments of Hekataios say nothing about Nurax being in central Europe (cf. Collis 2003, 188–9). Therefore, a link with *nurake*, Nora, and Norax of Tartessos is possible.

There were intense trade links between southern Hispania and southern Sardinia *c.* 1200–*c.* 750 BC: for example, numerous Huelva swords (similar to the Armorican carp's-tongue type) have been found at both Huelva (with 84 examples) and Monte Sa Idda in Sardinia near Nora (cf. Brandherm 2007, 92–9, for the relationship of the Iberian and Sardinian subtypes).

o- ✚, ua- ΛЧ are interpreted as phonological byforms of a compounding prefix, meaning essentially 'under', < *u(p)o- < Indo-European *(s)h₄upó, in the following examples: possibly [(o-)]lakⁱiuu ЧЧМΨΛ1✚] (MdC) |o̯o *lagi̯ṷ*| 'I [this inscribed stone] conceal/bury', ( )omuŕikᵃa[✚MͰϺͰͲΛ*[(J.16.2) |O̯omurikā| 'female of the kindred of O̯omuri- ("Under-sea being")' < *U(p)o-mori-, **o-ni-[l]akᵃatⁱi-śe** ΟΜΜΦΛΛΛͲΥΜ✚ (J.10.1) |o̯o ni l̯ăgati se| 'lies down under here', **oret°o** ✚ΛΟͰ✚(ΛΧ) (J.4.1.) |o̯o-reto| 'of rescue' < 'running under', **otᵉerkᵃa** ΛΛͰΟͰ✚ (J.1.4) |o̯o-derkā| 'grave (pit)' < 'under cavity'. The phonological variant /u̯a/, common in Brittonic, occurs in **kᵒtᵘuaratᵉe** 'has gone under, has delivered/rescued' (J.53.1).

One common innovation followed by two different phonological developments have conditioned the resulting byforms **o-** and **ua-**. First, the reflex of Indo-European *p was completely lost from Proto-Celtic *u(p)o. There is then no trace of an intermediate hiatus stage **u |o~. Rather the development appears to have been direct to monosyllabic *u̯o-. From this stage there was a split in the Tartessian treatments. If the mid back round vowel /o/ remained, the preceding glide was assimilated to give |o̯o| usually written **o**. Alternatively, *u̯o- might undergo dissimilation, in which the initial glide remained round, but the following vowel became unrounded. Both treatments are found also in Brittonic, frequently in the same word, and there is ample evidence for the same variation in Gaulish; see *Tartessian 2* §70.2. The conditioning determining which byform occurs is obscure. Rather there seems to have been something like a free variation in operation over centuries and across cognate dialects. In the case of **-tᵘ-ua-ratᵉe** | *tu-ua-rāte* | (J.53.1) < **to-u(p)o-rāte*, the phonetic environment might have been particularly favourable to the outcome of dissimilation, i.e. a round vowel in the preceding syllable and a long unround vowel in the following syllable with a non-labial consonant standing between. Another possible factor was the analogical influence of a related word *uamā* 'highest one' (feminine), as in the ancient place-name in the territory of the south-western Celtici, Οὐαμα *Uama* 'the highest place' (Luján 2001, 279), identical to the more archaic Tartessian superlative **uabᵃan** | *uaman* | (J.16.5) < **u(p)ₐmām*. Here, the **a** is the regular phonological outcome of the syllabic nasal following **p* in **U(p)ₐmā* ~ Lepontic UVAMO- in which the position of Indo-European **p* continues to be represented graphically (see *Tartessian 2* §§70.1, 97.2, 98), although that orthography could stand for /*uamo-*/.

Oestrymnin (accusative, name of a promontory: *prominentis iugi caput*), *(insulae) Oestrymnides, Oestrumnides, Oestryminicae, (sinus) Oestrymnicus, Oestrymnis, Oestryminicis* (Latin ablative plural). These names are amongst the archaic forms in Avienus's *Ora Maritima* (lines 90, 94, 95, 112, 129, 152, 153). They include references to 'islands' and inhabitants in a region rich in lead and tin, which had once been an important terminus of Tartessian maritime exchange (112–13: *Tartessiisque in terminos Oestrumnidum negotiandi mos erat*). Therefore, while the name may or may not itself be Tartessian, it has not improbably come to us through Tartessian. The references to the *Oestrymnides/Oestrumnides* as islands (95, 112) are very closely linked to mentions of 'the sacred isle' (probably Greek word play for Ἱερνη 'Ireland'), the populous *gens Hiernorum* 'Irish people', and the nearby *insula Albionum* 'island of the Britons'. Therefore, in that passage at least, the most straightforward interpretation is that *(insulae) Oestrumnides* mean Ireland and Britain. It is likely that Avienus has elided part of the Atlantic coastline owing to the similarity of this name and the early group name applied to westernmost Armorica, i.e. Ὠστιωνες in Staphanos of Byzantion and Ὀσισμιοι in Strabo (4.4.1) (Falileyev et al. 2010, 177), probably going back to Pytheas in the later 4th century BC, corresponding to Caesar's *Osismii* (*De Bello Gallico* 2.34, 3.9, 7.75). *Osismii* is clearly a Celtic superlative, cognate with Latin *postumus* 'last' and showing characteristically Celtic loss of Indo-European *p-*. It designates the 'last people', inhabiting the end of Gaul's long Atlantic peninsula (Delamarre 2003, 244–5). Though superficially similar to Ὠστιωνες, &c., *Oestrymnis* is more probably connected with Indo-European **u̯ésperos, *u̯ékeros* 'evening', hence 'place of the setting sun, west' and resembles most closely formations underlying Germanic as in Old English *westerna*, Old High German *westrôni*, Old Norse *vestránn* 'dwelling in the west, &c.' If this is the correct etymology, *Oestrymnis* is Indo-European. *Oest-* < Indo-European *μest-* parallels the development of Tartessian -**oir** < Indo-European *$\mu ih_x rós$* 'man, hero' (Wodtko et al. 2008, 726–9) in the name **ooŕoir** (J.19.2), similarly Welsh *ucher* 'evening' < *$oi\chi seros$* < Indo-European *$\mu ék(s)eros$* or *$\mu épseros$* alongside Welsh *gosber* < Latin *vesper(-)* (*ps* < Indo-European *sp* is also found in Celtic words for 'wasp'). On the phonological development of the initial *$\mu é$-*, note also Old Welsh *uceint* '20' < *$\mu oikanti$* < *$\mu ik_a ntī$*. Jordán Cólera (2002) explains *Oestrumnides* as the o-grade of an Old European root *eis-* 'to move fast, with impetus' compounded with the well-attested hydronymic element *-umni-/-umna-* < *up-n-*, *ub-n-*. But the *-tr-* is more easily accounted for if the first element is understood as 'west' < 'evening', thus *Oestrumni-* 'the Atlantic' < *$\mu estr$-ubn-* 'western stream(s)'. *Oestrumnides* would therefore have referred to 'Atlantic islands'. As an ancient Indo-European name for the western ocean, '*$\mu estr$-ubn-*' possibly contributed to the erroneous idea of Herodotus (§§2.34, 4.48) that the Danube, which had the similar name Ἴστρος, flowed all the way from the west, i.e. from the Atlantic.

——(o)ira A9M≠ (J.1.2)　　The context **na-kⁱi·bᵘu oira-uarbᵃan** can be approached both from the standpoint of meaning and of phonetics. **oira-** immediately precedes the formula word **uarbᵃan**, which is interpreted as an accusative of destination | *$\mu ar_a man$* | < *$u(p)er_a m\bar{a}m$* | 'highest being, place, state' (feminine); see note on **uar(n)bᵃan** and Appendix C below. The name of the deceased in the inscriptional text appears to be the unproblematical and abundantly paralleled **tⁱirtᵒos**, an o-stem masculine nominative singular. Therefore, it would be unnecessary to take **oira** as a feminine *ā*-stem nominative singular to fill that syntactic slot in the epitaph, nor would such a hypothetical feminine name be in agreement with other forms in the text (as is the most usual pattern with feminine names in the corpus) or correspond to comparanda elsewhere. Therefore, the interpretation offered is that **oira-** is the first element of a compound modifying the sense of **uarbᵃan**: | *$oira$-$\mu ar_a man$* | < *μiro-$u(p)er_a m\bar{a}m$* | '(to) the highest being, place, state of manliness, heroism, valour'. Though the syntax is different in J.1.2 (**o)ira- uarbᵃan**, the social concepts and institutions, as well as the words, are as in the Celtiberian VIROS VERAMOS 'supreme man' (Peñalba de Villastar; Wodtko 2000, 444; De Hoz 2007b, 202). An inherited Hispano-Celtic or Proto-Celtic collocation may be considered. Compare Celtiberian VIROS, Gaulish *uiros* in names, Old Irish *fer*, Old Welsh *g(u)ur*, cf. Lusitanian/North-west Hispano-Celtic personal names VIRIATIS, VIRIATVS, VIRONVS (Albertos 1985, 302): Proto-Celtic *$\mu iros$* < Indo-European *$\mu ih_x rós$* 'man, hero'. In the corpus, *$\mu iros$* 'man, &c.' often appears as (**i)ir-**, in which the initial labial glide [w] has been fully assimilated to the palatal articulation of the vowel. The reflex of [w] is never written with u ⴹ for this word. But oir(-), as in the present example, recurs: for example, the personal name ooŕoir ⴹⵎ⵾ⵀ⵿⵿ (J.19.2) and the gamonym ('wife's name') derived from it ooŕoire Oⴹⵎ⵾ⵀ⵿⵿ (J.19.1), and the compound uarbᵒoiir ⴹⵎⵎ⵾⊟ⴹⴰⴹ (J.22.1). soloir probably has as its first element Indo-Euroean *séh₂ul 'sun' (Wodtko et al. 2008, 606–11) or possibly *swel- 'turn' (Lambert 2008, with further possibilities). In all of these, the old labial sound is in some sense 'protected' by beginning the second element of a close compound. Or, it may simply be the composition vowel with its round articulation preserved by the former presence of [w] afterwards: for example, the nominative plural leb°o-iire Oⴹⵎⵎ⵾◻O⵿ (MdC). A chronological stratification is also possible, i.e. that *u̯iros first became oir(-) in all positions. oira- is not the second element of a compound in the present example. However, it does immediately follow a round vowel in what is probably a close phrasal group na-kⁱ·bᵘu oira-uarbᵃan. This context would have favoured the preservation of the labial quality of the glide.

——oiśaHa ᴀ⵿ᴀⵎⵎ⵾ (J.11.1) In the context kⁱielaoe:≡ oiśaHa ≡bᵃane≡ robᵃae n(a)ŕkᵉenii, it is likely that oiśaHa is placed in the middle of a lengthy naming phrase. oiśaHa stands out as lacking agreement with the other three forms preceding the standard formulaic closing n(a)ŕkᵉenii. The simplest solution is to take oiśaHa as the name of a dead woman, an ā-stem in the nominative singular. The other forms are then elaborations of oiśaHa's identification, inflected as a co-ordinative compound in the nominative/accusative dual: 'kⁱielaos's wife oiśaHa, foremost woman (?first wife, nominative singular *bena ro₄mā).' Compare the similarly structured naming phrase ⴹaitᵘura meleśae≡::≡bᵃaenae 'Lady of the Baeturians, sweet woman and wife' (J.15.1). For the form oiśaHa, I am unaware of any close comparandum for oiśaHa, and the phonetic value of the second-to-last sign is uncertain. Possibly compare Celtiberian ueizos, ueizui, ueiziai (Wodtko 2000, 437–9), which might mean 'inspector, witness' (De Hoz 2007b, 202), Primitive Irish and British TOVISACI 'of the leader' = Old Irish toísech, Middle Welsh tywyssawc: Indo-European *u̯eid- 'see, know (a fact)'. ś in oiśaHa could stand for a strong or double s developing from two dental consonants coming together in word formation, e.g. *u̯ēd-tu-, zero grade *u̯id-tu- 'vision, knowledge, wisdom'. There seems to be a comparable example of *u̯i- giving Tartessian oi in ooŕoir (J.19.2) < *u(p)er-u̯iros. Note also Oestrymnin above. However, there are more examples in which the labial glide has fully assimilated to the following high front vowel, i.e. iir < *u̯iros.

[o-]lakⁱiuu ⴹⴹⵎⴹᴀ⵿⵾ (MdC) As explained in Tartessian 2 (§§38.1–2), most of the first two signs of this sequence are now flaked away, though the second

is more legible than the first. In other words, the reading -akʲiuu is certain, (*)lakʲiuu is probable, and (o-)lakʲiuu conjectural, there being only a trace of a stroke in the appropriate position. lakᵉentʲi (J.53.1) appears to be inflected as a verb. With a stem syllable of this shape, as well as its context within a corpus of funerary inscriptions, it is likely that we are dealing with forms derived from Indo-European *legʰ- 'lie down'. Thus,)lakʲiuu would represent a thematic 1st person singular form corresponding, at least broadly, to the athematic 3rd plural lakᵉentʲi. From the standpoint of the form lakʲiuu and also the sense, causative *logʰéiō, transitive 'I lay down, cause to lie down', fits at least as well as the intransitive present *legʰō. This causative is behind Early Welsh go-lo, the usual verb for burying a man in heroic poetry, Old Breton past passive participle guoloetic 'covered, concealed', Middle Breton gueleiff 'to cover', which correspond to Old Irish fo·lugi 'conceals' < causative *u(p)o-logʰéiet(i). Note also Old Breton -cobloent 'they place, arrange' < *kom+logʰéiont(i), where the development of the ending resembles that of Tartessian lakᵉentʲi. The Insular Celtic compounds appear to share a preverb with Tartessian o-ni-[l]akᵃatʲi-śe (J.10.1), with o- | (o̦)o- | < *u(p)o- 'under' showing Celtic loss of Indo-European p. See further lak- above.

The 1st person singular in lakʲiuu from earlier -ō is a regular Celtic change in final syllables ∼ Gaulish regu 'I straighten' (Lezoux and Chamalières). Causative | logiu̯ū | or compound | (o̦)o·logiu̯ū | 'I conceal, lay down, cause to rest in the grave' of course suits the context and the attested semantics of derivatives of the root in Celtic. In the context, it would be the gravestone that is speaking, telling the reader that it 'conceals, buries' the deceased, Tillekurkos ⟨and⟩ Arga(n)stamos.

omuṛikᵃ*[✝ᛗᛈᛤᛁᛤᚾ⅄*[(J.16.2) opens the feminine naming phrase ( )omuṛikᵃa[≡]anbᵃatʲia≡iobᵃa[, comprising three forms in overt agreement; see anbᵃatʲia above. The suffix -ikᵃa[indicates that this form probably signifies the deceased woman's group comparable to the Celtiberian and other Hispano-Celtic 'gentilic' names of later periods, mostly attested in the genitive plural, e.g. mailikum, Teiuantikum, Toutinikum (all K.1.3; see Wodtko 2003, §56). ( )omuṛikᵃa[here would thus mean | Qomurikā | 'female of the Qomurikoi', i.e. '... of the group claiming descent from Qomuri-'. Thus, all together, 'woman of the kindred of Qomuri-, youngest daughter of Ambaχtos'; see the Commentary on the inscription. John Carey has suggested to me a possible link with the demonic Fomoire of Irish mythology (e.g. in the well-known tale Cath Maige Tuired), who might originally have had a more benign function in connection with the otherworld and afterlife. (While 'under-sea' is an obvious explanation for the Early Irish name Fomoire and how some of the tales clearly understood the name, it is not certainly the correct etymology; cf. Gray 1982, 132.) Following this suggestion, the deceased woman's group might have identified themselves as descendants of a mythological 'under-sea' (*$u(p)o$-mori-) ancestor. This word for 'sea' may occur also in the dative/ablative plural compound **alakⁱ-muŕbⁿ? ?◻ᚲᚣᚳᚣᚹᛈᚨᚔᚨ** (S. Martinho): Indo-European *$móri$ 'sea'. On the phonetic conditioning of Proto-Celtic *mori- to Tartessian -muŕi-, see *Tartessian 2* §91.

o-ni-↑akᵃatⁱi-śe ᚩᚳᚣᚩᚪᚾᚾᚨ↑ᚣᚣ‡ (J.10.1) ?= **o-ni-[l]akᵃatⁱi-śe** As discussed under the entry **lak-** above, this sequence can be interpreted as a paradigmatic form of a verb, attested in four other forms in the corpus. These can also be linked, as being derived from the same root, with the noun **lokⁿon** (J.1.1), **lokⁿon** (J.57.1), probably 'interment, funerary urn'. Apart from the long MdC text, the verb **lak-** does not occur together with the most pervasive formula word **naŕkᵉentⁱi**, &c. Therefore, the meanings of the two might be similar enough for one to render the other superfluous within the same statement. A basic sense 'lie down' < Indo-European *leg^b- is an obvious possibility. For the inscribed stone and text in general, which are unusual, see the Commentary on the inscription above. Taking the opening sequence **ariariśe** conventionally to be naming the deceased, this can be understood as 'this man Ariaris' | Ariaris-se | < *Ario-riχs+se. If so, that would be a prominent single opening name in the nominative singular, emphasized by a demonstrative, followed by a 3rd person singular present-tense verb, also emphasized by the same (or formally identical) demonstrative: **ariariś-e : o-ni-(l)akᵃatⁱi-śe** 'this man Ariaris now ?lies down under here' | Ariaris-se ọo ni lagặti se |. In this interpretation, a double -s-s- and a single s are both written with sign **ś** ᚳ. As discussed in *Tartessian 2* §115, there is, as yet, no apparent consistency in the corpus for distinguishing, **ś** ᚳ from **s** ‡. And here, the first -śe would have influenced the epigrapher's thinking as he carved the second, especially if they were the same word as proposed. On **o-** < *$u(p)o$- 'under' and **ni-** 'down(wards)', see the notes above. The basic statement can thus be understood as an elaboration of the minimal pattern of **akⁿo(l)ioś naŕkᵉetⁱi** 'Akolios now ?rests [here]' (J.56.1), in which the implicit 'here' has been made emphatically explicit.

ooŕoir ᚱᚣ‡ᚾ‡‡ (J.19.2) and **ooŕoire** ᚩᚱᚣ‡ᚾ‡‡ (J.19.1), both from the Pêgo necropolis, are clearly forms of the same name. The first occurs in the well-carved, minimal #**ooŕoir naŕkᵉen↑ⁱi#**, to be interpreted | Qor-ọir narkemi | 'I Qor-ọir now rest [here]' or | Qor-ọir narkenti | 'Qor-ọir [?and wife] now rest [here]'. **ooŕoire** in context with **bᵃane** 'woman, wife' is taken as a gamonym, part of the naming phrase of the wife:]l̲iirnestᵃakᵘun bᵃane≡ooŕoire 'woman of the kindred of Lir(a)nestos and wife of Ooŕoir'. Rather than taking **ooŕoire** as a form of genitive, it is more likely that it is a regular phonological development of a i̯ā-stem adjective of relationship: thus *$b_ạnai$≡U(p)er-u̯iri̯ặi 'woman/wife and female relative of *U(p)er-u̯iros’ > *...Qor-o̯ireāi by regular lowering of *i* to Tartessian **e** before *ă* (*Tartessian 2* §78), then *... Qor-o̯ireē by regular simplification of diphthongs (*Tartessian 2* §94). For the basic form *U(p)er-u̯iros 'Super-man, -hero', cf. Celtiberian VIROS VERAMOS 'supreme man' (Peñalba de Villastar; Wodtko 2000, 444; De Hoz 2007b, 202), which has the same two elements, but as a noun phrase, rather than a close compound, the second element of which is a superlative adjective based on the preposition *u(p)er 'over'. The elements go back to Indo-European *(s)h₄upér 'over' (with characteristically Celtic loss of Indo-European *p*) + *u̯ihₓrós 'man, hero'; both are extremely common in the name formation of all the ancient and medieval Celtic languages.

The phonetic variation in the reflexes of *u(p)er is found, to a greater or lesser degree, in all of the Celtic languages. The development of *u̯er > *u̯or is predominant in the Insular Celtic languages, but found also in Gaulish, e.g. DIVORTOMV alongside DIVERTOMV on the Coligny Calendar and the compound verb *de-uor-buet-id* (Lezoux); see *Tartessian 2* §§70.1–2. Celtiberian has VORAMOS and, as well as VERAMOS, accusative VERAMOM, so the development is obviously Hispano-Celtic too and occurs in this particular word, 'over'. Another probable example of this phonetic development is the well-attested divine epithet VORTEAECIO which occurs in Lusitania. As to the actual origin of the variation, a sound change is possible, as is an old Indo-European vowel-grade variation between *(s)h₄upér and *(s)h₄upor. The analogical interplay of the functional pair *u(p)er and *u(p)o is likely to have favoured the interchange of vowels.

orbᵃa ⧺ᛈᛉᚨ (J.53.1) occurs in the context of what is interpreted as the first of two sentences in a complete text: kᵒ-tᵘ-ua-ratᵉe tᵘn↑ⁱitᵉsbᵃan orbᵃa setᵃa. kᵒ-tᵘ-ua-ratᵉe is interpreted as a compound verb, 3rd singular perfect, taking the place, so to speak, of the formulaic tᵉe·ro-bᵃare. The two noun phrases, accusative feminine tᵘn↑ⁱitᵉsbᵃan and probable nominative feminine orbᵃa setᵃa, are seen as both, in different ways, taking the place of the formulaic uar(n)bᵃan. tᵘn↑ⁱitᵉsbᵃan does so as a feminine superlative accusative of destination, as well probably as the specific meaning of the word, see note on tᵘn↑ⁱitᵉsbᵃan below. orbᵃa is most probably the nominative singular of a phonological byform of uar(n)bᵃan | u̯arₐman |, i.e. | (o̯)orₐmā |, both from *u(p)eramā(-) 'highest' (feminine). In this interpretation, the phonological development of orbᵃa is like that of Celtiberian VORAMOS 'highest' masculine nominative singular, together with the regular assimilation of *u̯o- to | (o̯)o- | in Tartessian; see *Tartessian 2* §§70.1–3, 97.1–3. The fact that the find spot of this inscription was near Seville, i.e. closer to Celtiberia and far to the east of all the stones reading uar(n)bᵃan, may be significant. In other words, the form | u̯orₐmo- | might have been more common in the east and centre of the Peninsula.

An alternative possibility is to understand **orbᵃa** as 'heiress, inheritance, inherited', cf. the Hispano-Celtic family name [O]ʀʙɪᴇɴɪᴄ[ᴠᴍ] on an inscription from León (González Rodríguez 1986, 132), Old Irish *orbae, orb(b)* 'heir, inheritance', Early Welsh *wrvyδ* < Celtic **orbi̯om*, Gaulish personal names *Orbius, Orbia*, &c. (Delamarre 2003, 243), the Gaulish and British compound name ᴏʀʙɪᴏᴛᴀʟᴠs (Raybould & Sims-Williams 2007, 69) < Indo-European **h₂/₃orbʰos* 'orphan' (De Hoz 2007b, 197).

orbᵃa setᵃa ⧻P⟩A⧻O╳A (J.53.1)　　Following from the discussions on **orbᵃa** above and **setᵃa** below, this phrase would comprise the same two elements as in the Old Welsh compound *guorsed* 'tumulus, (fairy-)mound (*sídh*), throne, &c.' (cf. Ó Cathasaigh 1977–8; Falileyev 2010, 30). *Gorsedd* and **orbᵃa setᵃa** would differ syntactically in that the first element, a preposition 'over', has been supplied with a superlative suffix. **orbᵃa setᵃa** could be either a two-word phrase with agreeing endings, i.e. | (o̦)or̯ₐmā sedā | or a close compound | (o̦)or̯ₐma-sedā |. The latter would be a further example of the Tartessian composition vowel as -a-; see *Tartessian 2* §73.1. Either as a two-word phrase or full compound the basic sense would be 'highest seat, resting place, throne'. Welsh speakers may think along the lines of 'gorsedd, goruchaf sedd'. In either case **orbᵃa setᵃa** is not a name and does not function like the paired names, which take plural verbs, for example, the second sentence of this inscription, **lakᵉentⁱi ra⧧a≡kᵃaśetᵃana. orbᵃa setᵃa** and **tⁿnⵙitᵉsbᵃan** | *tumitesₐman* | can be traced by etymology as referring to different aspects of the physical burial (i.e. funeral vehicle and burial mound) and/or in afterlife belief; see note on **kᵒtᵘuaratᵉe** above.

oretᵒo ⧻△O⧼⧻ (J.4.1.)　　Until the stone was lost in recent times, the end of the inscription survived in tact and clearly closed with these five signs. The interpretation of this form as | o̦o-reto | 'of deliverance, of rescue, of running under', genitive singular of an *o*-stem verbal noun, 'to help, save, deliver' (< Indo-European **retₕ₂-* 'run') is supported by Celtic comparanda for the compound stem and case ending, the context of this sequence of signs within the inscription, and by a related find from the same site. To start with the last, there was also found at Benaciate a second stone of the same geological fabric and thickness as J.4.1, which carries a fragmentary and only partially legible right-to-left SW inscription, but more clearly the image of a horsewoman, viewed from the back, wearing a Greek helmet and riding side-saddle on a large horse. This relief sculptural image is reminiscent of some depictions of the Gaulish horse goddess Epona dating from the Roman period. The Benaciate horsewoman holds a long object in her left hand, probably the reins, which continue on behind the neck of the horse to its nose.

Nearly complete and well carved, the inscriptional text is unusual, and we cannot be certain that it belongs to the funerary genre: **?ibᵒoi̯ ion asune≡ uarbᵃan ≡ekᵘuŕine obᵃar bᵃara*******tᵃa oretᵒo/**. Given the iconography of the horsewoman, that **ekᵘuŕine** means 'horse queen' is an obvious lielihood, and equine associations for **asune** are also possible; see the notes on these forms above.

The Proto-Celtic compound verbal noun **u(p)o-reto-*, for which **o-retᵒo** would be the regular Tartessian phonological outcome in the genitive singular, means 'to help, deliver, rescue'. Literally and etymologically, the sense was 'to run under', like Latin *sub-curō*. Thus, the etymology invokes the idealized beneficial action of a horse or wheeled vehicle in combat. There are a few examples in the early medieval Celtic languages in which this older sense is preserved: e.g. Old Irish *fod rethat* 'that run under him' referring to chariot wheels in *Audacht Morainn* mentioned above, also in Early Welsh (the *Gododdin*) *eb̯ystrawr pasc a-e gwaredei* 'it was well-nourished steeds that were wont to run under him [i.e. the hero]'. Gaulish *uoreto-* occurs in names; cf. also Old Irish *fo reith*, Old Welsh *guoret*, Middle Welsh *gwaret*, *dywaret*, &c., and possibly the North-west Hispano-Celtic personal name VRETA (Albertos 1985, 302). Probably a form of the same verb is the perfect 3rd singular **kᵒ-tᵘ-ua-ratᵉe** 'has delivered' (J.53.1); see note.

—— **oteerkᵃa** ΛΛ9OᕀᗠΨ *or* **oteerkᵃaŕ*[** ΛΛ9OᕀᗠΨ (J.1.4)   Because of the fragmentary state of the stone and inscription—half or less survive—and absence of any of the formula words, interpretation is difficult. However, a meaning can be proposed on the basis of the close similarity to a Gaulish word, *uodercos*, *uoderce* (Larzac), the meaning of which would be appropriate in an epigraphic text commemorating a burial. The Gaulish means 'tomb' (Delamarre 2003, 326, citing Fleuriot) < 'under-cavity': **u(p)o-* + Indo-European **derk´-* 'glance at, see'. Old Irish *derc*, also *deirc*, does commonly mean 'cavity' as well as 'eye'. Cf. the personal name *Adercus* < Celtic **ad-derkos* in Vettonian territory (Luján 2007, 253, 256), and the Gaulish personal names INDERCILLVS, INDERCINIVS, INDERCVS (Raybould & Sims-Williams 2007, 63). The word possibly occurs again as **oᕀerbᵉe** OᏧ9Oᕀ₮ (J.10.1). If the segmentation is **oteerkᵃaŕ*[**, a compound with **oteerkᵃa** |*ǫo-derko-*| + a further element is possible. **u(p)o-* > Tartessian **o-** |*ǫo-*| is regular.

raᕀa≡kᵃasetᵃana ΡΑᕀΑΛΛΑΜΟᕁΑᏐΑ (J.53.1) is interpreted as a feminine co-ordinative compound, naming the deceased 'Raᕀa ⟨and⟩ the tin/bronze officer', the subject of the verb **lakᵉentⁱi** ᒥΑᏦΟᏐ⬤Ꮢ '"they" now lie down [here], have now lain down here'. See above **kᵃasetᵃana**, **lakᵉentⁱi**, and the Commentary on the inscription; also *Tartessian 2* 82–7. On the possible phonetic values and etymological origins of the SW sign ᕀ as used before Α **a**, see the notes on **ᘓaitᵘura** and **ᕀatᵃaneatᵉe** above. On the name **raᕀa**, if this is read as **raφa** with the reflex of a weakened *p*, then compare RAPPA in an inscription from the territory of the south-western Celtici, also an inscription from Rome RAPETIGVS MEDICVS, CIVIS HISPANVS. Luján regards neither comparandum as securely Indo-European (Luján 2001, 473). Nevertheless, they are indigenous Palaeohispanic names, and RAPPA reappears in the same region as **raⰓa**.

rinoeb°o ꟼ Ͷ Ͳ‡○日‡ (J.5.1) occurs in a series of datives/ablatives plural showing overt agreement: **ist̲a̲|ib°o rinoeb°o |anak^e enak^e:e|ib°o**, so in context it is surely a substantive, probably a name or common noun, and the segmentation— between **-b°o** and **+-b°o** is beyond doubt. The comparison **lok°ob°o≡niirab°o** 'for the divine Lugoues and for the chief men' (J.1.1) suggests that this may be an invocation and **rinoeb°o** thus a divine name. As explained in *Tartessian 2* §114, the phonetic distinction between r ꟼ and ŕ ͷ is uncertain. The form **naŕrk^e:n:** (J.23.1) implies that they were similar. ŕ does not occur in word-initial position, and it is common in the languages of the world, including the Celtic languages and modern languages of the Iberian Peninsula, for *r*-sounds to differ phonetically and sometimes phonemically at the beginning of a word or syllable. Therefore, dative/ablative plural **rinoeb°o** and the second element of the compound **ek^uuŕine** ○ͶͶͰͶ日○ (J.4.1) are more likely to be forms of the same word or name. Forms of **rig̲aní* 'queen' (~ Old Irish *rígain*, Sanskrit *rajñí*) would suit the contexts of both forms. Note that the cluster |g̲n| could not be represented directly in the SW writing system. Either the sign for the stop had to be omitted or |a̲n| had to be represented as two full segments, which was probably at odds with the phonemic structure of the language at the date the writing system became fixed (see *Tartessian 2* §69). Less probably, compare Gaulish *Rēnos* 'Rhine' < 'river' (Delamarre 2003, 257), Old Irish *rían* 'sea': Indo-European **rei-* 'flow'.

-ris ‡Ͷꟼ nominative singular 'leader, king' is probably the second element in the personal names **aib^uuris** (J.3.1) and *Gargoris*, the name of a mythological Tartessian king in Justin's Epitome. It is proposed that **ariariśe** beginning J.10.1 be read |*Aria-ris-se*| 'this man **Ario-rīχs*'. Compare Gaulish *Ambiorix, Biturix, Coticorix, Dumnorix, Secorix, Vercingetorix*, possibly Celtiberian *-rés* in *kombalkokores* (De Hoz 2007b, 197–8, 201; Wodtko 2000, 188–9), but *-ris* in Celtiberian *Caturis* (De Hoz 2007b, 203) < Indo-European **h₃rēg̑'s* 'king, ruler'.

ro ‡ꟼ can be interpreted in the following nine examples as a preverbal preposition reinforcing the perfective aspect of verbs derived from the Indo-European perfect: **t^e·ro·b^aare** ○ꟼΑ}‡ꟼ○日 (J.1.1, J.12.1), **t^ee·ro·b^aare** ○ꟼΑ}‡ꟼ○○日 (J.18.2), **ro·b^aare** Ͷ‡⟨ΑꟼO (J.16.3) ○ꟼΑ}‡ꟼ (MdC), probably also **ro·b^aak^e** Ͷ‡⟨ΑꟼO (J.16.3) to be read **ro·b^aare** (see p. 88 and **ro·b^aak^e** below), **ro-n·b^aare**

ⵔⵇA⸝ⵖ≠ⵇ (Monte Gordo), **ro·n·bᵃaren** ⵖⵔⵇA⸝ⵖ≠ⵇ (J.11.4), **ro-la[kᵘ]a** AⵔA⸀≠ⵇ (J.3.1); possibly also **ro·bᵃae** ⵔA⸝≠ⵇ (J.11.1).Tartessian **ro** corresponds exactly to Celtiberian (in *ro·biseti*), Gaulish, Old Irish, Old Breton *ro*, Old Welsh *ri* < Proto-Celtic **(p)ro* < Indo-European **pro* 'forward, ahead, &c.', showing loss of Indo-European *p* in Tartessian, a defining feature of Celtic. In J.11.4 and Monte Gordo, **ro** occurs as the first and only preverb, thus it would be capable of supporting a 'Wackernagel's' enclitic; therefore, **ro-n** ⵖ≠ⵇ in these examples can be understood as containing an elided accusative infixed pronoun or relative particle. For the syntax of **ro** in the Tartessian verbal complex and Celtic and Indo-European comparanda, see Appendix C below and *Tartessian 2* §§55.2–63.2. In J.55.1 the syntax of **ro-** is different. It begins the statement of a complete inscriptional text. It is possibly a simple preposition there, meaning 'for'.

robᵃa A⸝≠ⵇ (J.18.1) occurs within the naming phrase **bᵒotⁱieana**≡ **kᵉertᵒo** ≡**robᵃa**. It is possibly found again, if the graffito from Moura was written in the less common left-to-right orientation, as]***robᵃa na**[or]***robᵃan a**[ ]*ⵇ≠⸜AⵖA[, which could be either exactly the same form as in J.18.1 or its accusative, depending on the segmentation. In J.18.1, **robᵃa** agrees with the feminine personal name **bᵒotⁱieana**, which begins the inscription and surely identifies the deceased. The proposed etymology is to read **robᵃa** as | *roₐmā* | < Indo-European **pro-meh₂* 'first female' ~ Middle Irish *rom* 'early, too soon' < Indo-European **pro-mo-* (see further the Commentary on inscription J.18.1). For the Tartessian identification formula, compare **anbᵃatⁱia iobᵃa**[| *Amba(χ)tⁱā i̯ōₐmā* | 'youngest daughter of Amba(χ)tos' (J.16.2) and **tᵘurea iubᵃa** | *Tureā iūₐmā* | 'youngest daughter of Turos' (J.7.8) (*Tartessian 2* §§35.2–3). Together with these, **tⁱirtᵒos** 'Third' (J.1.2) would also show an identification system frequently resorting to prioritizing, probably expressing the birth-order of offspring, probably also Hispano-Celtic *Turos* 'Fourth'.

robᵃae ⵔA⸝≠ⵇ (J.11.1) can possibly be interpreted as **ro-bᵃae** | *ro· bāe* | 'has passed away', that is the perfect preverb **ro** together with a 3rd singular perfect of the same verb occurring in the compound **tᵉe·bᵃantⁱi** 'they pass away, they die' (MdC) ~ Old Iirsh *baïd* 'dies' < 'steps away'. However, in the context of this complete and legible inscription, which begins **kⁱielaoe:**≡ **oiśaHa** ≡**bᵃane**≡**robᵃae**, it is probable that **robᵃae** is the final element of a long naming phrase 'Kielaos's wife OiśaHā, foremost woman' or 'Kielaos's first wife OiśaHā'. In this case, **robᵃae** would be a case form of **robᵃa** | *roₐmā* | 'foremost, first woman' < **(p)roₐmā* in overt agreement with the 'gamonym' **kⁱielaoe** and **bᵃane** 'woman, wife'. **kⁱielaoe:**≡ **bᵃane**≡**robᵃae** would thus form an extended co-ordinative compound in the nominative/accusative dual.

ro·bᵃakᵉe P⧺{AKO (J.16.3) The damaged sign permits reading this sequence as the more usual formula word **ro·bᵃare** in the well-precedented epigraphic closing . . .**ro·bᵃare bᵃa naŕkᵉ[e]ntⁱi#** '. . . death/this grave has carried/taken, so now they remain [here]'; see Appendix C. **tᵉe(e)** is definitely absent as an initial preverb preceding **ro**, as is also the case with **ro·bᵃare** at MdC, see below. The opening line of the present inscription is obscure. It is therefore possible that there is a logical or syntactic reason that **tᵉe(e) | de |** 'away from' was not used.

ro·bᵃare O9A⦚⧺9 (MdC), compound verb 3rd singular perfect, with the probable meaning 'has carried' with 'death' or the grave or a particular deity being understood as the subject. That the compound verb is not **tᵉe(e)·ro-bᵃare** 'has carried away' (J.1.1, J.12.1, J.18.2) may be significant and purposeful. That preverb occurs in another compound verb **tᵉe·bᵃantⁱi** 'they pass away' earlier in the MdC text. There may be a grammatical or stylistic prohibition blocking the repetition of a preverb within one statement. Or it may be a matter of simple logic. If the deceased 'pass away' to the destination in present time, then death cannot already 'have carried [them] away' to that ultimate destination in past time. The journey away from this world is still ongoing. The logical, and probably the grammatical, object of **ro·bᵃare** would be the deceased **tⁱilekᵘurkᵘu=arkᵃastᵃamu**, named at the beginning of the text in the nominative/accusative dual. **tᵉe(e) | de |** 'away from' is also absent from the forms with the nasal orthography, **ro-n·bᵃare** (Monte Gordo) and **ro-n·bᵃaren** (J.11.4), see below.

ro-laꝾa AꝾA⊣⧺9 (J.3.1) ?= **ro·lakᵘa** The stem **lak-** occurs several times in the corpus; see above. **lakᵉentⁱi** ΓAKOⲨⱰⲚ (J.53.1) most especially appears to be a verb, both formally, and according to context. The preceding segment **ro** would also favour this interpretation. However, the sign Ꝿ would represent **tᵉ** before **e** or **kᵘ** before **u**, but is of uncertain value here preceding **a**. As 1st person singular perfect, **lakᵘa** could be compared with **bᵃarua** (J.7.9), for which a possible explanation could be the conflation of the inherited 1st person singular perfect ending with the higher-frequency 1st person singular thematic present tense in ~ū. See further the Commentary on the inscription.

ro-n·bᵃare O9A⦚Ⲩ⧺9 (Monte Gordo), **ro-n·bᵃaren** ⲨO9A⦚Ⲩ⧺9 (J.11.4) One could alternatively segment these as **ro·nbᵃare** and **ro·nbᵃaren** and take the forms merely as orthographic variants of **ro·bᵃare, ro·bᵃaren**, thus indicating that the initial consonant of the verb was not | b- | but | m- |, even though they are never written in their many occurrences with the unambiguous graphemes for | m- |, i.e. Ⲙ and ⲱ. The other detail arguing against reading these as more-or-less random graphic variants for ** | ro-mᵃre(n(t)) | is that **ro** is the only preverb in both these examples, rather than following **tᵉe(e)** as in the recurrent formulaic t^e e(e)·ro-b^a are. Therefore, there appears to be something not random about the presence of **n** in these examples, favouring the interpretation of an elided accusative singular infix; see note on **ro** above. In the Monte Gordo text, there is more than one possible antecedent for such an infix; see the Commentary on the inscription. With J.11.4 the naming phrase is hard to work out from the surviving 18th-century drawing. The provisional glosses are 'whom [death/this grave] have carried' and 'whom they have carried'.

sab^o oi ᛃ⊹日A⧧ (J.5.1) occurs as the first word of a long and complete inscription on a large stone. Three possible interpretations are canvassed in the Commentary, the preferred alternative being locative singular | *samoi* | 'in summer', commemorating a seasonal rite. Alternative possibilities include the dative singular of a personal name.

——**śaen** ᛃOAᛘ (J.27.1)   In the reading]uk^e e śaen b^a are nańk^e e*[ ] b^e eś**n*[, part of the formula is clear immediately following the four signs in question. In the extant 18th-century drawing, there is possibly room for another sign or two before]uk^e e, which could identify the deceased, if so feminine. There does not seem to be enough room for a form of **uar(n)b^a an**. Thus, **śaen** could be a different accusative singular taking its place in the syntax. An accusative demonstrative meaning 'to this [grave], here' is a possibility, cf. Celtiberian *stam*. A segmentation]uk^e eśa en b^a are is an alternative possibility with **en** as an accusative pronoun, thus corresponding to the nasalizing masculine accusative infixed pronoun of Old Irish.

—— **salsaloi** ⧧Aᛗ⧧Aᛗ⊹ᛃ or possibly **salsanoi** ⧧Aᛗ⧧Aᛗ⊹ᛃ (J.12.4)   This form begins the inscription (**salsaloi** 𝍌^i[|]b^a e b^a a lak^i in𝍌^i i) and so may be the name of the deceased, though the ending **-oi** could be that of a locative singular, referring to the place or time of the burial and its commemoration. The segmentation at the end is not certain: the first word could be **salsaloi**𝍌^i[. But the text's closing b^a a lak^i in𝍌^i i appears clearly to be a variant of the usual formulaic closing b^a a nańk^e ent^i i. The interpretation of **salsaloi**(-) is very uncertain. If a locative, ?cf. Gaulish *salico-* 'willow'. In the absence of any closely similar Celtic names, we should possibly consider the Numidian (Palaeo-Berber) names *Zelalsen* (a king of the 3rd century BC) and *Salsa* (a Christian martyr of the 4th century AD).

——**sarune** Oᛃ٩٩A⧧ (J.22.1, J.22.2) less probably to be segmented **saruneea** AOOᛃ٩٩A⧧, in either case significantly resembling **saru[?n]an** ⧧Aᛂᛈ☿ᛃAᛁ (MdC, see Guerra 2010, 71–3). As a personal name, SARONIS occurs twice in Roman Lusitania, at locations now in western Spain (Vallejo 2005, 394). Either

sarune or **saruneea** can be rationalized with ‡APH⌒☆AⱣ as forms of
ā-stem feminine singular | *Sarun(n)ā-* |, which can be etymologized as a divine
name, such as 'star goddess' < *$^{\prime}$Sərunnā*. On this form of the divine suffix,
Watkins (1999, 12–20) relates the formation of the Hittite theonym *Tarḫunnas*
to that of the Gaulish *C]ernunnos* as a shared Indo-European inheritance. Compare the well-attested Gaulish goddess *Sirona/Đirona* probably from a similar
preform with a long vowel in the root (Indo-European *$h_2st\bar{e}r$* 'star'), but also
Serona and *Serana* (Jufer & Luginbühl 2001, 62) with *e*-grade of the root as in
Old Welsh *ser-enn*, Old Breton *ster-enn*. Like Indo-European *$h_2n\bar{e}r$* 'man' (>
Tartessian **ni(i)ra-**), *$h_2st\bar{e}r$* 'star' had a complex paradigm with *e*-, lengthened,
and zero grades (Wodtko et al. 2008, 348–54): e.g. Greek nominative singular
ἀστήρ, plural ἄστρα, genitive singular ἀστέρος. The attested Celtic comparanda
show the reflexes of *e* and *ē*. **sarune** would reflect zero-grade *$h_2st\dot{r}V$-*, probably
with analogical syllabification (i.e. *-ar-* as a morphological zero-grade within a
paradigm also including alternation with *-er-*).

The fact that ‡APH⌒☆AⱣ has an unusual oversize sign with rays extending
from it is at least consistent with the 'star' interpretation. As discussed by Guerra
(2010), a more proportionally sized and differently orientated sign, similar in shape
to that used in MdC, occurs second-to-last amongst the 27 signs of the south-
western 'abekatu' from Espanca, south Portugal (J.25.1, p. 21). If **saru⌒an**
belongs to the same paradigm as **sarune** or **saruneea** (J.22.1, J.22.2), as seems
likely, then we expect the sign to stand for a nasal [n, nn], palatal nasal [n′, nn′]
or nasal + front vowel [ne], [ni]. John Carey has suggested to me that there might
be syncretism of **sarune** with Phoenician Astarte. Almagro-Gorbea (1988, 73)
mentions Tartessian images of the 'Dea Mater' type (reminiscent of the Phoenician Astarte) sometimes featuring 'éléments astraux'. Similarly now, with graffiti
on ceramics from the Medellín necropolis, five-pointed stars are a recurrent
image and have been plausibly linked to the cult of Astarte as a star goddess,
comparable to Aphrodite/Venus, also by Almagro-Gorbea (2008, 760–6).

Note that in the long MdC text the formula word **uar(n)bᵃan** | *uar$_a$man* |
'highest destination' is absent. But ‡APH⌒☆AⱣ is inflected like it, as a feminine
singular accusative, arguably taking the place of **uar(n)bᵃan**. Is this in fact an
underlying meaning, even the primary meaning, behind **uar(n)bᵃan**, i.e. the star
goddess, the Indo-Europeanized equivalent of Semitic Astarte? Again following
Carey's suggestion, we could compare the ideology behind the Romano-British
goddess called *Brigantia* 'the High One' and her Irish cognate *Brigit*, goddess and
saint, which of course have a bearing on the peoples called *Brigantes* in Britain
and Ireland, *Brigantium* in Callaecia, and the many places called *brigā* in ancient
Gaul and the Iberian Peninsula. As the Hispano-Celtic names *Uxama* and *Uama*,
both meaning 'highest place' (feminine), are built on a preposition *$^*u(p)o$*, rather

than adjectives or nouns, what then would have been the simple positive grade behind these superlatives? Surely, 'high place' was simply *brigā* (~ Welsh *bre*) with which *Uxama* and *Uama* stood as the suppletive superlatives. The concept and cult of the feminine lofty one was pervasive in the language and culture. Names with Celtic *Uχselo-* 'high' appear to be absent from the Iberian Peninsula (to surmise negatively from Falileyev 2010).

-sek^{u}ui ꓩꓩꓧꓳꓘ[(J.1.4)   The inscription is fragmentary, and there are no formula words. Therefore, interpretation is difficult, largely limited to forms of desinences and possible etymologies of word stems. Most of the first sign is missing, so the reading is doubtful. **-t^{e}ek^{u}ui** ꓩꓩꓧꓳꓩ[(which see) is somewhat more likely on the basis of the surviving carving. In the context of the line fragment]**sek^{u}ui uurk^{e}e ot^{e}erk^{a}a ŕ*[**, **uurk^{e}e** (which see) is recognizable as an attested Palaeohispanic element, thus providing the provisional segmentation, favoured also by the preceding signs **-ui**, which conform unproblematically to the form of an *o*-stem or *u*-stem dative singular case form. The forms of the surviving text and stone indicate that several signs have probably been lost at the beginning of this line. Therefore, one definite possibility is that]**sek^{u}ui** is the dative singular of a group name with an adjectival velar suffix, for example, **tuŕek^{u}ui** (J.14.1) 'for a man of the kindred of Turos' < **Turikōi*, also genitive plural]**t^{a}arnek^{u}un** (J.26.1) < **Tar$_a$nikōm*; see *Tartessian 2* §80. If that is the case, the actual eponym of the group has been lost in the surviving sequence]**sek^{u}ui**. Another possibility is that]**sek^{u}ui** is an example of the extremely common Celtic (including Hispano-Celtic) name element *segos* 'strong, bold, &c.', either as simplex man's name or as the second element of a compound name. Compare the Hispano-Celtic place-names *Segontia*, *Segovia*, *Segida*, and the personal names SEGIVS VIRONO MATIENI F., ANCOEMA DESICA SEGI. F., DOVID[EN]A CAELICA SEGEI, C(AIAE) AMBATAE ... SEGEI F., *Segumaros* (in the territory of the Celtici of the south-west [Vallejo 2005, 395, 471]), SEGIDIAECO (*L'Année épigraphique* 1967, 76, León), also Gaulish *Sego-dumnus*, ΣΕΓΟΜΑΡΟΣ, superlative *Segisami* = Hispano-Celtic *Segisama* (e.g. CANGILVS VIRONO SEGISAMI F. [Vallejo 2005, 396]), Old Irish *seg* 'force, vigour', Welsh *hy* 'audacious': Indo-European **seg'h-* 'conquer, victory' (Wodtko et al. 2008, 600–4). Another possibility is that]**sek^{u}ui** is the latter part of an incomplete personal name in which Celtic **ek^{u}os* 'horse', dative **| -ek^{u}ūi |*, is the final element.

set^{a}a ꓫꓳ✕ꓥ (J.53.1)   **orb^{a}a set^{a}a** (which see) is taken as a feminine nominative phrase showing overt concord, the subject of the compound 3rd singular verb in the syntagm **ko-tu-ua-rat^{e}e tun↑itesb^{a}an orb^{a}a set^{a}a** *| Ko(n) tu-ụa-rāte tumites$_a$man (ọ)or$_a$mā sedā |* 'the sublime resting place (*or* inherited resting place) has carried away safely (< has run under) to the best tumulus'; see further

Tartessian 2 §§47–53. **set^{a}a** is interpreted as 'seat, resting place, &c.', cf. Welsh *sedd* < Indo-European **sedes-*, **sed-*, 'resting place' ~ Early Welsh *seð* 'seat', *gorseð* 'burial mound, &c.', cf. North-west Hispano-Celtic NIMMEDO ASEDDIAGO (Mieres, Oviedo, Búa 2000, 270–1): Indo-European **sedes-*, **sed-* 'seat' (Wodtko et al. 2008, 590–600). Old Irish *síd* 'tumulus, fairy mound', also 'peace' (Welsh *hedd*) goes back to the same root with a long vowel (see further Ó Cathasaigh 1977/8). Lepontic *siteś* in the Prestino inscription (*c.* 500 BC) possibly belongs here, with 'seat' in the sense of 'monument, temple'. Another relevant semantic factor here is that Indo-European **sed-* is also the base for the Celtic terminology for chariots: e.g. Belgic Gaulish *assedon* 'war chariot' < **ad-sedo-*, British AÐÐEDOMAROS 'great in chariots', Old Irish *arae* 'charioteer' < **are-sed-s* (Koch 1987). The key verb in this connection is Celtic **u(p)o-ret-* 'help, deliver' < 'run under', and that is what we find here with perfect **-ua-rat^{e}e** (see *Tartessian* 2 §36).

sie: |OᛘǂN (J.12.1) The reading **sien̲** ᛙ̲OᛘǂN is also possible, but less likely. A significant feature of this unique inscription—as well as the warrior image in the middle of the writing field of the stone—is that the formula words are not in their usual order, i.e. **naŕk^{e}ent^{i}i**, which is frequently the closing word of the text, precedes **t^{e}e·ro-b^{a}are**: thus, **iru≡alk^{u}u—sie̲: naŕk^{e}ent^{i}i—mub^{a}a t^{e}e·ro-b^{a}are ⋭at^{a}anea̲t^{e}e**. Therefore, relative syntax could explain the modified word order: '. . . has carried away **iru≡alk^{u}u** who now lie here. . .' Such a syntactic function is consistent with the form **sie** ~ Gaulish *sies* (Larzac), which is probably a nominative plural demonstrative 'those ones, these women'. The ending without the final *-s* is the older, and Gaulish *sies* has been recharacterized as a plural on the basis of consonant-stem nouns. On the etymology, see further p. 248.

soloir ǂǂΓǂᛈP (J.11.3) The text does not survive complete, but we clearly have the beginning and end: **soloir uarb̲^{a}an̲**[ ]**in̲a o***[| n]**a̲ŕk^{e}enii**. The signs are enclosed within an inscribed line, and a vertical rule precedes **soloir**. As the clearly legible formula word **uarb̲^{a}an̲**[follows, there is no doubt about this form's segmentation. **uarb̲^{a}an̲** and the conventional closing n]**a̲ŕk^{e}enii** indicate that this is a Tartessian funerary inscription of the most common pattern and that **soloir** must be a one-term naming phrase identifying the deceased; see Appendix C. **soloir** is interpreted as the nominative of a compound man's name, with a second element **-ir** |*-i̯ir*| < **-u̯iros* 'man, hero'; see above **-iir**, **-ir**. Compare the Celtiberian 'family name' *Suoli*kum* (K.1.3 Botorrita, III–37) and another Hispano-Celtic family name SOLICVM on a funerary inscription from Navas de Estena, Ciudad Real (González Rodríguez 1994, 172), Cisalpine SOLA (Cureggio), Gaulish SOLIBODVVS, SOLICVRVS (2 attestations in Latin inscriptions), SOLIMARIVS (4 attestations), SOLIMARVS (12 attestations), SOLIRIX (2 attestations), SOLISETIVS, SOLORIX (Delamarre 2003, 287; Raybould &

Sims-Williams 2007, 74–6), ꜱᴠᴏʟɪᴄᴄᴇɴɪ, Galatian ΣΥΟΩΛΙΒΡΟΓΗΝΟΣ, British
ꜱᴠʟɪᴄᴇɴᴀ (Delamarre 2007, 174–5). The first element probably corresponds
to Old Irish *súil* 'eye', Old Welsh *houl* 'sun', probably also the Romano-British
divine name *Sūlis*, as worshipped at Bath/Aquae Sulis: Indo-European **séh₂ul*
'sun' (Wodtko et al. 2008, 606–11). There was a Hispano-Celtic place-name *Solia*
in the south-west, between the sites of inscriptions J.51.1 and J.55.1.

tᵃa-bᵉe ᴏ9ᴀ✕ (Monte Gordo), tᵃao bᵉe ←✝ᴀ✕ →6ᴏ (MdC), (?tᵃ)au
目ᴀ4 (J.10.1) are compared for their formal similarity and also their similar
placement within the ordering of elements in the inscriptions. In the Monte
Gordo text tᵃa-bᵉe is an 'amplification' of the basic formula (on which see
Appendix C below) following ro-n·bᵃare na[ŕ]kᵉen. tᵃao bᵉe in the long
MdC text similarly comes after the formula words, including the usual closing,
ro·bᵃare naŕkᵉ[e(n). The complete and legible J.10.1 is unusual, without any
formula words, at least not in their more recognizable form. However, er-bᵉeŕi
and ar·bᵃarie are probably forms of the same verb as the formula word tᵉe·ro-
bᵃare, &c., with a different preverb or different preverbs. (?tᵃ)au is the last word
in the text and distinguished by large signs and a change of orientation to the
less common left-to-right.

    As a matter of formal comparison and etymology tᵃa, tᵃao, tᵃau resemble
the Old Irish 'substantive verb', ·tá 'there is' < **stā(i)eti* 'stands', ·táu 'I am' <
*stā(i)ū 'I stand' < Indo-European **(s)teh₂-(i-)oh* 'I stand', cf. Latin *stō*, Oscan
stahu 'I stand' (Schumacher 2004, 623; Rix 2001, 590; McCone 1994, 149).
Oscan *stahu* and 3rd plural *stahint* were used on stelae to describe the monument
itself, and its inscription, standing. Welsh *taw* 'that it is' (probably attested as
Old Welsh *tau* in the Juvencus glosses) shows that Indo-European *s-* was either
absent or lost from this form at an early stage in Celtic. This interpretation raises
the question of the orthographic variation of tᵃa, tᵃao, tᵃau and the thematic
1st singular ending, which probably also occurs written -(u)u on lakⁱiuu (MdC)
and]naŕkᵉeuu[(Corte do Freixo 2). Considering the following segment in the
MdC and Monte Gordo texts, the variation can be explained as phonologically
conditioned. In J.10.1 tᵃau is clearly the last word in the inscription, but tᵃao bᵉe
(MdC) can be taken as | tāō-me | 'I stand' ~ Gaulish *uediíu-mí* 'I pray', *pissíiu-mí*
'I shall see', *dessu-mí-ís* 'I prepare them, I make them right'. Therefore, Pre-Celtic
*ō is not unambiguously in final position, as bᵉe could represent an enclitic
subject pronoun. tᵃa-bᵉe (Monte Gordo) might thus be read as | tā-me | with
loss of hiatus and simplification of the anomalous diphthong, or Pre-Celtic **ō*
has shared the fate of **ō* in non-final syllables. These examples would thus imply
a historical sequence: the suffixing of pronouns to verbs became an established
pattern before Pre-Celtic **ō* in final syllables became Proto-Celtic *ū*, the new
enclitic pattern thus blocked *ō* > *ū* in Tartessian. See further bᵉe above.

tᵃae·bᵃare O٩A〉OAX (J.14.1) is clearly a variant on the more common form of the formula word, a preverb+verb **tᵉe·bᵃare**, **tᵉe·ro·bᵃare** 'has carried away'; see notes below. A purely graphic variant is of course possible as the corpus shows other examples of interchange between **ae** and **e** (*Tartessian 2* §94). However, as discussed in the Commentary on the inscription, the syntax is unusual with what seems to be an opening sequence of an accusative singular followed by a dative singular: **tᵃalainon tᵘuřekᵘui or[ ]i[ ]noś tᵃae·bᵃare naŕkᵉen**. Therefore, it is possible that the preverb **tᵉe** is supporting an enclitic infix here, resulting in a long vowel or diphthong, written **ae**.

tᵃala-inon Y‡YꟼA٦AX (J.14.1) occurs as the first sequence in the same inscription as the previous item. As the beginning of the text is complete and the following item is not in doubt, the only possible uncertainty would be whether **tᵃalainon** comprises more than one word, though it is usually taken as a unit. Following on from the Commentary on the inscription, **tᵃalainon** is probably an o-stem accusative singular or nominative/accusative neuter. Allowing for the regular Tartessian loss of Proto-Celtic *u̯* (*Tartessian 2* §§97.1–3) and the tendency to lose dental stops after **n** seen in the variation **naŕkᵉentⁱi/naŕkᵉenii**, **tᵃala-inon** can be etymologized as Celtic **Tala(u̯)-u̯indom* 'having a fair front/brow', as a place-name 'country with a fair/blessed headland', thus the Celtic form underlying *sacrum Promontorium* or *cautes sacra* 'the sacred crag' in *Ora Maritima* (line 212), today Sagres point, the ultimate extremity of south-west Europe. Compare the Celtiberian family name *Talukokum* (genitive plural, Botorrita), Western Hispano-Celtic dative plural divine name ARABO͟ COROBELICOBO TALVSICO·BO (Arroyomolinas de la Vera, Cáceres, Spain [Búa 2000, 526]) and the personal name CRISSVS TALABVRI F. AEBOSOCELENSIS (*L'Année épigraphique* 1952, 42–3, Cáceres), the place-name *Tala-briga* (northern Portugal), and the personal names TALAIVS, TALAVIVS, TALAVI, TALAVICA, TALABARIVS (Albertos 1985, 295–7), SEGONTIVS TALAVI F(ILIVS) T͟A͟LABONICVM on an inscription from Yecla de Yeltes, Salamanca (González 1986, 133; Vallejo 2005, 406ff), the Cisalpine compound name TANOTALIKNOI (Briona, late 2nd century BC), *talu* on pottery from Verdello, Gaulish DANNOTALI, *Argio-talus*, *Dubno-talus*, *Cassitalos*, *Orbio-talus* &c. (Delamarre 2003, 288–9), Primitive Irish TALAGNI, Old Welsh *Talhaern*, Old Breton *Talhoiarn* 'Iron-brow'. The Old Irish common noun *tul*, *taul*, and Welsh *tal* < Celtic **talu-* have meanings including 'front, brow, headland, protuberance, shield boss'. A borrowing from Semitic *tel* 'hill, &c.' has been suggested (Vendryes 1960–, T-180–2). The second element is interpreted as Celtic **u̯indo-* 'white, fair, blessed', Gaulish *vindo-*, Lepontic *-uino-*, &c.: Indo-European **u̯eid-* 'see' (Wodtko et al. 2008, 717–22). The common Breton man's name *Gwendal* would contain both elements proposed here. The find spot of the inscription, Alcoforado, is in the far west of the zone with Tartessian inscriptions, but north of the cape and not immediately near Sagres. As to why the extreme south-western headland of Europe was called 'the sacred headland', the place beyond the horizon of the setting sun, is universally associated with the otherworld/ afterlife, as is the case in medieval Celtic legend with the Irish Tech Duinn and Gwales in the Welsh Mabinogi. Another possibility is a formation like TALANIO REBVRRINO F(ILIO) (Monte Cildá, Palencia; Vallejo 2005, 410) with epenthesis, again in the accusative singular.

tᵃarielnon ✗APᴎOᒋᕑ✝ᴎ (J.55.1)   In the text ṟo- kᵒoliọn eertᵃaune tᵃarielnon : lirniene narkᵉenai, segmentation can be deduced from ḻiirnestᵃakᵘun (J.19.1) and Celtiberian *uertaunei*; see the Commentary on the inscription and the note on **eertᵃaune** above. Taking (-)kᵒoliọn as a masculine *o*-stem accusative singular name or title, **tᵃarielnon** could be a two-element compound man's name in agreement with it. Both elements of such a compound can be analysed as Celtic, going back to a notional *Dari-ụelnos*. *Dari(o)-* is common in Gaulish proper names: *Dari-bitus, Dario-ritum* 'Vannes', &c. Delamarre (2003, 136) suggests a meaning 'furious' as in Welsh *cyn-ddaredd* 'rabies', cf. also the British genitive man's name DAARI (the husband of TVNCCETACE). *ụelno-* would be the older form of the common Old Celtic name element *ụello-* and probably means 'ruler'.

]tᵃarnekᵘ⟨ḵᵘ⟩un ᒋᕼᕼHOᒋᕑᗺᗞ✗ (J.26.1) for **tᵃarnekᵘun**   This form, like]ḻiirnestᵃakᵘun bᵃane≡oofoire (J.19.1), is a typical Hispano-Celtic genitive plural gentilic adjective ('clan name'). It similarly precedes **bᵃane** 'woman, wife' in the present example:]tᵃarnekᵘun bᵃane. The opening of the text has broken away.]tᵃarnekᵘun bᵃane is all that survives of the naming phrase. The underlying name behind this adjectival formation is probably that of an eponymous ancestor: 'wife/woman of the family descended from Tarn-'. Sounds that are written as simple nasals in Tartessian can correspond to *a* +nasal in other Celtic languages; see *Tartessian 2* §69. Therefore, a possible exact cognate is the Celtiberian family name *Turanikum* (genitive plural) ~ Old Irish *torann* 'thunder' (Wodtko 2000, 422), Old Breton *taran* 'thunder', the Gaulish dative divine name TAPANOOY (Matasović 2009, 384), also TARANVOS and suffixed TARANVCNO, and British TANARO (Latinized dative, without metathesis), an epithet of Jupiter. If these are the correct comparanda,]tᵃarnekᵘun 'of the kindred of Taranus' indicates either that Celtic *Taranus* also occurred as a personal name or, more probably, that kindreds could claim descent from mythological eponymous ancestors. The root of *Taranus* probably goes back to Indo-European *$(s)tonh_2r$-/$(s)tn̥h_2r$-os* 'thundering', in which case the Indo-European syllabic *n̥* either never developed as *an* in Tartessian | tarₐnekūn | or that development was not yet (consistently) recognized in the orthography.

Ταρτησσος, *Tartessus, Tartessii,* &c. On the references in Greek and Roman sources, see Freeman 2010. In Semitic sources the name usually occurs as *Taršīš*, hence *Tarshish* in the English versions of the Old Testament, which figures in the List of Nations in Genesis 10:4 as the name of a child of Javan, son of Japhet, thus connected with the Greeks and peoples of the Mediterranean. Tartessos is probably the meaning of Phoenician *tršš* on the stela from Nora, Sardinia, *c.* 850/775 BC. In the terms of the second treaty between Rome and Carthage of 348 BC cited by Polybius (III.24), Roman activities were curtailed beyond a place called Μαστια Ταρσηιον *Mastia Tarsēion,* i.e. 'Mastia in the country of the *Tarsēioi*', which probably identifies a place near Cartagena in south-eastern Spain. It appears, therefore, that a population name based on Semitic *Taršīš* (*Tarsēioi* in Greco-Punic form, with a possible Old Latin intermediary) had come to designate for the Carthaginians much of the southern Iberian Peninsula, including the non-Indo-European east (De Hoz 1989b, 25–40). On the Semitic forms, see further Lipinski (2004, 248–52), who does not seem to regard the name as of Semitic origin.

Villar (1995) reconstructs early byforms **Turta* and **Tartis,* going back at least to the 8th century BC or (if Semitic *Taršīš* means Tartessos) the later 2nd millennium. He connects these forms with numerous river-names in the Iberian Peninsula and regards them as Indo-European in origin (from **ter-* 'rub, bore, penetrate, &c.'; but contrast Untermann 2004, 207 n. 40). In *Ora Maritima* (line 54), *fretum Tartessium* clearly means the Straits of Gibraltar, the gap where *nostrum mare* (the Mediterranean) meets the outer ocean. This usage suggests an Indo-European and possibly Celtic etymology from **ter* 'through'—which is probably the same word ultimately as that proposed by Villar—or the verb derived from it, **terh₂-* 'cross over, overcome, pass through' ~ Old Irish *tar* 'across, over' (< **tares*), Welsh *tra* 'beyond', *trwy* 'through' (Old Welsh *trui*), Latin *trāns,* Sanskrit *tiráḥ,* Avestan *tarō* 'across', Sanskrit *tárati* 'crosses over, overcomes', Hittite *tarhuzzi* 'overcomes, is able' (Rix 2001, 633–4). Thus, the original primary sense of the name, highlighting the region's most significant feature for travellers, would have been 'where one passes through, crosses over, the place beyond, the country of transit' between the countries around the great inland sea and those of the outer ocean. Originally, the reference might have been to the world of the outer ocean in general—which would help to explain some apparent contradictions in the usages of *Tarshish* in the Old Testament—then secondarily focusing more specifically on the first important country immediately beyond the single maritime channel leading from the inner world to the outer. After the non-Indo-European Phoenicians increasingly dominated commerce through the straits and founded a great commercial town with the new name *Gadir,* the names *Taršīš, Tartessii,* and *Tartessos* came understandably to designate mainly the pre-Phoenician native population and their leading polity, still wealthy and influential about Huelva and the northern hinterland of the straits. According to *Ora Maritima* (line 85), Gadir was (?part of) what had formerly been called *Tartessus*. Another Celtic etymology, from 'dryness' (~ Old Irish *tart* 'thirst') was offered by Sims-Williams, albeit with apparent disbelief (2006, 226).

——t^{e}asiioonii ᛐᛘᛉᛂᛐᛘᛂᛉᚨᛄ (J.1.1)   This form is the last segment in the long, unique, and well-executed Fonte Velha 6 inscription. It lacks close parallels elsewhere in the corpus. Two possibilities are offered for consideration here. First, a masculine personal name, probably a case form of a *i̯o*-stem, 'son of *Tasgiog^{u}onos*' ~ British TASCIOVANOS, Gaulish *Tascouanos* < *Tasgiog^{u}onos*. If the Tartessian reflects this same name, Indo-European $g^{u̯h}$ in *$g^{u̯h}en$-* 'strike, kill' had become *$u̯$ in the subdialect of Proto-Celtic leading to Tartessian, as in British and Gaulish, then subsequently the usual development of *$u̯o$ in Tartessian was to |o̯o| written oo. The king's name *Argantonios* 'agent/devotee/relative of the divine silver' shows that Tartessian had formations in *-onios* as meaningful high-status occupational names. Note Vallejo's collection of comparable personal name formations from Roman-period Lusitania (2005, 626–7): *Albonius, Anonius, Arconius, Maelonius, Alionius, Albonia, Maelonia*. The second possibility and somewhat more likely, I now believe, is a 3rd plural future/desiderative |dāsi̯onji| < Pre-Celtic *dōsi̯ónti ~ Vedic *dāsyánti* 'they will give'. See further the Commentary on the inscription.

t^{e}e· Oᛂ (J.1.1, J.1.3, J.12.1, J.16.1, J.21.1, MdC, Vale de Águia), t^{e}ee· OOᛂ (J.18.2, J.23.1), t^{a}ae· OAX (J.14.1)   This prefix precedes forms clearly inflected as Indo-European (3rd person, present-marked) verbs as t^{e}e·b^{a}ant^{i}i (MdC) and t^{e}ee·b^{a}arent^{i}i (J.23.1). In this light, it can be interpreted in the same way, i.e. as a preverb, when found prefixed to the second stem with shorter endings, namely t^{e}e·b^{a}ar[e] (J.16.1), t^{e}e·b^{a}are (J.1.3, Vale de Águia), t^{e}e·b^{a}are (J.18.1), t^{e}ee·ro-b^{a}are (J.18.2), t^{e}e·ro-b^{a}are (J.1.1, J.12.1), and t^{a}ae·b^{a}are (J.14.1). The preverb which is found in western Indo-European languages with what are probably same verbs is *dē* 'out of, away from': thus Old Irish *dí-batar* 'they become extinct' < 'they step away', Latin *dē-ferō* 'I carry down, away', Early Welsh *dioferaf* 'I relinquish, offer up'. The earlier long *ē* has evidently become Tartessian i (showing the usual Celtic treatment) in the '*rīx*' names aib^{u}uris[(J.3.1), ariariś- (J.10.1), and *Gargoris*; see further *Tartessian 2* §81. Therefore, t^{e}e·, &c., probably reflects the short-vowel variant of *dĕ*.

t^{e}eaiona[ ]AᛘᛂᛐAOᛂ or t^{e}eaionk^{a}a[ ]AᛀᛘᛂᛐAOᛂ (J.4.3)   t^{e}eaionk^{a}a[is Untermann's reading. The more basic formation t^{e}eaiona[ ]AᛘᛂᛐAOᛂ is what appears to be on the stone today, but some restoration work is evident, and an undersized sign might have been lost. The inscription is incomplete. The second and final fragment of the text ... na]ŕkᵉentⁱi[shows that the inscription reflects the usual formulaic pattern (see Appendix C) and, therefore, tᵉeaiona[can be ascribed to the naming phrase near the beginning of the epigraphic statement. The form can be explained etymologically and phonologically as 'goddess' *Deiu̯onā developing regularly within Proto-Celtic to *Dēu̯onā with simplification of the long vowel ~ Gaulish *Deuonia* (Delamarre 2003, 142–3), the goddess name *Diiona* (Jufer & Luginbühl 2001, 37). Proto-Celtic already showed strongly the universal phonetic tendency for sounds to assimilate to the quality of the following vowel: *Dēu̯onā therefore tended to be articulated as [*Dᵉeew°onᵃaa]. In Tartessian this trend shows signs of having become phonologized early, resulting in |D´ẽ(o̯)onā| [*Dᵉeeo̯onᵃaa]. In the orthography, **ai** could be used for |ẽ| the reflex of *ei, because the Proto-Celtic diphthong *ai* had also become a simple vowel in Tartessian (see *Tartessian 2* §94), the result of which was evidently a long vowel similar or identical to the reflex of Indo-European *ei. Choosing to use **ai** to represent this long vowel determined that the epigrapher would have to use tᵉe- to accurately represent the palatal (*e*-quality) dental consonant and following syllabic onset. As further comparanda, note the Celtiberian family name *Teiuantikum* (interpreted as 'who swears'? by De Hoz 2007b, 203) and personal name *Teiuoreikis* /dẽu̯oríχs/. The suffix of tᵉeaiona[|D´ẽ(o̯)onā| may be the same as that in Ἀργανθωνιος and identical with the Gallo-Brittonic divine suffix -onā/-ono-. If we read tᵉeaionkᵃa[, that probably involves the adjectival -ko-/-kā suffix, thus 'she who is like the goddess, pertains to the goddess, of the kindred claiming descent from the goddess', or similar.

tᵉe·bᵃantⁱi ⋈⬭⬭⬭ (MdC)   In the context of the opening words of the long inscription tⁱilekᵘurkᵘu≡arkᵃastᵃamu tᵉe·bᵃantⁱi lebᵒo-iire, tᵉe·bᵃantⁱi can be understood as a 3rd plural compound verb |de·banti|, of which the logical and grammatical subject is the dual tⁱilekᵘurkᵘu≡arkᵃastᵃamu 'Tillekurkos ⟨and⟩ the man greatest in silver' and/or the nominative plural lebᵒo-iire < *Lemo-u̯iroi 'men/heroes of the elm wood'. On the etymology of the verb bᵃantⁱi, see the note above. The cognate compound is attested as Old Irish *dí-ba-* 'becomes extinct' (< 'goes away from'), *-dibatur* 'they became extinct' (Lewis & Pedersen 1989, §500), *dibad* 'destruction, extinction', possibly likewise Gaulish *dib(ato-)* 'end, extinction' (Delamarre 2003, 144). The common Early Welsh *difa* 'destruction, devastation, killing' is compared to the Middle Irish verb *di-baigim* 'I destroy' by GPC, but a connection with Old Irish *dí-ba-* could also explain the phonology and meaning. See further *Tartessian 2* §§34.1–5.

tᵉe·bᵃare ⬭⬭⬭ (J.1.3, Vale de Águia), tᵉe·bar[e] *⬭⬭⬭ (J.16.1), t̲ᵉe̲·b̲ᵃare ⬭⬭⬭ (J.18.1), t̲ᵉe̲·[bᵃ]are ⬭⬭ [ ]⬭⬭ (J.21.1)

Contexts:]ŕakᵘurś tᵉe·bᵃare naŕkᵉeni (J.1.3),]*******bᵃ tᵉe·bᵃare na[ŕkᵉe---] (Vale de Água), uursaau̱ *arbᵃan tᵉe·bar[e] bᵃa naŕkᵉentⁱi (J.16.1), bᵒotⁱieana≡ kᵉertᵒo≡robᵃa tᵉe·bᵃare bᵃa naŕkᵉentⁱi (J.18.1). In J.21.1, there is enough space to restore . . .]uarbᵃan t̲ᵉe̲[(e)·ro-bᵃ]are naŕkᵉenii.Like its longer variant tᵉe·ro-bᵃare, tᵉe·bᵃare recurs as an element of the Tartessian epigraphic formula, on which see Appendix C. Within the basic word order of complete epigraphic statements tᵉe·bᵃare is always medial. It always precedes a form of naŕkᵉentⁱi, which is always final in these examples. tᵉe·bᵃare always comes after the naming phrase. In the two examples where uarbᵃan is present, uarbᵃan precedes tᵉe·bᵃare directly.

tᵉee·bᵃarentⁱi (J.23.1; see below) is no doubt paradigmatically related to tᵉe·bᵃare. The former is plainly an active 3rd person plural compound verb with present-tense marking. Therefore, tᵉe·bᵃare is another form of the same compound verb. tᵉe·bᵃere (J.7.8) is apparently a variant orthography for the same form and possibly erratic as it violates redundancy, but see further below. The orthography tᵉe·bᵃere is significant in implying that the verb could also occur as *e*-grade *tᵉe·bᵉer-. The specific tense form of tᵉe·bᵃare, &c., is interpreted as a preterite < Indo-European perfect 3rd singular |*de·bāre*|. As a cognate of Latin *dē-ferō* 'carry down, away', the sense is well suited to the Tartessian funerary formula. Note also, Early Welsh *dioferaf* < **dē-u(p)o-ber-*, which in its earliest attestation means 'I relinquish [my patron at his death]'.

tᵉe·bᵃere Ο٩Ο⟩Ο⊟ (J.7.8) '(has) carried away, carries away'   On the implications of this orthography, see bᵃare and tᵉe·bᵃare above. The associated word order **kᵉe≡uuakᵉe*[|]ebᵒo tᵉe·bᵃere naŕkᵉen emun tᵘurea≡iubᵃa differs somewhat from that associated with tᵉe·bᵃare; see above. Namely, there is an 'amplification' with names after naŕkᵉen, a form of the type that often marks the formulaic closing. The text is therefore somewhat unusual, and it may be that tᵉe·bᵃere is not merely a slip, but an innovative attempt to write a different tense form of the verb, such as 3rd person singular imperfect |*de·beret*| or present |*de·beret(i)*| with an early apocope of final short -*i*.

tᵉee·bᵃarentⁱi Ϻ⦶Υ⦶٩Λ⟩ΟΟΗ (J.23.1)   A compound, 3rd person plural verb with present-tense marking; see notes on bᵃarentⁱi and tᵉe·bᵃare. This example shows that a Tartessian present-marked verb ending in -(n)tⁱi is not incompatible with a preverb; see further Appendix C.

]tᵉekᵘui ϺᛉΗΟⱶ[(J.1.4)   See the entry on]sekᵘui, another possible reading of this fragmentary form, which opens the line]t̲ᵉek̲ᵘui uurkᵉe otᵉerkᵃaŕ*[. In any event, -ekᵘui is probably the dative singular of an *o*-stem or *u*-stem name. If]t̲ᵉekᵘui is the correct reading, that could stand for |(-)*tekūi*| or |(-)*dekūi*|,

| (-)tegūi | or | (-)degūi | in the SW writing system, and there are comparanda in Ancient Celtic names across this range: Celtiberian *tekos konikum* (K.1.3), Lepontic TEKIALUI, Gaulish TECVSENVS, DEGOVEXI, ogam Irish -DECAS, DEGAS, British TECVRI.

t^ee·ro-b^aare O٩A3‡٩O目, HOP‡3APO (J.1.1, J.12.1), t^eee·ro-b^aare O٩A3‡٩OOH (J.18.2) are interpreted as the compound 3rd singular perfect verb | de·ro-bāre | 'has carried away' and/or the same with an infixed pronoun | de-e(n)·ro-bāre |, | de-e(d)·ro-bāre | 'has carried him/it away'. See notes on b^aare, ro, ro·b^aare, t^ee, t^ee·b^aare. Variants of this sequence occur repeatedly as part of the Tartessian epigraphic formula, on which see Appendix C.

Contexts: . . . naŕk^ee k^aakⁱiśiink°olob°o ii t^ee·ro-b^aare (b^e)e t^easiioonii# (J.1.1), . . . naŕk^eentⁱi—mub^aa t^ee·ro-b^aare ‡at^aaneat^ee# (J.12.1), uarb^a]an t^ee(-)e·ro-b^aare na[ŕk^ee(. . .) (J.18.2). In the extant examples, t^ee·ro-b^aare occurs in a medial position. J.1.1 and J.12.1 are both long, well executed, and generally remarkable inscriptions. And they both have unusual syntax in that naŕk^ee and naŕk^eentⁱi, forms of which often mark the close of the statement, precede t^ee·ro-b^aare. Therefore, the fragmentary J. 18.2 probably reflects that more basic and normal ordering of the formulaic elements.

tⁱilek^uurk^uu 4目٩4目O٦Μ① or tⁱilek^uulk^uu 4目٩4目O٦Μ① (MdC; see Guerra 2010, 67–73) is interpreted as the first element of the statement-initial co-ordinative naming phrase tⁱilek^uurk^uu=ark^aast^aamu 4ΨAX‡A٨٩A 4目٩4目O٦Μ①/, probably nominative/accusative dual case forms. Therefore, there is exact syntactic parallelism between MdC's initial naming phrase tⁱilek^uurk^uu=ark^aast^aamu and that of J.12.1 iru=alk^uu.

As explained in *Tartessian 2* §§31.1–33.6, tⁱilek^uurk^uu is a man's compound name, opening the inscription and probably the name of the deceased. For the first element, compare an inscription of AD 28 from Caurel, Lugo, Galicia: TILLEGVS AMBATI F SVSARRVS | AIOB[R]IGIAECO (Búa 2004, 387) with *Tillegus* probably reflecting an earlier *Tillikos*, showing the regular lowering of Celtic -iko- > -eko- in both Tartessian and the North-west Hispano-Celtic of the Roman Period; see *Tartessian 2* §80. The voicing of TILLEGVS < *Tillikos* is a common feature in the Western Hispano-Celtic names found in inscriptions of the Roman Period. The same Celtic man's name without the lowering or voicing occurs as the Gaulish genitive TILLICI (Les Poussots, Dijon).

For the second element, if the reading is -urk^uu, this has analogues in both the Indo-European and non-Indo-European indigenous languages of the Peninsula: cf. Celtiberian *urkala* and the Hispano-Celtic names *Urcala*, *Urcalonis*, *Urcalocus*, and *Urcico*, as well as the Iberian name element *urke* (Wodtko 2000, 461–2). If the reading is -ulk^uu, this could be Indo-European *ulk^uo- 'wolf', Sanskrit *vŕkaḥ*,

Avestan *vəhrka-*, Lithuanian *vil̃kas*, Gothic *wulfs*, common in Germanic compound personal names, also Celtic *Catuvolcus*. Compare ogam Irish (genitive) ULCAGNI, ULCCAGNI = Romano-British VLCAGNI, nominative VLCAGNVS (McCone 1985). A connection with Tartessian **alkᵘu** (J.12.1) is possible, but less likely. The indigenous second element of the Roman-period north-western place-name *Octaviolca* is not likely here, as it appears to be confined to place-names, for which suitable etymologies have been proposed (Búa 2007, 23–4).

tⁱirtᵒos ‡✝Δᕼᙏ◍ (J.1.2)   Because of the principles of the SW writing system, **tⁱirtᵒos** could stand for either | *Tirtos* | or | *Tritos* |. In theory, it could also stand for forms with one or two long vowels and/or one or two voiced dentals | *D_d_* |, but these latter possibilities do not lead to any promising comparisons. Thus compare Celtiberian *Tirtouios*, *Tirtunos*, *Tirtano*, *Tirtu*, family names *Tirtanikum* and *Tirtalicum*, *tirtotulu* 'triple' (Prósper 2007, 24–6), North-west Hispano-Celtic personal names TRITIA, TRITIVS, TRITEVS (Albertos 1985, 298), the divine epithet TRITIAECIO (Torremenga, Cáceres [Untermann 1985, 360; Búa 2000, 567]), TRITIAEGIO (Navaconcejo, Cáceres [Búa 2000, 563]), Gaulish personal names *Trito[s]*, *Tritus*, *Triti*, cf. Old Welsh *triti(d)* 'third', Latin *tertius* (Wodtko 2000, 297). The basic sense is the ordinal number. **tⁱirtᵒos** is possibly the third son, if not named for another **tⁱirtᵒos**. The form is unproblematically a masculine *o*-stem, nominative singular. Its position in the statement is not the most usual for the name of the deceased, i.e. it is not at the very beginning of the inscription. It does, however, begin the second of the complete inscription's two lines, which display a clear form of the most usual formulaic closing: **tⁱirtᵒos ne-bᵃa naŕkᵉeni**, probably a negation of the basic formula.

tᵒo ‡Δ (J.1.1) occurs as part of the long, complete, and unusual text, 'Fonte Velha 6': **lokᵒobᵒo niirabᵒo tᵒo aŕaiai**. This sequence shows remarkable similarity to Celtiberian TO-LVGVEI | ARAIANOM from the well-known, long inscription from Peñalba de Villastar (K.3.3). This comparison strongly suggests a shared and long-surviving Hispano-Celtic religious vocabulary, in connection with the cult of the pan-Celtic deity Lugus (cf. Jordán 2006). As De Bernardo Stempel has argued for the Celtiberian example (2008), the dative without TO would mean 'for' (para), but with TO 'to, towards' (hacia) with implied motion. The same principle is probably apt for the current example. Some sort of offering or ritual is made '*for* the divine Lugoues [and] chief men' **lokᵒobᵒo niirabᵒo**. On the other hand, something or someone 'has carried it away *to/towards araiā*' **tᵒo aŕaiai … tᵉe·ro-bᵃare**. 'Towards the ploughland' is one possible meaning. De Bernardo Stempel also argues for the essential identity of Hispano-Celtic TO and the preverb appearing in earlier Old Irish as *to*. See further **kᵒtᵘuaratᵉe** above and the next note below.

tᵘu ΔⱣ (J.53.1)   In **kᵒtᵘuaratᵉe** (see above), **tᵘu** is interpreted as a phonological development of the preposition and preverb **to*, Tartessian **tᵒo**. Proto-Celtic [-ou͜V-] has produced Tartessian **u Ⱳ** in this example, the reflex of **-to-u(p)er-rāte*, as in **iubᵃa** (J.7.8), the reflex of **iou͜ₐmā* 'youngest female'. **iobᵃa[** (J.16.2) reflects an earlier stage; see *Tartessian 2* §94. For *to* as a preverb, compare Cisalpine Gaulish тоšокотᴇ (Vercelli) = *to-śo(s)·ko(n)-de* 'has given these' (Koch 1983, 187–8), Old Irish *do*, Archaic Old Irish *tu*, Old Breton *do*, Old Welsh *di*.

tᵘn↑ⁱitᵉsbᵃan Δↁ↑ⱮH≢ƷAⱮ (J.53.1)   In the context of an opening sequence interpreted as a syntactic clause **kᵒ-tᵘ-ua-ratᵉe tᵘn↑ⁱitᵉsbᵃan orbᵃa setᵃa**, **tᵘn↑ⁱitᵉsbᵃan** is taken as a feminine singular superlative, an accusative of destination as the object of a verb of motion, a compound form of | *-rāte* | 'has run'. It is therefore comparable to the syntax of **uar(n)bᵃan** in the epigraphic formula; see Appendix C. What I now think is the most probable explanation of the etymology is to read it as **tᵘnbⁱitᵉsbᵃan** | *tumitesₐman* | 'the best, greatest tomb, tumulus' < **tumetisₐmām*; see further the Commentary on the inscription. The lowering of Proto-Celtic **i* before **ă* to Tartessian **e** is regular and amply paralleled in the corpus; see *Tartessian 2* §§78–80.

Another possibility is to read **tᵘn↑ⁱitᵉsbᵃan** as an anomalous orthography for | *tunkitesₐman* | 'most auspicious, fortunate', cf. the common Western Hispano-Celtic personal or divine name тоNᴄᴇтᴀмᴠѕ, тоNɢᴇтᴀмᴠѕ 'most fortunate' ([both attested at Fundão, Castelo Branco, Portugal; Búa 2000, 490–1] with a different but related superlative suffix [Albertos 1985, 298], connected with 'oath' by De Hoz 2007b, 203), Old Irish *tocad* 'fate, destiny', Middle Welsh *tynghet* 'destiny', Breton *tonket* 'luck', and the British personal name тᴠNᴄᴄᴇтᴀᴄᴇ 'Fortunatae' (genitive). On Tartessian superlatives, see also **uar(n)bᵃan** below.

tᵘurea ΔOↁↁΔ (J.7.8) and **tᵘuŕekᵘui ⱮↁⱻOↅↁΔ (J.14.1)** are interpreted as adjectival personal names of relationship derived from the common simplex Hispano-Celtic man's name *Turos*: so respectively nominative singular feminine | *Tureā* | < **Turiā* 'female relative (probably daughter) of Turos' and dative singular masculine | *Turekūi* | < **Turikōi* 'for a man of the kindred descended from Turos'. **tᵘurea≡iubᵃa** is a naming phrase in overt concord, meaning 'Turos's youngest daughter' | *Tureā iū͜ₐmā* |. Compare Celtiberian *Turos, Turaios, Tureibo, Turenta, Tures, Turo, Turaesos, Turanus*, family names *Turaku, Turanikum*, тᴠʀɪᴀѕɪᴄᴀ, *Turikum, Turumokum, Turanicus, Tureka*, North-west Hispano-Celtic (or Lusitanian) personal names тᴠʀᴀɪᴠѕ, тᴠʀᴇᴠѕ, тᴠʀᴇɪᴠѕ and the divine epithet тᴠʀɪᴀᴄо (Untermann 1985, 360; Búa 2000, 447), the place-names тᴠʀоʙʀɪɢᴀ (north of Huelva), тᴠʀᴠʙʀɪɢᴀ (attested also in Beja and Faro, south Portugal), тᴠʀɪᴠʙʀɪɢᴀ attested in the region of Badajoz, Spain (Búa 2000, 90–1, 641, 645), Cisalpine тᴜʀоκоѕ on pottery from Oleggio of the early 1st century BC. Gaulish *piχte* '5th(ly)' in the newly discovered inscription from

Ratiatum/Rezé in the country of the Pictones makes likely Lambert's explanation that that group name is derived from the ordinal and *Turones* (in Belgica) similarly based on *$(k^w)tur$- '4(th)' (Lambert & Stifter 2012, 151–2). In this light, compare the common Hispanic name *Turos* with t^{i}irt^{o}os '3rd' (see above) and the very common Hispanic names PENTVS, PENTIVS, PINTAMVS, &c. (Vallejo 2004, 370–4) probably from *$k^w en\chi to$-/*$k^w in\chi to$- '5th'. If not an adjectival gentilic name ('for a descendant of Turos'), t^{u}uřek^{u}ui could, less probably, be a compound with Indo-European *$h_1ek'\underset{.}{u}o$-s 'horse' as its second element.

t^{u}urₛn[ ] ㆔ (Abul), a graffito on pottery; see the previous entry and the Commentary on the inscription.

——]t^{u}urk^{a}aio[ ]△ᛁᛈ∧∧ᛘ≠[(J.51.1)   The segmentation is uncertain for this fragmentary text. This reading is more probable than]t^{u}ura̲aio[. It could be related to the two forms discussed in the entry on t^{u}urea (J.7.8) and t^{u}uřek^{u}ui (J.14.1) above.

uab^{a}an ㄱA≲A㄄ (J.16.5) | u̯aman | < *$u(p)_a mām$ 'highest one, place, being'   uab^{a}an is obviously related to the formula word uar(n)b^{a}an | u̯ar$_a$man | < *$u(p)_a eramām$ 'highest', feminine accusative singular. As the inscription is well executed and clearly legible, a simple mistake for uar(n)b^{a}an is unlikely. That explanation is also unnecessary. The comparanda discussed in the Commentary on the inscription show that *$u(p)_a mā$-/*$u(p)_a mo$- (without -r-) occurred widely in the Ancient Celtic languages, including specifically SW Hispano-Celtic, and was probably the more archaic form. See also the following item.

uarb^{a}an ㄱA㇋ᑫA㄄ (J.1.2, J.3.1, J.4.1, J.21.1), uar̲b^{a}an ㄱA≲ᑫA㄄ (J.9.1), uar̲b̲^{a}a̲n̲ ᛁAᛈ⟨A◣ (J.11.3), *arb^{a}an ㄱA㇋ᑫA* (J.16.1)   The syntactic contexts vary. Nonetheless, there are recurrent patterns to note. Usually, uarb^{a}an &c. occurs together with one or more of the other formula words, and it usually comes as the first of these. The most basic ordering of elements is seen in . . .]uarb^{a}an t^{e}e[(e)·ro-b^a]a̲re nařk^{e}enii (J.21.1) and uursaau *arb^{a}an t^{e}e·bar[e] b^{a}a nařk^{e}ent^{i}i (J.16.1). But also more loosely in k^{o}o-b^{e}elib^{o}o na-k^{i}i·b^{u}u oira uarb^{a}an t^{i}irt^{o}os ne-b^{a}a nařk^{e}eni (J.1.2), ?ib^{o}oi ion asune≡ uarb^{a}an ≡ek^{u}uři̲n̲e ob^{a}ar b^{a}ara*******t^{a}a oret^{o}o (J.4.1),]k^{a}anan uarb^{a}an eb^{e}e nař[k^{e}e . . . (J.9.1), soloir uar̲b̲^{a}a̲n̲[ ]i̲n̲a o*[n]a̲řk^{e}enii (J.11.3), and uuřerk^{a}ar ua[rb^{a}a]n k^{i}ik^{e}e≡ark^{a}are ro-n-b^{a}are na[ř]k^{e}en t^{a}a-b^{e}e anoři̲on (Monte Gordo). J.3.1 is thus exceptional: aib^{u}uris[ ]a̲ k^{i}inb^{a}ai⬆^{i}i ro·lak^{u}ua uarb^{a}an ub^u[u]i, and it could be that one perfect verb marked with ro has taken the place of the more usual t^{e}e·ro-bare. But even then, uarb^{a}an would be out of its usual position.

As argued in Appendix C, the core message of the Tartessian funerary formula —#naming phrase+uar(n)b^{a}an+t^{e}e·ro-bare+(b^{a}a+)nařk^{e}ent^{i}i#—is that

uarbªan ᴎA3ꟻAᴎ
(J.3.1)

the burial rites have already borne the deceased off to a sublime destination, but he/she also now lies here, so schematically ⎣**DECEASED**⎤. This paradoxical concept occurs in Christian funerary contexts and is fairly universal wherever the notion of a heavenly afterlife prevails.

In Celtic, there are several ways of saying 'highest', most of which are formed from the related prepositional bases *$*u(p)$-* and *$*u(p)er$-*. For example, Gaulish *uertamo-* and Old Welsh *guartham* < *$*u(p)ert_amo$-*. Hispano-Celtic shows three related formations. *$*u(p)_amo$-* gives Ούαμα *Uama* and the Latinized group name VAMENSI for a Roman-period settlement (Salvatierra de los Barros, Badajoz; Falileyev 2010, 228) in the territory of the south-western Celtici, situated high on the massif within the great bend of the Anas/Guadiana. Ούαμα probably originally designated the nearby conspicuous landmark, the highest summit of the region, Peña Utrera, at 813 metres. *$*u(p)s_amo$-* gives the recurrent Hispano-Celtic place-name *Uxama*; see **uśnee** below. It is noteworthy that the superlative place-names Ούαμα and *Uxama* are feminine singular, like the much more common place-name element *-brigā* 'high place, elevated settlement, hillfort'. In the conceptual hierarchy of toponyms, a place called *Uxama* would be claiming superiority over its region's places with *-brigā* names. *$*u(p)er_amo$-* gives Celtiberian masculine nominative singular VERAMOS, VORAMOS, accusative VERAMOM (Wodtko 2000, 444–5, 459–60), possibly also VRAMVS in Roman Lusitania (Vallejo 2005, 695). The derivation of **uarbªan** (J.1.2, J.3.1, J.4.1, J.21.1), &c., from Indo-European *$*(s)h_4upermo$-* 'over-most, highest' was first proposed by Correa (1992, 101).

For its phonological development, **uarbªan** should be taken together with **uabªan** (J.16.5), **uarnbªan** (J.20.1), **uarbºoś** (J.7.5), **uarbᵘu(i)** (J.23.1), and the compound **uarbºo-iir** (J.22.1). Old Welsh *guartham* alongside Gaulish *uertamo-* both < *$*u(p)ert_amo$-* show that Tartessian |*uar_aman*| could have developed in a similar way from Proto-Celtic *$*u(p)er_amām$* (feminine accusative singular). *$*u(p)er$* regularly becomes u̯ar as in Brittonic (e.g. Breton *war* 'on, over'; see *Tartessian 2* §§70.1–2). With Tartessian **uarbªan**, &c., the favourable conditions would have included both the general phonetic tendency for [we] to become [wa] and also the analogical influence from what was probably the older form—Ούαμα *Uama*, Tartessian **uabªan** |*u̯aman*|, and Lepontic UVAMO- < *$*u(p)_amo$-/$ā$*——where

the *a* in the first syllable had arisen from an Indo-European syllabic nasal within
Proto-Celtic. Celtiberian VORAMOS shows that the Hispano-Celtic reflex of
$*u(p)er$ was tending to share the vocalism of $*u(p)o$. It is thus unsurprising that
superlative | uar̩amā | would come to share the vocalism of *Uama*.

In the funerary formulas, **uabᵃan**, **uarbᵃan**, &c., may convey a purely abtsract
or unearthly sublime destination, but an ideologically significant terrestial height
or 'holy mountain' is also possible, such as Peña Utrera, at 813 metres, looming
above the ancient settlement called Ούαμα *Uama*. If we read **tᵘn↑ⁱitᵉsbᵃan**
(J.53.1; Alcalá del Río, Sevilla) as | tumites̩aman | 'the greatest tumulus', that
might mean the actual burial mound of the deceased, but could also refer to an
afterlife on an Olympian summit, real or figurative; for example, the name *Yr
Wyddfa* designates the highest mountain in Wales (English 'Snowdon') and means
literally 'the tumulus'. Another possible meaning is suggested by the proposed
glosses for **mubᵃa . . . ᶄatᵃaneat̲ᵉe** 'foster-mother to the winged one' (J.12.1)
and the feminine accusative of destination **saru[?n]an** 'the star goddess' (MdC).
In other words, the sublime destination of the deceased was possibly conceived
of as a feminine supernatural being residing in the sky. The Romano-British
goddess *Brigantia* 'the high one' and her Irish cognate, the goddess and saint
Brigit, may also be considered in this constellation. A system of religious ideas
and traditional religious phrases could easily accommodate these various ideas
simultaneously.

uarbᵒoiir ᑫᙏᙏ‡ᗺᑫᗅᐸ (J.22.1)   See the Commentary on the inscription and
the following item. **uarbᵒoiir** is interpreted as a compound name or epithet,
in the nominative singular | uar̩amo-i̩ir | 'supreme man, lord' < notional Indo-
European $*(s)h_4uperm^mo + uih_xro-$. These are the same elements as occur in the
Celtiberian phrase VIROS VERAMOS (K.3.18), which can thus be understood as
a shared development within Hispano-Celtic. The same elements are apparently
collocated again as (**o**)**ira-uarbᵃan** (J.1.2), which can be analysed as another
compound with the elements reversed, hence meaning 'to the heroic summit'.

———**uarbᵒoiir sarune** ᐳᑫᒪᑫᗅ‡ᑫᙏᙏ‡ᗺᑫᗅᐸ (J.22.1)   For **sarune**, see above.
In the first edition of this book and *Celtic from the West*, I suggested the segmenta-
tion **uarbᵒoiir saruneea** | Uar̩amo-i̩ir Sarun(n)e̩eā |, interpreting this as 'noble
consort of the star goddess', with the second element of the name or epithet as
an *ā*-stem genitive from earlier *-iās*, showing a development paralleled in ogamic
Primitive Irish. This is not impossible, but Indo-European and Proto-Celtic final
-s can be found preserved as Tartessian *-s* and *-ś* (*Tartessian 2* §115). This apparent
phonological inconsistency is unnecessary if we segment **uarbᵒoiir sarune /
ea** | Uar̩amoi̩ir Sarun(n)e̩ē | 'supreme man/husband *to* the star goddess' with the
second element as an *ā*-stem dative < $*U(p)eramo-uiros+^tSarunāi$. The inscription

as a whole is thus construable: **uarbᵒoiir sarune ea bᵃare naŕkᵉenii** 'U.S. "noble consort to the star goddess", she who has carried [him] away, they now remain'. See further the Commentary on the inscription and compare J.22.2.

This type of phrasal epithet has Indo-European parallels: e.g. Vedic *Dásyave vŕkaḥ* 'Wolf to the Dasyu [enemies of the Vedic Aryans]', and there is a second probable Tartessian example, **mubᵃa . . . ɸatᵃaneatᵉe**, 'foster-mother' (nominative singular) + 'to the winged one' (dative singular, probably an *i*-stem agent noun **(p)ataniatis*). This name/epithet type is otherwise unknown in the Ancient Celtic languages, but (with the second element in the genitive in Goidelic) a similar formation is common in personal names in the early medieval Celtic languages: e.g. Old Irish *Mael-Brigte* 'Servant of St Brigit', Cumbric *Gos-Patric* 'Servant of St Patrick', &c. Welsh *meudwy* 'anchorite' derives from a phrase with a petrified oblique case as its second member, either a genitive or a dative: **mogus dēui* 'slave of God' or **mogus dēu̯ū* 'slave to God'. The Tartessian construction may also have been influenced by the syntactic pattern (and ideology) of the very common Phoenician name-type of *Abd-Astart* 'Servant of [the goddess] Astarte', *Abd-Tanit*, *Gel-Melqart* 'Client of [the god] Melqart', &c. **uarbᵒoiir sarune** and **mubᵃa ɸatᵃaneatᵉe** can be viewed as forerunners of the characteristically Insular Neo-Celtic 'inversion compound' type illustrated above. Contact (intellectual and literate) with Semitic worked in favour of reinforcing this inherited Indo-European type. Though Sarunā might herself be an *interpretatio phoenica* of Astarte, the phrasal name is thoroughly Celticized, not only using Celtic elements rather than Semitic, but defining the relationship of mortal rulers to gods on the basis of a different predominant myth, not as priests of the gods, but rather as royal consorts linked to the tribal goddess through the *hieros gamos* (sacred marriage) of characteristically Celtic dynastic foundation legends. As John Carey has suggested to me, as 'lord consort of the great goddess in the sky' (see note on **sarune** above), **uarbᵒoiir sarune** comes close to the etymological meaning of Old Welsh *breenhin* 'king' < **brigantinos* 'consort of the elevated goddess *Brigantia*' (Binchy 1970), and the cognate form occurs as the Hispano-Celtic *birikantin* attested on coin legends.

— **uarbᵒo५ i[**]ᴎꞀ‡ᴏ٩ᴀᴄ [(J.7.5) Because the inscription is fragmentary, the segmentation is doubtful. The sign form Ꞁ is also of uncertain value. If this sign is read as a turned **n ꓵ**, then **uarbᵒon** represents |*u̯ar₄mon*| ∼ Celtiberian VERAMOM (K.3.11) < **u(p)er₄mom*, the masculine or neuter equivalent of feminine **uarbᵃan** |*u̯ar₄man*| 'the highest destination'. Possibly there can be a god as well as a goddess in this role in the funerary formula and corresponding afterlife beliefs.

uarnbᵃan Ч А Ϸ | ЧЯАЧ (J.20.1)   The context]uŕni bᵉelis̱on uarn|bᵃan e*
bᵃar[e]n naŕkᵉen[.. clearly presents a variant manifestation of the basic formula
... uarbᵃan tᵉe·ro-bᵃare naŕkᵉentⁱi#, on which see Appendix C. The variant
orthographies **uarnbᵃan** and **uarbᵃan** both suit |u̯ar̯man|, with a bilabial
nasal following *r*, < *u(p)er̯mām* 'highest' feminine accusative singular. See the
entry on **uarbᵃan** above.

]**uŕni** ЧЧ𝈁Ч (J.20.1)   In context (see previous entry),]uŕni bᵉelis̱on appears
to be a naming phrase (possibly truncated) at the beginning of a fairly typical
Tartessian funerary inscription. On the basis of philogical comparison, bᵉelis̱on
can be construed as an *i*-stem genitive plural (see above). Therefore,]uŕni is
probably the name, or part of the name, of the deceased. From the state of the
text on the stone now, it is possible that uЧ was the first sign originally, though
another sign preceding it may have broken away. If **uŕni** is complete, compare
the goddess name *Urnia* (Nîmes, Jufer & Luginbühl 2001, 67).

us̱nee ОⲞЧМЧ (J.23.1)   Another possible reading is **us̱nbᵉe** ОϱЧМЧ. As
explained in the Commentary on the inscription, the text, which survives complete, is an interesting variation on the Tartessian epigraphic formula (on which
see Appendix C), in which the usual inflexion of the formula words is changed:
bᵉetⁱisai tᵉe(-)e·bᵃarentⁱi iru≡arbᵘu i el naŕkᵉe:n: | us̱nee. As the final word
following naŕrkᵉe:n:, which is a variant of the recurrent closing, **us̱nee** figures
as a syntactic amplification as occurs in a minority of documents in the corpus.
Although {u}arbᵘu in iru≡{u}arbᵘu is a case form of the same word as the
formula word **uar(n)bᵃan**, its gender and grammatical and logical functions are
unusual. In other words. it cannot be the feminine singular destination of the verb
tᵉe(-)e·bᵃarentⁱi 'whom they carry away, have carried away'. Therefore, **us̱nee**
here could be a locative singular, related to Hispano-Celtic Οὐξαμα *Uxama* (e.g.
Pliny, *Naturalis Historia* 3.27, Ptolemy 2.6.55 Οὐξαμα Ἀργαιλα, 2.6.52 Οὐξαμα
Βαρκα), Celtiberian *Usama*, Old Breton *Ossam* 'Ouessant' ~ Welsh *uchaf*, thus
expressing the same idea usually conveyed by **uar(n)bᵃan** |u̯ar̯man| 'to the
highest destination'. If the reading is **us̱nbᵉe**, that could stand for the locative
of *Uxama*, i.e. |uχs̯mē| < *u(p)s̯mai* 'in the highest place'. Another possibility
along these lines is that **us̱nbᵉe** |uχs̯mē| is nominative plural from *u(p)s̯moi*
'the highest ones', an epithet describing iru≡arbᵘu and the deceased. Either of
these explanations for **us̱nbᵉe** (or any explanation of **us̱nee** < *u(p)s-*) would
imply the characteristically Celtic treatment of the Indo-European cluster *ps* in
Tartessian. Taking bᵉetⁱisai as the name of the deceased and a feminine *ā*-stem
in the dative singular, it apparently preserves the diphthong *āi* as **ai**. If **us̱nee** is
an *ā*-stem locative singular, **-ai** of bᵉetⁱisai could be purely graphic for /-ē/ (see
Tartessian 2 §94) or alternatively distinguish the reflex of *-āi* from that of *-ai*.

——=uuak^{e}e*[ ] *O)IA44 (J.7.8)   In the extant context, (*)**k^{e}e=uuak^{e}e*[
]eb^{o}o t^{e}e b^{a}ere naŕk^{e}en emun t^{u}urea=iub^{a}a, the first legible sign is preceded
by two or possibly three illegible signs. A version of the Tartessian epigraphic
formula is evident (on which see Appendix C), and there is an 'amplification'
after naŕk^{e}en which contains a two-term feminine identification in overt agreement t^{u}urea=iub^{a}a, probably a phrase 'youngest daughter of Turos'. Therefore,
form and syntactic position suggest that * *k^{e}e=uuak^{e}e could be another ā-stem
feminine naming phrase, the second element showing a characteristically Celtic
adjectival suffix, with nominative/accusative dual or dative singular case marking
< *U(p)ākāi. See further the Commentary on the inscription.

(])uult^{i}ina A4MO744([) (J.12.3)   The extant text is fragmentary: (])uult^{i}ina
ar-b^{e}ieŕit^{u}u la[. That this sequence consists of a feminine ā-stem personal
name of an individual in the nominative singular followed by a compound
verb is proposed on the bases of form and comparative etymology. Compare
the Celtiberian personal names *Ultinos* (Botorrita), *Ultia*, *Ultu*, *Ultatunos*, *Ulta*,
Lepontic dative/ablative plural UVLTIAUIOPOS (Prestino). *Ulti-* also occurs
as an Iberian name element, which has been argued to be a borrowing from
Indo-European, specifically Celtic, a variant of the Gaulish name element
u̯olti-, which probably means 'long-haired' (De Hoz 2005, 81) ~ Old Irish *folt*,
Old Breton *guolt*, Welsh *gwallt* 'human hair of the head'. With the double **uu**
in]uult^{i}ina—note likewise the orthography of Lepontic UVLTIAUIOPOS—a
zero-grade | ulti- | is possible, but it could also show a phonological change in
the o-grade: *u̯olti- > | u̯ulti- |. It would be a natural phonetic development for
[o] to be raised to [u] in this environment.

uuŕerk^{a}ar 9A∧9O)44 (Monte Gordo) is the initial sequence in a relatively
long and nearly complete inscription which includes the main elements of the
Tartessian epigraphic formula in their usual order. Therefore, it is probably
part of a nominative phrase identifying the deceased. Formally, it resembles
a compound and can be compared with the numerous forms in Celtiberian
inscriptions ending in *-kar*. This example raises the question of whether
Proto-Celtic *u(p)er-* 'over, super' could give Tartessian **uuŕ-** as well as **ooŕ-**,
as in **ooŕoir** (J.19.2) and **ooŕoire** (J.19.1). In Tartessian, as with Celtiberian
VORAMOS < *u(p)er$_a$mos, the analogy of the reflexes of *u(p)o- and its compounds and suffixed forms would have played a role.

uurk^{e}e O)I944 (J.1.4)   In the light of t^{i}ilek^{u}urk^{u}u at the beginning of the
Mesas do Castelinho inscription, it is probable that there was a Tartessian
name element | Urk- |. This would be connected with the Palaeohispanic name
elements Celtiberian *Urca-* and/or Iberian *Uŕke-*. However, the text appears

already to have a masculine name in the dative, preceding **uurkᵉe**:]t̲ᵉekᵘui **uurkᵉe otᵉerkᵃa ŕ*[**. Therefore, an alternative possibility may be considered, namely a perfect 3rd person singular 'has made', from the Indo-European root *$\underset{\sim}{u}erg'$- 'make, work'. The Early Welsh *guoreu* and Middle Breton *gueureu* 'did, made' reflect a reduplicated perfect *$\underset{\sim}{u}e$-$\underset{\sim}{u}r\bar{a}ge$ based on a variant form of the root *$\underset{\sim}{u}reg'$- found throughout the Brittonic paradigm. The Brittonic past tense forms, Middle Breton 3rd singular *greaz*, Welsh *gwnaeth*, show that British had a *t*-preterite formation *$wra\chi t$- or *$wre\chi t$- from the Indo-European aorist alongside the Indo-European perfect (whence *guoreu*, &c.). The orthography **uurkᵉe** may reflect a Proto-Celtic *$\underset{\sim}{u}o\underset{\sim}{u}orge$, cf. Greek perfect 3rd singular ἔοργε, Avestan *vauuarəza* (Rix 2001, 686–7). **iubᵃa** (J.7.8) |*iṵ̄ₐmā*| 'youngest female' < *$i̯ou_a m\bar{a}$ represents a comparable phonological development to what would be seen in **uurkᵉe** < *$\underset{\sim}{u}o\underset{\sim}{u}orge$.

——**uursaau** ᐅ𐌀𐌀‡ᔮ𐌀𐌀 (J.16.1)   In the context of the complete text **uursaau** [u]**arbᵃan tᵉe·bar[e] bᵃa naŕkᵉentⁱi**, which adheres closely to the norms of the Tartessian epigraphic formula, **uursaau** must be the name of the deceased. The only possible uncertainty in segmentation is whether the formula word might uniquely here have been written **uuarbᵃan** with an initial double **uu-**, preceded by **uursaa**. Untermann (1997, 168) compares the gentilic name *Ursius* from Lisbon and the (clearly Celtic) personal name *Ursacius* from Conimbriga. As with **uuŕerkᵃar** above, the question of the possible multiple reflexes of the common Celtic prefix *$u(p)er$ arises. Thus **uursa-** might continue Indo-European *$(s)h_4uper$-$steh_2$- 'stands above', with a sense opposite to that of Gaulish *uossos*, *uassos*, Old Irish *foss*, Old Welsh and Old Breton *guas* 'servant, lad' (also 'land, surface of the earth') < Celtic *$u(p)ost(a)o$- 'that which (he who) stands below' < Indo-European *$(s)h_4upo$-$steh_2$-. Since *$\breve{a}$ < *$(e)h_2$- is part of the root in these forms, the double **aa** in **uursaa** could be meaningful with hiatus preserved between vowel-final root and personal ending in the position of the lost laryngeal.

Tartessian Linguistic Elements

C. Grammatical Categories:
Summary of Provisional Interpretations

¶NOTE. In the narrative account of the many years of progress and reversals in deciphering the language of the SW inscriptions and the halting advance towards its classification as a Celtic language, the works of J. A. Correa are milestones. A view has gained currency that his proposal of Tartessian's Celticity (Correa 1989; 1992) was subsequently modified *cum* retracted due largely to the weight of (mostly unpublished) criticism from colleagues in Spain. For the objective of continued progress with the corpus, this account is not particularly helpful in that it takes attention off the basic scientific issues. There was a primary methodological barrier impeding the next stage of the decipherment. While the Celtic character of many of the personal names was apparent, the morphology of the noun remained unclear in several examples. So it did not seem possible to construe the syntax of the epigraphic statements in their entireties as belonging to an Indo-European and specifically Celtic language (Correa 1995; 1996).

When I began work on the corpus in 2006/7, I too saw this problem. On the other hand, it also seemed clear to me that Untermann (1995; 1997, 165) had been right that the portions of the texts that were not names contained elements inflected as Indo-European verbs, such as tᵉee-bᵃarentⁱi (J.23.1). Furthermore, these same verb forms often had the segment **ro** prefixed to them or infixed within them, such as in the recurrent formula word tᵉe(e)-ro-bᵃare. That looked very Celtic; see Appendix C. Nonetheless, many of the names ended merely in **-e** or **-u**. If those were all datives singular, then the sequences of signs appearing to be verbs only infrequently had subjects or direct objects. It would also follow that the o-stem dative singular could be sometimes the more conservative **-ui** (perhaps also sometimes an archaic **-oi**) as well as the more evolved **-u**, usually without any other clear-cut sign implying chronological stratification in their respective texts. Still, with Celtic names and Indo-European verbs with prefixed **ro**, the conclusion that the principal language of the SW corpus was Celtic was and remains, in my opinion, inescapable, even if the syntax of many of the epigraphic statements remained opaque.

The discovery of the Mesas do Castelinho inscription in 2008 and its publication by Guerra (2009; 2010) opened new possibilities. With this increased 'critical mass' in the corpus, it became possible to recognize two factors that had obscured the Indo-European character of Tartessian noun morphology. First, Tartessian's strong tendency to simplify diphthongs, especially in final syllables, could be confirmed. It was also possible to begin to describe this 'tendency' as a systematic phonological phenomenon; see *Tartessian 2* §94. Secondly, it became evident that feminine forms ending in **-e** and masculine forms in **-u** came in pairs. Therefore, they were probably not datives singular, but rather an archaic survival of the Indo-European co-ordinative compound in the nominative/accusative dual. Thus such compound identifications of the deceased provided probable objects for **t^{e}e(e)·ro-b^{a}are** 'has carried away' and/or subjects for the pervasive formulaic closing **nafk^{e}ent^{i}i** ?'now lie down, rest, remain [here]'.

DECLINABLE ELEMENTS: NOUNS, VERBAL NOUNS, AND ADJECTIVES

nominatives singular

(1) *o*-stem: **ak^{o}olioś** ᛗǂᛘ(ᒣ)ǂ⋈A (J.56.1), **t^{i}irt^{o}os** ǂǂΔ٩ᛘ⦶ (J.1.2);

with loss of Indo-European *-*os* in the reflexes **u̯iros* (as in Latin) — **ooŕoir** ٩ᛘǂ⩘ǂǂ (J.19.2), **soloir** ǂǂΓǂᛗP (J.11.3), **uarb^{o}oiir** ٩ᛘᛘǂ⊟٩A4 (J.22.1)

(2) *i̯o*-stem: Ἀργανθωνιος

(3) *ā*-stem: **b^{o}ot^{i}ieana** AᛘA☼ᛘ⦶ǂ□ (J.18.1), **ᛯait^{u}ura** A٩4ΛᛘAᛯ (J.15.1), **iob^{a}a**[ᛗǂ}A[, (J.16.2), **iub^{a}a** A}4ᛘ (J.7.8), **k^{a}aśet^{a}ana** ΛAᛗOXAᛗA (J.53.1), **mub^{a}a** A{4ᛘ (J.12.1), **raᛓa** PAᛓA (J.53.1), **rob^{a}a** A}ǂ٩ (J.18.1 and probably Moura), **set^{a}a** ǂOXA (J.53.1), ( )**uult^{i}ina** Aᛘᛘ⦶ᒣ44([) (J.12.3); probably ——**ośaHa** AHAᛗᛘǂ (J.11.1), **omuŕik^{a}***[ǂᛗᛗᛗ⩘ᛗΛ*[(J.16.2), **orb^{a}a** ǂP}A (J.53.1), **t^{e}eaiona**[ ]Aᛘǂᛘ AOH or **t^{e}eaionk^{a}a**[ ]AΛᛘǂᛘAOH (J.4.3)

possibly **k^{u}uik^{a}aosa** Aǂ*AΛᛘ4⊟ (J.17.1), ——**ot^{e}erk^{a}a** AΛ٩OFǂ (J.1.4), ——**uursaa** AAǂ٩44 (J.16.1)

(4) *i̯ā*-stem: **anb^{a}at^{i}ia** Aᛗ{A⦶ᛗA (J.16.2), **t^{u}urea** AO٩4Δ (J.7.8); probably **k^{e}eloia** Aᛘǂᒣ O⟩| (J.57.1), ——**mut^{u}uirea** AO٩ᛘ4Δ4ᛗ (J.1.5)

(5) consonant-stems: **aib^{u}uris**[ ]ǂᛘ٩4⋈ᛘA (J.3.1), probably **ariariśe** Oᛗᛘ٩Aᛘ٩A (J.10.1) = **ariaris-se, uuŕerk^{a}ar** ٩AΛ٩O⩘44 (Monte Gordo)

genitives singular

(1) *o-stem:* **k^{e}ert^{o}o** ǂΔ٩O⟩| (J.18.1), **oret^{o}o** ǂΔO٩ǂ (J.4.1)

(2) *i̯o-stem:* probably **k^{o}oŕb^{e}o** ǂ(|⩘ǂ⋈ (J.53.1)

datives singular

(1) *o*-stem: -*ekᵘui* ᴎᲣᕼO⊅[(J.1.4), *tᵘuŕekᵘui* ᴎᲣᕼᗺOᛕᲣᐃ (J.14.1); probably
al<u>b</u>ᵒoroi ᴎⵜᕊⵜ◻1Ａ (J.24.1);

possibly **alkᵘu** Უᕼ1Ａ (J.12.1), **arkᵃast<u>ᵃa</u>mu** ᲣᚷAX⧧Ａᐃᕊ (MdC), **isakᵃaoe**
O⧧ＡᐃＡ⧧ᴎ (J.24.1), **iru** ᕊᲣᴎ (J.12.1, J.23.1), NIΕΘΩΙ, **sabᵒoi** ᴎⵜᗺＡ⧧ (J.5.1),
——— **salsa<u>l</u>oi** ⧧Ａᒋ⧧Ａᒋⵜᛕ or **salsa<u>n</u>oi** ⧧Ａᒋ⧧Ａᛕⵜᛕ (J.12.4), **tᵢlekᵘur̄kᵘu**
Უᗺ1ᕊᗺO1ᴎⵙ or **tᵢlekᵘulkᵘu** Უᗺ1ᴎᗺO1ᴎⵙ (MdC), {u}ar̄bᵘui ᴎᲣᚷᕊAᲣ
(J.23.1), ——— **uur̄saa<u>u</u>** ᲣＡＡ⧧ᕊᲣᲣ (J.16.1)

(2) *i̯o*-stem: **aar̄kᵘui** ᴎᲣᕼᕊＡＡ (J.7.6)

(3) *ā*-stem |-*ái*| > |-*ê̄*|: **bᵉet̄isai** ᴎＡ⧧◍O◊ (J.23.1); probably **a<u>r̄</u>aiai** ᴎ<u>Ａ</u>ᴎＡᛕＡ
(J.1.1), ——— **sar̄une** OᴎᕊᲣＡ⧧ (J.22.1, J.22.2);

possibly **asune** OᴎᲣ⧧Ａ (J.4.1), **ekᵘur̄i<u>ne</u>** OᴎᴎᛕᲣᗺO (J.4.1), ——— **isakᵃaoe**
O⧧ＡᐃＡ⧧ᴎ (J.24.1), **kᵃalt̄e** Oᕼ1Ａᐃ (J.1.1), **nira-kᵃalt̄e** Oᕼ1ＡᐃＡᕊᴎᴎ
(MdC), **]kᵉeuuakᵉe** OᛕＡᲣᲣOᛕ[(J.7.8), **kⁱielaoe** O⧧Ａ1OᴎᕈＰ (J.11.1),
leoine OᴎᴎⵜO1 (J.10.1), **mele<u>s̄</u>ae** OＡᛖO1OᴎᲲ (J.15.1), **robᵃae** OＡ⦚⧧ᕈ (J.11.1)

(4) *i̯ā*-stem *-*i̯ái* > |-(ê)ê̄|: possibly **ar̄kᵃare** O⦚ＡᐃᕈＡ (Monte Gordo), **leoine**
OᴎᴎⵜO1 (J.10.1), **oor̄oire** Oᴎᴎⵜᛕⵜⵜ (J.19.1)

(5) *ā̊*-stem: possibly **bᵃaenae** OＡᴎOＡ⦚ (J.15.1), **bᵃane** OᴎＡ⦚ (J.11.1, J.19.1, J.26.1)

(6) *i*-stem: **<u>s</u>atᵃanea<u>t̄e</u>e** ᗺＡXＡᴎOＡᕼO (J.12.1)

(7) *u*-stem: possibly **ar̄aiu<u>i</u>** ᴎᲣᴎＡᛕＡ (J.1.1), **mutᵘui** ᴎᲣᐃᲣM (J.1.5)

(8) consonant-stem: possibly **ariaris̄e** OᴎᴎᕈＡᴎᕈＡ (J.10.1)

accusative singular

(1) *o*-stem: probably **kᵒoli<u>on</u>** ᴎⵜᴎ1⧧⋈ (J.55.1), **]kᵒoloion** (Monte Novo do
Castelinho), **tᵃarielnon** XＡＰᛕOᒋᴎⵜᛕ (J.55.1), ——— **uarbᵒo<u>s</u>** ⅃⧧◻ᕈＡᲣ [(J.7.5);

possibly **lokᵒon** ᴎ⧧Xⵜ1 (J.1.1), **lokᵒon** (J.57.1), **tᵃala-i<u>n</u>on** ᴎⵜᴎᴎＡ1ＡX (J.14.1)

nominative/accusative neuter: possibly **lokᵒon** ᴎ⧧Xⵜ1 (J.1.1), **lo<u>k</u>ᵒon** (J.57.1), **tᵃala-**
inon ᴎⵜᴎᴎＡ1ＡX (J.14.1), ——— **uarbᵒo<u>s</u>** ⅃⧧ᕈＡᲣ [(J.7.5)

(2) *ā*-stem: **tᵘnᵗⁱt̄esbᵃan** ᐃᛕᛎᴎᕼ⧧⦚Ａᛕ (J.53.1) probably to be read **tᵘnbⁱit̄esbᵃan**
|*tumites<u>a</u>man*|, **uabᵃan** ᴎＡⵜＡᲣ (J.16.5), **uarbᵃan** ᴎＡⵜᕈＡᲣ (J.1.2, J.3.1, J.4.1, J.21.1),
uarbᵃan ᴎＡⵜᕈＡᲣ (J.9.1), **uar<u>bᵃan</u>** ᕼＡＰ⟨Ａᛕ (J.11.3), **arbᵃan* ᴎＡⵜᕈＡ* (J.16.1),
uarnbᵃan ᴎＡ⦚ᕈᕼＡᲣ (J.20.1); probably **saru[ʔn]an** ⧧ＡＰᕼ⌖Ａᛕ (MdC);

possibly **iibᵃa<u>n</u>** ᲣＡ⦚ᴎᴎ (J.5.1), **]<u>k</u>ᵃanan** ᴎＡᴎＡ(ᐃ)[or **]aanan** ᴎＡᴎＡ(Ａ)[

(J.9.1), ——robᵃan Ρ‡ᚴΑ (Moura)

(3) *i*-stem: bᵉe:lin ᚤᛘᛖ|09 (J.17.4); probably kᵉenila(*)rin ᚤᛘᛖ(*)ΑᛐᛘᛘΟᛕ (J.17.4);

possibly **aalaein** ᚤᛘΟΑᛐΑΑ (J.15.3)

locative singular

(1) *o*-stem: probably bᵃastᵉebᵘuŕoi ᛘ‡ᛐᚤᛞᛞΟᛄ‡Αᚴ (S. Martinho), sabᵒoi ᛘ‡ᏴΑ‡ (J.5.1);

possibly —— **salsaloi** ‡Αᒋ‡Αᒋ‡ᛙ or **salsanoi** ‡Αᒋ‡Αᛙ‡ᛙ (J.12.4)

(2) *ā*-stem: probably **aliśne** ΟᛘᛘᛘᛐΑ (J.11.4), **uśnee** ΟΟᛘᛘᛘ or **uśnbᵉe** Ο9ᛘᛘᛘ (J.23.1);

possibly **liŕniene** ᒋᛙᛞᛘᛙΟᛞΟ (J.55.1)

(3) *i*-stem: probably **kᵃaltᵉe** ΟᏴᛐΑᐱ (J.1.1), **nira-kᵃaltᵉe** ΟᏴᛐΑᐱᐱΑ٩ᛘᛘ (MdC)

nominative/accusative dual

(1) *o*-stem: probably **alkᵘu** ᚤᏴᛐΑ (J.12.1), **arkᵃastᵃamu** ᚤᛞΑᚷ‡Αᐱ٩Α (MdC), **iru** ٩٩ᛘ (J.12.1, J.23.1), **{u}arbᵘu** ᚤᛞᛞ٩Αᚤ (J.23.1), **tⁱilekᵘuŕkᵘu** ᚤᏴ٩ᚤᏴΟᛐᛘᗕ or **tⁱilekᵘulkᵘu** ᚤᏴᛐᚤᏴΟᛐᛘᗕ (MdC);

possibly **kᵉeilau** ᚤΑᛐᛘΟᛕ (Cabeza del Buey IV)

(2) *ă*-stem: probably **asune** Οᛘᛘ‡Α (J.4.1), **bᵃaenae** ΟΑᛘΟΑᚴ (J.15.1), **bᵃane** ΟᛘΑᚴ (J.11.1, J.19.1, J.26.1), **ekᵘuŕine** ΟᛘᛘᛞᛘᏴΟ (J.4.1), **kⁱielaoe** Ο‡ΑᛐΟᛘᗭ (J.11.1), **kⁱikᵉe** Οᛕᛘᗭ |*Kikē*| (Monte Gordo), **meleśae** ΟΑᛞΟᛐΟᛥ (J.15.1), **robᵃae** ΟΑᚴ‡٩ |*roₐmāi*| (J.11.1)

possibly ——**isakᵃaoe** Ο‡ΑᐱΑ‡ᛘ (J.24.1), **uuakᵉe***[ ] *Οᛕ|Αᛘᛘ... (J.7.8)

(3) There are several examples of nominative feminine *ā*- and *iā*-stems in formal agreement in naming phrases, most probably identifying one individual, but they can occur together with 3rd plural verbs, presumably functioning as grammatical subjects, indicating that the phrases are syntactically dual or plural: e.g. bᵒotⁱieana≡ kᵉertᵒo =robᵃa Αᚴ‡٩‡ΑᛐΟᛕΑᛘΑ☆ᛘᗕ‡☐ (J.18.1), raᎶa=kᵃaśetᵃana ΡΑᎶΑᐱΑᛞΟᚷΑᛙΑ (J.53.1), tᵘurea=iubᵃa ΑᚴᛘᛘΑΟ٩ᛘᐱ (J.7.8).

(4) *iā*-stem: probably **arkᵃare** Ο٩Αᐱ٩Α (Monte Gordo), **ooŕoire** Ο٩ᛘ‡ᛞ‡‡ (J.19.1);

possibly **leoine** ΟΥΜ‡Ο1 (J.10.1)

nominative plural

(1) *o-stem:* **lebᵒo-iire** Ο۹ΜΜ‡□Ο1 (MdC), **linbᵒo-ire** Ο۹Μ‡□ΥΜ1 (J.11.2); probably **ire** Ο۹Μ (J.7.2, J.52.1)

nominative/accusative neuter plural o-stem: possibly **otᵉerkᵃa** ΑΛ۹Οﰠ‡ (J.1.4)

genitive plural

(1) *o-stem:* l̲iirnestᵃak̲ᵘun ΥΜΘΑΧ‡ΟΥ۹΄ΜΜ1 (J.19.1), ——nemun ΥΜΜΟΥ or ——emun ΥΜΜΟ (J.7.8),]tᵃarnekᵘun ΥΜΥΘΟΥ۹΄ΑΧ (J.26.1)

(2) *ă-stem:* possibly——bᵃaanon Μ‡ΥΑΑ} (J.11.4)

(3) *i-stem:* bᵉelis̲on̲ Μ‡ΜΜ1Ο9 (J.20.1)

datives/ablatives plural

anakᵉenak̲ᵉ:eibᵒo ‡ΘΜΟ |)(ΑΥΟ)(ΑΥΑ (J.5.1, group adjective), **bᵉelibᵒo** ‡□Μ1Ο9 (J.1.2), **istᵃaibᵒo** ← Χ‡Μ | → ᴎΘ‡ (J.5.1, demonstrative), —— (kᵃakⁱ)is̲iinkᵒolobᵒo ‡□‡1‡ΧΥΜΜΜΜ΄ΑΛ (J.1.1), **lokᵒobᵒo** ‡□‡Χ‡1 (J.1.1), **niirabᵒo** ‡□Α۹ΜΜΥ (J.1.1), **rinoₑbᵒo** PᴎΥ‡ΟΘ‡ (J.5.1);

possibly]aetᵉabᵒo*[ ]ΑΟ‡ΑН‡[(J.28.1),]aibᵒo‡□ΜΑ[(J.28.1), ——alakⁱimuŕbᵒ? ?□ΧΥΜΜ΄Α 1Α Υ▷◁Ο (S. Martinho), ——]antᵒonbᵒo̲ ‡□Μ‡ΑΥΑ [(J.8.1),]ebᵒo ‡□Ο[(J.7.8)

instrumental plural

possibly **kⁱinbᵃaiᴛⁱi** Μᴛ΄ΜΑ}ΥΜ΄ (J.3.1) = **kⁱinbᵃaib̲ⁱi**

PRONOUNS, DEMONSTRATIVES, AND PRONOMINALS

(1) personal pronoun, 1st singular: possibly **bᵉe** Ο9 (J.1.1, Monte Gordo), 6Ο (MdC)

(2) personal pronoun, genitive plural masculine: possibly——**emun** ΥΜΜΟ (J.7.8)

(3) relative pronoun, masculine accusative or neuter nominative/accusative: possibly **iion, -ion** (J.1.3, J.4.1, J.7.9) as suffixed relative, **s̲aen** ΥΟΑΜ (J.27.1 demonstrative

pronoun), -e (J.1.1, J.1.3 enclitic pronoun)

(4) possible relative pronouns, feminine: nominative **ea** AO, accusative **ean** ᛘAO, see note on the forms above.

(5) possible demonstrative, masculine nominative singular: **-śe** Oᛘ (J.10.1)

(6) possible demonstrative, feminine accusative singular: ——**śaen** ᛘOAᛘ (J.27.1)

(7) demonstrative, nominative plural masculine: **sie:** |Oᛘ‡ (J.12.1)

(8) demonstrative, dative/ablative plural: **ist^aaib°o** ←X‡ᛘ | →ᛗ日‡ (J.5.1)

INDECLINABLE FORMS: PREPOSITIONS, PREVERBS, CONJUNCTIONS, AND ADVERBS

ar ९A (J.10.1, J.12.3) < *(p)are*

b^aa A} (J.1.2, J.12.4, J.16.1, J.16.2, J.18.1)

er- ९O (J.10.1)

k°o ‡X (J.1.2), **k°** X (J.53.1) < **ko(m)*

o- ‡ (J.10.1), **ua-** A५ (J.53.1) < **u(p)o*

ro ‡९ < **(p)ro*, marking past-tense verbs as perfect J.1.1, J.3.1, J.12.1, J.16.3, J.18.2, MdC; possibly J.11.1; with accusative enclitic **ro-n** ᛘ‡९ J.11.4, Monte Gordo

t^aae OAX (J.14.1) possibly | *de* | with infixed object or relative pronoun

t^ee O日 (J.1.1, J.1.3, J.12.1, J.16.1, MdC, Vale de Águia) | *de* |

t^eee OO日 (J.18.2, J.23.1) possibly | *de* | with infixed object or relative pronoun

t°o ‡Δ (J.1.1) | *to* |

t^uu ΔΗ (J.53.1) < **to* before **u(p)o*

probably **na** A५ (J.1.2, J.7.1), **ne** O५ (J.1.2) negative preverbal particles

possibly **ane** O५A (J.1.1) < **ande*, **en_b^e** ᑲ५O (J.17.4)

VERBS

present 1st person singular

probably **lakⁱiuu** ꙮ or **(o-)lakⁱiuu** ꙮ (MdC) 'I lie down';

possibly **lakⁱinꭧⁱi** ꙮ (J.12.4) if read **lakⁱinbⁱi** | *lăgimi* |, **nař k^eenꭨⁱi**
ꙮ (J.19.2) if read | *narkemi* | or | *narkēmi* |,]**nař k^eeuu**[ ]ꙮ[
(Corte do Freixo 2) 'I lie still', **t^aa-b^ee** ꙮ (Monte Gordo), **t^aao b^ee**
ꙮ (MdC), (?t^a)**au** ꙮ (J.10.1). If we read J.16.2 as na]**ř k^eeo-**
io * * ꙮ[, this form may show that the older ō in the verbal ending was
preserved before the relative suffix, but **o** here might be purely orthographic: note
that this same inscription has **iob^aa**, contrasting with **iub^aa** in J.7.8.

present 3rd person singular active

probably **nař k^ee** ꙮ (J.27.1), **nař[k^e]e** ꙮ (J.1.1), **nař k^ee**
ꙮ (S. Martinho), **nař k^eetⁱi** ꙮ (J.56.1), **o-ni-ꭨak^aatⁱi-śe**
ꙮ (J.10.1) ?= **o-ni-[l]ak^aatⁱi-śe;**

possibly **t^ee·b^aere** ꙮ (J.7.8)

present 3rd person plural active

lak^eentⁱi ꙮ (J.53.1), **nař k^eeni** ꙮ (J.1.2, J.1.3), **nař k^eenii**
ꙮ (J.2.1, J.21.1), **nař k^eentⁱi** ꙮ (J.12.1, J.16.1, J.17.2,
J.18.1, J.19.2); probably **nař ken** ꙮ (J.7.5), **nař k^ee(n)** ꙮ (J.7.8),
nař rk^ee:n: | ꙮ (J.23.1), **t^ee·b^aantⁱi** ꙮ (MdC). Note also]**ntⁱi**
at the end of the fragmentary inscription from Monte Novo do Castelinho.

On the 'athematic' inflexion in **-entⁱi**, compare Lusitanian DOENTI 'they give' <
dōnti (Schmidt 1985, 337).

possibly **b^oolon** ꙮ (J.7.1) as a thematic verb with early apocope of *-i*,
ꙮ[or]**aanan** ꙮ (J.9.1), **lakⁱinꭧⁱi** ꙮ (J.12.4) if
read **lakⁱintⁱi**

3rd person plural present middle

possibly **nař k^eenai** ꙮ (J.7.1, J.55.1)

3rd person plural future

possibly ——tᵉasiioonii ᴎᴎᴎ⧻⧻ᴎᴎ⧻Aᕼ (J.1.1)

[NOTE. In the past tenses, the type known in comparative Celtic grammar as the 'suffixless preterite' or 'ā-preterite', which is derived from the Indo-European perfect, is well represented in the SW corpus. These forms are classified and translated here as perfect (expressing completed action) rather than as a simple past tense (preterite). However, the fact that the 'perfectivizing' Celtic preverbs **ro** (repeatedly) and **kᵒ** (probably once) are used with such etymologically perfect verbal forms suggests that Indo-European perfect might already have given rise to—or was merging into—a simple Celtic past tense in Tartessian, so that an additional marker was required to clarify the perfect aspect, as in early medieval Goidelic and Brittonic. See further Appendix C.]

imperfect 3rd person singular

possibly **ar·bᵉieŕi** ᴎ⋀Οᴎᗡ٩A (J.12.3), **tᵉe·bᵃere** Ο٩Ο⦚Οᕼ (J.7.8)

imperfect 3rd person plural

possibly **bᵒolon** ᴎ⧻1⧻◻ (J.7.1)

perfect 1st person singular

probably **bᵃara** A٩A⦚ (S. Martinho), **bᵃara**** **A٩A⦚ (J.4.1), **ro·laᴣa** AᕼA1⧻٩ (J.3.1) ?= **ro·lakᵘa**

possibly **bᵃarua-ion** ⦚APᖶAᴎ⧻ᴎ with suffixed relative? (J.7.9),]**bᵒoara**]◻/⧻A٩A (J.2.1)

perfect 3rd person singular

kotᵘuaratᵉe ⋈ΔᖶAPAᕼΟ (J.53.1); probably **abᵃre** Ο٩⦚A (J.52.1) = **bᵃare**, **ar·bᵃarie** Οᴎٜٜٜٜٜٜٜٜ٩A⦚٩A (J.10.1), **bᵃare** Ο٩A⦚ (J.7.10, J.26.1, J.27.1), **enbᵉ·kᵃa|rne** Ο٩٩|A)ᴵᗡᴎΟ (J.17.4), **ro·bᵃare** Ο٩A⦚⧻٩ (MdC, probably J.16.3), **ro-n·bᵃare** Ο٩A⦚ᴎ⧻٩ (Monte Gordo), **tᵃae·bᵃare** Ο٩A⦚ΟAⵝ (J.14.1), **tᵉe·bᵃare** Ο٩A⦚Οᕼ (J.1.3, Vale de Águia), **tᵉe·bar[e]** *٩A⦚Οᕼ (J.16.1), t̲ᵉe·b̲ᵃare Ο٩A[⦚]Οᕼ (J.18.1), t̲ᵉe·[b̲ᵃ]are Ο٩A[ ]Οᕼ (J.21.1), **tᵉe·ro·bᵃare** Ο٩A⦚⧻٩Οᕼ ᕼΟᖶ⧻⦚AᖴΟ (J.1.1, J.12.1), and **tᵉe(-)e·ro·bᵃare** Ο٩A⦚⧻٩ΟΟᕼ (J.18.2), **bᵘu(o)** (J.1.2)

possibly **bᵃareii** ᴎᴎΟ٩A⦚ (J.5.1), **ro-bᵃa** A⦚⧻٩ (J.18.1), —— **bᵘu(o)** ⧻ᴎ⋈ (J.1.2), **ro·bᵃae** ΟA⦚⧻٩ (J.11.1), **uurkᵉe** Ο)|٩ᴎᴎ (J.1.4)

[NOTE: Villar (1997, 931–2) interprets Celtiberian *kombalkez* and *terturez* as 3rd singular perfects in which the Indo-European secondary personal ending *-t* (whence Celtiberian *-z*) has been added to the inherited 3rd person singular perfect ending *-e*. Although we do not see such an innovation in Tartessian bᵃare, -ratᵉe, -k̲ᵃ | rne, and uurkᵉe, the writing system did not permit the representation of word-final stops, so it is not impossible that the spellings mean /*bāret, rātet*/, &c.]

perfect 3rd person plural active

probably bᵃar(e)n[ꟿꟼAꓘ (J.20.1) simplex, compound ro-n·bᵃaren ꓭOꟼAꓨꟿꟷꟼ (J.11.4), tᵉee·bᵃarentⁱi ꟿⴲꟿOꟼAꓨOOꟼ (J.23.1)

perfect 3rd person plural (medio-passive)

possibly bᵒo↑ir ꟼꟿ↑ꟷⵔ (J.7.1), ——kᵃaŕner-ion ∧A𐤷ꟿOꟼꟿꟷꟿ (J.7.2, with suffixed relative), akᵃa̲**ir-ion ∧**ꟷꟼ𐤷ꟷ𐤷A[(J.1.3) if read as a kᵃa̲[ŕn]ir-ion

imperative 3rd person singular

probably —— ar·bᵉieŕitᵘu ꟼ△ꟿ𐤷OꟿꟼꟼA (J.12.3)

verbal nouns

(1) genitive: oretᵒo ꟷ△Oꟼꟷ(AX) (J.4.1.).

(2) dative: eertᵃaune OꟿꟿAXꟼOO (J.55.1)

NOTES ON SYNTAX AND WORD ORDER

There are a number of obvious obstacles preventing a straightforward recovery of Tartessian syntax: the small size of the extant corpus, outstanding uncertainties of interpretation, the high proportion of fragmentary texts, the formulaic order-ing of elements required by the funerary context. Owing to the last consideration, the corpus might be more accurately taken as reflecting the Tartessian 'funerary inscriptional statement', rather than the Tartessian sentence. Nonetheless, there are a few noteworthy recurrent patterns, and some examples show ordering of elements similar to patterns found in other early Indo-European languages and better-attested Celtic languages.

THE POSITION OF THE VERB

The finite verb naŕkᵉentⁱi, &c., which occurs frequently in the formulaic language of the inscriptions, often appears at or near the ending of the statement (for example J.1.2, J.1.3, J.1.5, J.2.1, J.7.5, J.11.1, J.14.1, J.16.1, J.16.3, J.17.2, J.18.1, J.19.1, J.19.2, J.21.1, J.22.1, J.23.1, J.26.1, J.55.1; cf. J.7.1, J.11.4, J.11.5). J.56.1 **akᵒolioś naŕkᵉetⁱi** has been recognized as a simple sentence comprising a nominative singular name as subject of a 3rd singular verb, in that order. These examples favour the possibility that Tartessian, like Celtiberian and several other Ancient Indo-European languages, had a basic verb-final word order. However, this placement may also have had a semantic or logical factor behind it, if, as proposed here, the sense of **naŕkᵉentⁱi**, &c., is basically 'they lie down, rest, remain fixed, unmoving'. That would be the final thought in the funerary statement: the grave has been constructed, it has carried or taken (**bᵃare**) the remains, then finally the deceased (probably with grave goods) rests in place. Cf. J.1.3 **tᵉe·bᵃare naŕkᵉeni** '[this grave or death] has carried [the named deceased] away; "they" now rest [here]', **]bᵒoara naŕkᵉenii** 'I [the grave] have borne [the named deceased] "they" now rest [here]' (J.2.1). **sie̱: naŕkᵉentⁱi** (J.12.1) is unusual in this respect, with **naŕkᵉentⁱi** preceding the **tᵉe·ro·bᵃare** formula, as well as being a unique example of what appears to be a nominative pronoun or demonstrative preceding the verb as its subject; therefore, **sie̱:** (< Indo-European *$*t\!j̣oi$ ~ Vedic *tye*) may have relative force ('these men who now rest [here]'); if so, **naŕkᵉentⁱi** is not the main-clause verb in this case. J.12.1's final segment **ßatᵃaneat̲ᵉe**, probably a dative singular, appears unusual both syntactically and as regards the physical layout of the signs on the stone, oriented left-to-right, turning outwards, rather than spiralling inwards, as compelled by the image of the warrior at the centre. In J.12.4, the verb **lakⁱin↑ⁱi** 'I' or 'they lie down', 'I' or 'they have lain down' ends the statement. The fragmentary inscription from Monte Novo do Castelinho seems to end with a 3rd person plural verb.

Forms of **naŕkᵉentⁱi** are never found at the beginning of a complete inscriptional text, nor does **tᵉe·ro·bᵃare** which I take to be a compound perfective past-tense verb, meaning approximately '[this grave/death] has carried away'. Forms resembling Hispano-Celtic names begin several of the complete epigraphic texts. Therefore, Tartessian does not appear to have verb-initial basic order, at least the language of its funerary inscriptions does not. As discussed in Appendix C, there are some examples in the SW corpus of 'amplifications', in which segmentable elements follow a form of the recurrent closing word **naŕkᵉentⁱi**, whereas identifiable names and the usual formulaic elements precede **naŕkᵉentⁱi**, more or less in their usual order. In other words, in these longer texts we seem to be getting something extra after an already complete verb-final statement. The unusual text of J.3.1 may represent another type of verb-medial statement: **aibᵘuris[| kⁱinbᵃai↑ⁱi | ro-laßa | uarbᵃan ubᵘ[u |]i** (J.3.1).

Alcalá del Río (J.53.1) is remarkable in several respects: **kᵒ-tᵘ-ua-ratᵉe** tⁿnᐪⁱitᵉsbᵃan orbᵃa setᵃa lakᵉentⁱi raⱡa≡kᵃaśetᵃana 'The highest resting place/ throne (*or* the inherited resting place) has safely delivered to (<has run under towards) the greatest tumulus: Raφa and the bronze minister are now lain down [here].' There are six violations of the principle of redundancy (agreement between the stop consonant signs and the following vowel). In these six instances, the redundant vowel has been omitted, thus anticipating the subsequent Palaeohispanic writing systems. The text is arranged clockwise left-to-right. Its honorand seems to be a woman identified primarily by her professional standing. None of the formula words are used. Syntactically, it is most easily read as two clauses both beginning with verbs. The first verb kᵒ-tᵘ-ua-ratᵉe appears to be a 3rd person singular perfect with three preverbs. *to-u(p)o-rāte* 'has safely delivered to' is impeccably Proto-Celtic, but adding *ko(m)-* to the front of this is an innovation.

THE VERBAL COMPLEX

For many years now, a preoccupation of Celtic historical linguistics has been the derivation of the opposed 'absolute' and 'conjunct' forms of the finite verb as attested in Old Irish and early Brittonic, together with the associated preverbal particles, enclitic object pronouns, and related features. The light that the SW corpus might shed on these matters has been a focus of my research in the years after the first edition of this book appeared. Detailed discussions of this subject are presented in Appendix C below and in *Tartessian 2* §§56.1–63.2. These now supersede the treatment that appeared in this book's first edition. Note also the Syntactic Analyses in the catalogue of SW inscriptions above and in *Tartessian 2* §55.1.

NOUN PHRASES WITHIN THE STATEMENT

In J.1.1, the statement begins with the dative divine name lokᵒobᵒo niirabᵒo, probably co-ordinated with the following dative plural, 'for the Lugoues and for the chief men'. J.5.1 istₐ̲a̲|ibᵒo rinoebᵒo | anakᵉenak̲e̲:e | ibᵒo similarly shows datives plural in concord. In J.3.1 aibᵘuris[is possibly the name of the deceased as a detached nominative noun phrase at the beginning of the statement. J.19.2 and J.22.1 apparently begin with the name of the deceased in the nominative, ooŕoir < *u(p)erṷiros* and uarbᵒoiir *u(p)erₐmo-ṷiros*. J.7.6 aarkᵘui ... begins with a dative singular masculine name, probably naming the deceased. J.14.1 begins tᵃalainon tᵘuŕekᵘui, in which a noun in another case (accusative or nominative/accusative neuter) precedes what is probably an identification of the deceased in the dative; the initial noun tᵃalainon is interpreted as expressing the deceased's destination, 'the place of the fair/blessed headland'. If so, tᵃalainon would be taking the logical and syntactic place of the accusative formula word uar(n)bᵃan 'the highest destination', although

uar(n)bᵃan itself never occurs at the beginning of the statement. J.5.1 **sabºoi . . .** can be read as an initial locative singular ('in the summer') or as a further example of an initial dative singular, naming the deceased ('for Sabos, Samos'). The opening of the long San Martinho inscription **bᵃastᵉebᵘuŕoi . . .** is also probably a locative singular 'in the . . . yew wood'. A recurring pattern evident in several complete inscriptions is for the text to open with a complex naming phrase, including elements in concord probably in the nominative/accusative dual: **kⁱielaoe:≡|oiśaHa ≡bᵃane≡robᵃae. . .** 'Kielaos's wife OiśaHā, foremost woman' (J.11.1), **ɮaitᵘura meleśae≡::≡bᵃaenae. . .** 'Φaitura, sweet woman and wife . . .' (J.15.1), **bºotⁱieana≡ kᵉertºo ≡robᵃa. . .** 'Bōdⁱeanā ⟨and⟩ the first-born daughter of the artisan' (J.18.1), **iru≡alkᵘu. . .** 'the hero ⟨and⟩ Alkos' (J.12.1), **tⁱilekᵘur̲kᵘu≡arkᵃastᵃam̲u. . .** 'Tillekurkos ⟨and⟩ Arga(n)stamos (the man greatest in silver)' (MdC).

THE SYNTAX OF THE NOUN PHRASE

In J.18.1 **bºotⁱi☼ana kᵉertºo**, the nominative singular name is followed by an o-stem genitive singular, presumably used as a patronym, 'Bōdⁱeanā daughter of the artisan'. The noun phrase **raɮa≡kᵃaśetᵃana . . . kºoŕbᵉo** (J.53.1) is interpreted as name+title+genitive of an occupational patronym, 'Raφᵃa, the tin/bronze minister, [daughter] of Korbeos (the chariot maker/charioteer)'. In J.19.1,]**liirnestᵃakᵘun bᵃane ooŕoire**, the genitive plural group name precedes the nominative/accusative or dative singular of 'woman/wife' and a gamonym (wife's name) **ooŕoire** in apparent concord with **bᵃane** follows; note that the position of the genitive plural group name in]**tᵃarnekᵘun bᵃane** (J.26.1) is the same as in]**liirnestᵃakᵘun bᵃane**. **uarbºoiir sarune** (J.22.1) is interpreted as a loosely compounded or phrasal name similar to the 'inversion compounds' known in the medieval and modern Insular Celtic languages. In such loose compounds, the name comprises a noun phrase with a first element susceptible to case inflexion followed by a stereotyped case form, in the Tartessian examples probably datives singular, thus 'noble consort to the star goddess'. Compare examples like Old Irish *Mael-brigte* 'tonsured devotee of St Brigit', where the second element is genitive. In J.23.1 **iru≡{u}arbᵘu i el**, the first two elements could be datives singular in concord, but more probably form a co-ordinative compound in the nominative/accusative dual, thus literally 'man/ hero ⟨and⟩ the supreme one' < *$u̯irū$≡$u(p)er_amū$ 'the highest man/hero'. **iel** or **el** at the end could reflect a borrowing of one of the common West Semitic words for 'god' used by the Phoenicians.

THE SYNTAX OF THE SUPERLATIVE

Following Correa's proposals (1992, 101), the formulaic **uarbᵃan** (J.1.2, J.4.1, J.16.1, J.21.1) can be identified with the Celtiberian superlatives VERAMOS, VORAMOS < *$u(p)er_amo$- 'highest'. So, in the context of funerary inscriptions, it could possibly be construed as an honorific title or epithet, referring to the noble deceased, even though the inflexion of **uarbᵃan** did not agree with that of the personal names in the texts. Because **uarbᵃan** is formed as a superlative and most commonly ends with a nasal, I had at first (thus in the first edition of this book) thought it likely that the Tartessian superlative, like that of Old Irish, functioned syntactically as an inflexible nominative/accusative neuter singular, to be understood as a predicate 'the one who is most . . .'. However, the opening of the recently discovered Mesas do Castelinho inscription, **tⁱilekᵘur̲kᵘu≡arkᵃastᵃa̲m̲u̲. . .** 'Tillekurkos ⟨and⟩ Arga(n)stamos (the man greatest in silver)', indicated that Tartessian superlatives could occur with the full range of endings of o-/$\bar{a}$-stem adjectives. Therefore, the superlatives **uar(n)bᵃan** and **tᵘn↑ⁱitᵉsbᵃan** (J.53.1) were probably not honorific epithets of the deceased but feminine singular accusatives, which could be construed as expressing the destinations of adjacent verbs of motion in the texts. In other words, the deceased had gone to the 'highest' place, state, or feminine being, i.e. goddess. In the usual ordering of the epigraphic formula, **uar(n)bᵃan** follows the naming phrase (which no doubt identifies the deceased) and precedes **tᵉe·ro-bᵃare**, which can be construed as the verb of motion 'has carried away'. Like Celtiberian VORAMOS, Hispano-Celtic place-names *Uama* and *Uxama* likewise show a declinable superlative, not limited to a predicative function.

PREPOSITIONAL PHRASES are few in the Tartessian inscriptions in keeping with the syntactic possibilities of a fully inflected Ancient Indo-European language. **tᵒo araia̲|i** (J.1.1) shows the preposition **tᵒo** before a noun in the dative, which it presumably governs, thus directly comparable to the properties of the Celtiberian preposition TO in the phrase TO LVGVEI (K.3.3). As argued by De Bernardo Stempel (2008), the dative without a preposition would mean 'for', and with TO it would mean 'to, towards' with implicit motion. Thus, in J.1.1 a syntactic and logical contrast is being made between the two dative phrases that open the text: the independent datives plural **lokᵒobᵒo niirabᵒo**, then the prepositional phrase **tᵒo araiai**. With **kᵒo bᵉelibᵒo** (J.1.2), it is probable that the name or common noun inflected as a dative plural is the same attested in other case forms within the corpus as accusative singular **bᵉe:lin** (J.17.4) and genitive plural singular **bᵉeliśo̲n̲** (J.20.1). The force of the preposition **kᵒo** < *$ko(m)$ + dative is probably 'together with', so the phrase would mean 'together with the "stong ones", with the Belīs'. **r̲o- kᵒolio̲n̲** (J.55.1) could be a prepositional phrase with an accusative object, possibly meaning 'for Kolios, in the place of Koloios'.

THE RELATIVE

As discussed in the notes above on the forms **ea**, **ean**, **ion**, and **sie:**, there are examples in the corpus in which the syntactic context and the etymologies implied by historical phonology allow interpretation as relative clauses: **uarbᵒoiir sarune ea bᵃare naŕkᵉenii** (J.22.1) 'Uar(a)moiir Sarun(n)ē ("Noble Consort of the Star goddess"), she who has carried [him]; they now rest' with **ea** < *$ii\bar{a}$ (feminine nominative singular), **ean bᵃara** (S. Martinho) 'whom I [this grave] have carried' < *$ii\bar{a}m$ (feminine accusative singular), **bᵃarua-ion** (J.7.9) 'whom I [this grave] have carried' < *$iiom$ (masculine accusative singular), likewise **kᵃaŕner-ion** (J.7.2) 'whom they have entombed in a stone monument' or 'who is entombed', possibly also **kᵃa[ŕn]ir-ion** (J.1.3), **iru⹀alkᵘu—sie: naŕkᵉentⁱi** . . . (J.12.1) 'the man/hero ⟨and⟩ Alkos, these men who now rest [here]. . .' with **sie** < Indo-European *$tioi$. It is also possible that the preverbs that are represented as though they might have a long vowel or diphthong (e.g. **tᵃae** and **tᵉee**) result from the coalescence with an enclitic relative pronoun, likewise the examples of **ro-n** (J.11.4, Monte Gordo). Without further examples of recurrent patterns, it is difficult to confirm or eliminate any of these possibilities with confidence. If all of these forms, or a key subset of them, can be confirmed, then it appears that Tartessian had an inflected relative pronoun, like Celtiberian, rather than the inflexible *io* that is attested in Gaulish and must be reconstructed for Brittonic and Old Irish. This conclusion would have major implications for the dialectology of the Ancient Celtic languages. On a second point, the testimony of these examples would be more ambiguous. In some the relative would appear to be enclitic, as in Gaulish and the reconstructions implied by the Insular Celtic languages, and in others it would stand at the head of its clause, as an independent and probably accented word, as in Celtiberian and Vedic. It is not impossible that Tartessian was inconsistent or transitional with regards to this feature.

DIALECT AFFILIATION

Within the small number of recent publications considering specific details of the language of the SW inscriptions, some express the view that the primary or matrix language is Indo-European and specifically Celtic, as concluded in this book. Others allow that the corpus includes some sufficiently well-proven Indo-European content, but that the matrix language remains intractable and uncertain, and could thus be presumed to be non-Indo-European, much as Gaulish names and Celtic name elements have been found in Iberian texts. Either way—Tartessian simply is Indo-European/Celtic or Tartessian contains Indo-European/Celtic—the dialect affinity of that Indo-European/Celtic content remains an issue to be considered. These premises carry general implications for Indo-European and Celtic studies: workers in those fields cannot intentionally ignore the testimony of Tartessian unless they are prepared to defend the position that the corpus contains no Indo-European material at all. Otherwise, it represents, in either case, the oldest attested Indo-European language west of Italy (if not Greece). Although this section is written from the viewpoint that the language of Celtic elements and the matrix language are one and the same, anyone deferring that conclusion might still weigh the affiliation of the Indo-European 'element'.

The studies comprising *Tartessian 2* §§64–122 show that the signs used to represent the forms in the SW corpus with probable Celtic etymologies have a systematic relationship to the Proto-Celtic sound system and that this relationship is defined by regular sound laws. In all cases, there is more than one example to demonstrate each particular innovation from Proto-Celtic. Where more than one reflex of the Proto-Celtic sound in the same phonetic environment appears in the corpus, one of two factors obtains. (1) The unconditioned fluctuation is found also in another, or more than one other, early Celtic language: e.g., orbᵃa (J.53.1), uarbᵃan (J.3.1, J.4.1, J.21.1) < *u(p)er_ₐmā- ~ Brittonic and Old Welsh *Uertigernus, Uortigernus, Guarthigirn*. (2) The variation reflects the earlier and later phonologies, implying that the change was underway over the era of the corpus: e.g., ( )omurikᵃa[ ]anbᵃatⁱia . . . (J.16.2), in which Proto-Celtic short */i/ has been consistently preserved as Tartessian i, contrasting with the better-attested treatment in which lowering to e has occurred in these environments, thus]tᵃarnekᵘun (J.26.1) < *Tar_ₐnikōm, tᵘurekᵘui (J.14.1) < *Turikōi, tᵘurea (J.7.8) < *Turiā.

Although it is suggested that here Tartessian naŕkᵉentⁱi, &c., is equivalent to Greek ναρκάω 'grow stiff, numb, dead' in form and sense, it is not necessarily, nor even probably, a borrowing from Greek, rather the proposal is that it is a native Tartessian inheritance from Indo-European with a similar form and meaning to its Greek cognate due to their common source. There are Indo-European and specifically Celtic *comparanda* for a high proportion of the isolatable forms within the corpus. In many instances, the phonology of the words excludes the possibility of assigning them to any branch of Indo-European other than Celtic; the Tartessian forms show sound shifts that are the defining features of Celtic, as itemized in the following list.

INDO-EUROPEAN > COMMON CELTIC INNOVATIONS IN TARTESSIAN

(1) Loss of Indo-European *p*, initially before vowels and between vowels. There

are several derivatives of Indo-European *(s)h₄upér 'over', all with loss of *p*: ooŕ- (J.19.1, J.19.2, cf. J.53.1); the feminine accusative formula word | u̯arₐman | < *u(p)eramām 'highest' — uarbᵃan (J.1.2, J.3.1, J.4.1, J.21.1), uaṟbᵃan (J.9.1), uarbᵃa̱n̲ (J.11.3),]u̲arbᵃan (J.21.1), uarnbᵃan (J.20.1); cf. uarbᵒoiir (J.22.1) < *u(p)erₐmo-u̯iros, — uarbᵒoʃ (J.7.5), uarbᵘu( )i (J.23.1) < *u(p)erₐmū(i). The more archaic uabᵃan < *u(p)ₐmām 'highest one' (J.16.5). Indo-European *pro > Tartessian ro in ten examples (J.1.1, J.3.1, J.11.1, J.11.4, J.16.3, J.18.1, MdC, Moura, Monte Gordo), ro (J.55.1). Indo-European *(s)h₄upo- 'over, under' > Tartessian o-: oretᵒo 'save, run under' (J.4.1) < *u(p)o-reto- (*Tartessian 2* §77), otᵉerkᵃa(-) 'tomb' (J.1.4) < *u(p)o-derkā (cf. Gaulish *uodercos* 'tomb' Larzac). Tartessian ar continues the Indo-European preposition *peri in arᵇieŕitᵘu | ar-b'eritū(d) | probably 'let her carry on' (J.12.3) < *(p)ari-beretūd and arᵇᵃarie 'has carried onward'(J.10.1) < *(p)ari-bāre. Possibly Indo-European *pleir-o- 'very many' > Tartessian liir- 'ocean' (J.19.1). However, note Indo-European *ptn̥-: *pet(e)r- 'wing, feather' > Tartessian ⱻatᵃan- (J.12.1), where Indo-European *p has apparently not gone to zero in the phonetic environment at absolute initial position of a fully accented word and the following vowel is | a- |.

(2) Indo-European -ps- > Common Celtic -χs- > Tartessian ś: probably in uśne̱e̱ (J.23.1) or uśn̲be, i.e. | uχsₐmẽ | 'in the highest place' < *uχsₐmāi < *u(p)sₐmā-i.

(3) Another of one of the definitively Celtic sound changes is Indo-European *gᵘ > b. Thus Indo-European *gᵘénh₂ 'woman' (Wodtko et al. 2008, 177–85) > Tartessian bᵃane | banē | or, more probably, | bₐnē | (J.11.1, J.19.1, J.26.1) nominative/accusative dual or dative singular, feminine a-stem < *bₐnai, also written bᵃaenae (J.15.1), possibly genitive plural bᵃaanon (J.11.4), cf. Gaulish ?accusative singular *beni* (Châteaubleau), genitive plural *bnanom* (Larzac), accusative plural *mnas* (Larzac) < Celtic *bnam-s (see further Delamarre 2003, 72), personal names *Seno-bena*, *Uitu-bena*; Old Irish nominative singular *ben* 'woman, wife' < *bena, nominative/accusative dual *mnaí*, dative singular archaic *bein*, later Old Irish *mnaí*, genitive plural *ban* < *banom. tᵉeᵇᵃantⁱi (MdC) is probably | de-bānti | or | de-banti | 'they pass away' > 'they die': Indo-European *gᵘeh₂- 'go, step, pass'.

(4) Later (i.e. post-laryngeal) Indo-European ō in final syllables becomes Proto-Celtic ū: dative singular o-stem ending -ōi > Tartessian -ui in tuŕekᵘui (J.14.1), &c., genitive plural o-stem ending -ōm > Tartessian -un, in liirnestᵃakᵘun (J.19.1), (n) emun (J.7.8), &c., possibly also in the thematic present 1st person singular ending in]naŕkᵉeuu[(Corte do Freixo 2) 'I lie still' (or some similar meaning). Note also the probable masculine o-stem nominative/accusative duals with -u < -ō, such as iru (J.12.1) < *u̯irō 'two men, heroes'.

(5) Later Indo-European ō in non-final syllables to Common Celtic ā: Tartessian perfect -ratᵉe | rāte | (J.53.1) 'has run' < */rōte/, bᵃare 'has borne' < */bōre/.

The change is possibly not complete in]bᵒoara ▢ / ‡A٩A 'I have borne' (J.2.1) from older *bóra*.

(6) Later Indo-European *ē* > Common Celtic *ī*: **h₃rḗg´-s* 'king' probably in *Gargoris*, **aiburis** (J.3.1) and **ariariśe** (J.10.1) ?= **ariaris-se**.

(7) Although the other Indo-European branches also employ prepositional preverbs with verbs, the pattern observable in Tartessian appears particularly similar to what is found in the Celtic languages, especially the function of **ro** < **(p)ro*, in particular the mutual exclusivity of verbs marked with **ro** and verbs marked with Indo-European primary endings in *-i*; see Appendix C.

(8) As explained above (pp. 3–4), apart from the thorny **naŕkᶜentⁱi**, &c., the method behind this decipherment was generally not to seek Indo-European explanations based on etyma for which there was no Celtic cognate. However, for every fully developed Celtic sub-branch, there would undoubtedly be at least a few examples where an Indo-European root survived only in that one Celtic language. In the light of this methodology, it is of course in no way surprising that all the proposed Indo-European roots do include Celtic forms amongst the comparanda. Nevertheless, it is worth noting that items of Celtic core vocabulary with appropriate meanings do appear with remarkable frequency in the corpus, more than one would expect if the language of inscriptions belonged to some other (i.e. non-Celtic) branch of Indo-European.

TARTESSIAN IMPLIES A REVISED RECONSTRUCTION OF COMMON CELTIC in one phonological feature only. Indo-European syllabic nasals **/m̥ n̥/* show the usual Celtic treatment in Tartessian Ἀργανθωωιος |*Argantonios*| with 'silver' < Indo-European **h₂erǵ´ṇtom* 'silver'. However, in **ekᵘuŕine** OᲧᲧᚾᲧ𝌁O (J.4.1) and dative plural **rinoebᵒo** PᚾᲧ‡O𐌇‡ (J.5.1), Celtic **rigₐni* 'queen' < Indo-European **h₃rḗg´nih₂* (cf. Sanskrit *rājñī* 'queen') has not developed like Gaulish *rigani*, Cisalpine genitive *rikanas*, Old Irish *rígain* from Celtic **rigani* < a notional Indo-European **h₃rḗg´ṇⁿih₂* with a syllabic nasal. Similarly, *m* in the 'Italo-Celtic' superlative ending did not develop as *m̥* > *am* in Tartessian as in the other Celtic languages, for example: **uarbᵃan** ᲧA𐌙٩AᲧ (J.1.2, J.3.1, J.4.1, J.21.1) 'the highest one' < 'Italo-Celtic' **(s)uperm̥ᵐām* vs. Celtiberian masculine nominative singular VERAMOS, VORAMOS, accusative VERAMOM. **tᵘn↑ⁱitᵉsbᵃan** ᐃᲧ↑ᚾᲧᚼ𐌙ᑯᲧ probably |*tumitesₐman*| also shows a superlative ending in which the old syllabic nasal **m̥* is not represented as two segments. It appears that, in these examples, the syllabic nasal either never developed in the first place in Tartessian or ceased to be syllabic when a vowel followed. It is possible, however, that the throwback is largely a matter of representation. For example, if traditional poetry had been practiced, and especially if there had been some overlap in language learning between traditional oral poetry and new-fangled epigraphy, a situation might have prevailed in which the Indo-European syllabic nasals had come to be pronounced as two segments, as generally throughout the Ancient Celtic languages, but anachronistically still counted as one mora metrically.

A POSSIBLE AFFINITY WITH NON-CELTIC WESTERN INDO-EUROPEAN is suggested by a single recurrent detail, namely the possible analogical extension of the athematic 3rd plural active ending of **naŕkᵉentⁱi**, &c., as took place also in the Italic dialects of Oscan and Umbrian and is possibly also seen in Lusitanian DOENTI. However, it is not certain what the tense and mood of the various Tartessian verbs in -entⁱi are. Some might be causatives with -entⁱi < Indo-European -eįonti, or innovative perfects in which the personal marker -nt(i) from the present system has been added to the 3rd person singular in -e.

POST-COMMON-CELTIC INNOVATIONS IN TARTESSIAN

Despite its early date, the Tartessian linguistic evidence does not reflect an undifferentiated Proto-Celtic, i.e. a pre-dialectal state of affairs, but rather shows various points of agreement with the distinguishing innovations of sometimes Celtiberian, sometimes Gaulish, and also the 'Insular Celtic' languages, Goidelic, and Brittonic (this last, for present purposes, may be treated as a Gallo-Brittonic unity).

(1) Tartessian agrees with Celtiberian: *o*-stem genitive singular in **-o**, and probably *į*o-stem-**eo**: **kᵉertᵒo ‡ΔꟼΟ)ᛁ** (J.18.1) 'of the artisan', **oretᵒo** (J.4.1) 'of deliverance', **kᵒoŕbᵉo ‡◖ᛞ‡ᛝ** (J.53.1) 'of Korbos, of the chariot maker/charioteer' ~ Celtiberian *Aualo* 'of Aualos' (Froehner Tessera); *i*-stem genitive plural < -*isōm*, e.g. Tartessian **bᵉeliśon ᛁ‡ᛘᛑꟼΟᕼ** (J.20.1), Celtiberian *kentisum* 'of the sons' (Villar 1997, 918, citing Untermann); group affiliation expressed with genitive plural < -*kōm*, e.g. Tartessian **liirnestᵃakᵘun ᛁᕼᛞΑ✕‡Οᛑᛑᛑᛑ1** (J.19.1), **tᵃarnekᵘun ᛁᕼᛁᕼΟᛑᛩΑ✕** (J.26.1); Proto-Celtic χt > t, e.g. Tartessian **anbᵃatⁱia ΑᛑᏕΔ◖ᛝΑ** (J.16.2) < **ambaχtia* (though a false impression created by the SW writing system cannot be ruled out here), Celtiberian [*R*]*etukenos* < *Reχtugenos*; the Tartessian superlative **uarbᵃan** = Celtiberian VORAMOS 'most high, supreme' (cf. also **uabᵃan** corresponding to the Hispano-Celtic place-name *Uama* and the Lepontic name UVAMO-KOZIS), contrasting with Gaulish *uertamos* = Old Welsh *guartham* 'highest, summit'. Like Celtiberian and unlike Goidelic, Gaulish, and probably British, the Tartessian relative particle/pronoun appears to have case inflexion: e.g. **kᵃaŕner-ion ∧Α◖ᛑΟᛩᛘ‡ᛁ** (J.7.2) 'whom they have buried in a cairn', i.e. 'who has been entombed', vs. Gaulish DVGIIONTI-IO 'who serve'.

The Tartessian verbal noun **eert^{a}aune** O ᛃ ᛈ A X ⑨OO (J.55.1) and Celtiberian *uertaunei* (Botorrita) are probably identical formations. Celtic final *-ks* (> *-χs*) became Tartessian *-s* in *Gargoris*, cf. Celtiberian SEGOBRIS < *Segobriks* (Villar 1997, 912).

(2) Tartessian agrees with Gaulish (and, in the first example below, Western Hispano-Celtic): ablative/dative plural in *-bo*: **b^{e}elib^{o}o** ‡□ᛃ⑩O9 (J.1.2), **(k^{a}ak^i)iśiink^{o}olob^{o}o** ‡□‡1‡XᛃᛃᛃᛝᛝᛈAⴷ (J.1.1), **lok^{o}ob^{o}o** ‡□‡X‡1 (J.1.1), **niirab^{o}o** ‡□AᛈᛝᛃY (J.1.1), **rinoeb^{o}o** Ⲣᛉᛑ‡O⊟‡ (J.5.1), **ist^{a}aib^{o}o** (J.5.1 demonstrative pronoun), cf. Gaulish ATREBO 'to the fathers' (Plumergad); contrast Celtiberian *Arekoratikubos, Loukaiteitubos*, Lepontic UVL̲TIAUIOPOS, ARIVONEPOS (both Prestino). Old Irish *-aib* must reflect a different preform, with *-bis*. The Tartessian nominative plural pronoun **sie:** └Oᛃ‡ (J.12.1) is closely comparable to the Gaulish nominative plural *sies* occurring in the Larzac inscription.

(3) Tartessian agrees with Gaulish and British in the tendency for u̯o- or u̯e- to become u̯a- (see Koch 1992): Tartessian **k^{o}t^{u}uarat^{e}e** 'has run under towards, has safely delivered to' (J.53.1) /-u̯a rāte/ < Common Celtic *u̯(p)o rāte, also **uarb^{a}an** ᛃAᛝAᛃ 'the highest destination', but this form could be analogical to **uab^{a}an** ᛃAᛝAᛃ (J.16.5) < *u̯(p)$_a$mām with the same meaning (cf. the south-western Hispano-Celtic place-name *Uama*). However, Celtiberian may have shared this u̯e- > u̯a- tendency: Celtiberian *uarakos* has been derived from a Proto-Celtic *u̯u̯erákos (Wodtko 2000, 434). Tartessian also shows affinities with Gaulish and British with the name Ἀργανθωωιος |*Argantonios*|, which appears to show a divine suffix *-ono/ā* best paralleled in those Celtic languages.

(4) Tartessian appears to agree with Gaulish and Primitive Irish (probably British as well) in replacing a final *-m* with *-n*; however, the infrequency of the Tartessian character **m** ᛉ suggests that **n** ᛃ sometimes stands for a general nasal whose specific phonetic realization was determined by context.

(5) Tartessian agrees with Gaulish, Primitive Irish, and British in the simplification of the diphthong *ei* > *ē* in the example **eert^{a}aune** O ᛃ ᛈ A X ⑨OO (J.55.1) vs. Celtiberian *uertaunei* (Botorrita).

(6) The Tartessian system of writing the stop consonants (X t^a, ⊨ t^e, Φ t^i, △ t^o, ⋀ t^u, &c.) itself implies that consonants were perceived to have distinct qualities conditioned by the following vowel, as in the medieval and modern Goidelic languages. For a discussion of further evidence for 'vowel quality' in Tartessian, see *Tartessian 2* §§99.1–4. The system of phonemic consonant quality of Old Irish is not represented in the Primitive Irish ogam inscriptions. Therefore, that Tartessian as the first attested Celtic language should anticipate a feature of a sub-family of medieval and modern Celtic languages in this way will no doubt strike some

readers as unexpected and implausible. However, the fact that the ogam script is most probably derived from the Roman alphabet and that the bilingual ogams of Britain show a close, almost letter-for-letter, system of transliteration probably means that Irish consonant quality (as a system wholly alien to Latin and its alphabet) would have been impossible to represent in the earliest written Irish, even if it was then already phonemic. In fact, consonant quality is not represented consistently even in Old Irish, though there is no doubt of its phonemic status at that stage. It is a linguistic certainty that the vowel quality of Goidelic consonants goes back to a phonetic tendency that preceded the feature's grammaticalization by some indeterminant span of time. This could have been extremely deep, especially as its root cause is the linguistic universal that all segments tend to anticipate the articulation of the next. It is therefore not inherently implausible that two members of a language family that had a long-standing phonetic tendency of this type might grammaticalize the feature at widely different periods. That in both cases it came near the horizon of literacy and sweeping cultural change—the orientalization on one hand and the disintegration of Roman power and expansion of Christianity on the other—is not a coincidence. Rising bilingualism and the introduction of a new language of learning and social advancement—as affected the south-western Iberian Peninsula and Ireland at the respective horizons—can newly stimulate an awareness that a phoneme in one's first language is realized with multiple articulations corresponding to two or more phonemes in an acquired prestige language. This is especially likely to occur when the new language is learned diligently enough to augment the speaker's inventory of sounds, as unavoidably occurs if learners are to transfer a writing system with a phonetic basis from the learned language to their native language.

(7) Tartessian anticipates Old Breton and Old Welsh in the fluctuation of original -nti, with -n(i) in the terminations of 3rd person plural verbs: for example, naŕk^{e}eni (J.1.2, J.1.3), naŕk^{e}ent^{i}i ᛘ◻ᛘ◯)|ᛝAᛘ (J.12.1, J.16.1, J.17.2, J.18.1), naŕk^{e}en↑i ᛘ↑ᛘ◯)|ᛝAᛘ (J.19.2), naŕk^{e}enii (J.2.1), naŕk^{e}en (J.7.5, J.7.8), n[a]ŕk^{e}en ᛘ◯)|ᛝᛘ (Cabeza del Buey IV). The θ in Herodotus's spelling Ἀργανθωωιος may also be significant in this regard: cf. Old Welsh *hanter* 'half', also *hanther*, Middle and Modern Welsh *hanner*. This instability of inherited *nt* may have been incipient within Hispano-Celtic generally is suggested by Celtiberian *arkanta* 'silver' alongside *Arganda* and *turtunta / Tortonda* (Villar 1997, 904).

(8) In a further important respect, Tartessian appears to anticipate one of the defining features of the Insular Neo-Celtic languages, namely the weakening of some final and internal syllables, with the result that etymological *o* is sometimes written **a**. In the nominative of Celtic u̯iros 'man, hero, husband', the final syllable seems sometimes to be reduced (e.g. as a composition vowel in (o)ira- [J.1.2]), or simply lost in the nominative singular of this word (e.g. **ooŕoir** [J.19.2] <

*u(p)eruiros, **uarb°oiir** [J.22.1] < *u(p)er_amo-uiros), cf. also Latin *vir*. In inscriptions so old, this apparent precocity is surprising, though examples also occur in Gaulish, Galatian, and British, as well as systematically in Primitive Irish. It should be remembered that most of the evidence for the Ancient Celtic languages survives mediated through the writing systems of Greek and Latin, thus predicated—directly or indirectly—on a knowledge of one of those languages. This circumstance is likely to have contributed to an impression that Ancient Celtic had a sound system more like those of Greek and Latin and less like Neo-Celtic than was actually the case. With a literacy based mainly or wholly on Phoenician (a non-Indo-European language that didn't write vowels at all), the writing of Tartessian would not have been influenced by grammatical ideas derived from a cognate Old Indo-European language. In other words, it is unlikely that the language of the SW inscriptions has been misleadingly 're-Indo-Europeanized'. In this respect as well as its antiquity, Tartessian evidence may have special value in the reconstruction of Proto-Celtic.

(9) Tartessian loses Proto-Celtic */w/ in all positions, except before **a**, where it is written **u**. More precisely, the probable phonetic development was that */w/ was assimilated phonetically to the quality of an immediately following **u**, **o**, **i**, or **e**, but was preserved by dissimilation before **a**. The fact that Goidelic completely lost lenis w before the earliest written Old Irish raises the possibility of a common inherited basis. A plausible starting-point for this development would be for w to be lost when articulated weakly in some phonetic environments—a situation then systematized in the Goidelic mutational system—but extended more widely in Tartessian. As with vowel quality of consonants and the weakening of composition vowels, we should probably think of common phonetic tendencies leading to similar phonological innovations at widely different dates in Tartessian and Insular Celtic. Not only does the earliest evidence from Gaulish and Insular Celtic reflect a state of affairs before these changes were complete—if they had even begun—on the phonemic level, but also the precocious innovations as they appear in Tartessian are not identical to the Neo-Celtic transformations, merely suggestively similar. Of course, we should remember that the transformation of British to Neo-Brittonic and that of Primitive Irish to Old Irish were themselves similar, but not identical, so that at the end of the processes the languages were further apart than before.

In sum, then, Tartessian is well within the limits defining a Celtic language and not within the dialectically grey area of its more recently attested Indo-European neighbour to the north, Lusitanian. In other words, there is no need to expand the usual linguistic parameters of Celtic to include Tartessian in the family. Tartessian shares with Celtiberian a sufficient core of distinctive and probably innovative features to justify 'Hispano-Celtic' as a term for a linguistic sub-family as opposed to a purely geographical subgroup.

It is worth noting in this connection Pliny's statement (*Naturalis Historia* 3.13) that the Celtici (of south-west Hispania) and Celtiberians shared common religions, languages, and names for their fortified settlements (*Celticos a Celtiberis . . . aduenisse manifestum est sacris, lingua, oppidum uocabulis . . .*). On the other hand, innovations shared by Tartessian and British, and Goidelic, and most especially Gaulish, show that Tartessian's position in south-west coastal Hispania and within the Phoenician sphere of influence was—rather than being isolated and marginal—well placed for participating at an early date in linguistic innovations taking place in various parts of the wider Celtic-speaking world. The rapid economic and social development of the 10th–6th centuries BC could naturally have led to a 'gold-rush' situation favouring the mixing of dialects and acceptance of some innovative features within the resulting *koine*.

It appears, therefore, that Hispania had at least two, closely related, ancient Celtic languages: (1) a more easterly, inland branch attested at a somewhat later date in the far more extensive corpus of Celtiberian, and (2) a more westerly Celtic of the Atlantic zone, more meagrely attested, but to which the earlier inscriptional corpus of Tartessian may be assigned. In addition to these two, and in addition to the two non-Indo-European languages of Hispania—Iberian and Aquitanian/Palaeo-Basque—there are traces of a complex matrix of other pre-Roman Indo-European languages in the Hispanic Peninsula. Lusitanian is an Indo-European language found in five inscriptions from east-central Portugal and adjacent parts of Spain, which are written in Roman letters and date to the early centuries AD (see Wodtko 2009; 2010). In Lusitanian the word for 'pig' is the Indo-European PORCOM, which preserves Indo-European *p*. The loss of *p* is often considered a defining feature of the emergence of Celtic from Indo-European, often *the* pre-eminent defining sound change. Lusitanian thus lacks a key innovation and would require a rethinking of Celtic to accommodate it within the definition of that language family. As well as retained Indo-European *p* in PORCOM, Lusitanian also possibly shows *p* from Indo-European k^w in PVMPI and the pronominal PVPPID $< *k^uodk^uid$ (Búa 2007, 27; Wodtko 2010).

The term 'Hispano-Celtic' can be extended and further validated by the numerous parallels between Tartessian and the indigenous proper names from the west and central north of the Peninsula occurring in inscriptions and other sources of the Roman Period. In some features—such as the inventory of names and name elements, the dative plural in *-bo*, and the genitive plural in *-un*—Tartessian appears to agree closely with the indigenous Indo-European names found mixed with Latin in brief inscriptions widely distributed in areas north and west of

the Celtiberian area and north and east of the Lusitanian. One might conclude
that this uncategorized Hispano-Celtic represents the later stage of the same
language. However, this widespread material is likely to represent more than one
dialect. We find in it, for example, numerous examples of genitives plural in -um
and -on, as well as -un, and there is at least one inscription with datives plural in
-bor. Owing to the fragmentary and mixed nature of the evidence, attempts to
distinguish 'Vettonian', 'Callaecian', 'Cantabrian', and so on, present a formidable
challenge (cf. the approach of Untermann 1996), but one result of such an effort
might be to reveal a dialect continuum embracing the Celtiberian, Tartessian, and
Lusitanian *corpora*.

Considering the names of the SW corpus as a group, analogues are most forthcoming from Hispano-Celtic sources or, more generally and to include comparanda
of less certain classification, from inscriptions of the earlier Roman Period on
the Indo-European side of the Peninsula (i.e. north and west of the '*brigā*-line').
Such Indo-European Palaeohispanic comparanda, often extremely close, occurs for
the following items: aark^{u}ui (J.7.6), aib^{u}uris[(J.3.1), alb^{o}oroi[(J.24.1), anb^{a}at^{i}ia
(J.16.2), ’Αργανθωνιος, b^{e}elib^{o}o (J.1.2), b^{e}e:lin (J.17.4), b^{e}elis̱on (J.20.1), b^{o}ot^i-
ieana (J.18.1), -eb^{u}uṟoi (S. Martinho), Ʂait^{u}ura (J.15.1), iru≡{u}arb^{u}u (J.23.1), —
k̲^{e}eilau (Cabeza del Buey IV), k̲^{e}eloia (J.57.1), k^{i}ielaoe (J.11.1), leb^{o}o-iire (MdC),
linb^{o}oire (J.11.2), lok^{o}ob^{o}o (J.1.1), —mut^{u}uirea (J.1.5), oira-uarb^{a}a(n) (J.1.2),
ooṟoir (J.19.2), ooṟoire (J.19.1), raꟅa (J.53.1), sarune (J.22.1), s̱arune (J.22.2),
t^{a}alainon (J.14.1), t^{i}ilek^u-uṟk^{u}u (MdC), t^{i}irt^{o}os (J.1.2), t^{u}urea (J.7.8), t^{u}uṟek^{u}ui
(J.14.1), (uab^{a}an [J.16.5] and uarb^{a}an are probably not proper names), uarb^{o}oiir
(J.22.1), ([)uult^{i}ina (J.12.3), uurk^{e}e (J.1.4).

In Roman times, in the Indo-European zone of the Iberian Peninsula (the
north, west, and centre), names beginning with *p*-, and themselves having an Indo-
European appearance, occur in all major regions—Celtiberia, Vettonia, Callaecia,
Cantabria, and Lusitania (Untermann 1985/6). In numerous examples, it is not
immediately plain whether these have preserved Indo-European *p* or *p* from Indo-
European k^u as in P-Celtic and some Italic dialects: for example, in CASTELLANOS
PAEMEIOBRIGENSES and CASTELLANIS PAEMEIOBRIGENSIBVS which occur
on a bronze from Bembibre, León, the etymology of the first element of the
ethnonym, compounded with Celtic -*brigā*, is uncertain (Búa 2007, 20), and note
that *p*- is continued by *b*- in the modern name. Similarly, the Lusitanian divine
epithet PETRAṈIOI could contain Indo-European *k^uetr*- '4' (thus showing k^u to
p) or *petr*- 'feather, wing' with *p* preserved (contrast Old Welsh *eterinn* 'bird')
(Búa 2007, 26). The ancient place-name *Bletisama* occurs in the north-central
Peninsula, where it is today *Ledesma*, clearly cognate with Celtiberian *Letaisama*,
all from *$pletis_a$mā* 'broadest', showing a superlative suffix limited to the Celtic

and Italic branches of Indo-European. *Bletisama* can be explained by a two-stage transformation: first, the place-name **Pletis_ama* was rendered pronounceable by speakers of *p*-less dialects by substituting /b/ as the closest possible approximation for the absent phoneme /p/; then, the name was simply replaced by its obvious *p*-less Hispano-Celtic cognate *Letaisama*, whence modern *Ledesma* (see further Villar 2004; Búa 2007, 20, 33).

One hypothesis worth considering in the context of the study of Tartessian is that Celtic first emerged in Hispania. In *Bletisama/Letaisama* we have a doublet in which a *p*-less Celtic appears to be emerging from an Indo-European with *p* before our eyes. We might call the variety of Indo-European in which the name **Pletis_ama* was coined 'Hispanic' (or 'Peninsular'), to avoid 'Iberian' (which already designates a non-Indo-European language). This 'Hispanic' would be the common ancestor of Celtic (which lost Indo-European *p* in most positions) and Lusitanian (which did not). To refer to both branches as 'Celtic' strikes many historical linguists as a confusing self-contradiction, because, as explained above, loss of Indo-European *p* has been used to define Celtic. However, we could redefine Celtic on the basis of a different phonological change, such as Indo-European syllabic *l* and *r* becoming Celtic *li* and *ri* (as Dagmar Wodtko suggests to me). We could thus retain the old name 'Celtic', while expanding its definition to include Lusitanian and other evidence of the **Pletis_ama* type. With the loss of Indo-European /p/ in one dialect of this proto-language (whether we call that 'Celtic with Indo-European *p*' or 'Hispanic'), the *p*-less ancestor of most of the Celtic languages emerged. The conserving dialect or dialects did not participate in loss of Indo-European *p*, as reflected in the Lusitanian inscriptions and some of the pre-Roman Indo-European names of the Peninsula.

Against this background, the 43 pre-Roman town names from the south-western Peninsula containing forms of the element *-ippo* are somewhat perplexing. They are often considered 'Tartessian', as their geographic extent reflects the reach of the influence of the polity of Tartessos and its orientalizing civilization in the Early Iron Age. Most of the territory of their distribution overlaps with that of the SW inscriptions. On the other hand, the greatest densities of these two distributions do not correspond. The *-ippo*-names are thickest south of the lower Guadalquivir, while the SW inscriptions are concentrated in south Portugal with a thinner spread up the Guadiana. The language of the *-ippo*-names does not seem to have much in common with that of the SW inscriptions. With its abundance of *p*, these names look neither Celtic nor Iberian. All of this suggests that Greater Tartessos might have had two languages, one strongest in the south and another better evidenced in the lands of the Kunētes/Konioi. Whether these languages were actually in use at the same time is another question, as the place-names do not actually surface into the written record until the Roman period. Therefore, they might all conceivably postdate the fall of the Tartessos polity and the Orientalizing Period. The *Hippo* names of Numidia and a possible Carthaginian connection should not be overlooked.

In coming years, the alternative position, that is, the view that the principal language of the SW inscriptions is non-Indo-European or unclassified and (therefore) probably non-Indo-European (see p. 2 above) may quietly recede, or a vigorous debate might follow. In any reconsideration of the linguistic classification, it will be important to recognize that the decipherment work carried out within the framework of the 'Tartessian is Celtic' theory will not all be of equal relevance to the issue. Of those details of analysis most open to revision many will be merely tentative additions to sizeable categories made up of more clear-cut Celtic examples; these will not alter the basic picture if rejected. Many other points, raised within the context of the Celtic theory, will have no bearing one way or the other on Tartessian's classification.

At the core, there are four major factors, which, taken together, lead inevitably to the conclusion that the language of the inscriptions is of the Indo-European macro-family and Celtic family. If these four stand, the case stands. If Tartessian's classification is the overriding concern, everything else is a distraction or red herring.

1 The SW corpus contains an extensive representation of names that are closely comparable to attested Ancient Celtic names, the greatest proportion of which are specifically Hispano-Celtic (see above for examples). This material includes both names that can be classified as Celtic on the basis of comparative Celtic etymology and/or phonology and names that can be considered Celtic because the comparable forms occur in Celtic geographical and linguistic contexts, for example, comparanda are found repeatedly within the '-*brigā* zone' of the Iberian Peninsula and together with other Hispano-Celtic proper names.

2 These naming phrases in the corpus are most often inflected as Celtic nouns or occur with inflexions indistinguishable from those of Celtic, either as actually attested in the Ancient Celtic languages or as can be reconstructed from Old Irish and Indo-European: for example, datives/ablatives plural in -**b°o**, *o*-stem or *u*-stem datives singular in -**ui**, *o*-stem nominatives singular in -**os**/-**oś**, &c.

3 In the remainder of the inscriptional texts, i.e. what is not explicable as Celtic names, a sizeable proportion is made up of forms inflected as Indo-European verbs: for example, **b^arent^i** (J.23.1), **lak^eent^i** (J.53.1), **naŕk^eet^i** (J.56.1), **naŕk^eent^i** (J.12.1, J.16.1, J.17.2, J.18.1, J.19.2).

4   The stems found inflected as verbs are also found with recurring monosyllabic prefixes in the corpus: tᵉe(e)-, ro-, ar-, and o-/ua-. These prefixes correspond exactly to extremely common Celtic preverbs: *de/*di < *dě, *(p)ro, *(p)are, and *u(p)o-. In three of these four, Indo-European *p has been lost in the Tartessian. That sound change has traditionally been seen by linguists as the key diagnostic defining the emergence of Celtic from Indo-European. The behaviour of Tartessian ro- is particularly significant and consistent with the classification as Celtic (see Appendix C and *Tartessian 2* §§56.1–63.2).

If there is to be a valid argument for re-establishing the *status quo ante*—i.e. that the language of the SW inscriptions is undecipherable, thus unclassifiable, and thus somehow presumed to be non-Indo-European—it will not be a valid line of argument if the assumptions that led to this conclusion in the past are now recast as special rules for determining what can and cannot possibly be a Celtic language. It is not a defining criterion of Celtic that it cannot be written in *scriptio continua*. Most of the features of the SW writing system that appear ill-suited for representing an Ancient Indo-European language are also found in Linear B, the Cypriot syllabary, and the Celtiberian script. That the language of the SW inscriptions and that of the -ip(p)o- place-names can both be called 'Tartessian' and have been expected to be the same is a matter of modern terminology reflecting an a priori assumption and cannot stand as linguistic evidence that the former corpus cannot be Celtic because the latter appears not to be. Above all, the first indigenous language of western Europe to be represented in a small corpus with an adaptation of Semitic script would be hard for us to read no matter what family it belonged to. It cannot, therefore, be presumed to be non-Indo-European for this reason.

As McCone (1996, 43), Ballester (2004, 114–17), and now also Schrijver (2011) have suggested, the fact that the non-Indo-European language of the Iberian inscriptions of the eastern Peninsula also lacks p (as probably likewise Aquitanian/Palaeo-Basque) raises the possibility that it was prolonged exposure to the Iberian sound system that first led to the loss of Indo-European p in Celtic. Celtiberian and Tartessian both show numerous examples of loss of Indo-European *p. They were also both situated alongside the territory of the Iberians with whom they came to share a writing system. Across the Pyrenees, p-less Celtic was to find itself in contact with Italic and Germanic and other languages with p. It was here that Celtic developed, or restored, a sound system more like those of its central-European neighbours: inherited k^u came to be articulated as p, the defining criterion of the 'P-Celtic'.

The Gaulish (and Goidelic and British) affinities of Tartessian contrast with the conservative and relatively isolated character of Celtiberian. But, if one views the Atlantic maritime routes as the primary avenue of Celticization and subsequent innovations within Celtic, this is hardly surprising. Land-locked and wedged between non-Indo-European Iberian, non-Indo-European Aquitanian/Palaeo-Basque, and the Pyrenees, Celtiberian was ideally placed to be insulated from innovations affecting the other Celtic languages. No one has taken the possibility of Celtic coming from Hispania to the other Celtic countries seriously since we stopped taking *Lebar Gabála Érenn* (the 11th-century Irish 'Book of Invasions') seriously, but it is now at least worth pausing to review what it is that we think we know that makes that impossible.

**Hypothesis: Celtic emerged
in the Iberian Peninsula**

STAGE I: Indo-European

↓

STAGE II: l and r > li and ri,
defining Archaic Celtic or 'Hispanic'
[**Lusitanian**, Tartessian, Celtiberian, Goidelic,
Lepontic, Gaulish, Brittonic, Galatian]

↓

STAGE III: in contact with (p-less) Iberian,
p is lost in most positions,
defining Celtic as usually understood
[Tartessian, **Celtiberian, Goidelic,**
Lepontic, Gaulish, Brittonic, Galatian]

↓

STAGE IV: in contact with languages with p
in Gaul/central Europe, Celtic k^u becomes p,
defining the emergence of P-Celtic
[**Lepontic, Gaulish, Brittonic, Galatian**]

THE 'HAMITO-SEMITIC' HYPOTHESIS: LINGUISTIC ORIENTALIZATION?

Like this book's first edition and my contribution to *Celtic from the West* an essentially agnostic attitude is retained here towards the so-called 'Hamito-Semitic hypothesis' of the Insular Celtic languages. This term refers to the recurrently formulated idea that syntactic similarities between the medieval and modern Goidelic and Brittonic languages, on the one hand, and various non-Indo-European languages of Middle East and north Africa, on the other, reflect a substratum effect or some other situation of contact in antiquity between Celtic and a language of the Afro-Asiatic group (Gensler 1993; Jongeling 2000). Conversely, the present conclusions are relevant to that hypothesis, whose chief weakness heretofore has been the absence of any documented historical or archaeological mechanism for contact between the relevant language families (Isaac 2007). As related phenomena of the first half of the 1st millennium BC, the 'orientalization' of the material culture of western Hispania—that of the Tartessian culture most especially—and the invention of the SW writing system both imply a context of Phoenician-Celtic linguistic contact. However, in drawing attention not just to the script and language of the SW inscriptions, but also to Tartessos as a historical phenomenon and the Orientalizing Period as an archaeological phenomenon, we are reminded that Hispano-Celtic was directly and profoundly interacting in multiple social domains with a Semitic language (one very similar to Hebrew, which has often been drawn into the Hamito-Semitic argument). The hybrid 'orientalizing' Tartessian culture of the 9th to 6th centuries BC was the outcome of unique circumstances where the (Levantine) Mediterranean Early Iron Age and Atlantic Late Bronze Age exchange networks—fundamentally different in ethos—truly overlapped (cf. Cunliffe 2001, 275–89).

After the faltering of Tyrian independence *c.* 573 BC, south-west Hispania remained within the Semitic influence of Tyre's daughter cities Gadir and Qart-hadašt (Carthage) until Rome captured Punic Gadir in 208 BC. According to Strabo (1.3.2, 2.13–14), Phoenician/Punic was still spoken in Turdetania in south-west Hispania (that region's name at least is probably the successor of Tartessos) in his own time about the turn of the 1st centuries BC/AD. In the notes on words above, I suggest that Tartessian had borrowed the Phoenician divine name *El* 'god' (J.23.1) and that the Tartessian personal name **uarb°oiir sarune** 'noble consort to the star goddess' (J.22.1) was an early 'inversion compound' modelled on the highly common Semitic name type: office + divine name, e.g. *Abd-Astart*. Although having a bearing on the 'Hamito-Semitic' question, these details are merely possibilities offered for consideration.

Let us finally reconsider the story of Arganthonios (Herodotus 1.163–5; see pp. 148, 269, 281) and its linguistic implications. He was a ruler with a Celtic name or title and enormous wealth. His policies can be seen in modern terms as ambitious geopolitics: outreach to recruit client states thousands of kilometres away across the sea, a door wide open to culturally advanced colonists, and financing the costly defence of a distant statelet to play against the rising world power of Media/ Persia. Was Arganthonios a 'once off' or rather nearly the last representative of the essence of the brilliant Tartessos phenomenon going back to the Late Bronze Age? Certainly the legendary longevity of the king of Tartessos—known already to Anacreon in the 6th century BC (cf. Freeman 2010, 304)—shows that to the Greek mind the Age of Arganthonios was no fleeting moment. There are details not included in Herodotus's account, but which we can conclude beyond doubt. First of all, there must have been well-placed bilinguals and/or multilinguals in Arganthonios's inner circle, men and probably women who exerted great influence over long distances through the medium of their second languages. Inevitably, this means that the power of Tartessos was often exercised through agents speaking one language with the phonetics and syntax of another. Such people were emulated for their wealth and power.

Secondly, for Herodotus the world ended at Sagres point in the land of the Kunētes, but surely it did not end there for Arganthonios. The archaizing late Latin poem *Ora Maritima* of Avienus, despite its ornate language, is fairly clear in stating that the *Tartessii* had once been wont to frequent the waters about the sea-girt country of the *gens Hiernorum* 'Irish people' and the nearby *insula Albionum* 'island of the Britons' (lines 111–13; Freeman 2010, 308). Even without Avienus, we could infer that Tartessian influence spread along the Atlantic routes. On a socio-linguistic level, this means Tartessian sea captains using an Indo-European wearing the stamp of Iberian and/or Semitic bilingualism to communicate with indigenous groups further north. Something like this situation, which we glimpse at the horizon of proto-history, would already have obtained in later prehistory: an Indo-European in intense contact with a non-Indo-European had special prestige and influence along the western seaways.

Most often, the Hamito-Semitic Hypothesis has seen its only possible mechanism as non-Indo-European aboriginals in Britain and Ireland overlain by an intrusive Celtic élite. This premise leads to a startling conclusion about the former extent of the Afro-Asiatic macro-family. But is that really necessary? How certain are we that the known contacts between Celtic and non-Indo-European—converging on Tartessos—cannot explain the distinctive typology revealed when Insular Celtic first appears to us in sentences?

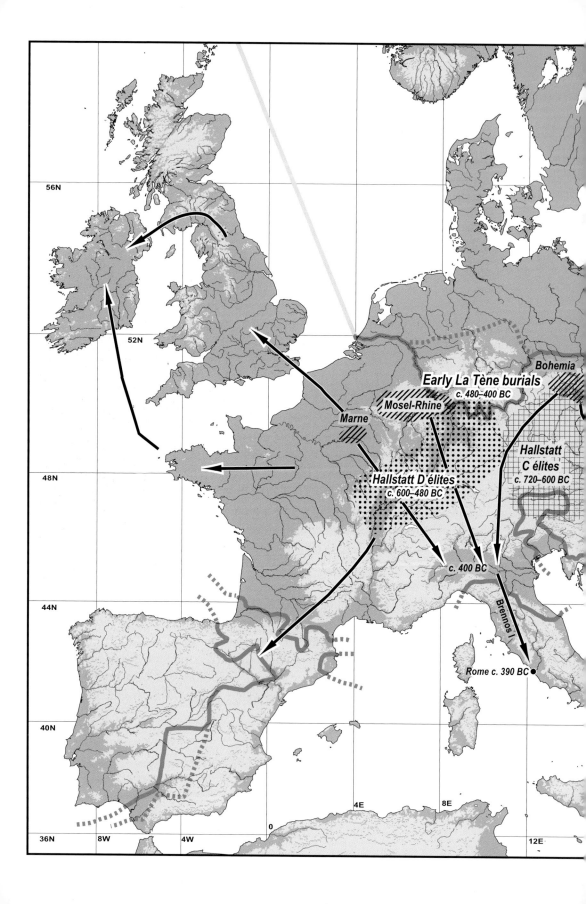

56N

52N

48N

44N

40N

36N

8W

4W

0

4E

8E

12E

Bohemia

Early La Tène burials
c. 480–400 BC

Mosel-Rhine

Marne

**Hallstatt
C élites**
c. 720–600 BC

Hallstatt D'élites
c. 600–480 BC

c. 400 BC

Brennos I

Rome c. 390 BC

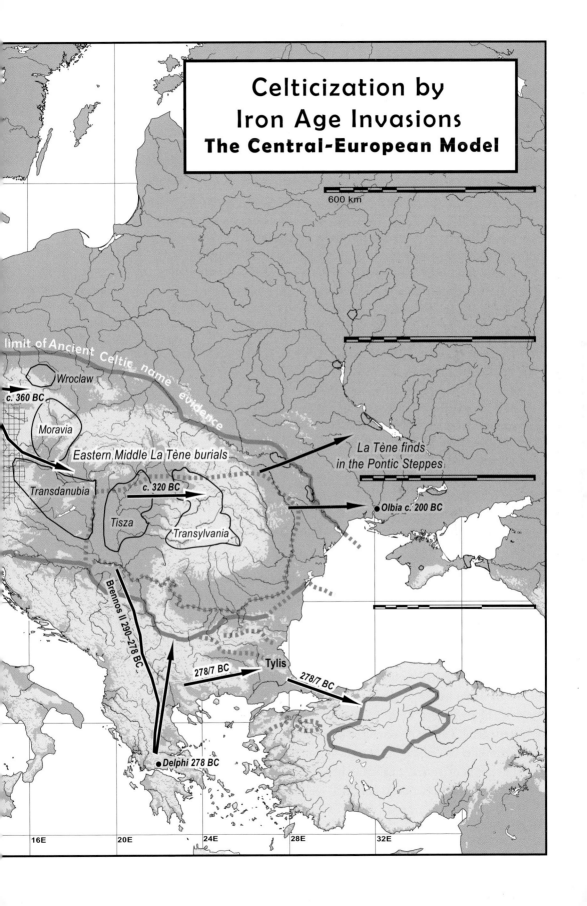

Celticization by
Iron Age Invasions
The Central-European Model

600 km

limit of Ancient Celtic name evidence

Wroclaw

c. 360 BC

Moravia

Eastern Middle La Tène burials

La Tène finds
in the Pontic Steppes

Transdanubia

c. 320 BC

Olbia c. 200 BC

Tisza

Transylvania

Brennos II 290–278 BC

278/7 BC

Tylis

278/7 BC

Delphi 278 BC

16E   20E   24E   28E   32E

Appendices

O'DONNELL LECTURES 2008

The following text is based on Celtic Studies Lectures given in spring 2008 under the terms of the bequest of Charles James O'Donnell: 'Was the Atlantic Zone the Celtic Homeland? Early Linguistic Evidence' (University of Edinburgh 24 April), 'People called Keltoi, the La Tène Style, and Ancient Celtic Languages: the Threefold Celts in the Light of Geography' (Swansea University 29 April, Bangor University 6 May, Aberystwyth University 13 May). In preparing the second edition of this book, no significant changes have been made in the lectures' text apart from some of the translations of the Tartessian forms. To avoid inconsistency and confusion, these have now been brought into line with the interpretations offered in the Catalogue above.

THE modern concept of the Celts equates three categories of evidence:

- (first) people called *Keltoí* by the Greeks,
- (second) the ancient Celtic languages, and
- (third) the Hallstatt and La Tène archaeological cultures.

To locate the origins of the Celts in time and space, the last category has been given priority, which gives priority to central Europe, specifically the lands about the Alps and the Watershed Zone where the great rivers come together—the Danube, Rhine, and Marne and Seine, Loire, Rhône and Saône, and the Po. The key period is the Early Iron Age, about 750–400 BC.

The traditional Celtic studies narrative has therefore tended to view Britain as peripheral, a zone of secondary expansion. Like Ireland, Armorica, and the Iberian Peninsula, or Galatia in the east—Iron Age Celtic Britain is often represented as one spoke of several emanating from the central European hub.

Although this model is not often spelled out in words in this way, it is an accurate description of many maps drawn to show Celtic expansion, in which radiating black arrows still seem to imply invasions or mass migrations, even though the 'Invasion Hypothesis' has been obsolete for forty years in British archaeology. The Iron Age central-European model of Celticization is such an ingrained habit of thought— underpinning innumerable orthodox subtheories—that neither maps nor explicit words are necessary and alternative explanations tend to be overruled quickly on the basis of any number of things that we think we already know.

The main point that I want to make in this lecture is that for two of the three components of the synthetic Celts—namely, as people called Keltoí and as speakers of Ancient Celtic languages—there is earlier and better evidence in the Atlantic west than in the central European Watershed Zone. Therefore, we should no longer associate those three traditional indicators of Celticity so closely as to assume that the Celtic languages must have originated in the same time and place as the Hallstatt and La Tène cultures. In fact, a shift of focus from Iron Age central Europe to the Atlantic Bronze Age is indicated as the more meaningful starting place for a new narrative Story of the Celts. Such a new account of Celtic origins will have more to do with the exchange of ores, ingots, and prestige metalwork and less with expansionist warbands—though both factors were present in both periods.

The proposed paradigm shift would affect how we understand early Britain in a number of ways. Not only would Britain have become Celtic, in the sense of Celtic-speaking, at an earlier date than usually allowed, but probably by different mechanisms and possibly from a different direction. West Britain, as well as remaining Celtic speaking longer, possibly became Celtic speaking earlier.

After uncoupling Hallstatt and La Tène from the Celtic proto-language, there is no longer any a priori reason to rule out the possibility that Britain was an integral part of the region in which Celtic first evolved from Indo-European. In other words, the question 'when did the Celts come to Britain' may have built into it an assumption that is no longer valid.

You've now heard my conclusions. Let's proceed to the evidence, starting with Herodotus's famous statements about the Keltoí. Writing around 430 BC, he stated that they inhabited the lands near the source of the river Ister, that is, the Danube.

§2.34. I am willing to believe that [the Nile] rises at the same distance from its mouth as the [Danube], which has its source amongst the Keltoí at Pyrēnē and flows right through the middle of Europe, to reach the Black Sea at Miletos's colony of Istri. The Keltoí live beyond the Pillars of Hercules, next to the Kunēsioi who are the most westerly people of Europe.

§4.48. ... the [Danube], that mighty stream which, rising amongst the Keltoí, the most westerly, after the Kunētes, of all the European nations, traverses the whole length of the continent before it enters Scythia.

[adapted from translations of de Sélincourt]

References to Keltoí on the upper Danube coincide well with the established theory of central-European origins, bringing us close to Hallstatt itself and such important Hallstatt and Early La Tène sites as the Heuneberg hillfort and Dürrn-berg-bei-Hallein. And many modern writers have drawn attention to this apparent confirmation. Unfortunately, the passages themselves alert us to the likelihood that Herodotus was profoundly ignorant about the upper Danube. He wrote that the river was as long as the Nile, flowed across the whole of Europe, and that its source lay beyond the Straits of Gibraltar and near Pyrēnē, a name apparently connected with the Pyrenees. One possible explanation is that he knew of people called Keltoí on both the upper Danube and in the Iberian Peninsula, but being unaware of the course of the river, he assumed these were the same group and that the Danube therefore began in Spain. Given this level of geographical confusion, fine tuning and second guessing today cannot rehabilitate these passages as solid evidence for Keltoí in the centre of Europe in the 5th century BC.

In these same passages, Herodotus gives much clearer information about the other Keltoí in the extreme south-west, where they lived next to the Kunēsioi or Kunētes, the westernmost people in Europe. From later sources we know that the Kunētes inhabited the Algarve and that their eastern limit was at or near the river Anas, now the Guadiana, which forms the southern border between Portugal and Spain. According to Trogus Pompeius (44.4), the Cunetes inhabited the forests of the Tartessians. Thus, we can place this group of Herodotus's Keltoí exactly where later classical sources located the Celtici, in south-west Spain. Before 350 BC Epho-ros likewise wrote that *Keltikē* extended as far south-west as Gades near Gibraltar. According to Strabo (3.3.5), other tribes also called *Celtici* (Greek *Keltikoi*) inhabited north-west Spain and shared a common origin with the Keltikoi on the Anas in the south-west.

In tending to ignore the Keltoí who were certainly in the far south-west in favour of those doubtfully at the source of the Danube, there has also been a general tendency to overlook the fact that *Kunētes* looks like a Celtic name. We may compare it to the place-name *Cunētio* in Roman Britain, or Old Welsh *Cinuit*, the name of the founder of the leading dynasty of Dark Age Strathclyde. This same *Cynwyd* is also a place-name in north Wales.

Unlike the upper Danube, Herodotus was apparently well informed about the kingdom of Tartessos in what is now south-west Spain. This is not surprising, since Greek imports were common in the rich orientalizing archaeological culture of Early Iron Age Tartessos, about 775–550 BC. These finds include ceramics and other manufactured luxuries from Cyprus, Phokaia, Rhodes, Samos, and Attika, alongside Phoenician imports from Tyre and Tyre's colonies in north Africa and southern Spain. A key factor was Tyre's colony at Cádiz (Phoenician *Gadir*) near the Straits of Gibraltar and on the southern edge of Tartessos.

As well as information on a species of Tartessian weasel (4.192), Herodotus provides accounts of two remarkable Greek voyages to Tartessos. The first was led by a ship's captain named Kolaios, who sailed from Samos between 650 and 638 BC. Kolaios returned from metal-rich Tartessos with silver worth 60 talents, a tenth part of which was spent to commission an enormous bronze ritual vessel (4.152).

The second expedition came from Phokaia, when this Greek state was under threat from the Medes of western Iran during the 550s BC.

§1.163 [The] Phocaeans were the first Greeks to make long sea voyages, discovering the Adriatic and Tyrrhenia and Iberia and Tartessos. They did not sail in cargo ships but in vessels with fifty oars. When they arrived at Tartessos they made friends with the king of the Tartessians named Arganthonios [Ἀργανθώνιος]. He ruled Tartessos for eighty years and lived to be one hundred and twenty. They were so friendly to the king that he tried to persuade them to leave their own country and settle anywhere in his land they might wish. But when he was not able to persuade them, having learned how the power of the Medes was increasing, he gave them money to build a wall around their city. He gave this money generously, for the circuit of the wall is many stades long, all made of large stones fitted closely together.

[trans. Freeman 2010, 314]

Arganthonios is a transparently Celtic name or title, meaning something like 'agent of divine silver' (**Arianhonydd* if the name existed in Welsh today). *Arganthonios* is, in fact, the only clearly Celtic personal appellation in all of Herodotus's Histories. The basis of the fabled wealth of Tartessos was metals, silver most especially, but also gold and copper, and tin transhipped from Galicia, Brittany, and Cornwall. It was need of great quantities of silver, demanded as tribute by the Assyrians, that had impelled sailors from Tyre in what is now Lebanon to Tartessos.

According to the Roman historian Velleius Paterculus, the Tyrians founded Gadir 80 years after the Trojan war, or about 1100 BC. Phoenician metalwork occurs together with Atlantic Late Bronze Age types in the Huelva deposition of about 950 BC. But the Phoenician colony of Gadir is not archaeologically detectable until about 770 BC, early in the Tartessian Orientalizing Phase of the Iberian First Iron Age. In 573 BC, Babylon conquered Tyre, and there was afterwards a downturn of eastern luxuries reaching the Tartessian aristocracy, which explains Arganthonios's eagerness, about 20 years later, for the Phokaians to found a colony 'anywhere they liked' in Tartessos.

Orkas

56N

GOIDELIC
?VI/IV BC–
Iverio

Albiones

BRITTONIC
VI/IV BC–

52N

Kantion

Viktis

La Tène A V BC

Uxantis

Ostimioi

48N

Hallstatt D
VI BC

Hallstatt
VIII–VII E

Atlantic
LBA
XIII–VIII BC

GAULISH
VI BC–IV AD

LEPONTIC
VI–I BC

GAULISH

Oestrumnis

44N

Hispano-
Celtic names
Roman
Period

CELTIBERIAN
III BC–I AD

40N

TARTESSIAN
VIII–V BC

4E   8E

36N   8W   4W   0   12E

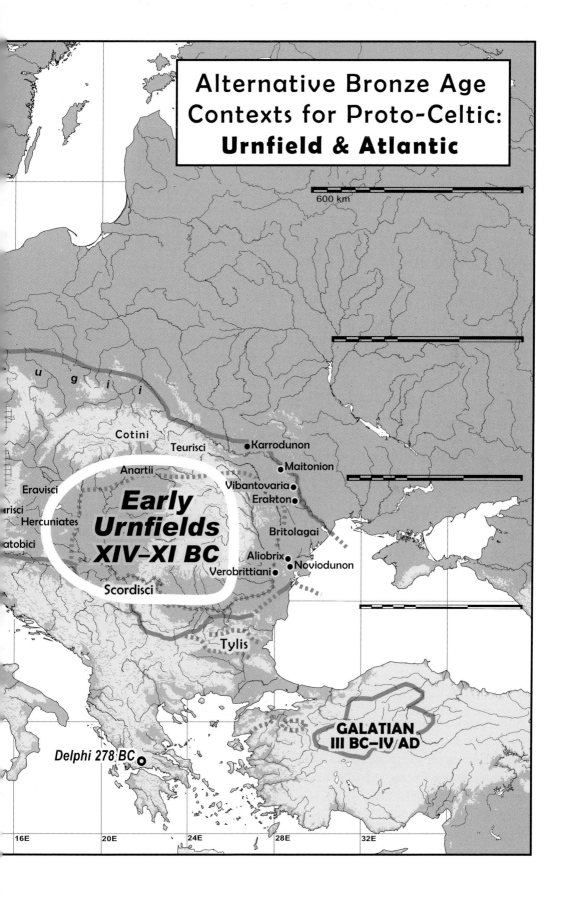

Alternative Bronze Age Contexts for Proto-Celtic: **Urnfield & Atlantic**

600 km

u   g   i   i

Cotini

Teurisci

Anartii

Eravisci

...risci

Hercuniates

...atobici

Karrodunon

Maitonion

Vibantovaria

Erakton

Britolagai

Aliobrix

Noviodunon

Verobrittiani

Early Urnfields XIV–XI BC

Scordisci

Tylis

Delphi 278 BC

GALATIAN III BC–IV AD

As well as the etymology, a further indication that *Arganthonios* 'Agent of Divine Silver' might be a title or office rather than a mere name is Herodotus's improbable statement that Arganthonios ruled Tartessos for 80 years. Since the Phokaians' visit came near the end of this long reign, one possible explanation is that the Tartessian potentate who had enriched Kolaios 80 years before was also called 'Agent of Divine Silver' and Herodotus assumed that this was the same *Arganthonios*. Note that ARGANTODANNOS, meaning 'silver minister', was a Gaulish title and recurs on pre-Roman silver coinage.

For the present subject, the most significant import from the east was alphabetic writing. The first written language in western Europe occurs on roughly 75 [about 100 by 2012] inscribed stones concentrated in south Portugal and a further 15 from south-west Spain. This script and language are sometimes called simply 'south-western', referring to their location in the Peninsula, though that name also suits their situation in Europe overall. Alternatively, they are lately often called 'Tartessian', which is the correct historical and archaeological identification if we understand Tartessos to refer to a sizeable region rather than narrowly to that civilization's chief proto-urban concentration at Huelva. There are closely datable contexts for a few of the Tartessian inscriptions. However, many are associated with necropolises of the Iberian First Iron Age, about 800–550 BC. Some scholars see an admixture of Greek orthographic principles behind the Tartessian script, but the most obvious primary source was the Phoenician alphabet, and in some letter forms, specifically a version of the Phoenician alphabet in use about 825 BC. It is also relevant to the questions of origins and dating that the Tartessian inscribed stones continue a Late Bronze Age tradition of pre-literate funerary stelae depicting weapons, armed warriors, and sometimes wheeled vehicles, dancing figures, and lyre-like musical instruments.

Since the 1990s, the sounds represented by most of the letters of the Tartessian 319 have been known. We don't have enough time to go into all the particulars of the writing system, but one key detail is that the voiceless and voiced stop consonants—*t* and *d*, *k* and *g*—are not distinguished. A second peculiarity is that the stop consonants have different forms depending on what vowel follows—thus *tᵃ, tᵉ, tⁱ, tᵒ, tᵘ*—even though the redundant vowel is written afterwards:

⟨ AX OⱯ ⵋⴲ ⵜA ⵉⴷ ⟩

[the consonant-vowel pairs are printed here in their more common right-to-left arrangement]. In other words, the system itself implies consonant qualities broadly reminiscent of the sound system of Goidelic.

José Antonio Correa, a classical philologist from Seville, had proposed that the inscriptions contained Celtic proper names and titles. No one until now has unreservedly agreed with this idea, and Correa now regards Tartessian as an unclassified language. In the light of the early references to Keltoí in the south-west and the Celtic names *Kunētes* and *Arganthonios*, as well as many further Ancient Celtic place- and group names recorded in the region in Roman times, I decided that the possibility that the language of the Tartessian inscriptions was Celtic was worth re-examining. At present, the established list of Ancient Celtic languages is as follows:

- Lepontic (the oldest, attested in northern Italy from about 550 BC),
- Celtiberian in east-central Spain,
- Gaulish in France and central Europe,
- Goidelic (the ancestor of Scottish Gaelic and Irish),
- Brittonic or British (the ancestor of Welsh, Breton, and Cornish),
- and Galatian (in the east, about Ankara in central Asia Minor).

Having studied the inscriptions for about a year now, I think that the Tartessian language should be added to this list. It is therefore the first attested of the Celtic languages. It is also about 2,000 kilometres west of Hallstatt and 1,500 from La Tène. Tartessian has affinities with Celtic names attested in Galicia as well as with Celtiberian—as might be expected—but also with Gaulish and even Gaelic and Brittonic. It is the longer, most complete, and best preserved inscriptions where Celticity is most apparent. And most of the elements—names, common nouns, verbs, and prepositional preverbs—are not rare but occur in the core vocabulary of one or more of the other Celtic languages.

EXAMPLES FROM THE TARTESSIAN INSCRIPTIONS AND TENTATIVE TRANSLATIONS

[J.7.2] O⚎MM‡MⵕOⵉⵀA∧AA*| ⵕA⧓‡A‡□ [read right-to-left] b^oot^oo⧓ar[|]*aa k^aaŕner-ion ire 'Bōdo- (< Boudo-) or Bod$\underset{\frown}{u}$o- ... whom the men/heroes have entombed.'

[J.1.4] A∧ⵕOㅐ ‡O⟩ⵉⵕⵕMⵕㅐO‡ [read right-to-left]]t^eek^{u}ui uurk^{e}e ot^{e}erk^{a}a '... has made the grave(s) for (-)Tegos ...' or '... for Degos, -(s)-ek$\underset{\frown}{u}$os, Segos.'

[J.1.1] MMⵉ‡MMⵉ AㅌO9O ⵕA⸝‡ⵕOㅌMMⵉ □‡⇑‡✗ MMMMⵕⵔA∧O⟨⟩⟨KAⵕOⵉAⵉ ‡✗‡⇑OㅌⵕA∧M AⵉAKA‡A‡□AⵕMMⵉ‡O‡✗‡⇑ [read right-to-left beginning here] lok^{o}ob^{o}o≡niirab^{o}o t^{o}o aŕai$\underline{a}$i k^{a}alt^{e}e lok^{o}o|n ane naŕk^{e}e k^{a}ak^{i}śiin|k^{o}olob^{o}o|o ii t^{e}e·ro-b^{a}ar|e (b^e)e t^{e}a|siioonii 'For the divine Lugoues and for the chief men—and for all the "heroic ones"—a burial rests unmoving within the sacred grove that has carried away [the offering/deceased] towards the ploughland, so they might give [benefit].'

[J.18.2] . . ⌐ ⟨script⟩ ⌐ . . [read right-to-left]]an tᵉe(-)e·ro-bᵃare na[r̂kᵉe(. . .)ˊ . . . [this grave/death] has carried (him/it) away; remain(s).ˊ

[J.4.1] ⟨script⟩ [|] ⟨script⟩ [read right-to-left beginning here] ?ibᵒoi ion asune꞊ uarbᵃan ꞊ekᵘuŕine obᵃar bᵃara*******tᵃa oretᵒo/ (or ibᵒon ion) ‘In the town(??) . . . I [this stone monument] have carried to the highest one, to Asunā (??the divine she-ass/mare) and Ekᵘu-r̄i(g)nī (the horse queen) . . . of deliverance (< running under)ˊ: cf. Gaulish *Assuna*; Welsh *ebol*, *Mynydd Epynt*, Old Irish *ech* ‘corseˊ; Welsh *rhiain* ‘noble ladyˊ < ‘queenˊ; oretᵒo ‘run underˊ > ‘deliverˊ; Gallo-Roman EPONAE REGINAE ‘to the Horse Goddess Queenˊ, Welsh *Rhiannon*.

[J.5.1] ⟨script⟩ [left-to-right, other lines right-to-left] istᵃₐlibᵒo rinoebᵒo |anakᵉenak̲ᵉ:e|ibᵒo ‘for these indwelling queens (goddesses).ˊ

[J.19.2] ⟨script⟩ [read right-to-left] ooŕoir naŕkᵉenↃⁱi ‘Ooŕoir (*U(p)eruiros): I (or they) now remain here.ˊ

[J.19.1] ⟨script⟩]liirnestᵃakᵘun bᵃane꞊ooŕoire bᵃa[re naŕ]kᵉenii ‘[This grave/death] has carried a woman of the kindred of Lir(a)nestos (“man near the sea”)] ⟨and⟩ wife of Ooŕoir (< *U(p)er-uiros). “They” now remain [here].ˊ

[J.18.1] ⟨script⟩ bᵒotⁱieana꞊ kᵉertᵒo ‘Bōdⁱeanā daughter of the artisanˊ.

[J.53.1] ⟨script⟩ [read left-to-right] ⟨script⟩ [right-to-left] kᵒ-tᵘ-ua-ratᵉe tᵘnↃⁱitᵉsbᵃan orbᵃa setᵃa lakᵉentⁱi raⱶa꞊kᵃaśetᵃana || bᵒbᵉ kᵒoŕbᵒo bᵃarleǁ ‘The highest resting place/throne (or the inherited resting place) has safely delivered (<has run under) to the greatest tumulus: Raꝓa and the bronze minister are now lain down [here] — ?daughter of Korbeos (?“charioteer, chariot-maker”) . . .ˊ: cf. Welsh *gwared* = Tartessian oretᵒo < *wo-reto- ‘run underˊ; Old Irish *síd*, Welsh *gorsedd*, Old Welsh *asedd* ‘Celtic war-chariotˊ; Gaulish *cassidannos* ‘tin/bronze ministerˊ, ARGANTODANNOS ‘silver minister, moneyerˊ; Old Irish *Corb*, *Corb-macc* > *Cormac*.

[J.12.1] ⟨script⟩ [read right-to-left] ⟨script⟩ [read left-to-right] iru꞊alkᵘu — sie:̲ naŕkᵉentⁱi — mubᵃa tᵉe·ro-bᵃare ⱶatᵃaneatᵉe ‘Mumā Φataneatē (“the foster-mother to the winged one”) has carried away the hero ⟨and⟩ Alkos, these men who now lie [here]ˊ: for Hatᵃaneatᵉe, cf. *Y Gododdin*: *aer edenawc*; *aer seirchyawc* ‘winged in battle, harnessed in battleˊ.

Tonight, this handful of examples will have to do to show that the oldest written language of western Europe can be read as Celtic without excessive ingenuity, that is, with little recourse to rare Celtic words or Indo-European roots otherwise unattested in Celtic.

How do we make sense of this additional evidence? The less disruptive course would be to retain the central-European model for Celtic origins, but move it back several centuries to allow the Celts time to radiate out farther from the epicentre at an earlier date. In other words, we could identify the Proto-Celtic community with the Urnfield Late Bronze Age of about 1350–750 BC, rather than the Hallstatt Iron Age of about 750–450 BC. We could thus retain the basic shape—including most of the arrows—of the established 'Story of the Celts'.

But I sense that we are now past the 'tipping point' and therefore should consider a new paradigm. How do we avoid attaching the label 'Celtic' to the spectacular orientalizing culture of Tartessos, which was more certainly Celtic speaking and more certainly inhabited by *Keltoí* than Hallstatt?

Incidentally, in the Carpathian Basin, the home of the Urnfield Culture, Celtic place- and group names are thin, though it is surrounded by them.

The most ancient names of Ireland and Britain—*Īveriō* and *Albiōn*—are also relevant. Both are probably Celtic, though a Semitic etymology has been proposed for *Īveriō*, and they were in use at least as early as the date of the voyage of Pytheas of Marseilles about 325 BC and probably the expedition of Himilco of Carthage about 500 BC.

It is also suggestive that the Iberian Peninsula, as well as being the home of Celt-iberian and Tartessian, had other Indo-European languages, similar to Celtic—in the way they formed the superlative, for example—, but retaining Indo-European *p* and, therefore, by definition not Celtic. So, it is in the west that we come closest to seeing Celtic evolving from Indo-European before our eyes.

One barrier to the hypothesis that Celtic spread from the Atlantic to the Watershed Zone is that we know—or think we know—that Indo-European, the parent language of Proto-Celtic, came from eastern Europe or western Asia. However, that doesn't mean that no Indo-European language ever developed on the periphery and then moved back towards the centre. In fact, none of the languages which replaced Celtic in the Watershed Zone is native to the region, but instead all came from homelands in more marginal regions of Europe and continue to occupy those homelands—Romance, Germanic, and Slavic. For Germanic and Slavic, their expansion into central Europe coincided with turmoil, contraction, and the collapse of the Western Roman Empire in the 4th to 6th centuries AD.

Around 1200 BC, something broadly similar occurred with the collapse of the great Late Bronze Age civilizations of the Aegean and Anatolia. In other words, at this point, the engine went into reverse. Economic power and cultural influence ceased to pulse outward from the Aegean. Peoples, cultures, and languages—such as Phrygian—were sucked down from the barbarian hinterland into the troubles of the civilized world. The effects of the implosion were thus transmitted outward, into central Europe. Barbarian Europe's prolonged Late Bronze Age (about 1300–750 BC) thus provides a possible context for a language of the Atlantic west gaining ground in the Watershed Zone.

I'll conclude with a distribution map of the Gündlingen swords. This type dates to about the 8th century BC. A generation ago, these swords were often cited as evidence of Hallstatt Celts coming as invaders from central Europe to Britain and Ireland. More recently, it is suggested that the Gündlingen type is of British origin.

Even so, I hesitate to close here by reversing the arrows of the familiar Story of the Celts to make them point from the Atlantic west towards Hallstatt. For *An Atlas for Celtic Studies*, our team plotted the archaeological evidence of Iron Age Europe and the early linguistic evidence together—without arrows. We now have new evidence in view—not just from the Canolfan's projects, but also Aberystwyth University's ancient Celtic place-name project and the constant advance of archaeology. We could just leave this evidence to air for a while before re-imposing a new superstructure of arrows or a new definition of the Celts.

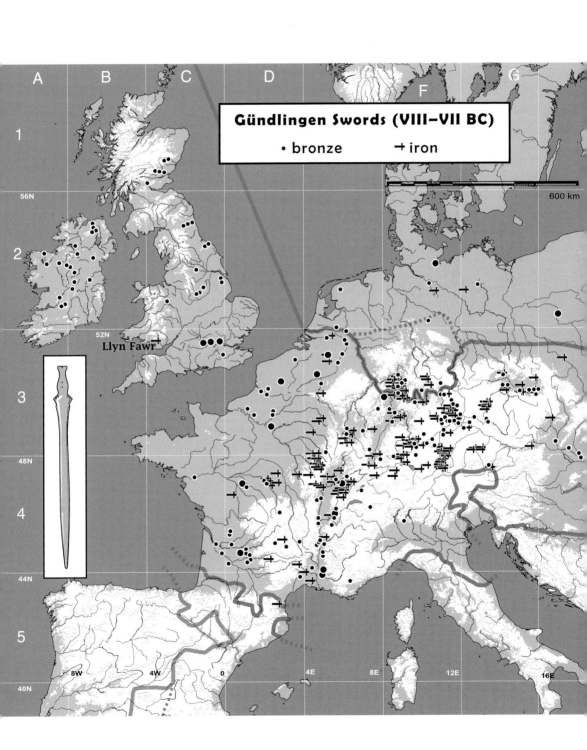

Gündlingen Swords (VIII–VII BC)

• bronze   + iron

600 km

Llyn Fawr

Traddodwyd y ddarlith hon yn y Babell Lên yn Eisteddfod Genedlaethol Cymru, Caerdydd a'r Cylch, 9 Awst 2008. Wrth baratoi testun y ddarlith hon ar gyfer yr ail argraffiad yn 2012, fe'i gadawyd fel y gwreiddiol ac eithrio rhai cyfieithiadau o'r enghreifftiau Tarteseg a newidiwyd er mwyn osgoi anghysondeb gyda'r deongliadau yn y catalog o arysgrifau uchod.

Tartesos: Cartref y Celtiaid yn y De-orllewin Pell?

WRTH sôn am gartref y Celtiaid yn y De-orllewin pell, yr hyn yr wyf yn ei olygu yw'r Penrhyn Iberaidd, sef Portiwgal a Sbaen heddiw.

MYTH A DIRGELWCH TARTESOS

I ysgrifenwyr Groeg a Rhufain, yr oedd Tartesos yn lle a oedd yn llawn cyfoeth naturiol anhygoel mewn arian ac aur, teyrnas wedi ei lleoli mewn man amhendant yn ne-orllewin eithaf Ewrop, y tu hwnt i Golofnau Ercwlff. Tua 430 CC, pan oedd Herodotos, 'Tad Hanes', yn ysgrifennu, yr oedd teyrnas Tartesos eisoes wedi darfod; perthynai i'r gorffennol cyn-glasurol cyn dyfodiad Cyrws Fawr ac Ymerodraeth Persia.

Yr oedd dylanwad y syniad o Dartesos ar y dychymyg clasurol yn eithriadol o rymus. Oherwydd hynny, adleolwyd nifer o orchestion Ercwlff—a leolwyd yn wreiddiol yn ardal ddwyreiniol Môr y Canoldir—i'r wlad chwedlonol y tu hwnt i Gulfor Gibraltar. Ac felly y daeth yr enw Colofnau Ercwlff.

Sonnir hefyd am 'longau Tarsis' yn aml yn yr Hen Destament. Bu'r llongau hyn yn teithio'r cefnfor yn gyforiog o foethau mor bell yn ôl â chyd-fenter Solomon a'r brenin Phoenicaidd Hiram yn y ddegfed ganrif Cyn Crist. Er bod gwahaniaeth barn ar y pwnc, un hen syniad cyffredin oedd fod y 'Tarsis' hwn hefyd yn cyfeirio at Deyrnas Tartesos.

Yn archaeolegol, y mae Tartesos yn gyfystyr â 'Chyfnod y Dwyreinio' [*el Período Orientalizante*/the Orientalizing Period], cyfnod byr ac ysblennydd yn ystod yr Oes Haearn Gynnar yn y Penrhyn Iberaidd de-orllewinol, rhwng tua 775–550 CC. Yr adeg honno yr oedd trefedigaeth Phoenicaidd Gadir—sef Cádiz heddiw, ar arfordir deheuol yr Iwerydd yn Sbaen—yn gatalydd ar gyfer diwylliant byrhoedlog disglair a hybrid.

Yn y cyfnod cyn Cyfnod y Dwyreinio, yr oedd Tartesos yn rhan ddeheuol o Oes Efydd yr Iwerydd rhwng tua 1250–750 CC. Y mae'r gorwel diwylliannol cynharach hwnnw yn cael ei ddiffinio gan gleddyfau [gweler t. 16], blaenau gwaywffyn, a def-nydd gwledda arwrol, gan gynnwys peiriau, ffyrc a chigweiniau efydd. Ac yr oedd tiroedd Oes Efydd yr Iwerydd yn estyn o Dartesos i Galicia, Llydaw, Prydain ac Iwerddon.

Erbyn 800 CC yr oedd gorsafoedd masnachu Phoenicaidd yn Ne Sbaen wedi datblygu yn drefedigaethau llawn. Yn yr wythfed ganrif Cyn Crist tyfodd elît new-ydd yn gyflym ymysg partneriaid masnachu brodorol y Phoeniciaid. Y mae'r pena-ethiaid Tartesaidd hyn yn weladwy yn bennaf yn eu mynwentydd mewn gorseddau claddu. Yr oedd y gorseddau hyn yn gyforiog o nwyddau angladdol moethus o

Amffora win Phoen-icaidd a ddarganfu-wyd ger Cádiz, Sbaen, 7fed/6ed ganrif CC, Museo de Cádiz

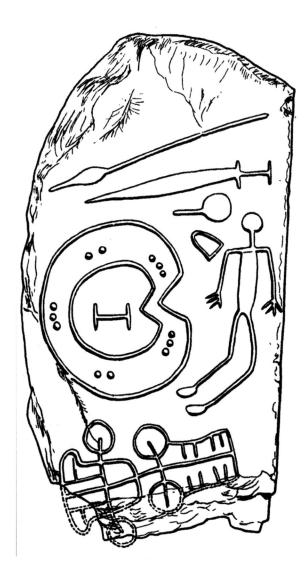

Coflech rhyfelwr/
estela de guerrero,
Solana de Cabañas,
Cáceres, gorllewin
Sbaen, yn dangos tarian
rhicyn-V, cleddyf
siâp deilen, a gwaywf-
fon bigfain, drych a
cherbyd, tua 1200 CC
[llun: R. J. Harrison]

ddwyrain Môr y Canoldir—gan gynnwys gemwaith, colur, delweddau bychain o
dduwiau, cerbydau addurnedig, gwin ac olew.

Cwympodd mamddinas Gadir, sef yr ynys-ddinas Tyrws (hynny yw 'Tyre'), rhan
o Libanus heddiw, i Nebuchadnesar brenin Babilon ym 573 CC. Yn fuan wedyn,
cyfyngwyd ar lwybr economaidd yr elît Tartesaidd i'r dwyrain, a daeth y beddau
goludog i ben.

Ysgrifennodd Herodotos fod grŵp o Roegiaid o Phocaea yng ngorllewin Asia
Leiaf wedi ymweld â Thartesos tua 550 CC, gan dderbyn croeso brwd a chyfoeth
enfawr gan y llywodraethwr Tartesaidd, Arganthonios [Ἀργανθώνιος]:

§1.163 [Y] Phocaeaid oedd y Groegiaid cynharaf i ymgymryd â mordeithiau hir: hwy oedd y rhai a ddarganfu'r Môr Adriatig, a Tyrrhenia, ac Iberia, a Thartesos . . . Pan ddaethant i Dartesos daethant yn ffrindiau â brenin y Tartesiaid, a elwid Arganthonios.

Yn ei enw yntau gallwn adnabod y gair Celteg am 'arian', *airgead* yn yr Wyddeleg, *arian* yn Gymraeg, *arganto-* yn iaith y Galiaid. Gwelwn hefyd yr ôl-ddodiad dwyfol neu fytholegol a geir mewn enwau Cymraeg megis *Mabon, Modron,* a *Rhiannon*.

Y mae'n ddigon dealladwy fod Arganthonios yn awyddus i'r Groegiaid o Phocaea sefydlu trefedigaeth 'yn unrhyw fan a fynnent ar ei dir'. Ond ni allai'r Groegiaid achub Tartesos. Tua 540 CC cwympodd Phocaea i Cyrws y Persiad. Yn fuan wedi hynny, pan oedd Arganthonios wedi marw, dinistriwyd gweddill y llynges Phocaeaidd gan lu cyfun Etrusgaidd-Carthaginiaidd ger Alalia yn Corsica. Wedi hynny yr oedd Culfor Gibraltar ar gau i longau o wlad Groeg.

Ond yr oedd gan yr Iberiaid fynediad parhaus at fasnach Roegaidd a Charthaginiaidd ar arfordir Canoldirol Sbaen. O ganlyniad, disodlwyd Tartesos gan y diwylliant Iberaidd fel parth mwyaf cyfoethog a deinamig y Penrhyn yn ystod y bumed ganrif Cyn Crist.

YR ARYSGRIFAU TARTESAIDD

Un o ganlyniadau parhaol Cyfnod y Dwyreinio gynt a'i ddylanwad Phoenicaidd oedd fod y boblogaeth frodorol wedi mabwysiadu ysgrifennu alffabetig, yn y de-orllewin i ddechrau. Y mae'r nifer o arysgrifau Tartesaidd ar garreg y gwyddys amdanynt bellach dros naw deg, ac y mae'r nifer yn cynyddu'n gyson wrth i rai newydd ddod i'r golwg drwy'r amser. Y mae'r rhain wedi eu crynhoi yn ddwys yn Ne Portiwgal. Ceir gwasgariad ehangach o ryw bymtheg ar draws de-orllewin Sbaen. Y mae'r arddangosfa orau o'r arysgrifau i'w gweld yn y Museu da Escrita do Sudoeste, amgueddfa newydd ac arloesol yn nhref daleithiol hyfryd Almodôvar.

Yn y lleiafrif sylweddol o achosion lle y cafodd y cerrig eu darganfod yn eu hamgylchiadau gwreiddiol, a lle y mae hyn wedi'i gyhoeddi, y mannau darganfod yw mynwentydd o'r Oes Haearn Gynnar Iberaidd (tua 775 tan 500 CC). Dengys hynny fod yr arysgrifau'n perthyn i draddodiad angladdol. Yn hyn o beth y mae'r cerrig arysgrifedig Tartesaidd fwy na thebyg yn ffurfio cyfres ddi-dor gyda'r 100 'coflech rhyfelwr' [*estela de guerrero*] gyn-lythrennog o'r Oes Efydd Ddiweddar Iberaidd [*la Edad de Bronce Final*] (o 1250–750 CC). Mewn tri chofadail sydd, fe ymddengys, yn cynrychioli cyfnod o drawsnewid, cyfunir delweddau arwrol â thestunau Tarteseg ar yr un garreg [e.e. J.12.1].

Iaith Semiteg sy'n perthyn yn agos i'r Hebraeg a chyda gwyddor sydd hefyd yn debyg i'r Hebraeg yw'r iaith Phoeniceg. Seiliwyd y llythrennau Tartesaidd ar siapiau llythrennau Phoenicaidd a ddefnyddid yn ail hanner y nawfed ganrif Cyn Crist. Ond y mae'n glir nad yw'r arysgrifau Tartesaidd wedi eu hysgrifennu yn yr iaith

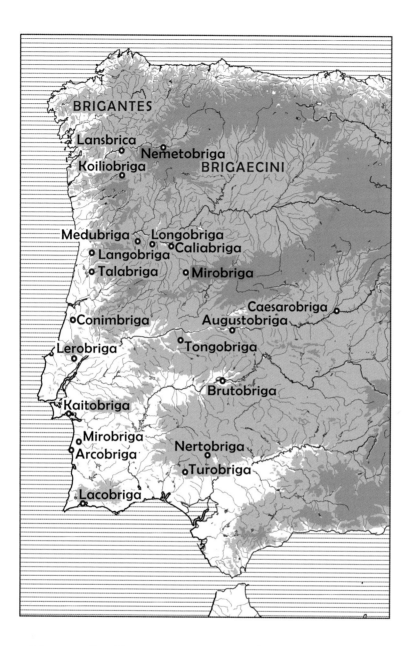

Rhai enwau lleoedd a grwpiau gyda'r terfyniad *-brigā* yn y Penrhyn Iberaidd gorllewinol

Phoeniceg, na hyd yn oed yn defnyddio'r union wyddor Phoenicaidd mewn iaith arall. Yn hytrach y mae'r sgript Dartesaidd yn cynrychioli ailfeddwl sylweddol o'i ffynhonnell Semitig. Ac felly y mae'r sgript hon wedi cyflwyno her aruthrol i ymchwilwyr modern o ran dehongli neu ddadgodio.

Nid oes arwyddion llafariaid yn yr wyddor Phoenicaidd, ac ychwanegodd pwy bynnag a ddyfeisiodd yr wyddor Dartesaidd bump ohonynt. Y darganfyddiad unigol pwysicaf wrth ddehongli'r sgript Dartesaidd oedd gweld bod y tair atalsain—*k*/*g*, *t*/*d*, a *b*—yn wahanol gan ddibynnu ar ba un o'r pum llafariad a oedd yn dilyn. Felly, er enghraifft, defnyddir un arwydd ∧ ar gyfer *k* neu *g* pan fydd *a* yn dilyn, ond un gwahanol o flaen *e*, neu *i*, neu *o*, neu *u* [sef)| φ Ⴟ ฿]. Mewn geiriau eraill, y mae'r wyddor Dartesaidd yn adlewyrchu dealltwriaeth sylfaenol fod y cytseiniaid yn rhannu ansawdd ffonetig y llafariad sy'n dilyn. Gallai unrhyw un sy'n gyfarwydd â'r Wyddeleg neu Aeleg yr Alban weld yn y manylyn hwn awgrym cryf ynglŷn â pha deulu o ieithoedd y mae'r Darteseg yn perthyn iddo.

Erbyn dechrau'r 1990au yr oedd consensws digonol wedi ymddangos o ran gwerthoedd ffonetig y llythrennau Tartesaidd a oedd yn digwydd amlaf. Felly, yr oedd modd cynnig darlleniadau o'r rhan fwyaf o'r arysgrifau gyda llai a llai o fylchau ac ansicrwydd.

Yn ystod y cyfnod hwn ceid ambell si fod rhai grwpiau o lythrennau Tartesaidd (wedi eu dadgodio) yn ymdebygu i enwau Celteg. Dilynodd gwrth-ddadl gref. Wedi hynny, cytunodd dyrnaid o arbenigwyr ar gyfaddawd. Hynny yw: y gallai'r arysgrifau gynnwys ychydig o 'elfennau' Celteg, ond, at ei gilydd, y dylai'r iaith aros yn y categori 'heb ei dehongli'. Ac yn fwy na thebyg na ellir ei galw yn Gelteg, na hyd yn oed Indo-Ewropeeg o gwbl. Ond nid yw hynny'n golygu bod Tarteseg yn edrych yn neilltuol debyg i unrhyw iaith arall.

YR IAITH GELTEG HYNAF?

Hyd yma, nid yw'r lledawgrym petrus fod elfennau Celteg yn yr arysgrifau Tartesaidd wedi cael ystyriaeth haeddiannol oherwydd diffyg sylw arferol ysgolheigion Celtaidd ym Mhrydain, Iwerddon a Gogledd America tuag at ddarganfyddiadau o'r Penrhyn Iberaidd. Gŵyr y rhan fwyaf o arbenigwyr astudiaethau Celtaidd mai iaith Gelteg oedd yr iaith Geltibereg a siaredid yn nwyrain canol Sbaen yn ystod y canrifoedd olaf Cyn Crist. Gwyddant hefyd am nifer o enwau lleoedd ac enwau grŵp Celteg yn y Penrhyn gorllewinol (enwau gyda'r terfyniad -*brigā* 'bryngaer' yn cyfateb i Gymraeg *bre* 'bryn', er enghraifft). Ond dyna hyd a lled y mater fel arfer. Y mae'r ddadl Dartesaidd wedi ei chadw o fewn y cylch cyfyng o arbenigwyr sy'n canolbwyntio ar olion enfawr ieithoedd cyn-Rufeinig Sbaen a Phortiwgal. Y mae'r holl gyhoeddiadau perthnasol wedi bod yn yr ieithoedd Sbaeneg, Almaeneg a Phortiwgaleg.

Ond gallwn ddod at y Darteseg o gyfeiriad arall, o safbwynt yr ieithoedd Celteg gyda mwy o dystiolaeth ar eu cyfer—y Gymraeg, Gwyddeleg, Llydaweg a'r ieithoedd Hen Gelteg o ochr arall mynyddoedd y Pyreneau. Ac wedyn, y mae Tarteseg yn edrych yn fwy yn hytrach nag yn llai Celteg. Yr ydym eisoes wedi nodi

Arganthonios, y pendefig arian mewn enw a gweithred.

Cyfeiriodd Herodotos hefyd at y Kunētes, trigolion yr Algarve, 'pobl fwyaf gorllewinol Ewrop' a chymdogion y Keltoi (hynny yw y Celtiaid). Ymddengys fod yr enw *Kunētes* yn cynnwys y gair 'ci' (lluosog 'cŵn'), sydd hefyd yn cael ei ddefnyddio'n drosiadol i olygu 'rhyfelwr, arwr' (er enghraifft, yr uwch-arwr Gwyddelig *Cú* Chulainn). Ceir yr enw gyda'r union ôl-ddodiad yn yr Hen Gymraeg: *Cinuit* o'r *Kynwydyon*, sylfaenydd prif linach Ystrad Clud (o'r Frythoneg *Cunētio*, *Cunētiones*). Yn ôl *Bonedd Gwŷr y Gogledd*, llu o ryfelwyr oedd y Kynwydyon. Y mae'n bosibl, felly, fod enw'r *Kunētes* yn Ne Portiwgal hefyd yn golygu 'llu o ryfelwyr'.

Gan droi at yr arysgrifau Tarteseg, gellir ychwanegu llawer at y rhestr o enwau a geiriau cyffredin sy'n edrych yn Gelteg. Yn enwedig yn yr arysgrifau hwyaf a'r rhai heb eu torri a mwyaf darllenadwy, y mae rhywbeth fel mas critigol yn ymddangos, ac y mae'n ddigon o fas critigol i gymeradwyo'r ddamcaniaeth mai iaith Gelteg yn ei chyfanrwydd sydd yn yr arysgrifau, yn hytrach nag ambell 'elfen Gelteg' hwnt ac yma. Ac felly, gallwn wrthod yr hen syniad mai iaith unigryw ac anhysbys yw Tarteseg.

Y mae'r geiriau sy'n ymddangos yn Gelteg yn addas iawn mewn beddargraffiadau; a dyna beth yw'r arysgrifau. Er enghraifft, y mae pum rhes o lythrennau Tarteseg sy'n cyfateb i eiriau mewn ieithoedd Celteg eraill sy'n golygu 'bedd' neu 'carnedd' neu 'twmlws' neu, fel berfau, 'adeiladu carnedd'.

Gan ein bod yn yr Eisteddfod Genedlaethol, yr wyf am ganolbwyntio ar esiamplau o eiriau yn y Gymraeg sy'n gytras â geiriau Tarteseg yn y testunau sy'n dilyn. Ond y mae digon o eiriau cytras hefyd yn yr Wyddeleg a hen ieithoedd Celteg y Cyfandir.

CASGLIAD O ENGHREIFFTIAU

[J.7.2] Yr un gyntaf yw carreg arysgrifedig o Vale dos Vemelhos, yn Ne Portiwgal (sydd bellach yn yr Amgueddfa Drefol yn Loulé). Gan amlaf, y mae datganiad yr arysgrif yn cychwyn ag enw—enw dyn neu fenyw a oedd dan y garreg, neu enw dwyfol. Darllenwch yn groes i'r cloc: ᗒ᛭ᛘᛣᚿ ᛣᛙᛆᛣᚿᛉᗒᗒᗒᗒ*᛭ ᛙᗒᛝᛘᛆᛞᛔ b°ot°oⱵar[|]*aa kᵃaŕner-ion ire 'Boddwar (*neu* Buddar) a adeiladodd y gwŷr/arwyr ei garnedd'.

Y mae **ire** yn golygu 'gwŷr': Hen Gelteg *wiroi.

Y mae'n debyg fod enw'r gŵr ei hun wedi ei seilio naill ai ar *budd* megis *Buddug*, neu ynteu *boddw*, megis enw'r sant *Elfoddw*.

[J.1.4] Yr esiampl nesaf yw carreg o Fonte Velha, De Portiwgal—dim ond un darn a thri gair arno sydd wedi goroesi. Darllenwch yn groes i'r cloc eto: ᗒᗄᛙᚿᛈ ᛭ᚿᛘᛙᛆᛆᛘᛊᛊᚿᛉ . . .]tᵉekᵘui uurkᵉe otᵉerkᵃa 'y mae [rhywun] wedi gwneud bedd i (-)Tekos . . .' *neu* '. . . i Degos, -(s)-ekᵤos, Segos.'

Y mae *[-t]ekui* neu *[-s]egui* yn y cyflwr dadiol yma [dative case]. 'Dewr' yw'r

ystyr, a'r gair cytras i -*segos* yn Gymraeg yw *hy*, fel '*ga' i fod mor hy?*' Posibilrwydd
arall yw darllen yr enw fel *[-t]ekui* ac felly, hynny yw fel enw wedi'i seilio ar 'teg' fel
sawl enw Cymraeg.

Y mae **uurkᵉe** yn cyfateb i'r ferf Gymraeg Cynnar *gworau* sy'n golygu 'gwnaeth, wedi
gwneud'.

Yr un yw'r gair Tarteseg **otᶜerkᵃa** â'r gair *uodercos* sy'n golygu 'bedd' yn iaith Gelteg
Gâl.

[J.1.1] Un o'r arysgrifau Tarteseg hwyaf a mwyaf darllenadwy yw 'Fonte Velha 6':

ᐱᴎ ᴎᴎᐱ‡‡ ᴎ ᴎᴎ‡ ᗅᗷOᗡO ᕈᗅᗱ‡ᕈOᗷᴎᴎ‡ ▢‡ᐱⵝ ᴎᴎᴎᴎᴎᕈᗅᗅO[)[]
ᛕᗅᴎOᴎᗅᴎ ‡ⵝ‡ᐱOᗷᐱᗅᗅ ᴎ ᴎᴎᗅ ᛕᗅ‡ᗵ‡ᗅᕈᴎᴎᴎ‡▢‡ⵝ‡ᐱ (darllenwch
yn groes i'r cloc yn cychwyn fan hyn) **lokᵒobᵒo≡niirabᵒo tᵒo aŕaiai kᵃaltᵉe lokᵒon
ane naŕkᵉe kᵃaki̇śiinkᵒolobᵒo ii tᵉe·ro-bᵃare (bᵉ)e tᵉasiioonii** 'i dduwiau
Lugus a'r arweinwyr—ac i'r holl ddynion arwrol—, y mae claddedigaeth yn gorffwys yn
awr yn ddisymud yn y llwyn cysegredig sydd wedi cario'r aberth i ffwrdd tua'r tir âr er
mwyn iddynt roi [lles].'

Y mae'r enw lluosog dwyfol **lokᵒobᵒo** yn gytras â *Lleu Llaw-gyffes* yn y Mab-
inogi, a *Lugh*, enw brenin llwyth mytholegol y Tuatha Dé Danann yn y traddodiad
Gwyddelig. Ceir yr un duw fel grŵp yn y cyflwr dadiol fel LVCVBO dair gwaith yn
Galicia (gogledd-orllewin Sbaen) ac fel *Lugouibus* yn Celtiberia yn nwyrain Sbaen.

Parthed **niirabᵒo**, dengys yr hen air Cymraeg *nêr* sy'n golygu 'arglwydd' fod yr
enw yn Gelteg. Ac yr oedd llwyth o'r enw *Neri* neu *Nerii* yn Galicia yn ystod y cyfnod
Rhufeinig.

Yr esboniad mwyaf tebygol ar gyfer y gair Tarteseg **aŕaiai** (ac ARAIANOM yn
y Geltibereg) yw fel gair cytras â *tir âr* ac *aradr*.

Yn Hen Gelteg yr Eidal, sef *Gallia Cisalpina*, ceir y gair LOKAN yn yr ystyr 'bedd'
(VRNVM yng nghyfieithiad Lladin y testun Celteg) ac mae *go-lo* yn hen air Cymraeg
sy'n golygu 'claddu mewn bedd'. Yn wreiddiol y mae'r ffurf hon yn ferf sy'n
golygu 'gorwedd i lawr'. Ceir sawl ffurf o'r ferf hon yn yr arysgrifau Tarteseg:
lakᵃatᵢi 'y mae'n gorwedd i lawr', **lakᶜentᵢi** 'y maent hwy yn gorwedd i lawr' a
lakᵢinↂᵢi (efallai 'yr wyf yn gorwedd i lawr'), a **ro·laHᵃa** 'yr wyf wedi gorwedd
i lawr'.

Darn aml o iaith fformiwläig yr arysgrifau Tarteseg yw'r ferf gyfansawdd
Oᕈᗅᗱ‡ᕈOOⴳ **tᵉe(-)e·ro-bᵃare** 'cariodd [y bedd hwn/angau] i ffwrdd.'

[J.18.2] Dyma enghraifft arall o'r fformiwla hon: | ᗅᴎOᕈᗅᗱ‡ᕈOOⴳᴎᗅ | · ·
[yn groes i'r cloc]**an tᵉe(-)e·ro-bᵃare na[ŕkᵉe(...)** Y mae pob elfen o'r cyfansodd-
dair yn digwydd yn Gymraeg—rhagddodiaid, rhagenw mewnol a bôn y ferf, sef ail
hanner *arfer* a *cymer*. Y mae'r defnydd o'r geiryn **ro-** yn rhagflaenu bôn y ferf yn
nodweddiadol o'r ieithoedd Celteg. Y mae'n gytras â'r geiryn perffeithiol Hen

Wyddeleg *ro* a Chymraeg Cynnar *rhy*, a ddefnyddiwyd yn yr un ffordd yn union.

[J.19.2] Y mae dau feddargraff Tarteseg o fynwentydd yr wythfed i'r seithfed ganrif Cyn Crist yn Pêgo, Portiwgal. Darganfuwyd sgarab Eifftaidd o 800 CC ymhlith y beddau hyn. Y mae'r arysgrif fyrrach yn coffáu dyn o'r enw ᑫᙏ‡ᚋ‡‡ ooŕoir, sef cyfansoddair o *gor-* a *gŵr*, Celteg *u̯or* a *u̯iros*, *Gorwr* yn Gymraeg fel petai, Proto-Gelteg *U(p)er-u̯iros*.

[J.19.1] Y mae'r un hwy yn coffáu Oᑫᙏ‡ᚋ‡‡OᑌᗑᛉᙏᎸAᚷ‡Oᑫᑫᙏᑫ
]**liirnestᵃakᵘun bᵃane≡ooŕoire**. Yr wyf yn deall hynny fel 'benyw o'r bobl sy'n byw nesaf at y llŷr (*neu'r môr*)', hynny yw 'ger y lli'. Ac y mae hi hefyd yn fenyw, sef yn wraig, i'r un *Gorwr* a enwir ar y garreg arall o fynwent Pego.

    Gyda llaw, y mae'r gair Gwyddeleg *bean*—sy'n cyfateb i'r gair Tarteseg **bᵃane**—yn golygu 'gwraig' yn ogystal â 'benyw'. Ceir **bᵃane** mewn sawl arysgrif Darteseg arall, bob tro yn golygu 'benyw' neu 'wraig' neu'n ddwy yn ôl y cyd-destun. Y mae'r ffurf luosog enidol **bᵃaanon** yn digwydd un waith.

[J.18.1] Y mae rhai cerrig Tartesaidd yn coffáu menywod yn eu henwau eu hunain, er enghraifft, yr arysgrif gyntaf o 'Mealha Nova', Portiwgal: ‡AᑫOᐟAᑌAᚕᙏⵔ‡◻ **bᵒotⁱeana≡ kᵉertᵒo** 'Buddan ferch y cerddor'. Seiliwyd ei henw ar yr un bôn â'r enw *Buddug*—Hen Gelteg *Boudica*, enw arwres enwog y Brythoniaid—hynny yw, yr elfen *budd*, *buddugoliaeth*, ac yn y blaen.

    Gallwn ystyried mai tad Buddan, y cerddor, a oedd yn gyfrifol am gerfio ei beddargraff, ac yr oedd y **kᵉertᵒoi**, hynny yw cerddorion neu grefftwyr Tartesos, yn gyfrifol am y ffenomen o lythreniaeth.

[J.53.1] Y mae arysgrif o Alcalá del Río yn ardal Sevilla, Sbaen, yn dangos menyw yn dal swydd uchel ei statws, un rymus yn yr economi Dartesaidd a seiliwyd ar gyfoeth metelau: ᛉ ᐃᑭAᑭAᕼOᐃᙏⵔᙏᕼ‡ᗑAᙏ‡ᑭᛤAᚕOᚷAᒥAᛉOᑌ OᙏᑭAᛉA ᐠAᙏOᚷAᙏA [darllener yn glocwedd] ᕼOᑫᑫA ‖ ‡ᗡᚋ‡ᛉ [darllener yn groes i'r cloc] **kᵒ-tᵘ-ua-ratᵉe tᵘnↃⁱitᵉsbᵃan orbᵃa setᵃa lakᵉentⁱi raᛤa≡kᵃaśetᵃana || bᵒbᵉ kᵒoŕbᵒo bᵃarleᕼ** 'Y mae'r orsedd uchaf wedi ei gwaredu i'r twmwlws gorau: y mae **raᛤa**, merch y saer cerbydau, a'r gweinidog efydd, yn gorwedd [yma] nawr'.

    Yr un ferf yw'r Darteseg **uaratᵉe** â *gwared* yn Gymraeg. Yn etymolegol, y mae *gwared* yn golygu 'rhedeg o dan', felly yn mynegi gweithred cerbyd neu geffyl. Ac y mae pump ar hugain o gerrig Tartesaidd o'r cyfnod cyn ysgrifennu sy'n dangos cerbydau.

    Yr ail air **tᵘnbⁱitᵉsbᵃan** yw y *twmpath* neu'r *domen* fwyaf, wedi'i *thyfu* fwyaf, gyda therfyniad y radd eithaf.

Yr wyf yn deall **orbᵃa setᵃa** fel cyfansoddair cytras yn ei ddwy elfen i *gorsedd*. Mae'r elfen gyntaf yn y radd eithaf, felly *goruchaf sedd* neu *gorsedd fwyaf, orau*. **setᵃa** yw *sedd*, lle eistedd, y bôn yn *gorsedd*, hefyd yn *asedd*, gair Hen Gymraeg am gerbyd rhyfel Celtaidd.

kᵃaśetᵃana yw'r ffurf fenywaidd sy'n cyfateb i'r teitl swyddogol gwrywaidd *cassidannos* 'gweinidog efydd' a geir sawl gwaith yn Hen Gelteg Gâl, lle y ceir ARGANTODANNOS 'gweinidog arian' yn aml hefyd.

Yr un yw **kᵒoŕbᵉo**, enw tad yr ymadawedig, â'r enw gwrywaidd Hen Wyddeleg *Corb* a hefyd hanner cyntaf yr enw Gwyddeleg cyffredin iawn *Cormac, Corbmacc* yn wreiddiol. Mae'r gair Hen Wyddeleg *corb* yn digwydd hefyd i olygu 'cerbyd'. Felly, mae'n debyg fod **kᵒoŕbᵉo** yn enwi tad **ra♮a** yn ôl ei grefft.

Gyda llaw, y mae rhyw fath o odl neu gynghanedd yn cysylltu enw'r ymadawedig **ra♮a** â'r ferf *gwared*, ac eto **orbᵃa** 'goruchaf' ag enw ei thad **kᵒoŕbᵉo**, yn ogystal â chytseinedd rhwng **tᵘ-ua-ratᵉe** a **tᵘnbⁱitᵉsbᵃan**.

> **kᵒt̲ᵘuaratᵉe**
> **t̲ᵘnbⁱitᵉsbᵃan** *orbᵃa*
> **setᵃa lakᵉentⁱi ra̲H̲ᵃa**
> **kᵃaśetᵃana** *kᵒoŕbᵒo*

[J.4.2] Y mae delwedd Dartesaidd o un o'r duwiesau Celtaidd enwocaf yn ymddangos ar ddwy garreg doredig o'r un deunydd ac o'r un trwch a ddarganfuwyd yn Benaciate, San Bartolomeu de Messines, Portiwgal. Ar y gyntaf (J.4.2), y mae rhai llythrennau Tartesaidd yn ddarllenadwy uwchben delwedd o ferch yn marchogaeth wysg ei hochr ar geffyl mawr ac yn chwifio gwialen hir yn ei llaw chwith.

[J.4.1] Y mae'r ail garreg o Benaciate yn darllen: **ʔibᵒoi ion** (*neu* **ibᵒon ion**) **asune≡ uarbᵃan ≡ekᵘuŕine̲ obᵃar bᵃara*******tᵃa oretᵒo**/ 'Yn y dref (??) . . . yr wyf i [h.y. y cofeb hwn] wedi cario i'r un uchaf, i Asunā (??yr asen-dduwies/ caseg) a'r Farch-Frenhines . . . o waredigaeth (< rhedeg o dan).'

Ceir *Assuna* fel enw menyw yng Ngâl.

Ar gyfer **ekᵘuŕine̲** cymharer y gair Cymraeg *ebol* am yr elfen gyntaf, a *rhiain* yn yr ystyr wreiddiol 'brenhines' neu 'dduwies' am yr ail elfen.

[J.5.1] Y mae'r gair Tarteseg am frenhines neu dduwies yn digwydd mewn arysgrif arall sy'n galw ar grŵp o dduwiesau: **ist̲ᵃa|ibᵒo rinoebᵒo |anakᵉenak̲ᵉ:e|ibᵒo** 'i'r duwiesau brodorol hyn', neu gyda'r un geiriau Celteg yn Gymraeg 'i'r rhianedd anianol hyn'.

[J.4.1] **oretᵒo** yw'r berfenw sy'n cyfateb i **ua-ratᵉe** 'wedi gwaredu / wedi rhedeg odanodd' a drafodais i eisoes.

Y mae ugeiniau o gysegriadau i'r farch-dduwies *Epona* wedi eu darganfod yng Ngâl. Yn aml, cyfeirir ati yn llawn fel EPONAE REGINAE 'i'r Farch-Dduwies Frenhines', sy'n cyfateb yn union i ddwy elfen **ekᵘu-ŕine̲** yn yr iaith Darteseg. Ceir nifer o gerfluniau yn dangos Epona yn marchogaeth ar geffyl neu ferlyn. Yn y

Mabinogi y mae *Rhiannon* yn ymddangos fel marchog dirgel ar bwys gorsedd hudol. Y mae ei henw hi yn golygu 'Brenhines Ddwyfol' ac yn cynnwys ail elfen **ekᵘu-ṟine**.

Ceir digon o dystiolaeth archaeolegol am gwlt ceffylau ymhlith y Tartesiaid, megis y cerfluniau hyn o'r ganolfan gwlt yn Marchena ger Sevilla [gweler t. 46].

[J.12.1] Yr arysgrif Dartesaidd fwyaf ffotogenig yw'r rhyfelwr o Abóboda, sy'n ffurfio cyswllt clir rhwng yr arysgrifau a choflechi'r rhyfelwyr o'r Oes Efydd Ddiweddar. Y mae'r testun yn darllen: ᚼᚪᛂᚼᛗᛘᚻᛦᛆᛘᚻᚪᛦᛁᛁᛆᛘᚵᚼᚻᛁᚪᚻᚻᛘ [darllener yn groes i'r cloc] ᛆᛒᚵ ᛃᚪᛒᛆᚷᚪᚷᛆᛦᛆᚪᚻᛆ [chwith i'r dde] **iru≡alkᵘu — sie: naṟkᵉentⁱi — mubᵃa tᵉe·ro-bᵃare** ⸔**atᵃaneatᵉe** 'Mae Mumā ϕpataneatē ("mamaeth i'r un adeiniog") wedi dwyn ymaith yr arwr ⟨ac⟩ Alkos, y rhain sy'n gorwedd [yma] yn awr'.

Y mae ⸔atᵃaneatᵉe 'i'r un adeiniog', o bosibl, yn cyfeirio at agwedd arswydus y rhyfelwr: mewn arfwisg a harnais, y mae'n chwifio gwaywffyn byr mewn dwy law wedi'u hestyn allan. Y mae un o'r arwyr ym marwnadau'r *Gododdin* hefyd yn cael ei alw yn 'adeinawg mewn brwydr', ac yn gwisgo harnais brwydr. Ymladdai arwyr y *Gododdin* hefyd â gwaywffyn byr.

Dyma esiamplau o waywffyn Tartesaidd o'r teip perthnasol mewn casgliad cyfoethog o fetelwaith o Huelva, Sbaen, sy'n dyddio o'r ddegfed ganrif Cyn Crist [gweler t. 76].

GOBLYGIADAU

Gallwn estyn y casgliad gan restru llawer mwy o eiriau ac enwau cysylltiedig o'r Llydaweg, Gwyddeleg a Chelteg y Cyfandir yn ogystal â'r Gymraeg. Os yw'r casgliad hyd yma yn ddigon i ddangos bod yn y Darteseg fwy nag ambell elfen Gelteg, y mae sail dros ailddehongli llawer o'r athrawiaeth safonol am y Celtiaid a hyd yn oed Celtigrwydd Cymru.

Y syniad cyffredin yw fod yr ieithoedd Hen Gelteg wedi lledaenu o famwlad yng nghanolbarth Ewrop, lle'r oeddynt mewn cyswllt agos â diwylliannau La Tène a Hallstatt yr Oes Haearn (tua 800–50 CC). Serch hynny, ychydig sydd i'w weld yn gyffredin rhwng Tartesos a Hallstatt a La Tène. Mewn gwirionedd, yr oedd Tartesos wedi dod i ben cyn i'r deunydd La Tène cynharaf gychwyn yn y bumed ganrif Cyn Crist, ac y mae'n debyg fod yr arysgrifau Tartesaidd hefyd wedi darfod cyn cychwyn La Tène.

Ar y llaw arall, yr oedd Ynysoedd Prydain a de-orllewin Iberia wedi bod yn aelodau llawn o Oes Efydd yr Iwerydd.

Cydnabuwyd ers tro fod cyfatebiaeth agos rhwng lluniau'r arfau ar goflechi'r rhyfelwyr Iberaidd ac arteffactau go iawn o'r Oes Efydd Ddiweddar yn Iwerddon a Phrydain: hynny yw, tarianau gyda rhicyn-V, cleddyfau siâp deilen a gwaywffyn pigfain.

Felly, hoffwn ailgyfeirio ein meddyliau oddi wrth Hallstatt a La Tène i edrych tuag at berthnasau tramor Prydain ac Iwerddon yn ystod eu Hoes Efydd Ddiweddar gyfoethog a rhyngwladol hwy. Ac wedyn, efallai nad yw'n gymaint o syndod fod Tartesos o'r diwedd yn datgelu rhai o'i ddirgelion mewn iaith y gellir ei chymharu â'r Gymraeg.

AIL GASGLIAD

Y mae'r cysyniad modern o'r Celtiaid wedi ei seilio ar dri chategori o dystiolaeth:

- (yn gyntaf) pobl a alwyd yn Keltoí gan y Groegiaid;

- (yn ail) yr ieithoedd Hen Gelteg;

- (yn drydydd) diwylliannau archaeolegol Hallstatt a La Tène.

Er mwyn lleoli gwreiddiau'r Celtiaid mewn amser a gofod, rhoddwyd blaenoriaeth i'r categori olaf, sy'n pwysleisio canolbarth Ewrop, yn benodol y tiroedd o gwmpas mynyddoedd yr Alpau a'r parth lle y mae'r afonydd mawr yn dod at ei gilydd— Daniwb, Rhine, a Marne a Seine, Loire, Rhône a Saône, a Po. Gwelwyd yr Oes Haearn Gynnar fel cyfnod allweddol, tua 800–400 CC.

Casgliad y ddarlith hon yw fod tystiolaeth well a chynharach ar gyfer dwy allan o'r tair elfen uchod yn rhanbarth Tartesos nag yng nghanolbarth Ewrop: hynny yw, Celtiaid fel pobl a elwid yn Keltoí ac fel siaradwyr ieithoedd Hen Gelteg.

Ymddengys fod datganiad enwog Herodotos fod y Keltoí, sef y Celtiaid, yn byw ar ran uchaf afon Daniwb wedi ei seilio ar ei syniad dryslyd fod yr afon yn tarddu'n agos at 'Pyrēnē', hynny yw, mynyddoedd y Pyreneau. Tua 430 CC, ysgrifennodd fel a ganlyn:

§2.34. [Y mae afon Daniwb], a chanddi ffynhonnell ymhlith y Keltoí [Celtiaid] yn Pyrēnē, yn rhedeg drwy holl ganolbarth Ewrop cyn cyrraedd y Môr Du yn Istri, trefedigaeth Miletos. Y mae'r Celtiaid yn byw y tu hwnt i Golofnau Ercwlff, yn nes at y Kunēsioi [Kunētes], y bobl fwyaf gorllewinol yn Ewrop.

Ac ysgrifennodd Herodotos hefyd:

§4.48. . . . Y mae Afon Daniwb, y ffrwd rymus honno,—sy'n codi ymhlith y Celtiaid, y bobl fwyaf gorllewinol, ar ôl y Kunētes, o holl bobloedd Ewrop— yn croesi ar hyd y cyfandir cyn cyrraedd Scythia.

Yn amlwg, yr oedd gan Herodotos fwy o wybodaeth pan ysgrifennodd am y Celt-iaid yn 'byw y tu hwnt i Golofnau Ercwlff', wrth ymyl y Kunētes, nag am ddyffryn Daniwb. Felly, yr oedd y Celtiaid yn yr ardal lle y diflanasai teyrnas Tartesos cyn y flwyddyn 500 CC.

Versions of this talk were given at the Department of Irish and Celtic Studies, Queen's University Belfast, in May 2011 and at the XIV Congress of Celtic Studies at Maynooth in August 2011.

A Celtic Verbal Complex in Tartessian?

I. INTRODUCTION

§ 0. If we were just discovering Gaulish now, many of the names would fit Proto-Brittonic-Goidelic as previously reconstructed. But we could not have foreseen the most prevalent sentence type or verb forms—*ieuru, auuote, ΔΕΔΕ*, and KARNITU. Despite impressive advances, our understanding of the Proto-Celtic verb remains incomplete, and ideas will have to be revised as new evidence continues to appear.

§ 1. As the South-western (SW) or Tartessian inscriptions of south Portugal and south-west Spain became more reliably decoded, commentators noted sequences of signs resembling Indo-European verbs with primary endings: for example, **naŕk^{e}et^{i}i, naŕk^{e}ent^{i}i, lak^{e}ent^{i}i** (e.g. Untermann 1997). With the last two, compare Lusitanian DOENTI 'they give'.

There are also recurrent prefixes found with these Tartessian forms: for example, **t^{e}ee-b^{a}arent^{i}i** and **t^{e}e-b^{a}ant^{i}i**. I suggest that the last, from the recently unearthed Mesas do Castelinho stone, be understood as | *de·bānti* | 'they pass away', i.e. 'they die'.

That long text allows a breakthrough, significantly increasing the corpus and confirming previously proposed word divisions by recombining attested stems, endings, and prefixes. At present, the prefix **ro** is found eight times with the same stem syllables as those occurring with Indo-European primary endings, though **ro** never occurs together with those inflexions: for example, **ro-la[k^u]a, ro-n-b^{a}aren, ro-n-b^{a}are**, possibly **ro-b^{a}ae**, and the frequent **t^{e}e(e)-ro-b^{a}are**. My working hypothesis is that the last means | *de-ro-bāre* | 'has carried away', understood as '[this grave/death] has carried away'. The minority of SW inscriptions found in documented archaeological contexts come from burial grounds of the Early Iron Age.

§ 2. It was the occurrence of **ro** together with stems found inflected as verbs that convinced me that the principal language of the SW corpus was Celtic. What I want to talk about today is this pattern of verbs and preverbs and what light that might throw on the persistent uncertainties in deriving the early Neo-Celtic verbal complex.

But first, as the idea that Tartessian is Celtic is still fairly new, I will supply more evidence favouring the Celticity of the corpus, particularly names, naming formulas, and their inflexions. Relevant examples include:

1 nominative singular masculine o-stem tⁱirt°os (J.1.2) well-attested in Hispano-Celtic;

2 dative singular t^uuŕek^uui (J.14.1), which can be understood as 'for a male of the kindred of Turos', a name, formation, and case ending all known in Celtiberian;

3 the typical Hispano-Celtic genitive plural family name]t^aarnek^uun (J.26.1), probably 'of the kindred of Taranus';

4 the dative plural (with preposition) k°o b^eelib°o (J.1.2).

5 Compare tⁱilek^uurk^uu opening the Mesas do Castelinho text with a heavily Celtic inscription dating to AD 28 from Caurel, Galicia: TILLEGVS AMBATI F SVSARRVS | AIOB[R]IGIAECO, also the Gaulish genitive TILLICI. Note that the adjectival suffix ~iko~ is found lowered to ~eko~ in both Western Hispano-Celtic and Tartessian.

6 I suggest taking anb^aatⁱia iob^aa[and t^uurea iub^aa as | amba(χ)tiā i̯ō‚mā | 'young-est daughter of Amba(χ)tos' and | Tureā i̯ū‚mā | 'youngest daughter of Turos'. Both fathers' names are common in Hispano-Celtic. The latter shows two sound shifts paralleled elsewhere in the corpus: i lowered to e before a and o from the diphthong ou raised to u.

7 A similar formula is b°otⁱieana k^eert°o rob^aa, which I understand as | Bōdⁱeanā kerdo ro‚mā | 'Bōdieanā the craftsman's first-born daughter', | kerdo | being an o-stem genitive, formed as in Celtiberian. Names in both Boudi- and Bouti- were very common in the western Peninsula during the earlier Roman period. The diphthong simplified to o occurs in these. With rob^aa for | ro‚mā |, compare Middle Irish rom 'early, too soon' < Indo-European *pro-mo-, Homeric πρόμος 'foremost man'. Note also that the distinctive SW signs for [m] are rare; more commonly the series for b+vowel was used. rob^aa, or its accusative rob^aan, recurs in the recently discovered graffito from Castelo de Moura.

8 lok°ob°o niirab°o opening the long inscription of Fonte Velha 6 (J.1.1) is strikingly similar to early Roman-period dedications from Galicia: LVCVBO ARQVIENOBO (Sober, Lugo), LVCOVBV[S] ARQVIENI[S], DIBVS M[.] LVCVBO, and LVCOBO AROVSA[-] (Lugo). I take the Tartessian as co-ordinated datives plural, meaning 'for the divine Lugoues and for the chief men'.

9 With ra‡a kᵃaśetᵃana | kas(s)edannā | (J.53.1, Alcalá del Río), I think the dead woman's name (~ Hispano-Celtic *Rapa*) is co-ordinated with the feminine equivalent of the Gaulish title *cas(s)idan(n)os* 'tin or bronze minister' (Graufesenque). Note again *i* lowered to **e** before **a**.

10 That shift happens again in **meleśae**, a feminine case form equivalent to the Gaulish man's name *Meliððus*, meaning 'sweet'.

II. PATTERNS IN THE TARTESSIAN VERBAL COMPLEX

§ 3. Romanized transcriptions of the longer and more complete SW inscriptions—those for which syntax can be considered—are gathered in *Tartessian 2*, 93–8 and can be found individually in the catalogue above (pp. 29–134).

The forms with **ro** never show the primary endings. Where there are two or more instances of the various recurrent verbs on one stone, the pattern is that **ro** never occurs twice and that the primary endings never occur twice. It is also possible for verbs to have neither feature. The other preverbs—**tᵉe(e)** being the most frequent of these—never occur twice in one text either.

§ 4. The verbal expressions thus appear to avoid marked agreement. By contrast, the forms that are recognizable as names by their Celtic and/or Palaeohispanic analogues often occur with another element in exact formal agreement: dative ablative plural pairs in -**bᵒo** + -**bᵒo**, masculine pairs ending in -**u** + -**u**, and feminine in -**a** + -**a** or -**e** + -**e**. I take these doublets as co-ordinative or *dvandva* compounds to be translated with 'and'. The masculine and feminine forms are inflected as nominative/accusative duals and can be the subjects of plural verbs.

§ 5. The most common of the forms resembling Indo-European verbs is **naŕkᵉetⁱi**, **naŕkᵉentⁱi**, and numerous other endings. This stem never occurs with a prefix resembling a Celtic or Indo-European preposition, but **naŕkᵉentⁱi** can be preceded by the segment **bᵃa**.

The complete minimal text **akᵒolios naŕkᵉetⁱi** resembles a masculine name, o-stem nominative singular, followed by a present-tense active verb, 3rd person singular. In the light of the probably funerary function of the corpus, **naŕkᵉetⁱi** would mean, or at least function, as 'rests, remains, lies' or the like.

bᵃa before **naŕkᵉentⁱi** could stand phonetically for | *ma* | and thus be equivalent to Old Irish *ma* 'if'. Etymologically, this has been related to the Vedic enclitic *smá* and Greek μήν used in oaths. Both forms added affirmative force to a statement. The recurrent **bᵃa naŕkᵉentⁱi** could thus mean something like 'so they now rest [here]'.

§ 6. In the longer inscriptions, there are variations on a recurrent formula (cf. De Hoz 2010, 400). The most common elements and sequence of this are as follows:

1   name of deceased (often including two substantives in concord),

2   **uar(n)bᵃan**   (once **uabᵃan**),

3   **tᵉe(e)·ro-bᵃare**,

4   **(bᵃa) nařkᵉentⁱi**.

My working interpretation of this formula is: '[This grave *or* death (understood)] has carried away (*de·ro-bāre*) the deceased X=and=Y to the highest destination (*uarₐman* < **u(p)erₐmām*); (so) they now rest [here]'. **nařkᵉentⁱi** or one of its variants frequently ends the statement as a formulaic closing, although this is not always the case, and in some of the longer inscriptions there can be an 'amplification' after **nařkᵉentⁱi**.

§ 7.   For formula words 2 and 3, preceding **(bᵃa) nařkᵉentⁱi**, an Early Welsh analogue is worth noting. In the canon of poems generally classed as the earlier or historical content of the 14th-century manuscript known as the 'Book of Taliesin' ('Llyfr Taliesin', National Library of Wales, Peniarth 2), 'Dadolwch Vryen' is addressed to the 6th-century ruler Urien Rheged. Anticipating his patron's death, this 'historical Taliesin' declaims: *namyn y·Ðuw vchaf | ny-s dioferaf* 'except to the highest God I will not give (< carry) him away'. The key words and concepts in these lines are *vchaf* < **u(p)samo-* 'highest' (= Hispano-Celtic *Uxama*) and *dioferaf* < **di-u(p)o-ber-* 'carry away'. So the Welsh *Cynfardd* (earliest poet), like the Tartessian epigraphers, articulates the wish for his patron to be carried off at death to the highest destination. And they use cognate vocabulary to express these ideas. I would see the parallel as a shared inheritance with the following reconstructable starting point:

'carry away [the deceased patron]	to the highest destination/god(dess)'
*dĕ-ber-	**u(p)ₐmām, *u(p)erₐmām, *u(p)sₐmām*
tᵉe(e)·(ro-)bᵃare	**uar(n)bᵃan/uabᵃan**
dioferaf	*y·Ðuw vchaf*

The chief poetic elaboration in the Welsh is the double negation. The underlying, and no doubt earlier, formulation would be the straightforward 'to the highest (deity) carry him off'.

§ 8.   When one or more of the formula words are missing in an SW inscription, their place sometimes appears to be taken by forms that have a similar grammatical form or arguably have a similar sense, or both: such as, a different accusative of destination or some other expression of a sublime afterlife, a different verb expressing conveyance or deliverance of the deceased grammatically marked as completed action, or a different present-tense verb expressing the current repose of the deceased. Thus, the essential logical content is preserved. For example, in the long and complete, but now lost, inscription from Alcalá del Río near Seville (J.53.1), **uar(n)bªan** 'highest destination' is absent, but we find **orbªa setªa**, possibly meaning 'inherited resting place' or 'highest resting place', compare Old Welsh *guorsed*. **tᵉe(e)·ro-bªare** 'has taken away' is absent; **kº-tᵘ-ua-ratᵉe** 'has delivered to' < 'has run under (with) towards' (compare Old Irish *fu·rráith*, Old Welsh *guo-raut* < **u(p)o-rāte*) arguably expresses the same notion in the same tense and person. There is no **naŕkᵉentⁱi**, but instead **lakᵉentⁱi** (possibly 'they lie down' or 'they are now lain down') precedes the co-ordinative compound naming the deceased **ra♭a≡kªaśetªana** 'Ra♭a ⟨and⟩ the bronze minister'.

§ 9. Why are these verbs (most often in the second clause and) with present marking **naŕkᵉentⁱi**, &c., usually 3rd person plural? I see more than one possibility. First, the name of the deceased is often expressed with two, or sometimes three, names in agreement, often inflected like nominative/accusative duals. Whether these naming phrases referred to one or more persons, they were probably not singular grammatically. Secondly, the idea of the formula is, I think, that the deceased has been carried away by the memorialized grave to the highest place, state, or deity: so 'they' (the mortal and the immortal grave and/or the sublime) now rest together.

§ 10. The recurrent **uar(n)bªan** | *u̯arₐman* |, which I take as an accusative of destination, could refer to an ideal or actual place. The variant **uabªan** | *u̯aman* | is the exact cognate of Οὔαμα, the ancient name of a settlement below the highest summit of the south-western Celtici. But in some of the variants of the formula in which **uar(n)bªan** is absent, there may be a feminine personage instead. For example, my interpretation of the text with warrior relief of Abóboda 1 (J.12.1) is as follows:

iru≡alkᵘu — sie: naŕkᵉentⁱi — mubªa tᵉe·ro-bªare ♭atªaneatᵉe
| (i)*irū≡Alkū — siē narkenti — Mumā de·ro-bāre φataneatē* |

'She who is nurturer to the winged one (i.e. she who feeds the [battle-field] bird and the armed warrior [as pictured]) has carried the hero and Alkos away, these men (who) now rest [here]'.

On | *Mumā φataneatē* | 'foster-mother to the winged one', compare *Sanas Cormaic's*

Búanann Mume na Fian 'B. Foster-mother of the warband'. On the warrior armed with short spears as wingèd, Welsh *aer-edeinauc* 'winged in slaughter' expresses this idea in *Y Gododdin*.

§ 11. In the inscription from Monte Nova do Visconde— **bᵉetⁱisai tᵉee·bᵃarentⁱi iru≡{u}arbᵘu i el naŕrkᵉe:n: uśnee** — the stem **bᵃar-** occurs with the primary ending **-entⁱi**. From this example, it appears that this usage excludes **ro** with **bᵃarentⁱi**. The other verb has the form **naŕrkᵉe:n:**, rather than the frequent **naŕkᵉentⁱi**. There is thus a reversal in forms, though the usual sequence remains. **tᵉee** (probably | *de* | 'away from', possibly with an enclitic infix here) is compatible with primary **bᵃarentⁱi**.

§ 12. Proto-Indo-European **pro* was high frequency and had many non-temporal meanings. This situation continued with both the Goidelic and Brittonic reflexes of **pro*. Therefore, as Celtic **(p)ro* had functions other than tense, its close contrastive relationship with the primary endings might have provided an analogical basis for extending the opposition outside the tense system.

The 'Mealha Nova 1' inscription (J.18.1) has **ro** in a nominal compound, in concord with the name of the deceased. This excludes **ro** from the usual formula **tᵉe-ro-bᵃare**:

bᵒotⁱieana≡ kᵉertᵒo ≡robᵃa tᵉe-bᵃare bᵃa naŕkᵉentⁱi
| *Bōd´eanā≡ kerdo ≡roₐmā de-bāre; ma narkenti* |

'[this grave] has carried away Bōdⁱeanā ⟨and⟩ the first-born daughter of the artisan; so "they" now rest [here]'.

§ 13. The inscription of Barradas (J.5.1) has no **ro** and only one verb, to which **-ii** is added:

sabᵒoi : ist̲ᵃa̲|ibᵒo rinoe̲b̲ᵒo| anakᵉenak̲ᵉ:e|ibᵒo iibᵃan bᵃare̲i̲i̲

My tentative interpretation is

| *samoi istəbo rī(g)anəbo an(d)əgenākəbo ippan bāre-i* |

'In summer, for these indwelling queens [this altar stone] has now carried offerings to ʔippā (the important place/town)'.

So the usual **ro** and **naŕkᵉentⁱi** are absent, but the final **-(i)i** turns up on **bᵃare-**, as though the ending is gravitating to the only available slot.

§ 14. The contrastive pattern of **ro** and the primary endings possibly signifies a sequence of actions and states. **ro** with verbs that mostly resemble Indo-European perfects marks completed actions. Primary endings without **ro**, but with or without other preverbs, mark actions or states continuing through the present.

narkᵉen as well as **narkᵉentⁱi** in variants of the same Tartessian formula suggest that the *-i of the Indo-European primary endings was sometimes being lost. Note also the form **ar·bᵉieritᵘu**, probably a compound verb with **ar** < Indo-European *peri*; compare South-west Hispano-Celtic ARBRVNVS ARCELTI F.

A system like that seen in the SW corpus—contrasting present-tense verbs with final -i and completed action marked by *(p)ro*—was thus vulnerable at two points to a non-temporal reanalysis, producing a pattern similar to that in Old Irish:

1 the survival of lexical *(p)ro* with the present tense and

2 the emergence of present-tense verb endings with apocopated 3rd person singular -t and 3rd person plural -nt.

III. TARTESSIAN AND ABSOLUTE AND CONJUNCT THEORIES

§ 15. Do the patterns in Tartessian favour or disprove any of the accounts tracing the Old Irish and early Brittonic verbal complex to their Indo-European sources? Those explanations diverge widely at two points:

1 the origins of the opposition of absolute and conjunct verb forms (a system not found in any other branch of Indo-European);

2 the non-lenition of verbs, object pronouns, and second preverbs after main-clause-initial preverbs that originally ended in a vowel.

§ 16. The explanations can be subdivided into four broad categories. Comparing these with Tartessian potentially illuminates not only what happened between Indo-European and the attested Celtic languages, but also when it happened—at the Proto-Celtic stage or later in a sub-branch nearer Old Irish.

1 Absolute and conjunct from Indo-European primary and secondary. It has long been recognized that the Old Irish pattern (absolute *beirid*, conjunct ·*beir*; 3rd plural absolute *berait*, conjunct ·*berat*) can be reconstructed like Sanskrit present *bharati* 'carries' < Indo-European *b^hereti*, *bharanti* 'they carry' < *b^heronti*, and *á-bharat* 'used to carry' < *b^heret*, plural *á-bharant* < *b^heront*. In the theories of Watkins and Meid, both published in 1963, Old Irish absolute and conjunct had not lost tense as the original significance of the contrast, rather Celtic alone

reflected an early stage of Proto-Indo-European before the final *-*i* had become a fixed feature of present-tense endings. The Tartessian contrast of primary endings versus **ro** prefixed to perfects is easier to understand as a development from Indo-European as usually reconstructed than by the Watkins/Meid theories.

2   Particle theories go back to Thurneysen (1907). The most influential was Cowgill's (1975). In these, an enclitic particle in Wackernagel's position—i.e. second in its clause—became obligatory in most sentences in a proto-language ancestral to both Goidelic and Brittonic. Its presence produced the absolute endings for simplex verbs at the head of their sentences and non-lenition after sentence-initial preverbs. Forms and etymologies of the particle vary. As in Celtiberian and Gaulish, no 'Cowgill' particle announces itself in Tartessian. But the particle theories often claim relevance only for Insular Celtic and in this require a special shape for the Celtic family tree. A common thread unites particle theories with types 3 and 4 coming up. They derive the conjunct endings from the Indo-European primary endings with an apocope of final short *-*i* in the common ancestor of Goidelic and Brittonic. Such an apocope has possibly occurred in Tartessian **naŕkᵉen** versus **naŕkᵉentⁱi**, and **ro-n-bᵃaren** versus **tᵉee-bᵃarentⁱi**.

3   'Enclitic-deletion' theories. In these (notably McCone 1979; 2006; Sims-Williams 1984) there is no particular Wackernagel's enclitic. However, various enclitics in second position are pivotal as the proto-language or languages of Goidelic and Brittonic shift from verb-final to verb-initial order. So, an infrequent inherited type #*bereti-E . . .#, in which the enclitic has shielded the primary *-*i* from apocope, gives rise to the unmarked absolute-verb-initial #beirid . . . # by analogical suffix deletion. And inherited #*to-E . . .beret(i)# gives #do·bbeir . . . # by infix deletion. The changes are thus bound up with both the emergence of verb-initial syntax and the beginning of morphophonemic mutations. The key changes are explicitly late—Late Iron Age or Roman Period—and limited to Insular Celtic. But do we have something like the final stage already in Tartessian, e.g. **lakᵉentⁱi raⱡa≡kᵃaśetᵃana**? However clearly not **tᵉee-bᵃarentⁱi** or **akᵒolios naŕkᵉetⁱi**.

4   The prosodic theory is based on the premise that the Proto-Indo-European verb—as reflected in Vedic—was unaccented in main clauses, except in the less common type where the verb began the sentence. In Celtic the result was that the verb shows features otherwise characteristic of enclitics: early apocope of final *-*i* (giving rise to the conjunct verb forms in non-initial position) and doubling of initial consonants. So unlenited *do·bbeir* < *tó beret(i)* has the same enclitic gemination as *do-t* 'to thy' and *do-m(m)* 'to my'. Since I published this

idea in 1987, developments include De Hoz's (1997) conclusion that it accounted better for the Continental Celtic evidence than the alternatives. Hock (2005) argues that the unaccented verb of Vedic and the apocope creating the conjunct series are both results of universal tendencies for sentential intonation to cause sentence-final words to lose their word accent and for unaccented words to lose final sounds. So, the Vedic enclitic verb and Old Irish conjunct series are both consequences of Proto-Indo-European verb-final basic order.

§ 17. As I see it now, the Tartessian evidence is most compatible with the 'enclitic-deletion' or 'prosodic' explanations, but doesn't conclusively prove either or exclude all alternatives. Though suggesting the Indo-European primary endings as the source of the absolute series, the relevant forms seem to mark the Tartessian present tense, ruling out the similar approaches of Watkins and Meid. **naŕkᵉentⁱi** and **naŕkᵉen**, **tᵉee-bᵃarentⁱi** and **ro-n-bᵃaren** suggest apocope of final *-i as a factor. But there is no obvious 'Cowgill' particle.

In very broad outline, it might now be possible to glimpse a succession of stages: (1) the primary-secondary opposition marking present and past tenses as usually reconstructed for Proto-Indo-European, (2) an opposition of marked present-tense non-**ro**-forms contrasting with marked perfect **ro**-forms as found in the SW corpus, possibly reflecting the Proto-Celtic situation, (3) the absolute and conjunct opposition observable in Old Irish, which still has some relation to the tense-aspect system, particularly in the matter of the *ro*-forms.

Bibliography

Albertos Firmat, Mª. L. 1985 'La onomástica personal indígena del noroeste peninsular (astures y galaicos)', *Actas del III Coloquio sobre Lenguas y Culturas Paleohispánicas*, ed. J. de Hoz, 255–310. Salamanca, Universidad de Salamanca.

Almagro Basch, M. 1952 'La invasión céltica en España', *Historia de España* I (2), ed. R. Menéndez Pidal, 1–278. Madrid, Espasa-Calpe.

Almagro-Gorbea, M. 1988 'Société et commerce dans la péninsule Ibérique aux VII–Vᵉ siécles', *Les princes celtes et la Méditerranée*, 71–9. Paris, La Documentation Française.

Almagro-Gorbea, M. 2002 'Una probable divinidad tartésica identificada: Niethos/Netos', *Palaeohispanica* 2, 37–70.

Almagro-Gorbea, M. 2004 'Inscripciones y grafitos tartesicos de la necrópolis orientalizante de Medellín', *Palaeohispanica* 4.13–44.

Almagro-Gorbea, M. 2005 'La literatura tartésica. Fuentes históricas e iconográficas', *Gerión* 23/1.39–80.

Almagro-Gorbea, M. (ed.) 2007 *La necrópolis de Medellín I: la excavacíon y sus hallazgos* (Bibliotheca Archaeologica Hispanica 26/Studia Hispano-Phoenica 5). Madrid, Real Academia de la Historia.

Almagro-Gorbea, M. (ed.) 2008 *La necrópolis de Medellín II: estudio de los hallazgos* (Bibliotheca Archaeologica Hispanica 26–2/Studia Hispano-Phoenica 5–2). Madrid, Real Academia de la Historia.

Almagro-Gorbea, M. (ed.) 2008b *La necrópolis de Medellín III: estudios analíticos; IV: interpretacíon de la necrópolis; V: el marco histórico de Medellín-Conisturgis* (Bibliotheca Archaeologica Hispanica 26–3/Studia Hispano-Phoenica 5–3). Madrid, Real Academia de la Historia.

Almagro-Gorbea, M. 2010 'La colonización tartésica: toponimia y arqueología', *Palaeohispanica* 10, 187–99.

Almagro-Gorbea, M., & M. Torres Ortiz 2009 'La colonización de la costa atlántica de Portugal: ¿Fenicios o Tartesios?' *Palaeohispanica* 9, 113–42.

Anthony, D. W. 2007 *The Horse, the Wheel, and Language: How Bronze-Age Riders from the Eurasian Steppes Shaped the Modern World*. Princeton, Princeton University Press.

Arruda, A. M. 2011 'Indígenas, fenicios y tartésicos en el occidente peninsular: mucha gente, poca tierra', *Fenicios en Tartesos: nuevas perspectivas*, ed. Manuel Álvarez Martí-Aguilar, BAR International Series 2245, 151–60. Oxford, Archaeopress.

Aubet, M. E. 2001 *The Phoenicians and the West: Politics, Colonies, and Trade*, trans. M. Turton. 2nd edn. Cambridge, Cambridge University Press. 1st English edition, 1993.

Ballester, X. 2004 'Hablas indoeuropeas y anindoeuropeas en la Hispania prerromana', *Real Academia de Cultura Valenciana, sección de estudios ibéricos. Estudios de lenguas y epigrafía antiguas — ELEA* 6, 107–38.

Beekes, R. (with L. van Beek) 2010 *Etymological Dictionary of Greek*, 2 vols. Leiden Indo-European Etymological Dictionary Series 10. Leiden and Boston, Brill.

Beltrán Lloris, F. 2002 'Les dieux des celtibères orientaux et les inscriptions: quelques remarques critiques', *Dieux des celtes (Études luxembourgoises d'Histoire & de Sciences des religions* 1, 39–66. Luxembourg.

Binchy, D. A. 1970 *Celtic and Anglo-Saxon Kingship*. O'Donnell Lectures 1968. London, Oxford University Press.

Blázquez, J. M. 1993 'El enigma de Tarteso en los escritores antiguos y en la investigación moderna', *Los enigmas de Tarteso*, eds. J. Alvar & J. M. Blázquez, 11–30. Madrid, Cátedra.

Bosch Gimpera, P. 1943 'Two Celtic Waves in Spain', Sir John Rhŷs Lecture (1939), *Proceedings of the British Academy* 26.

Brandherm, D. 2007 *Las Espadas del Bronce Final en la Península Ibérica y Baleares*, Prähistorische Bronzefunde IV/16. Stuttgart, Franz Steiner Verlag.

Brandherm, D. 2008 'Greek and Phoenician Potsherds between East and West: A Chronological Dilemma?', *A New Dawn for the Dark Age? Shifting Paradigms in Mediterranean Iron Age Chronology / L'âge obscur se fait-il jour de nouveau? Les paradigmes changeants de la chronologie de l'âge du Fer en Mediterranée*, BAR International Series 1871, eds. D. Brandherm & M. Trachsel, 149–74.

Brandherm, D. 2008/9 'Sobre los supuestos arreos de caballo y piezas de carro de la Ria de Huelva', *Boletín de la Asociación Española de Amigos de la Arqueología* 45, 27–34.

Broderick, G. 2010 'Die vorrömischen Sprachen auf der iberischen Halbinsel', *Handbuch der Eurolinguistik*, ed. U. Hinrichs, 287–320. Wiesbaden, Otto Harrassowitz Verlag.

Bromwich, R. (ed. & trans.) 2006 *Trioedd Ynys Prydein / The Welsh Triads*. 3rd edn. Cardiff, University of Wales Press. First published, 1961.

Brun, P. 2006 'L'origine des Celtes: Communautés linguistiques et réseaux sociaux', *Celtes et Gaulois, l'Archéologie face à l'Histoire, 2: la Préhistoire des Celtes*, dir. D. Vitali. Bibracte 12/2, 29–44.

Búa Carballo, J. C. 2000 'Estudio lingüístico de la teonima lusitano-gallega', Tesis Doctoral, Salamanca.

Búa Carballo, J. C. 2003 *Cosus. Una exemplo da epigrafía e relixíon*, Boletín Avriense.

Búa Carballo, J. C. 2004 'Tres cuestións relacionadas coa toponimia antiga en -*bris*, moderna -*bre*', *Novi te ex nomine: Estudios filolóxicos ofrecidos ao Prof. Dr. D. Kremer*, ed. A. I. Boullón Angelo, 381–99. Instituto da Lingua Galega, A Coruña.

Búa Carballo, J. C. 2005 'Zur Etymologie der deutschen Konjunktion *und*', *Sprachwissenschaft* 30/2, 111–25.

Búa Carballo, J. C. 2007 'O *Thesaurus Palaeocallaecus*, un proxecto que quere botar a andar', *Onomástica galega con especial consideración da situación prerromana. Actas do primeiro Coloquio de Trier 19 e 20 de maio 2006*, ed. D. Kremer, 15–40. Verba, Anuario Galega de Filoloxía, Anexo 58. Universidade de Santiago de Compostela.

Burgess, C., & B. O'Connor 2008 'Iberia, the Atlantic Bronze Age and the Mediterranean', *Contacto cultural entre el Mediterráneo y el Atlántico (siglos XII–VIII ANE), La precolonización a debate*, Serie Arqueológica 11, eds. S. Celestino, N. Rafel & X-L. Armada, 41–58. Madrid, Escuela Española de Historia y Arqueología en Roma-CSIC.

Catalán, M. P. 1993 'Crítica analítica de la arqueología tartesia y turdetana', *Lengua y cultura en la Hispania prerromana, Actas del V Coloquio sobre Lenguas y Culturas Prerromanas de la Península Ibérica*, eds. J. Untermann & F. Villar, 189–207. Salamanca, Ediciones Universidad de Salamanca.

Celestino Pérez, S. 1990 'Las estelas decoradas del s.w. peninsular', *La cultura tartesica y Extremadura*, 45–62. Cuadernos Emeritenses 2. Mérida, Museo Nacional de Arte Romano.

Celestino Pérez, S. 2001 *Estelas de guerrero y stelas diademadas: La precolonización y formación del mundo tartésico*. Barcelona, Edicions Bellaterra.

Celestino Pérez, S., & C. López-Ruiz 2006 'New light on the warrior stelae from Tartessos (Spain)', *Antiquity* 80.89–101.

Chamorro, J. G. 1987 'Survey of Archaeological research on Tartessos', *American Journal of Archaeology* 91/2.197–232.

Charles-Edwards, T. M. 1978 'The Authenticity of the Gododdin: An Historian's View', *Astudiaethau ar yr Hengerdd: Studies in Old Welsh Poetry*, eds. Rachel Bromwich & R. Brinley Jones, 44–71. Caerdydd, Gwasg Prifysgol Cymru.

Clackson, J. 2007 *Indo-European Linguistics—An Introduction*. Cambridge, Cambridge University Press.

Collis, J. 2003 *The Celts: Origins, Myths & Inventions*. Stroud, Tempus.

Correa, J. A. 1985 'Consideraciones sobre las inscripciones tartesias', *Actas del III Coloquio sobre Lenguas y Culturas Paleohispánicas*, ed. J. de Hoz, 377–95. Salamanca, Universidad de Salamanca.

Correa, J. A. 1989 'Posibles antropónimos en las inscripciones en escritura del SO. (o tartesia)', *Veleia* 6.243–52.

Correa, J. A. 1992 'La epigrafía tartesia', *Andalusien zwischen Vorgeschichte und Mittelalter*, eds. D. Hertel & J. Untermann, 75–114. Cologne, Böhlau.

Correa, J. A. 1993 'El signario de Espanca (Castro Verde) y la escritura tartesia', *Lengua y cultura en la Hispania prerromana, Actas del V Coloquio sobre Lenguas y Culturas Prerromanas de la Península Ibérica*, eds. J. Untermann & F. Villar, 521–62. Salamanca, Ediciones Universidad de Salamanca.

Correa, J. A. 1995 'Reflexiones sobre la epigrafía paleohispánica de la Península Ibérica', *Tartessos 25 años después: Congreso Conmemorativo del V Symposium Internacional de Prehistoria Peninsular*, 609–17. Ayuntamiento de Jérez de la Frontera.

Correa, J. A. 1996 'La epigrafía del Sudoeste: Estado de la cuestión', *La Hispania Prerromana, Actas del VI Coloquio sobre Lenguas y Culturas Prerromanas de la Península Ibérica*, eds. F. Villar & J. d'Encarnação, 65–75. Salamanca, Ediciones Universidad de Salamanca.

Correa, J. A. 2002 'Crónica epigráfica del sudoeste', *Palaeohispanica* 2.407–9.

Correa, J. A. 2004 'Crónica epigráfica del sudoeste', *Palaeohispanica* 4.283–4.

Correa, J. A. 2005 'Del alfabeto fenicio al semisilabario paleohispánico', *Palaeohispanica* 5.137–54.

Correa, J. A. 2006 'Crónica epigráfica del sudoeste', *Palaeohispanica* 6.295–8.

Correa, J. A. 2008 'Crónica epigráfica del sudoeste IV', *Palaeohispanica* 8.295.

Correa, J. A. 2009 'Identidad, cultura y territorio en la Andalucía prerromana a través de la lengua y la epigrafía', *Identidad, cultura y territorio en la Andalucía prerromana*, ed. F. Wulff Alonso & M. Álvarz Martí-Aguilar, 274–95. Málaga, Universidad de Málaga.

Correa, J. A. 2011 'La leyenda indígena de las monedas de *Salacia* y el grafito de Abul (Alcácer do Sal, Setúbal)', *Lucius Cornelius Bocchus: Escritor Lusitano da Idade de Prata da Literatura Latina*, ed. J. L. Cardoso, M. Almagro-Gorbea, 103–12. Lisboa/Madrid, Academia Portuguesa da Historia / Real Academia de la Historia.

Correa, J. A., & J. Á. Zamora 2008 'Un graffito tartesio hallado en el yacimiento del Castillo de Doña Blanca', *Palaeohispanica* 8.179–96.

Correia, V. H. 1996 *A epigrafia da Idade do Ferro do Sudoeste da Península Ibérica*. Porto, Etnos.

Correia, V. H. 2005 'The Collection of Pre-Latin Writing in the Museum of Faro', *Paths of the Roman Algarve*, 14–19. Faro, Câmara Municipal de Faro.

Correia, V. H. 2009 'A escrita do sudoeste: uma visão retrospectiva e prospectiva', *Acta Palaeohispanica* X / *Palaeohispanica* 9, 309–21.

Cowgill, W. 1975 'The Origins of the Insular Celtic Conjunct and Absolute Verbal Endings', *Flexion und Wortbildung: Akten der V. Fachtagung der Indergermanischen Gesellschaft, Regensburg, 9.–14. September 1973*, ed. H. Rix, 40–70. Wiesbaden, Reichert Verlag.

Cowgill, W. 1975b 'Two Further Notes on the Origin of the Insular Celtic Absolute and Conjunct Verb Endings', *Ériu* 26, 27–32.

Criado, A. J. 1996 'El misterio de la Piedra Escrita', *Diario Córdoba*, 25 de Febrero de 1996.

Cunliffe, B. 1997 *The Ancient Celts*. Oxford, Oxford University Press.

Cunliffe, B. 2001 *Facing the Ocean: The Atlantic and its Peoples 8000 BC–AD 1500*. Oxford, Oxford University Press.

Cunliffe, B. 2008 *Europe between the Oceans, 9000 BC–AD 1000*. New Haven, Yale University Press.

Cunliffe, B. 2009 'A Race Apart: Insularity and Connectivity', *Proceedings of the Prehistoric Society 75*, 55–64.

Cunliffe, B. 2010 'Celticization from the West: The Contribution of Archaeology', *Celtic from the West: Alternative Perspectives from Archaeology, Genetics, Language and Literature*, Celtic Studies Publications 15, eds. B. Cunliffe & J. T. Koch, 13–38. Oxford, Oxbow Books.

De Bernardo Stempel, P. 1998 'Minima Celtica zwischen Sprach- und Kultur-geschichte', *Man and the Animal World: Studies . . . in memoriam Sándor Bökönyi*, eds. P. Anreiter, L. Bartosiewucz, E . Jerem, W. Meid, 601–10. Budapest, Archaeolingua.

De Bernardo Stempel, P. 2006 'Language and Historiography of Celtic-speaking Peoples', *Celtes et Gaulois, l'Archéologie face à l'Histoire: Celtes et Gaulois dans l'Histoire, l'historiographie et l'idéologie moderne*, ed. S. Rieckhoff, Bibracte 12/1, 33–56.

De Bernardo Stempel, P. 2008 'Cib. *to Lvgvei* "hacia Lugus" frente a *Lvgvei* "para Lugus": sintaxis y divinidades en Peñalba de Villastar', *Emerita* 76/2, 181–96.

De Bernardo Stempel, P. 2008b 'Linguistically Celtic Ethnonyms: Towards a Classification',

Celtic and Other Languages in Ancient Europe, ed. J. L. García Alonso, 101–18. Salamanca, Ediciones Universidad de Salamanca.

De Hoz, J. 1989 'El desarrollo de la escritura y las lenguas de la zona meridional', *Tartessos: Arqueología Protohistórica del Bajo Guadalquivir*, ed. M. E. Aubet Semmler, 523–87. Barcelona, Sabadell.

De Hoz, J. 1989b 'Las fuentes escritas sobre Tartessos', *Tartessos: Arqueología Protohistórica del Bajo Guadalquivir*, ed. M. E. Aubet Semmler, 25–43. Barcelona, Sabadell.

De Hoz, J. 1992 'The Celts of the Iberian Peninsula'. *Zeitschrift für celtische Philologie* 45.1–37.

De Hoz, J. 1996 'El origen de las escrituras paleohispánicas quince años después', *La Hispania Prerromana, Actas del VI Coloquio sobre Lenguas y Culturas Prerromanas de la Península Ibérica*, eds. F. Villar & J. d'Encarnação, 171–204. Salamanca, Ediciones Universidad de Salamanca.

De Hoz, J. 1997 'When did the Celts lose their verbal **-i?*', *Zeitschrift für celtische Philologie* 49/50.107–17.

De Hoz, J. 2005 'Epigrafías y lenguas en contacto en la Hispania antigua', *Acta Palaeohispanica IX, Palaehispanica 5*, 57–98.

De Hoz, J. 2007 'The Mediterranean Frontier of the Celts and the Advent of Celtic Writing'. *Crossing Boundaries / Croesi Ffiniau: Proc. XII International Congress of Celtic Studies 24–30 August 2003*, eds. P. Sims-Williams & G. A. Williams. *Cambrian Medieval Celtic Studies* 53/54.1–22.

De Hoz, J. 2007b 'The Institutional Vocabulary of the Continental Celts', *Gaulois et Celtique continental*, eds. P.-Y. Lambert & G.-J. Pinault, 189–214. Genève, Librairie Droz.

De Hoz, J. 2010 *Historia lingüística de la Península Ibérica: I. Preliminarties y mundo meridional prerromana*, Manuales y Anejos de "Emerita"—L. Madrid, Consejo Superior de Investigaciones Científicas.

De Hoz, J., et al. 2005 *Catálogo de estelas decoradas del Museo Arqueológico Provincial de Badajoz.*

De Mello Beirão, C. 1993 'Novos dados arqueológicos sobre a epigrafia da I Idade do sudoeste da Península Ibérica', *Lengua y cultura en la Hispania prerromana, Actas del V Coloquio sobre Lenguas y Culturas Prerromanas de la Península Ibérica*, eds. J. Untermann & F. Villar, 683–96. Salamanca, Ediciones Universidad de Salamanca.

De Sélincourt, A. (trans.) 1954 *Herodotus: The Histories*. Harmondsworth, Penguin.

Delamarre, X. 2003 *Dictionnaire de la langue gauloise: une approche linguistique du vieux-celtique continental*. Collection des Hespérides. Paris, Errance. First published, 2001.

Delamarre, X. 2007 *Nomina celtica antiqua selecta inscriptionum*. Paris, Errance.

Díaz-Guardamino Uribe, M. 2008 'Iconical Signs, Indexical Relations: Bronze Age stelae and statue-menhirs in the Iberian Peninsula', *Journal of Iberian Archaeology* 11, 31–45.

Díaz-Guardamino Uribe, M. 2010 'Estelas decoradas del Bronce Final en la Península Ibérica: datos para su articulación cronológica', *Siderreum Ana II, El río Guadiana en el Bronce Final*, ed. J. Jiménez Ávila. Mérida, Anejos del Archivo Español de Arqueología de Mérida.

Fabião, C., & A. Guerra 2008 'Mesas do Castelinho (Almodôvar): um projecto com vinte anos', *al-madan* II(16), 92–105.

Fabião, C., & A. Guerra 2010 'Mesas do Castelinho (Almodôvar): A Case of a Failed Roman Town in Southern Lusitania', *Changing Landscapes: The Impact of Roman Towns in the Western Mediterranean. Proceedings of the International Colloquium, Castelo de Vide 15th–17th May 2008*, eds. C. Corsi & F. Vermeulen, 325–46. Bologna, Ante Quem soc. coop.

Falileyev, A. 2005 'In Search of Celtic Tylis: Onomastic Evidence', *New Approaches to the Celtic Place-names in Ptolemy's Geography*, eds. J. de Hoz, E. R. Luján, P. Sims-Williams, 107–33. Madrid, Ediciones Clásicas.

Falileyev, A. 2007 *Celtic Dacia: Personal Names, Place-names and Ethnic Names of Celtic Origin in Dacia and Scythia Minor*. Aberystwyth, CMCS.

Falileyev, A., with A. E. Gohil & N. Ward 2010 *Dictionary of Continental Celtic Place-Names: A Celtic Companion to the* Barrington Atlas of the Greek and Roman World. Aberystwyth, CMCS.

Faria, A. M. de, & A. M. M. Saores 1998 'Uma inscrição em caracteres do Sudoeste proveniente da Folha do Ranjão (Baleizão, Beja)', *Revista Portuguesa de Arqueologia* 1.1, 153–60.

Ferrer i Jané, J. 2010 'El sistema dual de l'escriptura ibèrica sud-oriental', *Veleia* 27, 69–113.

Fortson, B. W. 2004 *Indo-European Language and Culture: An Introduction* (Blackwell Textbooks in Linguistics). Oxford, Blackwell.

Freeman, P. M. 1996 'The Earliest Greek Sources on the Celts', *Études Celtiques* 32, 11–48.

Freeman, P. M. 2001 *The Galatian Language: A Comprehensive Survey of the Language of the Ancient Celts of Greco-Roman Asia Minor*, Ancient Near Eastern Texts and Studies 13. Lampeter, Edwin Mellen Press.

Freeman, P. M. 2010 'Ancient References to Tartessos', *Celtic from the West: Alternative Perspectives from Archaeology, Genetics, Language and Literature*, Celtic Studies Publications 15, eds. B. Cunliffe & J. T. Koch, 303–34. Oxford, Oxbow Books.

Gamito, T. Júdice 1988 *Social Complexity in Southwest Iberia 800–300 BC—The Case of Tartessos*. Oxford, BAR.

Gamito, T. Júdice 1993 'The Internal and External Dynamics of the Development and Collapse of Tartessos. A Possible Explanatory Model', *Lengua y cultura en la Hispania prerromana: Actas del V Coloquio sobre Lenguas y Culturas Prerromanas de la Península Ibérica* (Colonia, 25–28 de Novembre de 1989), eds. J. Untermann &F. Villar, 127–42. Salamanca, Ediciones Universidad de Salamanca.

Gaspari, A. 2006 'Scordisci', *Celtic Culture: A Historical Encyclopedia*, ed. J. T. Koch, 1569–71. Santa Barbara, ABC–Clio.

Gensler, Orin David 1993 'A Typological Evaluation of Celtic/Hamito-Semitic Syntactic Parallels'. Ph.D., University of California.

Godley, A. D. (trans.) 1920 *Herodotus: The Persian Wars, Books I-II*. Loeb Classical Library. Cambridge Massachusetts, Harvard University Press.

Gómez-Moreno, M. 1949 *Misceláneas. Historia, Arte, Arqueología. Primera serie: la antigüedad*. Madrid.

González Rodríguez, Mª. C. 1986 *Las unidades organizativas indígenas del área indoeuropea de Hispania*, Veleia Anejo 2. Vitoria/Gasteiz.

González Rodríguez, Mª. C. 1994 'Las unidades organizativas indígenas II: *addenda et corrigenda*', *Veleia* 11, 169–75.

Gorrochategui Churruca, J. 1984 *Estudio sobre la onomástica indígena de Aquitania*. Bilbao, Servicio Editorial Universidad del País Vasco.

Gray, E. A. (ed.) 1982 *Cath Maige Tuired: The Second Battle of Mag Tuired*, Irish Texts Society 52. London, Irish Texts Society.

Guerra, Amílcar 2002 'Novos monumentos epigrafados com escrita do Sudoeste de vertente setentrional da Serra do Caldeirão', *Revista Portuguesa Arqueologia* 5/2.219–31.

Guerra, A. 2009 'Novidades no âmbito epigrafia pré-romana do sudoeste hispânico', *Acta Palaeohispanica X / Palaeohispanica* 9, 323–38.

Guerra, A. 2010 'Newly Discovered Inscriptions from the South-west of the Iberian Peninsula', *Celtic from the West: Alternative Perspectives from Archaeology, Genetics, Language and Literature*, eds. B. Cunliffe, J. T. Koch, 65–78. Oxford, Oxbow Books.

Guerra, A., A. C. Ramos, S. Melro, I. A. Pires 1999 'Uma estela epigrafada da Idade do Ferro, proviente do Monte Novo do Castelinho (Almodôvar)', *Revista Portuguesa de Arquelogia* 2/1, 143–52.

Harrison, R. J. 1988 *Spain at the Dawn of History: Iberians, Phoenicians and Greeks*. London, Thames and Hudson.

Harrison, R. J. 2004 *Symbols and Warriors: Images of the European Bronze Age*. Bristol, Western Academic & Specialist Press.

Hawkes, C. F. C. 1977 *Pytheas: Europe and the Greek Explorers. A Lecture Delivered at New College, Oxford on 20th May 1975*. J. L. Myres Memorial Lecture 8. Oxford, Blackwell.

Hock, H. H. 2005 'The Insular Celtic Absolute/Conjunct Distinction Once Again: A Prosodic Proposal', *Proceedings of the Sixteenth Annual UCLA Indo-European Conference, Los Angeles, November 5–6, 2004*, ed. K. Jones-Bley, M. E. Huld, A. Della Volpe, M. R. Dexter, 153–72. Journal of Indo-European Monograph Series, No. 50. Washington DC, Institue of the Study of Man.

Isaac, G. R. 2004 'The Nature and Origins of the Celtic Languages: Atlantic Seaways, Italo-Celtic and Other Paralinguistic Misapprehensions', *Studia Celtica* 38.49–58.

Isaac, G. R. 2007 'Celtic and Afro-Asiatic', *The Celtic Languages in Contact: Papers from the Workshop within the Framework of the XIII International Conference of Celtic Studies. Bonn 26–27 July, 2007*, ed. H. L. C. Tristram, 25–80. Potsdam, Potsdam University Press. (e-book: http://opus.kobv.de/volltext/2007/1568)

Isaac, G. R. 2007b 'A New Conjecture on the Origins of the Absolute and Conjunct Flexion', *Ériu* 57, 49–60.

Isaac, G. R. 2007c *Studies in Celtic Sound Changes and their Chronology*. Innsbruck, Innsbrucker Beiträge zur Sprachwissenschaft.

James, S. 2000 *The Atlantic Celts: Ancient People or Modern Invention?* London, British Museum Press.

Jongeling, Karel 2000 *Comparing Welsh and Hebrew*. CNWS Publications 81. Leiden, Research School of Asian, African and Amerindian Studies, Universiteit Leiden.

Jordán Cólera, C. 1993 *Nueva revisión y valoración de isófonas e isomorfas compartidas por itálico y griego*, Zaragoza.

Jordán Cólera, C. 2002 'De las *Oestryminides*, la *Garumna* e de hidrotopónimos relacionados', *Emerita, Revista de Lingüística y Filología Clásica* 70/2, 213–30.

Jordán Cólera, C. 2005 *Celtibérico*, Zaragoza, Ediciones del Departamento de Ciencias de la Antigüedad.

Jordán Cólera, C. 2006 '[K.3.3]: Crónica de un *teicidio* anunciado', *Real Academia de Cultura Valenciana, sección de Estudios Ibéricos "D. Fletcher Valls", Estudios de lenguas y epigrafía antiguas – ELEA* 7, 2006, 37–72.

Jordán Cólera, C. 2007 'Celtiberian', *e-Keltoi* 6: *The Celts in the Iberian Peninsula*, 749–850.

Joseph, L. S. 1990 'Old Irish *cú*: A Naïve Reinterpretation'. *Celtic Language, Celtic Culture: A Festschrift for Eric P. Hamp*, eds. A. T. E. Matonis & D. F. Melia, 110–30. Van Nuys, Calif., Ford & Bailie.

Jufer, N., & Th. Luginbühl 2001 *Les dieux gaulois: répertoire des noms de divinités celtiques connus par l'épigraphie, les textes antiques et la toponymie*. Paris, Errance.

Koch, J. T. 1983 'The Sentence in Gaulish', *Proceedings of the Harvard Celtic Colloquium* 3, 169–216.

Koch, J. T. 1987 'Prosody and the Old Celtic Verbal Complex', *Ériu* 38, 141–74.

Koch, J. T. 1990 'Some Etymologies Relevant to Mythology in the Four Branches', *Proceedings of the Harvard Celtic Colloquium 1988/1989*, 1–11.

Koch, J. T. 1991 'Ériu, Alba, and Letha: When was a Language Ancestral to Gaelic First Spoken in Ireland?', *Emania* 9.17–27.

Koch, J. T. 1992 '"Gallo-Brittonic" vs. "Insular Celtic": The Inter-relationships of the Celtic Languages Reconsidered'. *Bretagne et pays celtiques—langues, histoire, civilisation: Mélanges offerts à la mémoire de Léon Fleuriot*, eds. G. Le Menn & J.-Y. Le Moing, 471–95. Saint-Brieuc, Skol Uhel ar Vro.

Koch, J. T., et al. 2007 *An Atlas for Celtic Studies: Archaeology and Names in Ancient Europe and Early Medieval Ireland, Britain, and Brittany*. Celtic Studies Publications 12. Oxford, Oxbow Books.

Koch, J. T. 2010 'Paradigm Shift? Interpreting Tartessian as Celtic', *Celtic from the West: Alternative Perspectives from Archaeology, Genetics, Language and Literature*, Celtic Studies Publications 15, eds. B. Cunliffe & J. T. Koch, 185–301. Oxford, Oxbow Books.

Koch, J. T. 2011 *Tartessian 2: The Inscription of Mesas do Castelinho, ro and the Verbal Complex, Preliminaries to Historical Phonology*. Aberystwyth, Centre for Advanced Welsh and Celtic Studies.

Koch, J. T., & J. Carey, eds. 2003 *The Celtic Heroic Age: Literary Sources for Ancient Celtic Europe & Early Ireland & Wales*. 4th edn. Celtic Studies Publications 1. Aberystwyth.

Kristiansen, K. 1998 *Europe Before History*. New Studies in Archaeology. Cambridge, Cambridge University Press.

Lambert, P.-Y. 1994 *La langue gauloise*, Collection des Hesperides. Paris, Editions Errance.

Lambert, P.-Y. 2008 'Gaulois *Solitumaros*', *Études Celtiques* 36, 89–101.

Lambert, P.-Y. & D. Stifter 2012 'Le plomb gaulois de Rezé', *Études Celtiques* 38, 141–64.

Lewis, H., & H. Pedersen 1989 *A Concise Comparative Celtic Grammar.* 3rd edn. Göttingen, Vandenhoeck and Ruprecht. First published, 1937.

Lipinski, E. 2004 *Itineraria Phoenicia.* Studia Phoenicia 18, Orientalia Lovaniensia Analecta. Leuven, Peeters.

Lorrio, A. J., & G. Ruiz Zapatero 2005 'The Celts in Iberia: An Overview', *e-Keltoi* 6 http://www4.uwm.edu/celtic/ekeltoi/volumes/vol6/6_4/lorrio_zapatero_6_4.html

Luján, E. R. 2001 'La onomástica de los *Celtici* de la Bética: estudio lingüístico', *Réligión, lengua y cultura prerromana de Hispania*, eds. F. Villar & Mª. P. Fernández-Álvarez, 271–81. Salamanca, Ediciones Universidad de Salamanca.

Luján, E. R. 2007 'L'onomastique des Vettons: analyse linguistique', *Gaulois et celtique continental*, eds. P.-Y. Lambert & G.-J. Pinault, 245–75. Genève, Librairie Droz.

Luján, E. R. 2008 'Galician Place-names Attested epigraphically', *Celtic and Other Languages in Ancient Europe*, ed. J. L. García Alonso, 65–82. Salamanca, Ediciones Universidad de Salamanca.

McCone, K. R. 1979 'Pretonic Preverbs and the Absolute Verbal Endings in Old Irish', *Ériu* 30, 1–34.

McCone, K. R. 1985 'Varia II', *Ériu* 36.169–76.

McCone, K. R. 1994 'An tSean-Ghaeilge agus a Réamhstair', *Stair na Gaeilge in ómós do Pádraig Ó Fiannachta*, in eagar ag K. McCone, at al., 61–219. Roinn na Sean-Ghaeilge, Coláiste Phádraig, Maigh Nuad.

McCone, K. R. 1996 *Towards a Relative Chronology of Ancient and Medieval Celtic Sound Change*, Maynooth Studies in Celtic Linguistics I, Department of Old and Middle Irish, St Patrick's College, Maynooth.

McCone, K. R. 2006 'Greek Κελτός and Γαλάτης, Latin *Gallus* "Gaul"', *Die Sprache* 46, 94–111.

McManus, D. 1991 *A Guide to Ogam.* Maynooth Monographs 4. Maynooth, An Sagart.

Mallory, J. P. 1989 *In Search of the Indo-Europeans: Language, Archaeology and Myth.* London, Thames and Hudson.

Mallory, J. P., & D. Q. Adams 2006 *The Oxford Introduction to Proto-Indo-European and the Proto-Indo-European World.* Oxford, Oxford University Press.

Marco Simón, F. 2005 'Religion and Religious Practices of the Ancient Celts of the Iberian Peninsula', *e-Keltoi 6: The Celts in the Iberian Peninsula*, 287–345.

Marzoli, D., F. López Pardo, J. Suárez Padilla, C. González Wagner, D. P. Mielke, C. Leon Martín, L. Ruiz Cabrero, H. Thiemeyer, M. Torres Ortiz 2010 'The Beginnings of Urbanism in the Local Societies of the Gibraltar Area: Los Castillejos de Alcorrín and its Territory (Manilva, Mála3ga)', *Menga* 1, 277–87.

Matasović, R. 2009 *Etymological Dictionary of Proto-Celtic.* Leiden/Boston, Brill.

Mayrhofer, M. 1992–2001 *Etymologisches Wörterbuch des Altindoarischen.* Heidelberg, Carl Winter Universitätsverlag.

Mederos Martín, A. 1996 'La connexión Levantino-Chipriota. Indícios de comercio atlántico con el Mediterráneo Oriental durante el Bronce Final' (1150–950 AC), *Trabajos de Prehistoria* 53(2), 95–115.

Mederos Martín, A. 1997 'Cambio de rumbo. Interacción comercial ente el Bronce Final Atlántico ibérico y el micénico en el Mediterráneo Central (1425–1050 AC)', *Trabajos de Prehistoria*, 54(2), 113–34.

Mederos Martín, A. 1999 'Ex occidente lux. El comercio micénico en el mediterráneo central y occidental (1625–1100 AC)', *Complutum* 10, 229–66.

Mederos Martín, A. 2008 'Carros micénicos del Heládico Final III en las estelas decoradas del Bronce Final II–IIIA del suroeste de la Península Ibérica', *Contacto cultural entre el Mediterráneo y el Atlántico (siglos XII–VIII ane). La precolonización a debate*, ed. S. Celestino, N. Rafel, X.-L. Armada, 437–63. Madrid, Escuela Española de Historia y Arqueología en Roma.

Mederos Martín, A. 2009 'La sepultura de Belmeque (Beja, Bajo Alentejo). Contactos con el Egeo durante el Bronce Final I del suroeste de la Península Ibérica (1625–1425 AC)', *Veleia* 26, 235–64.

Mederos Martín, A., & L. A. Ruiz Carbrero 2001 'Los inicios de la scritura en la Península Ibérica: grafitos en cerámicas del Bronce Final III y Fenicias', *Complutum* 12, 97–112.

Meid, W. 1963 *Die indogermanischen Grundlagen der altirischen absoluten und konjunkten Verbalflexion*. Wiesbaden, Harrassowitz.

Meid, W. 2008 'Celtic Origins, the Western and the Eastern Celts', Sir John Rhŷs Memorial Lecture, *Proceedings of the British Academy* 154, 177–99.

Mitchell, S. 1993 *Anatolia: Land, Men and Gods in Asia Minor*. 2 vols. Oxford, Clarendon.

Morandi, A. 2004 *Celti d'Italia. Tomo II. Epigrafia e lingua*. Roma, Spazio Tre.

Moret, P. 2006 'La formation d'une toponymie et d'une etnonymie grecque de l'Ibérie: étapes et acteurs', *La invención de una geografía de la Península Ibérica. 1. La época republicana*, eds. G. Cruz Andreotti, P. Le Roux, P. Moret, 39–76. Madrid.

Murillo Redondo, J. F., J. A. Morena López, & D. Ruiz Lara 2005 'Nuevas estelas de guerrero procedentes de las provincias Córdoba y de Ciudad Real', *Romula* 4, 7–46.

Ó Cathasaigh, T. 1977–8 'The Semantics of "Síd"', *Éigse* 17, 137–55.

Olmos, R. 1989 'Los griegos en Tartessos: una nueva contrastación entre las fuentes arqueológicas y las literarias', *Tartessos: Arqueología Protohistórica del Bajo Guadalquivir*, ed. M. E. Aubet Semmler, 497–521. Barcelona, Sabadell.

Parsons, D. 2010 'Tracking the Course of the Savage Tongue: Place-names and Linguistic Diffusion in Early Britain', *Celtic from the West: Alternative Perspectives from Archaeology, Genetics, Language and Literature*, Celtic Studies Publications 15, eds. B. Cunliffe & J. T. Koch, 169–84. Oxford, Oxbow Books.

Peckham, B. 1998 'Phoenicians in Sardinia: Tyrians or Sidonians?', *Sardinian and Aegean Chronology*, eds. M. S. Balmuth, R. H. Tykot, 347–54. Studies in Sardinian Archaeology 5. Oxford, Oxbow Books.

Pereira Sieso, J. 1989 'Nuevos datos para la valoración del hinterland tartésico. El enterramiento de la Casa del Carpio (Belvis de la Jara, Toledo)', *Tartessos: Arqueología Protohistórica del Bajo Guadalquivir*, ed. M. E. Aubet Semmler, 395–409. Barcelona, Sabadell.

Pingel, V. 1993 'Bemerkungen zu den ritzverzierten Stelen im Südwesten der Iberischen Halbinsel', *Lengua y cultura en la Hispania prerromana, Actas del V Coloquio sobre Lenguas y Culturas Prerromanas de la Península Ibérica*, eds. J. Untermann & F. Villar, 209–31. Salamanca, Ediciones Universidad de Salamanca.

Pokorny, J. 1913 'Altirisch *muimme* "Pflegemutter"', *Zeitschrift für vergleichende Sprachforschung* 45, 362–4.

Pokorny, J. 2002 *Indogermanisches etymologisches Wörterbuch*. 4th edn. 2 vols. Tübingen, A. Francke.

Prósper Pérez, B. M.ª 2002 *Lenguas y religiones prerromanas del occidente de la Península Ibérica*. Salamanca, Ediciones Universidad de Salamanca.

Prósper, B. M.ª 2007 *Estudio lingüístico del plomo celtibérico de Iniesta*. Acta Salmanticensia, Estudios Filológicos 319. Salamanca, Ediciones Universidad de Salamanca.

Prósper, B. M.ª 2011 'The Instrumental Case in the Thematic Noun Inflection of Continental Celtic', *Historische Sprachforschungen* 124, 224–41.

Raybould, M. E., & P. Sims-Williams 2007 *The Geography of Celtic Personal Names in the Latin Inscriptions of the Roman Empire*. Aberystwyth, CMCS.

Renfrew, C. 1987 *Archaeology and Language: The Puzzle of Indo-European Origins*. London, Pimlico, 1998. First published, London, Cape.

Rix, H. 2001 *Lexikon der indogermanischen Verben*. Wiesbaden, Ludwig Reichert.

Rodríguez Ramos, J. 2000 'La lectura de las inscripciones sudlusitano-tartesias', *Faventia* 22/1.21–48.

Rodríguez Ramos, J. 2002 'Las inscripciones sudlusitano-tartesias: su función, lengua y contexto socio-económico', *Complutum* 13.85–95.

Ruiz, M. M. 1989 'Las necrópolis tartésicas: prestigio, poder y jerarquás', *Tartessos: Arqueología Protohistórica del Bajo Guadalquivir*, ed. M. E. Aubet Semmler, 247–86. Barcelona, Sabadell.

Ruiz-Gálvez Priego, M. 1995 'Cronología de la Ría de Huelva en el marco del Bronce Final de Europa occidental', *Ritos de paso y puntos de paso. La Ría de Huelva en el mundo del Bronce Final europeo*, ed. M. Ruiz-Gálvez, 79–83. Madrid, Editorial Complutense.

Ruiz-Gálvez Priego, M. 2000 'Weight Systems and Exchange Networks in Bronze Age Europe', *Metals Make the World Go Round: Supply and Circulation of Metals in Bronze Age Europe*, ed. C. F. E. Pare, 267–79. Oxford, Oxbow Books.

Ruiz-Gálvez Priego, M. 2008 'Writing, Counting, Self-Awareness, Experiencing Distant Worlds. Identity Processes and Free-lance Trade in the Bronze Age/Iron Age Transition', *Contacto cultural entre el Mediterráneo y el Atlántico (siglos XII–VII ane). La precolonización a debate*, eds. S. Celestino, N. Rafel, X.-L. Armada, 27–40. Madrid, Escuela Española de Historia y Arqueología en Roma.

Ruiz-Gálvez Priego, M. 2009 '¿Qué hace un micénico como tú en un sitio como éste?

Andalucía entre el colapso do los palacios y la presencia semita', *Trabajos de Prehistoria* 66/2, 93–118.

Salinas de Frías, M. 2006 *Los pueblos prerromanos de la península Ibérica*. Madrid, Ediciones Akal.

Sánchez Moreno, E. 1996 'A proposito de las *gentilitates*: los grupos familiares del área vetona y su adecuación para la interpretación de la organización social prerromana', *Veleia* 13, 115–42.

Schmidt, K. H. 1976 'Zur keltiberischen Inschrift von Botorrita', *Bulletin of the Board of Celtic Studies* 26/4.375–94.

Schmidt, K. H. 1985 'Contribution to the Identification of Lusitanian', *Actas del III Coloquio sobre Lenguas y Culturas Paleohispánicas*, ed. J. de Hoz, 319–41. Salamanca, Universidad de Salamanca.

Schmidt, K. H. 1996 *Celtic: A Western Indo-European Language?* Innsbruck, Innsbrucker Beiträge zur Sprachwissenschaft.

Schmoll, U. 1961 *Die südlusitanischen Inschriften*. Wiesbaden, Harrassowitz.

Schrijver, P. 2004 'Der Tod des Festlandkeltischen und die Geburt des Französischen, Niederländischen un Hochdeutschen', *Sprachtod und Sprachgenurt*, eds. P. Schrijver & P.-A. Mumm, 1–20. Bremen, Hempen Verlag.

Schrijver, P. 2005 'Early Celtic Diphthongization and the Celtic–Latin Interface', *New Approaches to Celtic Place-names in Ptolemy's Geography*', eds. J. de Hoz, E. R. Luján, P. Sims-Williams, 55–67. Madrid, Ediciones Clásicas.

Schrijver, P. 2011 'Pruners and Trainers of the Celtic Family Tree: the Rise and Development of Celtic in the Light of Language Contact' (handout), XIVth International Congress of Celtic Studies, Maynooth.

Schulten, A. 1945 *Tartessos*. Madrid, Espasa-Calpe.

Schumacher, S. 2004 *Die keltischen Primärverben: Ein vergleichendes, etymologisches und morphologisches Lexikon*, Beiträge zur Sprachwissenschaft 110. Innsbruck, Institut für Sprachwissenschaft.

Schumacher, S. 2005 '"Langvokalische Perfekta" in indogermanischen Einzelsprachen und ihr grundsprachlicher Hintergrund', *Sprachkontakt und Sprachwandel: Akten der XI. Fachtagung der Indogermanischen Gesellschaft*, eds. G. Meiser & O. Hackstein, 592–626. Wiesbaden, L. Reichert.

Schwerteck, H. 1979 'Zur Deutung der großen Felsinschrift von Peñalba de Villastar', *Actas de II Coloquio sobre Lenguas y Culturas Prerromanas de la Península Ibérica, Tübingen 1976*, eds. A. Tovar, M. Faust, F. Fischer, M. Koch, 185ff. Salamanca.

Sims-Williams, P. 1984 'The Double System of Verbal Inflexion in Old Irish', *Transactions of the Philogical Society*, 138–201.

Sims-Williams, P. 1998 'Celtomania and Celtosceptism', *Cambrian Medieval Celtic Studies* 36 (1998) 1–35.

Sims-Williams, P. 2006 *Ancient Celtic Place-names in Europe and Asia Minor*. Publications of the Philological Society 39. Oxford, Blackwell.

Sims-Williams, P. 2007 *Studies on Celtic Languages before the Year 1000.* Aberystwyth, CMCS.

Sverdrup, H., & R. Guardans 2002 'A Study of the Tartessian Script and Language', *Languages and their Speakers in Ancient Eurasia: Studies in Linguistics and Cultura; Language Reconstruction Presented in Honour of Prof. Aharon Dolgopolsky*, eds. V. Shevoroshkin & P. Sidwell, 115–48. Association for the History of Language Monographs and Serials 4. Canberra, Association for the History of Language.

Thurneysen, R. 1907 'On Certain Initial Changes in the Irish Verb after Preverbal Particles', *Ériu* 3, 18–19.

Thurneysen, R. 1975 *A Grammar of Old Irish,* trans. D. A. Binchy & O. Bergin. Rev. and enlarged edn. Dublin, Dublin Institute for Advanced Studies. First published, 1946.

Tomlin, R. S. O. 1988 'The Curse Tablets', *The Temple of Sulis Minerva at Bath: Volume 2 The Finds from the Sacred Spring,* ed. B. Cunliffe, 59–277. Oxford, Oxford University Committee for Archaeology, Monograph 16.

Untermann, J. 1962 'Das silbenschriftliche Element in der iberischen Schrift', *Emerita* 30, 281–94.

Untermann, J. (ed.) 1980a *Monumenta Linguarum Hispanicarum II. Die Inschriften in iberischer Schrift aus Südfrankreich.* Wiesbaden, Ludwig Reichert.

Untermann, J. 1980b 'Namenkundliche Anmerkungen zu lateinischen Inschriften aus Kantabrien', *Beiträge zur Namenforschung* 15, 367–92.

Untermann, J. 1985 'Los teónimos de la región lusitano-gallega como fuente de las lenguas indígenas', *Actas del III Coloquio sobre Lenguas y Culturas Paleohispánicas,* ed. J. de Hoz, 343–63. Salamanca, Universidad de Salamanca.

Untermann, J. 1985/6 'Lusitanisch, Keltiberisch, Keltisch', *Veleia* 2/3, 57–76.

Untermann, J. 1992 'Anotaciones al estudio de las lenguas prerromanas del noroeste de la Península Ibérica (1)', *Galicia: da romanidade á xermanización, Problemas históricos e culturais. Actas do encontro cientifico en homenaxe a Fermín Bouza Brey (1901–1973),* 369–97. Santiago de Compostela.

Untermann, J. 1995 'Zum Stand der Deutung der "tartessischen" Inschriften', *Hispano-Gallo-Brittonica: Essays in Honour of Professor D. Ellis Evans on the Occasion of his Sixty-Fifth Birthday,* eds. J. F. Eska et al., 244–59. Cardiff, University of Wales Press.

Untermann, J. 1996 'VII. La onomástica de Botorrita 3 en le contexto de la Hispanica indoeuropea', *El tercer bronce de Botorrita (Contrebia Belaisca),* ed. F. Beltrán, Collección Arqueología 19, 167–80. Zaragoza, Gobierno de Aragon.

Untermann, J. (ed.) (with D. S. Wodtko) 1997 *Monumenta Linguarum Hispanicarum IV. Die tartessischen, keltiberischen und lusitanischen Inschriften.* Wiesbaden, Ludwig Reichert.

Untermann, J. 1997b 'Neue Überlegungen und eine neue Quelle zur Entstehung de althispanischen Schriften', *Madrider Mitteilungen* 38, 49–66. *Deutsches Archäologisches Institut Abteilung Madrid. Mainz, Verlag Philipp von Zabern.*

Untermann, J. 2004 'Célticos y Túrdulos', *Palaeohispanica* 4.199–214.

Untermann, J. forthcoming 'La aportación de la toponimia a la definición de las lenguas ibérica y tartesia'.

Vallejo Ruiz, J. M. 2005 *Antroponimia indígena de la Lusitania romana*. Vitoria/Gasteiz, Anejos de Veleia, Series Minor 23.

Vendryes, J. et al. 1960– *Lexique étymologique de l'Irlandais ancien*. Dublin, Dublin Institute for Advanced Studies/Paris, CNRS.

Villar, F. 1995 'Los nombres de Tartesos', *Habis* 26, 243–70.

Villar, F. 1997 'The Celtiberian Language', *Zeitschrift für celtische Philologie* 49/50.898–949.

Villar, F. 2004 'The Celtic Language of the Iberian Peninsula', *Studies in Baltic and Indo-European Linguistics in Honor of William R. Schmalstieg*, eds. P. Baldi & P. U. Dini, 243–74. Amsterdam, John Benjamins.

Villar, F., & B. Mª. Prósper, C. Jordán, & Mª. Pilar Fernández Álvarez 2011 *Lenguas, genes y culturas en la prehistoria de Europa y Asia suroccidental*. Salamanca, Ediciones Universidad de Salamanca.

Watkins, C. W. 1963 'Preliminaries to a Historical and Comparative Analysis of the Syntax of the Old Irish Verb', *Celtica* 6, 1–49.

Watkins, C. W. 1969 'On the Prehistory of Celtic Verb Inflexion', *Ériu* 21, 1–22.

Watkins, C. W. 1999 'A Celtic Miscellany', *Proceedings of the Tenth Annual UCLA Indo-European Conference, Los Angeles, May 21–23, 1998*, eds. K. Jones-Bley, M. E. Huld, A. Della Volpe, & M. Robbins Dexter, 3–25. Journal of Indo-European Studies Monograph Series No. 32. Washington DC, Institute of the Study of Man.

Wodtko, D. S. 2000 *Monumenta Linguarum Hispanicarum 5.1, Wörterbuch der keltiberischen Inschriften*, ed. J. Untermann. Wiesbaden, Ludwig Reichert.

Wodtko, D. S. 2003 *An Outline of Celtiberian Grammar*, Freiburg http://www.freidok.uni-freiburg.de/volltexte/747/

Wodtko, D. S. 2009 'Language Contact in Lusitania', *International Journal of Diachronic Linguistics and Linguistic Reconstruction* 6.1–48.

Wodtko, D. S. 2010 'The Problem of Lusitanian', *Celtic from the West. Alternative Perspectives from Archaeology, Genetics, Language, and Literature*, eds. B. Cunliffe & J. T. Koch, 335–67. Oxford, Oxbow Books.

Wodtko, D. S., B. Irslinger, & C. Schneider 2008 *Nomina im Indogermanischen Lexikon*. Heidelberg, Universitätsverlag Winter.

Index

Linguistic and General